Plains Farmer

NUMBER FOUR

The Clayton Wheat Williams

TEXAS ★ LIFE ★ SERIES

Major funding for this series was provided by
CLAYTON W. WILLIAMS, JR.

Plains·Farmer

The Diary of William G. DeLoach, 1914–1964

EDITED BY JANET M. NEUGEBAUER

ILLUSTRATED BY CHARLES SHAW

TEXAS A&M UNIVERSITY PRESS : COLLEGE STATION

The paper used in this book meets the
minimum requirements of the American National Standard
for Permanence of Paper for Printed Library Materials, Z39.48-1984.
Binding materials have been chosen for durability.

LIBRARY OF CONGRESS CATALOGING-IN-PUBLICATION DATA

DeLoach, William G. (William Green), 1880–1967.
Plains farmer : the diary of William G.
DeLoach, 1914–1964 / edited by Janet M.
Neugebauer ; illustrated by Charles Shaw. –
1st ed.
p.   cm. – (The Clayton Wheat
Williams Texas life series ; no. 4)
Includes bibliographical references (p.   )
and index.
ISBN 0-89096-422-X
1. Farm life–Texas–Crosby County–
History–20th century.   2. Farm life–Llano
Estacado–History–20th century.   3. Agri-
culture–Texas–Crosby County–History–
20th century.   4. Agriculture–Llano
Estacado–History–20th century.   5. Crosby
County (Tex.)–Social life and customs.
6. Llano Estacado–Social life and customs.
7. DeLoach, William G. (William Green),
1880–1967–Diaries.   8. Farmers–Texas–
Crosby County–Diaries.   9. Crosby County
(Tex.)–Biography.   I. Neugebauer, Janet M.,
1935– . II. Title. III. Series.
F392.C85D45   1991
976.4'84806'092–dc20
[B]   90-21701
                                        CIP

Contents

Illustrations

M·A·P

Preface

Few people have heard of William G. DeLoach, for he did not distinguish himself by accumulating wealth or power. He was an ordinary man who saw the Texas Plains change from ranching empires to farm factories. He did distinguish himself, however, by leaving a firsthand account of this epic experience. He kept a daily diary.

In 1979, when I joined the staff of the Southwest Collection at Texas Tech University, people were still talking about DeLoach's fifty-year farm diary that the Southwest Collection had received in 1975. For sixteen years I lived on a farm within eighty miles of DeLoach's place, and after losing many battles with the elements and the markets I was fed up with the whole business. I couldn't understand why anyone would want to spend fifty years writing about farming. When the thought would not go away, I made time to read the diary. As I turned the pages I found myself farming again, and it soon became evident that this man had a powerful story to tell. I was tired after walking behind a mule all day, I counted every egg that was gathered, and I looked for rain as hard as DeLoach did. Believing that other readers would find the story as engrossing as I did, I requested permission from the director of the Southwest Collection, Dr. David J. Murrah, to edit the diary for publication. He also thought it should be published and gave my request his blessings.

During the course of the project I received tremendous support from others; I could not have done it alone. A chance conversation in an airport with Dr. James F. Lovell from the Development Office at Texas Tech University started the wheels in motion toward finding grant money that would provide release time from my regular duties to complete a manuscript. Unfortunately, he accepted a position at another university before everything was in place, but Dr. William M. Pearce took up the cause. Dr. Pearce knew about the diary and encouraged Dr. Lauro F. Cavazos, former U.S. Secretary of Education, but president of Texas Tech at that time, to ask Mr. W. B. "Dub" Rushing, of Lubbock, to provide money from the Rushing Foundation. The answer was a resounding "yes." Like those of DeLoach, Mr. Rushing's roots go deep into the Texas Plains. It has been especially meaningful to me to know that the contributions of two West Texans made this publication possible. I believe William DeLoach would have liked this kind of cooperation.

Support also came from Preston Lewis of the University News Bureau and David Pasztor of the *Dallas Times Herald*, who teamed up on news coverage that brought nationwide attention to the project.

A special thanks goes to graduate students David Marshall and Yolanda Romero, who fulfilled my responsibilities at the Southwest Collection while I was at home working away on my computer. Yolanda also spent many extra hours checking footnotes; Holle Humphries and Penny Mason helped her. Vicky Vaughan, Beth Snell, and Tommie Davis did yeoman service in producing a typescript of the diary that saved wear and tear on the original. Additionally, I would like to thank the staff of the Southwest Collection who did everything possible to bring this project to its conclusion.

I am grateful to the Texas Tech Library staff in the Government Documents Section, especially Tom Lindsey, Tess Trost, Mary Ann Higdon, and Tom Rohrig, who found a government report to support every idea I had. Jane Olm and Norma Reger from the Law Library also helped by uncovering some interesting facts about "estrays." T. Lindsay Baker, at the Strecker Museum in Waco, helped with information about windmills. Thanks.

I am indebted to Roy Sylvan Dunn, former director of the Southwest Collection. He saw the diary first and, understanding its importance, worked closely with DeLoach's daughter, Jimmie DeLoach Moorhead, to get it into the Southwest Collection for preservation and permanent storage. He was also responsible for adding the right periodicals, newspapers and photographs to the repository's holdings to aid some future researcher who he hoped would work with the diary.

Sensing that a very demanding relationship was developing between DeLoach and me, my friends accepted my need to be alone. They greeted me teasingly with "How's your farmer?" I appreciate their understanding and their interest. One friend, however, fulfilled a different need. The hours Richard Mason spent talking to me about agriculture provided valuable clues for many of the footnotes. The exchange of ideas was very important to me.

Perhaps the greatest help a beginning writer can receive is an offer to read the manuscript and suggest improvements. I had two offers! Dr. James W. Graves, professor of agricultural economics at Texas Tech, read my first draft, and William C. Billingsley, professor of history at South Plains College, read the final draft. I followed their suggestions and found encouragement in their comments. I needed both.

My deepest appreciation goes to the DeLoach family, especially Jimmie De-

Loach Moorhead, Mr. & Mrs. Robert E. (Bud) DeLoach, and their children Robert Edwin (Buster) DeLoach and Wanda DeLoach Swart, for helping me through the rough spots. When I ran out of other places to look for answers, they always invited me to visit. They were full of information. Together we marveled at how perceptive DeLoach was and shared many laughs about his humorous entries. Robert (Bud) and Jimmie told me their dad was a very gentle and loving person, but he was always serious. It was a treat to discover this hidden facet of his personality. Having already grown quite fond of the diarist, I found it easy to like his family.

Finally, I would like to thank my children, Gayle Sandidge and Joel Neugebauer, for their support and encouragement. They told all of their friends their mom was writing a book that would soon be on the market. With that kind of confidence I had to succeed.

William DeLoach's diary has been edited for readability rather than attempting to duplicate the original. Examples of writing by people who lack literary skills are plentiful, but firsthand accounts of the sweeping changes in U.S. agriculture during the twentieth century are rare.

Even though I favored substance over form, I did not try to improve DeLoach's writing when correcting his grammar, punctuation, or spelling. In fact, I generally corrected only those words which I found distracting. When the wrong tense broke my train of thought or when his phonetically spelled words made me hesitate, I made corrections. Likewise, when DeLoach made two words out of one, such as "to day" and "fore noon," I often consolidated them. However, I left intact errors of form that were unobtrusive or that gave me a better feel for the man and his times. Words that DeLoach obviously overlooked in haste were added in italics and square brackets. Narrative I supplied is in wider measure. Titles of books and newspapers were italicized throughout, regardless of how he treated them (quotes, underline, etc.). Finally, all ellipses are mine.

Annotations intentionally combine folksy and scholarly information. I believe this is in keeping with the tone of a story that sheds light on the dilemmas farmers faced when adjusting to sophisticated urban economics.

Names of community members were changed to protect privacy, but all family names were retained, including in-laws. Unless otherwise identified, people mentioned are DeLoach's friends and neighbors.

Besides my imposed yearly divisions, the format I used for the diary entries is very close to the one DeLoach used when making the original entries in his account ledgers.

Introduction

Do you know what it was like to travel in a covered wagon, what happens when the wind gets its sandy clothes on, or how much a team of mules was worth as the downpayment on a new tractor? Will DeLoach knew all these things, and he wrote about them in a diary he kept from 1914 to 1964. As the diary was written, DeLoach created a friend, a confidant, who always listened. As we read, we find two interesting stories that he shared with his friend. The larger story chronicles the change in farming from a simple, independent way of life to a complex, interdependent business. Woven into this is a colorful narrative about West Texas, one of the last frontiers in the nation.

DeLoach was born in 1880 in Ellenville, Georgia, the eldest son of Emmanuel P. and Elizabeth Bowden DeLoach, former plantation owners. After the Civil War, financial reverses dogged his father's footsteps, and in 1887 the family moved to Parker County, Texas. Will grew up here, attending a one-room schoolhouse three or four months a year for seven years.

In 1898 Will struck out on his own to the Texas Plains, where he got a job working cattle and mending fences on the Two-Buckle Ranch in Crosby County. By 1879 barbed wire had made its way to the Southern Plains, ending the open-range era. When ranchers fenced their land, they hired fence riders to repair the broken sections. Will learned about Crosby County from two of his sisters, who moved there before the turn of the century. Their husbands were in the vanguard of pioneer farmer-stockmen moving onto the Plains as the big ranches broke up.

Will didn't say why he left the Plains, but by 1901 he was back with his family, which had moved to Old Greer County, Oklahoma. In 1896 the U.S. Supreme Court, ruling on a boundary dispute between Texas and Oklahoma, decided that Greer County actually belonged to Oklahoma instead of Texas.[1] After arrangements allowed longtime settlers to claim their lands, unappropriated land was opened to homesteaders, and the Emmanuel DeLoach family left Parker County to file on 160 acres in Greer County.

The DeLoach's path was the path of opportunity for many people leaving the Old South after the Civil War—through Parker County, Texas, to Greer County,

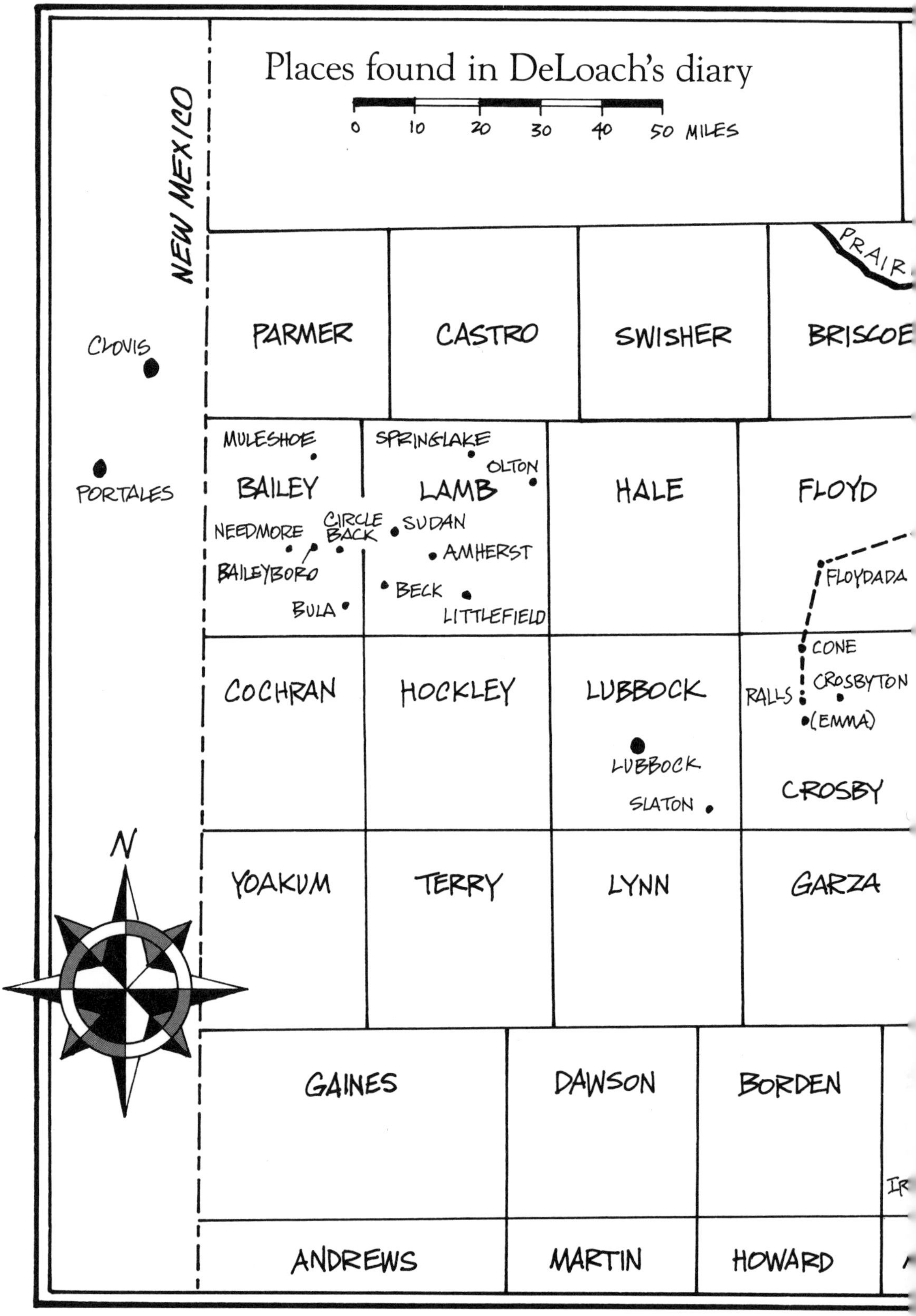

Places found in DeLoach's diary

0   10   20   30   40   50 MILES

NEW MEXICO

PRAIR

CLOVIS

PORTALES

PARMER   CASTRO   SWISHER   BRISCOE

MULESHOE   SPRINGLAKE
                         OLTON
BAILEY   LAMB   HALE   FLOYD

NEEDMORE   CIRCLE   SUDAN
            BACK
BAILEYBORO   AMHERST
                                      FLOYDADA
      BULA   BECK
                  LITTLEFIELD

                                      CONE
COCHRAN   HOCKLEY   LUBBOCK   RALLS   CROSBYTON
                                         (EMMA)
                  LUBBOCK
                      SLATON   CROSBY

N

YOAKUM   TERRY   LYNN   GARZA

GAINES   DAWSON   BORDEN

                                      IR

ANDREWS   MARTIN   HOWARD

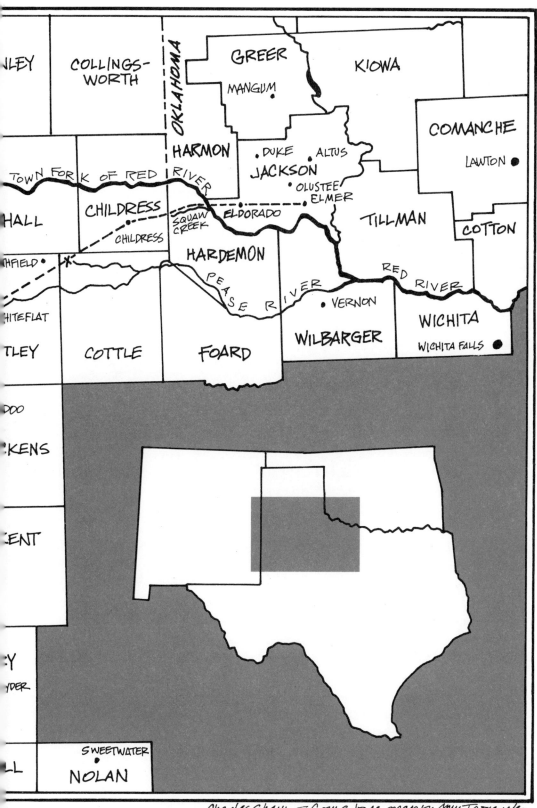

NLEY

COLLINGS-
WORTH

OKLAHOMA

GREER

MANGUM

KIOWA

COMANCHE

LAWTON

HARMON

DUKE   ALTUS

JACKSON

OLUSTEE

ELMER

TOWN FORK OF RED RIVER

CHILDRESS

HALL

SQUAW
CREEK

ELDORADO

TILLMAN

COTTON

CHILDRESS

HARDEMON

HFIELD

HITEFLAT

PEASE RIVER

RED RIVER

VERNON

WICHITA

TLEY

COTTLE

FOARD

WILBARGER

WICHITA FALLS

DDO

KENS

ENT

Y

YDER

SWEETWATER

NOLAN

LL

Charles Shaw — from a base map by Amy Troyansky

Oklahoma, and finally onto the Texas Plains. The big attraction was cheap land and a new chance for success.

In Oklahoma Will met a Mr. Newton, who hired the young man to work his land on halves. Newton furnished the land, seed, and equipment; DeLoach furnished the labor; and they split the crops equally.

Newton's wife was bedridden and the household duties fell to a niece, Sallie, who had been living in the Newton home since her mother's death. Will, a boarder, was attracted to this pretty eighteen-year-old girl, and he courted her by putting notes under the coffee pot at breakfast. She responded with an answer under the same coffee pot at noon, thus setting the stage for two lifelong commitments—writing and Sallie.

His diary entry of January 13, 1953, describes their wedding: "This night 50 years ago I left my father's home in Old Greer Co., Okla. about 10 P.M. to drive a two horse rig near Elmer, Okla., 35 miles away to get my future wife. I did not have roads to drive over. One just took a course, and it was up to me to keep a southeast course, where my girl lived. I arrived at her home about 2:00 or 3:00 A.M. on January 14, 1903. We had breakfast and let my horses rest. She and I pulled out and the long drive started for an old preacher that lived in a dug out. We got to his place and were married about 5:00 P.M. on the 14th day of January, 1903."

The newlyweds lived in Acme, Texas, where Will worked in a brick factory. It was probably there that he heard stories about the brick factory in Thurber, an industrial town on the Texas frontier that had been built for Texas and Pacific Coal Company workers. The company operated coal mines, supplying fuel to the Texas and Pacific Railroad (no connection with the coal company), as well as a brick factory to use the low-grade coal. Wages were attractive, as were the modern conveniences, such as electricity and up-to-date medical facilities.[2]

The DeLoaches moved to Thurber, where Will got a job in the mines, but the Labor Day Strike of 1903 quickly introduced him to one of the disadvantages of an industrial society. He had to wait until the strike was settled before he could work. He continued in the mines until 1908, moving up to crew chief before he returned to Oklahoma to farm and run a shoe store.

Then, in March of 1913, tragedy struck. Sallie and Will's four-year-old daughter, Mildred, burned to death after igniting her clothes with some matches she found in a rocking chair. This accident, followed by a droughty summer, made Will read more thoughtfully the news articles about opportunities for settlers in West Texas. He hoped a new home would ease the grief of his family, which by this time included three other children: Harold Grady born in 1904, Robert Emmet born in 1906, and Dorothy Irene born in 1910. He sold his crops in the field and his interest in the shoe store. In September of 1913 they loaded their possessions in a covered wagon and headed for Emma in Crosby County, Texas. Their third daughter, Jimmie Lee, was born that Christmas Eve.[3]

In 1913, Emma was a village of about twenty-five families, where DeLoach's two sisters lived. A brother-in-law agreed to let him rent a farm north of town. The farm was just three miles south of Ralls, a growing community on the Santa Fe line.

During the first two decades of this century small towns sprang up all over West Texas as wave after wave of settlers arrived. Four main factors drew them into the area: a series of wet years in which the rainfall exceeded twenty inches; Texas land laws that were reshaped to provide cheap land and liberal credit terms for farmers under the Four Section Act of 1895; railroads that brought settlers in and transported their farm products to market; and finally, the ever-rising price of agricultural commodities that made farming attractive.[4]

Most West Texas ranchers actually promoted settlement rather than trying to stop it. The absence of natural water streams helped prevent the conflict between ranchers and farmers so characteristic of other areas in the West. Windmills pumped water where it was needed and spared ranchers the problem of settlers' fencing off water sites. A compatible economic relationship quickly developed when farmers found a local market for surplus forage crops and ranchers were assured a supply of winter feed without having to hire extra hands to grow it. In fact, many farmers rented land from ranchers, keeping two-thirds of the crop and giving the landlord one-third as rent.

Even though conflict between ranchers and settlers was minimal, bitter intercommunity rivalries often developed as the railroad streaked its way across the Plains. It bypassed some towns, such as Emma, which was already in its death throes by the time DeLoach arrived, and went through others, such as Ralls, which grew into a marketing and shipping point.

DeLoach planted the farm mostly in grain sorghums to feed the livestock he considered his primary source of income. As late as 1914 the economy of West Texas was still based on barter and the sale of livestock, although cotton was gaining acceptance as a cash crop. A 500-pound bale, which could be produced on one to three acres, averaged sixty dollars. By comparison, a yearling steer, requiring nearly fifteen acres for grazing, averaged only thirty dollars.[5] Despite this, most pioneer farmers still associated cotton with the humid regions to the east and were reluctant to reduce their acreage planted in grain sorghums, long recognized as the premier drought-resistant crops, to gamble on something less certain. Consequently, cotton was forced to wait until the inflated prices of World War I dramatically increased production before taking its place as a primary crop in Crosby County.[6] It proved to be a hardy crop that could withstand droughty conditions. In 1927 Lubbock, Texas, a regional marketing center, boasted of being the second largest inland cotton market in the world. It had seven gins, a cotton oil mill, two compresses with a capacity of thirty-five hundred bales daily, rail outlets connecting it with 175 gins on the Llano Estacado, and 150 buyers with an office representing every major cotton company in the world.[7] By 1947 the Llano Estacado was recognized as one of the most prolific cotton-producing areas in the United States,[8] and during the following decade, Lubbock became one of the nation's top "spot cotton" markets.[9]

Llano Estacado means Staked Plains, but there is no general agreement in Texas concerning the origin of the term. The Llano Estacado is a vast plateau, 3,240 feet high, that covers approximately thirty-two thousand square miles extending from the central western part of Texas northward over most of the Panhandle and westward into eastern New Mexico. Thrusting up nearly 1,000 feet higher than the surrounding area, it is a conspicuous region known locally by several names – South Plains, West Texas, Caprock, Southern High Plains, and, simply, the Plains.[10]

The Plains is not hospitable country. Native vegetation has had to withstand adverse conditions, and farm crops have also had to adjust to the environment to be successful. Grain sorghums adapted easily. These native African plants are known as drought escapers; they mature quickly, in 90 to 120 days, and can be harvested before summer dry spells become severe. Additionally, their dwarf stature and small leaf area reduce the amount of water they need, allowing them to use available moisture more slowly. Distantly related to corn, they produce heads instead of ears, but chemically the two are very similar, with sorghum having 90 percent of the nutritional value of corn.[11] From pioneer days until mechanization, it was common practice to plant at least a third of the farm's acreage in these crops. Kaffir corn and milo maize, "the sorghums that fed the draft animals used to plant and plow the Plains," became the foundation of the modern Texas grain sorghum industry.[12]

Farming west of the ninety-eighth meridian also requires different methods than those used in the humid east. Dry farming has proven most successful. This is not farming without moisture; rather, it is farming on nonirrigated land where annual rainfall averages only ten to thirty inches. Soil is prepared by plowing it deeply for maximum absorption of available moisture that can be stored in the ground until used by plants. The next task is keeping it there. As heat from the sun and hot winds cause evaporation on the surface, moisture rises from below, through capillary action, to supply the drying surface. Plowing the soil after each rain breaks the crust, creating a dust mulch that prevents further evaporation. Subsurface moisture then rises only to the level of the dust mulch, within reach of plant roots.[13]

The soil of the Llano Estacado is composed principally of sandy loam with a clay subsoil that reaches down to the calcareous rock below. The clay subsoil aids in the retention of moisture during periods of scant rainfall. The sandy loam surface absorbs moisture readily, losing very little to runoff, and forms a natural mulch that retains the subsoil moisture for long periods, unless removed by plant growth. This retentive nature makes it possible to produce abundant crops with an annual rainfall of only twenty inches. Equally important is the fact that 80 percent of the total falls between April and October, when it is needed most.[14]

DeLoach wrote frequently about the weather. Like every farmer, he was preoccupied with this unpredictable factor in farm life, but his comments also reflect the wide range of weather conditions characteristic of the Great Plains. Extreme changes often occur from one day to the next, or even within a single day. Located between two mountain ranges, the Plains acts as a corridor for cold, dry air masses descending from the arctic circle and for warm, moist air masses coming up from the Gulf of Mexico. Fronts, formed where two or more masses meet, might produce light gentle rains or violent thunderstorms with hail and tornadoes. High winds sweep freely across the flat land, often blasting everything with dust and scorching temperatures, or freezing man and animal alike with a blizzard.[15]

Why would anyone want to farm on the Plains? When the rains came, the fertile soil produced so abundantly that most people forgot how terrible the droughts were, and the crisp coolness of a summer morning, or the fire-like glow of a fall sunset, made the dust storms and blizzards fade from memory. Furthermore, the wind that brought so much aggravation also powered the windmill that brought water to every farmer's door. At times the wind even seemed to amuse DeLoach; he wrote about listening to it howl and watching it make the sand strut or walk about. People, like vegetation, learned to adapt. Only the strong and persistent remained, and they taught newcomers how to take it all in stride. The weather still gets a lot of attention in West Texas, where being able to read the sky is an esteemed talent.

The price of land, which rose steadily in West Texas until all the farming areas were settled, was often a hedge against poor crops for pioneer farmers. Several times from 1917 through 1929 DeLoach bought grassland, broke it for cultivation, and sold it for a profit when opportunity beckoned elsewhere. In fact, he often made more money selling land than he did selling crops.

After settling on a farm located close enough to Ralls to easily market his crops and buy supplies, Will's attention turned to moisture for planting. He had to buy livestock feed from his neighbors during the first winter, because it was not practical to bring it from Oklahoma. He did bring with him, however, memories of the dry summer before, memories that made him watch every cloud anxiously. And after a good rain one Saturday, he made the first entry in his diary, which he started in an old ledger left over from his shoe store days. It grew to fill twelve ledgers, most of them legal size. Each night for the next fifty years, before any part of it could fade, he recorded his memory of the day. When he was away from home, he made entries on a tablet and later transferred them to the ledger without making corrections.[16] In fact, when he was in a hurry, DeLoach did not tarry long over grammar or punctuation. He just jotted down thoughts quickly, often spelling words phonetically. However, when he was troubled, or in a reflective mood, his entries resembled vignettes, with description that was very close to dialogue.

This lengthy account of a working man's life is unusual, because those who labor for a living are usually too tired at the end of the day to write about ordinary experiences. Moreover, the everyday tasks of life require most of their time. Until the 1940s DeLoach farmed with mules and gathered his crops by hand. When his family needed a place to live he built a house; when they needed food he butchered a hog or steer and processed his own meat; when a neighbor was in distress he helped fix a windmill, looked for stock that had broken out, or dug a grave.

Even though farm diaries usually have little literary value, they are an excellent way to trace a day-to-day farming operations over an extended period of time. They provide useful information about prices of products sold and supplies bought, varieties of seed planted, the evolution of farm equipment, type of livestock raised, how farm families handled their everyday problems, and what those families did for entertainment. Students of agricultural history are grateful for the hours some tired farmer spent with his diary by lamplight, writing his personal account of "how it really was."[17]

DeLoach's diary was obviously intended for his eyes only, because he shared many secrets with his special friend who always had time to listen to the troubles others did not seem to understand. His attachment to the diary is obvious from the confidential, sometimes intimate, tone of his writing, his pleasure in using new words, his jovial entries when things were going well, and his long laments when troubles weighed heavily. Family members recall some feelings of isolation as their father sat in a corner, writing, while they were often left to spend the evening alone. According to DeLoach's youngest daughter, Jimmie, family members relied on the diary to settle disputes about dates. Even though the ledgers were kept in an open desk, the family never read more than was necessary. Understanding the strong bond between their father and his ledgers, the family respected his privacy, but it didn't bother the kids to take his pens to school!

Until the late 1940s DeLoach didn't realize his diary would ever be of interest to others. Over the years, when one ledger was nearly full, someone gave him another as a Christmas or Father's Day gift, and his writing continued. In the early 1950s when the local newspaper published excerpts from his diary, he began to realize the significance of his long record. During this time, also, he wrote of reading newspaper accounts of other diarists and compared the length of their diaries to his. After he retired from farming, his entries began to contain a greater amount of explanation and reminiscing, as though he anticipated a reader at some later date. He was also thinking about a final resting place for the diary, and a way to preserve it. Having made a decision, he wrote on August 4, 1958: "I waited till 2:20 for the people from Texas Technological College to come. They arrived about 3:00 P.M. A Mr. Sylvan Dunn and a young man, by name David Ramsey. They looked over my 9 completed Ledgers, March 28, 1914 to Aug. 5, 1958. They made 4 pictures of me and my Ledgers. I think this is the best way to do it, as I could not just single out one of the 5 children and give them the diary, and I never wanted them separated. It is hard to make a decision like this."

So hard, in fact, that in November, 1958, DeLoach asked the Southwest Collection to return his diary. He said he had had it so long he was just lost without it, but promised all of the ledgers to the repository after his death.

William G. DeLoach died in 1967, and in 1975 Sallie DeLoach returned the ledgers to the Southwest Collection, where I discovered them.

After reading the diary, I realized its importance in what it reveals about the lives of countless pioneers who settled the Plains—their struggles, their accomplishments, and their defeats. It also provides an insight into why they farmed, how farming changed during the first half of the twentieth century, and the evolution of some of the agricultural problems Americans face today.

Overproduction and low prices in agriculture have been persistent problems in the United States since World War I. Prior to 1914, surplus agricultural commodities were easily used to settle U.S. debts to European financiers. During the war European dependence on American food and fiber increased as Allied demands grew beyond all expectations. At every turn farmers were admonished to do their patriotic duty by increasing production. Newspapers advertised, "Win the war by preparing the land, sowing the seed and producing bigger crops,"[18] and the Department of Labor even became a clearinghouse, directing laborers into the wheat harvest.

Peace was declared in November, 1918, and by mid-1920 the foreign markets had collapsed. During the war an important shift in the balance of trade occurred. Instead of continuing as a debtor nation, the United States became the largest creditor nation in the world, and war-torn European countries could no longer afford to buy American produce. Additionally, war-inflated prices caused other nations, such as Egypt, India, and Brazil, to increase their cotton production, creating competition in a dwindling market. To make matters worse, the home market for feed grains was greatly reduced as automobiles replaced horses and mules for transportation.

Moreover, U.S. manufacturing was growing rapidly, making the nation less dependent on imported goods. Also, high protective tariffs, designed to limit competition from imported industrial products, severely restricted the trade basis that had formerly been the foundation of American agricultural prosperity. Since nations tend to buy where they can sell their products, foreign sales dropped.

When demand slackened, agricultural prices fell, but taxes and prices of purchased items remained high. Farmers with debts from wartime expansion were not able to make the necessary downward adjustment in production; instead, they looked for ways to increase production in order to maintain their wartime level of income. A long battle against the cost-price squeeze grew out of this situation. DeLoach described the farmer's problem vividly when he wrote, "Money seems to go nowhere."

During the 1920s, most Americans enjoyed a period of unprecedented prosperity, but farmers were hit hard; thousands of them faced disaster. In their severe economic distress, many sought legislation as a quick remedy, and the Farm Bloc, a coalition of congressmen committed to serving farming interests, emerged in 1921. Subsequently, laws favoring cooperative marketing were enacted.[19]

Most agricultural leaders were not ready to accept the idea that the world would never again need the amount of American agricultural commodities that it had used in the past. They believed cooperatives, managed by farmers, could gain a measure of monopolistic control over the market and sell agricultural products more aggressively. The difficulty of organizing farmers limited the success of this movement. Farming is an industry of small, diverse units whose conflicting needs make cooperation difficult without government intervention.

By the mid-1920s the importance of production controls was gaining acceptance but producing less presupposes a reduction of labor. Families provided the labor on family farms. Less than full use of available labor and reduced production made no sense to the farmer who was having difficulty making ends meet by using the entire family to produce as much as possible. The vicious cycle of overproduction and low prices simply reduced the standard of living for most farm families rather than reducing production. Nonfarm employment was a solution for many young people, and a path that grew ever-wider over the years was cut from farm to city.

When Herbert Hoover entered the White House, he addressed the farmers' problems by signing the Agricultural Marketing Act of 1929 that created the Federal Farm Board. This board consisted of eight presidentially appointed members who were charged with the task of "improving the marketing organization, bargaining power, and financing arrangements of agriculture."[20] The board launched into national marketing associations, organized along commodity lines, only to discover the basic weakness of their plan—a lack of managerial experience that successful cooperatives acquire through slow, steady growth. Unfortunately, farmers could not wait for slow, modest gains; they needed immediate, large-scale improvement of their financial condition.

In October, 1929, the stock market crash set off a chain of events that greatly reduced the buying power of domestic and foreign buyers. No downward adjustment of agriculture could offset the effects of the Great Depression. Texans did not immediately notice the stock market crash, because very few of them owned stocks or bonds. In fact, most Texas farmers were not aware a depression existed until it was severe. Nearly 60 percent of the state's population lived on farms or in small rural towns, compared with a national average of 43 percent.[21]

These people had lived with low agricultural prices in the previous decade, and during the 1930s their attention was focused primarily on the savage drought that gripped the Plains states. Ultimately, it caused more misery and greater fundamental changes than the financial crisis.

Sandstorms became legendary. As a wall of dirt two hundred feet high crossed the Texas Panhandle on April 14, 1935, many feared the end of the world was at hand. People still remember exactly what they were doing when that boiling mass of dust darkened the sky, turning day into night. After the blow, songwriter Woody Guthrie left the Texas Plains for California, where he wrote *So Long, It's Been Good to Know You*, commemorating "Black Sunday."

Sandstorms raged across West Texas during the drought-ridden 1930s, because few farmers had either tractors to plow the land quickly enough to stop the blowing dirt or irrigation wells to allow the planting of cover crops. Drought and high winds were not new to the Plains; broken, bare land was. Today powerful farming equipment, irrigation wells, and conservation measures greatly control wind erosion.

When the price of cotton fell to a nickel a pound, the small, self-sufficient farms in West Texas quickly turned to dairy cattle, hogs, and chickens for their income. During the depression the South Plains became a poultry and dairy center, furnishing nearly one-fourth of all the butter manufactured in Texas. "In those money-scarce, drought-ridden years cream and egg checks became the chief medium of exchange, passing from hand to hand until there was no more space for endorsement."[23] Along with the increased poultry and cream production, feed grains that had little market value were used to fatten hogs and cattle. Cows, hogs, and chickens stood between farmers and failure.

Despite hard times, the depression and Dust Bowl days were an era of progress for many farmers; tractor power replaced animal power, general farming gave way to cash crop agriculture, and the federal government became a new farmhand.

New Deal agricultural legislation changed a way of farming that was six thousand years old. Individual independence shifted toward group interdependence. Farmers were organized as never before through thousands of local committees operating in a quasi-legal manner under a vast government bureau. Cooperative movements during the 1920s had been largely unsuccessful because free-riding farmers stood aside while cooperating farmers paid for the benefits that all shared. Federal programs corrected this by providing monetary benefits only to those who participated in production control.[24]

DeLoach's diary entries during the 1930s reveal a grass-roots reaction to FDR's farm program. Initially, the Agricultural Adjustment Act provided payments for plowing up cotton to control production. The drought that severely restricted planting on the Plains denied many farmers an opportunity to participate in the program. Resentment grew when some, who were lucky enough to get a shower or two to start the crops, collected their checks. Farmers were confused, and federal officials failed to understand how local needs could be contradictory to national policy. These were early indications of the difficulty of establishing a single policy, or goal, for all farmers.

More important, though, DeLoach was almost prophetic in his concern that small farmers would not benefit from government programs as much as large farmers. It was not until the mid-1950s that national attention focused on the plight of family farmers, whose small acreage of cash crops, such as cotton, had been reduced even further by government allotments. Improved prices meant little to people with nothing to sell. Moreover, these small farmers planted too few acres to qualify for most federal credit programs to purchase improved equipment or additional land. By the end of the decade 40 percent of the nation's farmers sold 90 percent of all products. The remaining 60 percent suffered from limited resources more than surpluses.[25] American farmers were rapidly dividing into the haves and the have-nots. DeLoach became resigned to the rules of the game and learned to wait for his government check before he paid his bills.

During the 1940s and 1950s, favorable crop prices brought on by World War II, the postwar economic boom, and the Korean conflict all encouraged maximum production. In addition, the technological revolution in agriculture that produced powerful machinery, high-quality seed, and chemical fertilizers made it possible to expand farming operations. Finally, widespread irrigation lent an element of predictability to farming, speeding the transition to cash crop monoculture. On the Llano Estacado, "farming grew to mean the production of large quantities of cotton for sale on the world market. Farmers were replaced by producers; and production replaced husbandry as the goal of agriculture."[26] Modern commercial farming had become a highly competitive enterprise that closely resembled other businesses in the industrial economy.

Living conditions on West Texas farms improved greatly during the 1940s. Rural electrification, farm-to-market roads, telephones, and gas lines brought the rural standard of living to the level enjoyed by city dwellers.

Unfortunately, this picture of prosperity has a dark side. Ever-increasing amounts of capital were required to raise crops whose market price was still subject to fluctuation. It was the same old gamble, but now the stakes were higher. An added worry was evidence that the water table in the Ogallala Aquifer was declining rapidly. The aquifer is a vast underground bed of water-bearing sand that stretches from Midland, Texas, to South Dakota. Recharge comes only from rain that slowly percolates down to the water sands, and since the onset of large-scale irrigation, consumption has greatly exceeded recharge.

As farmers moved toward a single cash crop after World War II, West Texas agriculture became increasingly vulnerable. When cotton prospered, so did farmers, but when cotton fell on hard times, farmers quickly accumulated staggering debts. The mechanism for diversification was not in place as it had been on the general family farm.

During the 1960s foreign growers and synthetic fabrics undermined the cotton market, creating a large surplus. South Plains growers and businesses joined forces to produce a quality of cotton that satisfied the needs of the textile mills. Next they waged an effective advertising campaign to create a demand for West Texas cotton.

Similar programs were started in other areas of agriculture, but headlines of the 1980s testify to the fact that relief was not permanent. American agriculture is still plagued with overproduction and low prices. In reality, too many farmers are producing too abundantly. Mechanical, genetic, chemical, and management "revolutions" have made it possible for one person to produce twenty times as much as a person could at the turn of the century. Because of this, many rural people live near the poverty level. Social scientists are stressing the importance of a move away from programs that keep marginal farmers hanging on and a move toward retraining programs designed to ease the transition of people out of agriculture into other jobs.

DeLoach retired in 1952 and rented his land to a younger neighbor. He realized that it was more profitable for a small farmer to own land than to farm it. His farm was free of debt, and the rent he received was all profit, while the ever-increasing expenses and headaches belonged to someone else.

DeLoach typified the rural American for whom life changed drastically after the 1920s, and his writing reflects this change. In the early years of the diary, all the animals had names, but he simply planted so many acres of cotton, or "planted feed all day." He wrote that Lady Cow pleased him by "finding" a heifer calf (his cows "found" their calves), that Bess Cow disappointed him with a bull calf, or that Nancy, his mule, was stubborn. However, beginning in the late 1930s, and increasingly during the 1940s, the animals were no longer mentioned by name, whereas he wrote about planting Martin Maize and Oklahoma 44 or Paymaster cotton. He also wrote about tractors, combines, and irrigation wells. Farmers quickly accepted the science and technology that radically changed their way of life.

Prior to widespread use of the automobile, lodge meetings, singings, and ice-cream suppers were popular forms of entertainment. By the mid-1920s a new era was emerging. As the number of cars increased, more people spent Saturday in town, where movies provided an escape from the drudgery of farm life. More important, they lured people away from their traditional life-styles by providing images that were soon reflected in their lives. By the end of the 1920s, DeLoach was writing about style shows, bridal and baby showers, and Chamber of Commerce meetings.

Listening to the radio became another popular pastime. Daily news of social and political changes broke the bonds of isolation, and worldwide agricultural developments and market conditions were now available in the farmer's living room. The radio encouraged West Texans to think and talk like other Americans.

Despite the convenience of modern technology, the homespun pleasures of rural life were still gratifying for many of DeLoach's generation. "Car visiting" was so popular that everyone tried to get to town as early as possible on Saturday to get a good parking place, and friendships of many years' duration developed over a domino game or coffee at the local drugstore.

Sunday was still a day of rest, a day to bring friends home from church for dinner, go for a ride in the car, watch a baseball game, or just make a "pop call" on some of the neighbors. It was also a good day to catch up on the week's newspapers that had been put aside because of work.

Revivals, box suppers, and youth activities helped rural churches retain their influence in society, but by the late 1930s DeLoach was writing nostalgically about the days when he knew everyone at church and people had time to visit after services. The old order was passing.

After World War II, the world grew much smaller as the countryside became the outskirts of regional marketing centers. Saturday was no longer the traditional day for going to town, and town was no longer a rural community. Any day of the week DeLoach's automobile might speed over the highway to Lubbock, where the traffic jams and choice of merchandise were dizzying. However, the shopping was always finished in time to get home for favorite television programs, the same programs the rest of America was watching, further blurring the line between rural and urban life-styles.

Within a single lifetime the foundation of our national values and mores changed from rural to urban, and an eyewitness with an urge to write sat in a corner describing it all.

N·O·T·E·S

1. Edwin C. McReynolds, *Oklahoma: A History of the Sooner State*, pp. 301–302. Oklahoma divided the territory into three new counties—Jackson, Harmon, and Greer—and part of a fourth, Beckham.

2. W. G. DeLoach family to David Murrah, Feb. 21, 1975, Oral History Files, Southwest Collection, Texas Tech University, Lubbock, Texas (hereafter cited as SWC).

3. The ground was covered with several inches of snow when Sallie started labor about sundown on Christmas Eve, 1913. Will took the kitchen table outside, turned it over, and hitched a team of horses to the two front legs. He used the table as a sled to go for the doctor in Ralls, three miles away. It was after dark when they returned and the children were sent to bed while Will and the doctor took care of Sallie. When Jimmie Lee was born and Sallie was comfortable, the doctor, who had a long white beard, went into the bedroom where Robert and Harold were sleeping and got into an empty bed to catch a few winks before daybreak. When the two boys awakened the next morning they were quite excited because they thought Santa had spent the night at their house. Indeed he had, and he had left a baby sister. Robert E. DeLoach, interview with Janet Neugebauer, Sudan, Tex., Mar. 17, 1987.

4. Donald E. Green, *Land of the Underground Rain: Irrigation on the Texas High Plains, 1910–1970*, pp. 62–73.

5. USDA, *Yearbook of Agriculture, 1913*, p. 425; Joseph F. Gordon, "The History and Development of Irrigated Cotton on the High Plains of Texas" (Ph.D. diss., Texas Tech University, 1961), pp. 104–34.

6. U.S. Bureau of the Census, *Cotton Production in the United States, Crop of 1916*, p. 26; U.S. Bureau of the Census, *Cotton Production in the United States, Crop of 1920*, p. 22. Cotton production in Crosby County increased from 8,035 bales in 1914 to 20,639 in 1919.

7. *The Hub* 1, no. 1 (Dec., 1927), p. 8.

8. Richard Mason, "The Cotton Kingdom and the City of Lubbock: South Plains Agriculture in the Postwar Era," in *Lubbock from Town to City*, ed. Lawrence L. Graves, pp. 1–4; Max M. Tharp and E. Lee Langford, "Where Our Cotton Comes From," in *Yearbook of Agriculture, 1958*, p. 134.

9. *The Hub* 3, no. 9 (Apr., 1942), p. 2; *Charter, Rules and Bylaws of the Lubbock Cotton Exchange*, comp. Lubbock Cotton Exchange (Lubbock: Board of Directors, Lubbock Cotton Exchange, 1951). On August 2, 1954, the Lubbock Cotton Exchange was designated a bona fide cotton market with daily quotations and sales.

10. Walter Prescott Webb et al., eds., *The Handbook of Texas* 2, pp. 69–70.

11. Carleton R. Ball, "The Grain Sorghums: Immigrant Crops That Have Made Good," in *Yearbook of Agriculture, 1913*, p. 228.

12. J. Roy Quinby, "The Development of Grain Sorghums," *West Texas Historical Association Yearbook* 33 (Oct., 1957): 45–48.

13. John Widsoe, *Dry Farming*, pp. 1–10, 136–64, 326–27, 416; Walter Prescott Webb, *The Great Plains*, pp. 369–74.

14. R. E. Karper and D. L. Jones, *Varieties of Cotton in Northwest Texas*, p. 5; Lubbock Chamber of Commerce, *Texas Technological College Locating Brief*, (Lubbock, 1923), pp. 7–10.

15. Norman J. Rosenberg, "Climate of the Great Plains Region of the United States," *Great Plains Quarterly* 7, no. 1 (Winter, 1987): 22–32.

16. Entries for three months during the summer of 1915 were not transferred to the ledger. They were written on pages from a lined stationery tablet and stuck in the back of Ledger #1, where they remain.

17. Rodney C. Loehr, "Farmer's Diaries," *Agricultural History* 12, no. 4 (Oct., 1938): 313–25.

18. *McLean (Texas) News*, Mar. 8, 1918, p. 6.

19. Gilbert C. Fite, *American Farmers: The New Minority*, pp. 38–50.

20. Murray R. Benedict, *Farm Policies of the United States, 1790–1950*, pp. 256–58.

21. *Texas Almanac and State Industrial Guide*, 1929, p. 46; U.S. Bureau of the Census, *Fifteenth Census of the United States: 1930*, vol. 1, p. 8.

22. Roy Sylvan Dunn, "Agriculture Builds a City," in *A History of Lubbock*, ed. Lawrence L. Graves, p. 261.

23. Clarence Poe, "What's New in Agriculture?" *Progressive Farmer* 48, no. 6 (June, 1933): 18–21.

24. USDA, *Report of the Secretary of Agriculture, 1959*, pp. 62–63.

25. Mason, "Cotton Kingdom," p. 3.

DeLoach Family

William Green DeLoach — Diarist
Sallie Edna (Newton) DeLoach — DeLoach's wife
Harold Grady (H. G.) DeLoach — DeLoach's first son
Dellie Shipman DeLoach — Harold's wife
Walter McMahan — Harold's stepson
Leonard DeLoach — Harold's son
Wayne DeLoach — Harold's son
Robert (Bud) Emmet DeLoach — DeLoach's second son
Ida Rene Crain DeLoach — Robert's wife
Wanda DeLoach Swart — Robert's daughter
Robert (Buster) Edwin DeLoach — Robert's son
Mildred Texas DeLoach — DeLoach's first daughter
Dorothy (Dot) DeLoach Blackman — DeLoach's second daughter
Almeda Faye Blackman — Dorothy's daughter
Jimmie (Jim) DeLoach Coward Moorhead — DeLoach's third daughter
Arlois Coward — Jimmie's first husband
Kalah Yvonne (Kay) Coward — Jimmie's daughter
Stanley Arlois Coward — Jimmie's son
Glenda Lee Coward — Jimmie's daughter
William Alvah (Bill) Coward — Jimmie's son
Billy Roland DeLoach — DeLoach's third son
Noma Jean Seeds DeLoach — Billy's wife
Billy Roland DeLoach, Jr. — Billy's son
C. C. Newton — Sallie's father

Plains Farmer

1·9·1·4

Will DeLoach was thirty-four when he started his diary. At the outset, he didn't say why he started it or how long he intended to keep it. Entries were brief—really just notes he could refer to later. The fact that he began during his first year on the Plains suggests he believed his farming experiences in a new environment were too important to be trusted to memory.

M·A·R·C·H

· Sat 28. Finished plowing. Went to Ralls. Sold 10 doz. eggs. Came a good rain tonight. 10:30 p.m.
· Sun 29. Rec'd of English Bros. $15.00 for looking after wind mill and water for his cows for the month of April & May.

The English Brothers were nearby ranchers. Ranchers often hired settlers to water, feed, and look after cows known to have trouble at calving time. The cows were kept in a stock lot on the settler's farm, or the settler made frequent trips to the pasture. This practice, less expensive for ranchers than hiring year-round hands, added to the settler's cash income and illustrates the working relationship that generally existed between ranchers and farmers on the Llano Estacado.

A·P·R·I·L

· WED 1. . . . Bought 140 bundles of millet, 4¢ per bundle. Went to Ralls.
Put in application to join Woodmen of the World. . . . Bought 1 ton
of maize off Mr. John Ralls @ $15.00 per ton. Will go tomorrow after
same.

After arriving too late in 1913 to plant forage crops, DeLoach had to buy
winter livestock feed from neighbors. This was one of the most expensive aspects of moving for pioneer farmers. The millet bundles he bought were pearl,
or cattail (the head of grain resembles a cattail spike), millet. It was fed to poultry and livestock. He also bought yellow milo maize, a popular grain sorghum
in semi-arid areas because it produces high yields under droughty conditions.
Maize was fed, primarily as threshed grain, to all types of livestock. The stalks
did not make good forage because they were fairly dry and not sweet (See Ball,
"The Grain Sorghums," in *Yearbook of Agriculture, 1913*, pp. 221–38; John H.
Martin, "Sorghum Improvement," *Yearbook of Agriculture, 1936*, pp. 523–42).
Woodmen of the World was an insurance lodge that provided fellowship. A dis-
tinctive monument was placed on the grave of every deceased member. It was
a six-foot-high granite tree trunk with nubby branches all around and bark-like
grooves textured into the stone along with the fraternal seal (See Charles W.
Ferguson, *Fifty Million Brothers: A Panorama of American Lodges and Clubs*, pp.
136–44; David L. Caffey, *The Old Home Place: Farming on the West Texas Frontier*, p. 46). In 1908, John R. Ralls, a Georgia native, traded a business in Oklahoma for ten thousand acres of grassland in Crosby County, Texas. He later
colonized this land with farmers to establish the town of Ralls, Texas (See Nellie
Witt Spikes and Temple Ann Ellis, *Through the Years: A History of Crosby County,
Texas*, p. 440).

· FRI 3. It is raining this morning. That is fine. A good sod season in the
ground now. Will break some at once.
· SAT 4. Went and got my sod plow today. Cost $6.00. Payed $2.00 down.

The plow that broke the Plains was made of steel. A moldboard, located just
behind the share, was the most prominent part. It was shaped to twist the furrow slice and turn it over, leaving the land fairly smooth for planting. A team
of two mules or horses pulled the plow. The driver walked behind, guiding and
adjusting it to suit the ground by bearing down, or letting up, on the handles.
Fourteen inches of plowed land was a "through," and twenty-eight inches was
a "round" (See Percy W. Blandford, *Old Farm Tools and Machinery: An Illustrated
History*, p. 48).

· Mon 6.   Broke sod all day. Was very tired at night. I don't like that marching behind a sod plow. . . .

A sod plow was called a footburner because a farmer's feet got tired and sore after following one all day. Turning over an unbroken ribbon of sod that went half a mile or more was considered a good job of plowing, and breaking two or three acres was considered a good day's work (See W. J. Morton, Jr. *Snowstorms, Dust Storms and Horses' Tails*, p. 15).

· Wed 22.   Bought team of mules off Yates, $180.00.

Many farmers preferred mules because they required little food, were stronger than horses, and were highly resistant to heat, flies, and disease. Their smaller feet were desirable for working cotton, especially during cultivation. They were thought to be more intelligent than horses because they balked at being worked past their endurance. However, they never completely replaced horses (See Delmar Hayter, "South Plains Agriculture: 1880–1950" [Master's thesis, Texas Tech University, 1981], p. 51).

· Sun 26.   . . . Came [a] cyclone 2 mi. north of our house. Kill[ed] all of Mr. Hicks' horses. Wrecked his house.

Very likely DeLoach is referring to a tornado, nature's most violent storm, with winds up to 325 miles an hour. Tornadoes were sometimes called cyclones (See Donald R. Haragan, *Blue Northers to Sea Breezes: Texas Weather and Climate*, pp. 45–48).

· Mon 27.   . . . Sallie wants me to dig storm cellar.
· Tues 28.   Went to Emma after lumber to fix cellar. Got Mr. Bowen's planter. Came by town. Bought side meat, 20¢ per lb. Too high to eat. Keep a little to look at.

M · A · Y

· Fri 1.   Finished up dug out [*storm cellar*]. Am proud of it. If it was my own place I would be lots prouder [*he was renting from his brother-in-law George Witt*].
· Wed 6.   . . . I planted water melons, roasting ear patch, and a little cane for early feed for hogs. My other sow brought 5 pigs. 2 died. She disappointed me as I thought she would bring 8 or 10. They are sure fine ones. (thanks)

· Tues 19.   Warm and nice all day. Worked on cultivator in A.M. Planted cotton in P.M. 24 rows. Not much of ½ day's work. Could not crowd Mike [*a mule*] for he is sick with distemper. Have not smoked any cigaretes since Fri 15. Yes, I bummed 3 or 4 since then, but will try to quit for a while at least.

· Wed 20.   . . . I planted peanuts in morning and cotton in P.M. . . . Put up another cow. That makes 6 of 2 E's [*English Brothers*] cows. 8 with my two. Get lots of milk. My hogs left milk in the trough today.

· Mon 25.   Planted cotton 'til about 3 P.M. Finished up about 40 or 45 A[*cres*] in cotton. If it makes that will be a plenty and if it don't make enough to lose. Go-deviled some feed. I think the go-devils are a huge joke. Would not have one at all if I had not already bought [*it*]. My maize and other feed stuff that is up, is in the weeds to beat the band.

DeLoach was apprehensive about planting cotton on the arid Plains, because historically it was considered suited only to humid areas. Also, forty to forty-five acres of cotton was enough to gather at harvest time since laborers were very scarce on the South Plains. A go-devil was a piece of farming equipment used by most West Texas farmers. It had long sharp knives attached to each side, which slipped through the dirt beside young crops and cut the weeds off just under the top of the ground. Perhaps DeLoach was upset because some weeds continued to live in the moisture-conserving mulch of dirt that go-devils left around the young plants (See Spikes and Ellis, *Through the Years*, p. 89).

· Thurs 28.   11:30 o'clock. Big cloud in southwest. Looks bad. All are asleep, but if I were to holler "storm" they would be up like a bunch of quail and down in the cellar they would go. Went to Hardy Witt's after planter, but if it rains can't plant feed tomorrow. Will go to bed soon.

Hardy Witt was George Witt's nephew and was also DeLoach's brother-in-law.

J·U·N·E

· Thurs 11.   . . . a stray calf came up with my milch cows. Branded 3 on left thigh, undercrop the ear. Don't know who he belongs to. 3 or 4 weeks old. Rather young to be branded.

The calf was marked with a registered brand, and the bottom of its ear was cut with a knife for further identification. The spring cow work on neighboring ranches would have been finished before this calf was born, but the influx of settlers probably made its owner apprehensive about waiting until fall branding time. Unmarked calves were easy prey for thieves (See William Curry Holden, *The Spur Ranch*, pp. 112–19).

- TUES 16.   Harrowed cotton. Putting same in fine shape. Water getting scarce. No wind. Tank sprang leak. Nearly all water ran out [*of*] surface tank.
- FRI 19.   Plowed cotton all day. . . . Yates and I helped cow deliver calf. She was about dead. Largest calf I ever saw. Cow left calf as soon as she got strength enough to get up and walk off and she has not come back to it.
- SAT 20.   . . . Cow won't claim calf at all. Went after her. Could not drive her. She was on the prod and fought my horse and I had to leave her.
- SUN 21.   . . . Old cow won't take her calf at all.
- MON 22.   The orphan calf died about 2 or 3 o'clock P.M. Skinned him. . . .
- SAT 27.   Plowed cotton. Harold did. Brother [*DeLoach's second son, Robert Emmet, usually called Bud*] & I hoed. We went to town in P.M. Boys sold their calf hides, 16½¢ per lb. They weighed 4 lbs.

Weeds missed with the plow were hoed out to conserve scarce moisture. Hides were a minor source of income for farmers, and they often gave the money to the children who had helped care for the animals.

J·U·L·Y

- MON 6.   Planted cane in forenoon. Sun was hot. Mules sweated awful. . . . Gnats were a fright. Awful hot all day. Thunderheads all around.
- WED 15.   Month ½ gone and not done work yet. . . . Mike gave plumb out. Had to take him out. He is awful poor. No feed, hard work will make any one poor.

DeLoach fed his animals sparingly because he was buying feed. Farmers always hoped for good sorghum crops so that their animals could eat abundantly and work harder.

- FRI 31.   . . . The wolves came and killed one of the old turkey hens. Caught her out in the garden. She had 11 little ones. Can't find all of them. English Bro. cut hefer yearlings out [*removed from the herd*] and delivered them at $30.00 per head. Hot and no prospect for a rain. Would be fine on late feed stuff, but cotton don't need any. . . .

Lobo wolves were a menace in Crosby County. This large wolf was also known to kill and eat grown cows (See Spikes and Ellis, *Through the Years*, p. 284).

Shipping problems and fear of an embargo destroyed the cotton market during the early months of World War I, reports in the *Fort Worth Star-Telegram* (Sept. 27, Sept. 30, and Oct. 4, 1914) indicated. In August, 1914, it dropped from twelve to six cents per pound. Because more than half of U.S. cotton was exported, pandemonium broke out in the New Orleans and New York cotton exchanges, forcing them to close until order was restored. Local remedies were devised to provide some relief for farmers. The Fort Worth Chamber of Commerce initiated a "buy-a-bale" program, encouraging merchants in the Cotton Belt to buy a bale of cotton for ten cents per pound; however, it was impossible to absorb the bumper crop waiting to be harvested. Bradford Knapp, an official with the Department of Agriculture, pleaded with farmers to plant less cotton in 1915 and diversify to food products. He predicted food would remain high and cotton low throughout the war.

S·E·P·T·E·M·B·E·R

· Fri 4. Cut one load of maize. The mules got out of the lot with the harness on and I could not pen them on the pony I bought off Yates. I gave him $20.00 for him and his saddle. He got all he was worth. The boys will have something to fool around on and when school starts can ride to school. Andrew [*a temporary hand*] started in to cutting maize.

Ripe maize had large golden heads of grain that crooked down toward the ground. The heads were cut off by hand and thrown on a wagon that mules pulled slowly down the row. When full, it was hauled to the "stack" lot. The grain was either thrown on the ground for threshing later, or it was stored, for use as winter feed, by covering the stack of maize heads with sorghum bundles (See Spikes and Ellis, *Through the Years*, p. 66).

· Wed 16. Cut maize till noon. Hauled [*to*] Ralls. Rent to stack lot. . . .
Bought 22 yds cotton sacking at 14 cts per yd. 116 lbs spuds @ 3 cts per lb.

Before the evolution of a cash economy, rent was paid in crops. Every third load of forage crops and every fourth bale of cotton went to the landlord. In later years, it became customary to pay the landlord a similar portion of the total cash received from crops raised on his land.

Millet   Crook neck maize   Feterita

· Sun 27. Cut patch of feterita that was shattering out. Had to cut it or lose it. Don't like to work on Sunday. Ought to rest. Lots of work. No one to do it but me and boys. Cotton sure is opening. I think I have at least 15 bales of cotton open now. Looks little bit like rain. Hope will not rain. Would do lots of harm.

Feterita is a variety of sorghum native to Egypt (Sudan) that is characterized by erect heads, fairly dwarf stature, early maturity, and extreme drought resistance. A popular feed for work stock, cattle, and chickens, harvested feterita was tied into bundles using either twine or a few stalks of green cane that were twisted around the bundle. It was then shocked up and allowed to dry for about three weeks before stacking (See Ball, "The Grain Sorghums," pp. 221–38). Cotton harvesting began about mid- to late September and lasted until the youngest bolls were cracked by a hard freeze and their lint dried. Each field was gone over two or three times; the last time, bolls were harvested that had only partially matured before frost stopped their growth (See Gordon, "The History and

Development of Irrigated Cotton," p. 134). DeLoach was concerned about rain because it wets the bolls and stains the lint, which reduces its price.

> · MON 28. . . . I picked 211 lbs cotton this afternoon. My best ½ day's work. . . . Clear & cool. Picking on 3rd bale. . . .

Cotton was harvested by hand. Lint, containing seeds, was pulled out of the open boll, put into a sack, then dumped on a wagon after being weighed. The cotton sack, often called a tow sack, was dragged between the rows of cotton by a shoulder strap (See Hayter, "South Plains Agriculture," p. 70).

> · WED 30. . . . Payed up a few ac'cts. B. [*Bennett*] Bros [*Grocery*] $15.00, Botts [*Mercantile*] $10.00, Bedingfield [*Hardware*] $17.50, Woodman dues, $2.55, $8.30 [*apparently $4.15 per bale*] for ginning. Took all I had in bank. Money & I can't stay together.

O·C·T·O·B·E·R

> · FRI 23. The whole earth is covered with water. Walked to town. My mules are all out and can't get them up. It came another hard rain. Filled the lake full. That finished fixing [*ruined*] the cotton.

Water stands on the level Plains, giving the impression that "the whole earth is covered with water." October, 1914, was an unusually wet month. Lubbock, Texas, 28 miles west of Ralls, recorded 7.12 inches of rain for the month and 31.44 inches for the year, well above the yearly average of 19 inches (See USDA, *Climatological Data for the United States by Sections* 1, part 5: Annual Summary, 1915, p. 151). The lake DeLoach referred to was probably a wet-weather lake, common on the Llano Estacado. Even today these low places are planted in crops when the water has evaporated. If a heavy rain comes before the crops are harvested, the standing water destroys everything.

> · SUN 25. Cloudy, but not raining. Went to Hardy's in afternoon. They sure have the blues. Not any worse than I though.
> · TUES 27. . . . Rented a room in the old court house. Will move soon. Cotton was off. Yates came down. Will stay all night.

The farm on which DeLoach was living sold and he had to move. He rented a room in the original Crosby County courthouse, which was built in Esta-cado, Texas, when it was the county seat. In 1891 the county seat was moved to Emma, where the courthouse also went. After the Santa Fe Railroad came to Crosbyton, in 1911, the county seat was moved there, but the courthouse did not follow this time. It was sold to a private owner who moved it to Cedric, about four miles away from Emma, where it was converted into a rooming house. Scarcity of wood on the treeless Plains encouraged adaptive reuse of buildings long before the concept was popularized by historical preservationists.

· WED 28. . . . Killed a shoat. Sure did hate to kill them. They were so young. I thought that we were all meat hungry, but not so. All are filled already. Give me plenty of milk & butter and I don't care much for meat.

Historically, pork has been a major meat source for Texas farm families. Hogs are smaller and easier to slaughter than cattle, there is a diversity of pork products, and cured pork keeps dependably (See John A. Kincannon and John G. McNeely, *An Economic Appraisal of the Texas Hog Industry*, pp. 3, 16).

N·O·V·E·M·B·E·R

· SAT 7. Took cotton to gin. 2 bales. One weighed 538 [*pounds*], the other 545. Was offered 5½¢ [*per pound*]. Would not sell for that, for my cotton was graded middling and was worth more. Will hold a few days.

Raw cotton is sold in bales of ginned lint, averaging five hundred pounds each. Price, per pound, received for a given bale depends on the class assigned to a sample taken from that bale. In August, 1914, Congress passed the Cotton-Futures Act, which set standards for determining the quality and value of cotton. Initially only nine classes existed; today there are thirty-seven, ranging from Good Middling to Below Grade. Middling cotton has a good white color, is free of foreign matter, and has good fiber confirmation. To receive this classification lint has to be picked from the boll. DeLoach harvested his cotton by picking the lint out of the open bolls, therefore the grade was very likely high. Today, fiber length, known as staple, is also a factor in determining the class of a cotton sample (See "Report of the Secretary," in *Yearbook of Agriculture, 1915*, pp. 44–47; Terry Kuhlers, cotton classer, U.S. Department of Agriculture, interview with Janet Neugebauer, Lubbock, Texas, Feb. 25, 1987).

· MON 16. Awful cold all day. Our first killing frost this morning.
· WED 18. Still cold and cloudy. Could not pick cotton. Went to town. Was offered 5¢ for my cotton. Would not take it. Stayed and finely got 6¢. One bale weighed 545, 564, and 538. Payed my cow note, $21.25.

Bennett Bros., I payed them $40.00. Ordered the *Star-Telegram* $3.25, so nearly all my cotton money went today. The boys set the cotton pile on fire, or at least I think they did it. They claim "fire of unknown origin." Did not damage it much, I don't think, but scared the devil out of them. They were in bed when I came home. "Had gone to sleep."

The *Fort Worth Star-Telegram* originated in 1879 and was widely read throughout Texas and southwestern Oklahoma.

· THURS 19.   The boys "came clean with the goods." They finely made a confession and told me how they set the cotton on fire. It was just as I said.

Robert (Bud) and Harold were smoking cigarettes made from cotton leaves when they dropped one in the cotton pile. It immediately burst into a blaze, and after putting the fire out the two boys "high-tailed it" to bed before their father could question them (Robert E. DeLoach, interview with Janet Neugebauer, Sudan, Tex., Mar. 17, 1987).

· THURS 26.   This is Thanksgiving day. Went to Hardy Witt's after some posts and wire to fix cow lot. . . . Helped brand & dehorn some cows. I ate turkey dinner at sister's (Curtie's). She has lots of work to do. Feel sorry for her.

D·E·C·E·M·B·E·R

· MON 7.   Went to town. Made a sale of cotton seed . . . got 2415 lbs cotton seed. Sold to O. M. Morgan for $15.25 per ton.
· THURS 10.   Went to town. Got some wood for lard rendering. Made 12 or 13 gal. of lard and about 40 lbs. of sausage. Will pack my meat tomorrow.

Wood had to be imported and purchased on the treeless Plains. Sausage was preserved by frying it in patties, packing the patties in stone jars, and pouring melted lard on top to seal the contents (See Edward Everett Dale, *Frontier Ways: Sketches of Life in the Old West*, pp. 126–27).

1·9·1·5

Cotton was a bad gamble in 1914. Its price dropped so low that it was hardly worth picking, so DeLoach built a boll puller to finish gathering his crop, then swore off cotton. In 1915 he planted grain sorghums on newly broken sod land—which was weed-free because the sod was so tight that it denied weeds a place to grow—and spent the summer harvesting wheat in Oklahoma.

J·A·N·U·A·R·Y

· FRI 1. New year. Did not make any new resolutions but will try to do
better than I did last year so I started the new year by helping Sallie do
an awful big washing. It took us nearly all day. . . .

Water was heated, outdoors, in a big cast iron pot. Clothes were first scrubbed on a washboard, then put into the pot to be boiled. The dried cowchips that were commonly used for fuel produced a hot fire but burned very quickly, so one person was kept busy feeding the fire. When available, mesquite grubs (the stump and root system that had been grubbed out of the ground) or cotton-wood and hackberry branches from nearby canyons were used to make a fire that burned longer without refueling, as the weekly wash for a family required several hours (See Morton, *Snowstorms, Dust Storms, and Horses' Tails*, p. 14).

· THURS 14. Sold my feterita heads for $12.25 per ton. Made 3 loads. Let
Taggart have a team of mules to haul feed for Haney. Am to get $1.50

for them. Will not let him have another at all. He jerks them too much.

· Tues 19. . . . Got my sled and fixed me up a cotton puller.

DeLoach's homemade boll puller was a box affair mounted on sled runners. The front end was open and had a row of non-adjustable, steel fingers in the middle. Mules, hitched to each side of the open end, pulled the box down the row as the steel fingers stripped the bolls off each cotton stalk. It harvested only one row at a time. DeLoach stood behind the fingers forking the cotton bolls into the back end of the box. The term cotton sled, which developed from these early mechanical harvesters, was a misnomer because the bolls were stripped from the plant. It was actually a cotton stripper, which this type of equipment was called after the 1940s. Low prices caused many farmers in northwest Texas to experiment with mechanical harvesters in 1914–15; however, DeLoach's record is the earliest known personal account of mechanical cotton harvesting in Texas. The movement toward mechanization was retarded because gin equipment could not adequately separate unopened bolls, burrs, and other trash from the lint. Foreign matter lowered the price farmers received (See D. L. Jones, W. M. Hurst, and D. Scoates, *Mechanical Harvesting of Cotton in Northwest Texas*, pp. 1–9; Robert E. DeLoach, interview with Janet Neugebauer, Sudan, Tex., Mar. 16, 1987).

· Wed 20. Did not work good. Left so much cotton I layed it aside. Went and got another slide. It does very well.

Generally, the term *slide* describes long knives attached to metal runners to prepare beds for planting, but DeLoach's reference to a slide indicates he was probably using metal runners to drag the cotton puller more easily along the ground. The earliest sleds had wooden runners that would have been difficult to pull across the wet ground after all of the moisture in the fall of 1914 and winter of 1915. Ground losses from the use of this crude instrument were heavy, and DeLoach probably thought he could correct the problem with smoother runners. The varieties of cotton available in 1915 had expansive branches and bolls that opened wide for ease of hand-picking the lint. Exactly the opposite characteristics were bred into varieties that ultimately made stripper harvesting efficient and profitable.

· Sun 24. Still cold and bad weather. Tim Andrews came and got his gilt that I traded him for cotton patch. I traded cotton patch I got from Tim Andrews to Taggart for a sow and kitchen cabinet. Would not

14

have traded if I could of handled it my self, but could not. I think I made the sow clear on the deal.

Before the establishment of a cash economy, DeLoach bartered whenever possible, saving his small supply of cash to use with merchants, banks, etc. and to pay taxes.

· Wed 27. Went to Crosbyton [*the county seat*] to pay my taxes. . . . My taxes were $6.07. . . .

F·e·b·r·u·a·r·y

· Sat 13. Pulled cotton till noon. Took a load of cotton to Lorenzo. Had on 2436 lbs at $1.25 per cwt. Will be glad when I get through with this cotton but I am making money out of it. Can't break sod and I have plenty of time for the old land.

Each new gin that was built was better equipped to extract the burrs as the trend was toward pulled, rather than picked, cotton. Approximately fourteen hundred pounds of picked cotton, compared to nearly twenty-nine hundred pounds of sledded cotton, was required to make one five hundred-pound bale. Burrs in the sledded cotton explain the difference in weights. At six cents per pound, DeLoach's hand-picked cotton averaged $30.00 per bale, and he also made about $7.50 on seed. His expenses would have been $4.15 for ginning, plus labor costs for harvesting. Thus, net income per bale, before labor, was $33.35, compared to approximately $27.50 per bale equivalent of sledded cotton (containing unopened bolls), which had no labor expense. Entries do not indicate how much cotton DeLoach harvested with his boll puller (See Jones, Hurst, and Scoates, *Mechanical Harvesting of Cotton in Northwest Texas*, p. 17).

· Sun 14. . . . I roached [*cut an animal's mane so the remainder stands upright*] Nig and Mike. Hauled a load of cane.
· Wed 24. We moved in our new house. Sure was lots to do. I fixed up the cow lot and moved them over but did not move the mules, chickens nor hogs. My big black sow is gone. Don't know where. She "came in" and "went out." Will not try to plow any this week on acc't of so much work to do.

DeLoach rented another farm and moved into the house located on it.

M·A·R·C·H

· TUES 2. . . . Is raining like the devil now 10:30 P.M. Got letter with notice
that 3 checks I got from Lorenzo Hardware Co. had been protested.
That sure did give me the wide eye. I will go to Lorenzo tomorrow to
see about it.

DeLoach apparently sold his ginned cotton to the owner of the hardware
store in Lorenzo and received checks that would not clear the bank. The market for selling cotton and feed grains was just as good in small towns as nearby
cities, and local merchants often acted as middlemen in the transfer of agricultural products from grower to processor.

· SAT 6. Went over to Burrell's after my sow. They charged me 10 cents per
day while she stayed over there. Don't want her to go over there any
more. $1.20. I could have fed her on a whole lot less than that. . . .

According to Texas laws, when stock entered the enclosed lands of any person other than the owner, the person in lawful possession of such lands could
impound the stock, legally described as estrays, and detain them until fees and
damages were paid to the person impounding the stray animals. The price
DeLoach paid was not too high. Ten cents per day was permitted for each hog
(See *Texas Jurisprudence: A Complete Statement of the Law and Practice in the State
of Texas* [Stock Laws: Chapter Five, Articles 7222 and 7224; Chapter Six, Articles 7249 and 7251]).

· MON 8. . . . now snowing to beat the band. 9:00 o'clock P.M. All gone to
bed but me. I bought a bottle of Livertone and will take it for my
"sickness."

The average pioneer settler spent an astonishingly large percentage of his
meager cash for patented medicines, which were purchased from the local drug-
gist. "Liver regulators," were popular for biliousness (See Dale, *Frontier Ways*,
p. 200).

· THURS 18. Sent for the man up at Taggarts'. Will keep him one month if
I can. . . . Am to pay Mr. Marvin $25.00 per month.
· SUN 21. Went over and stirred my cotton again. It is not damaged as
much as I thought yesterday. I did think it sure was ruined.

Cotton that was piled on the ground after pulling had to be turned over, or
stirred, several times after a rain or snow to protect the lint from molding or
staining due to contact with the wet bolls.

· WED 24. Plowed till noon. . . . Went to town in P.M. Borrowed $60.00 at
   bank. Would not have had to borrow any money from the bank if I
   could have sold my cotton but the bad weather kept my cotton
   wet. . . .

A·P·R·I·L

· SUN 11. . . . Made a trade with Watson for his 2 row planter. Gave him
   a nice gilt and a cultivator. Sure did hate to let the hog go but I can do
   without her and I have to have a planter.

M·A·Y

· MON 3. Took load of cotton to the gin. It was hard looking. Had it
   ginned. Only got 320 lbs. lint. I am utterly disgusted with cotton.
   Don't think I'll plant a seed for myself. I traded what cotton I have
   planted to Warren for his 20 A. sod. Warren broke sod today. . . .
· SAT 8. . . . Sold my cotton for 4½ cents per lb. Not much. Did not settle
   my gin acc't. Came back home and plowed the afternoon.
· FRI 28. . . . Sallie and I went to Lorenzo. I bought me a new wagon. Cost
   $90.00 but I need it.
· SAT 29. I went to Ralls to get a rod to my planter fixed. Came by Cedric.
   Brought the organ. $7.55 freight charges on it.

An organ was ordered from a marketing center, possibly Fort Worth because
DeLoach regularly read the *Fort Worth Star-Telegram*. Sallie received musical
training during her youth; in 1903, she taught piano lessons in Acme, Texas,
earning enough money to buy a lounge. There is no record of teaching after
starting a family, but her musical ability made the DeLoach home a popular
gathering place.

· SUN 30. Hardy Witt & family came over. We had a little singing. I did
   not attend much. I was busy trying to get ready to go.

The DeLoach family returned to Oklahoma to work in the wheat harvest
during the summer of 1915. They traveled in a covered wagon. When DeLoach
was away from home it was his habit to record the day's happenings on a tablet and transfer this information to his ledger upon returning home. Entries from
May 31, 1915, to August 11, 1915, however, were not transferred to the ledger.

They were recorded on pages from a tablet and inserted in the back of ledger #1, where they remain.

· MON 31.   We made ready and started for Okla. I sent Warren & Gordon [*hired men who went to Oklahoma to help DeLoach harvest wheat*] by Ralls for a wagon sheet. I did not have but one and I had that one on my wagon that Sallie & little ones ride in. Harold & Bud drove the wagon that Warren & Gordon drives. Harold & Bud bring up the rear with the buggy. Charley & Lippy [*are the*] two saddle horses. We did not stop for noon meal. Warren & Gordon caught us at Cone. We made Floydada for over nite camp [*campsites were twenty to twenty-five miles apart, which was apparently a day's travel in a wagon*].

J·u·n·e

· TUES 1.   We were up early and on our way. We made nite camp east of White Flat. Looks rainy back in the West. All tired. Sallie & little ones rode quite a lot in the buggy. Boys rode the saddle horses.

· WED 2.   We made a good day's drive. Camped for the nite across North Pease River, east of Northfield.

· THURS 3.   We were on the road early. Made Childress by noon. Noon stop in east edge of Childress. Night camp 5 to 8 mi. west of Squaw Creek crossing on Red River. Rainy looking.

· FRI 4.   We were up early. But could make no time much. Came a rain during nite and the roads were muddy. We made noon camp on Red River. Crossed OK. Just east of Eldorado, Okla. a bad cloud caught us and we stayed with some people—a Mr. & Mrs. Springer. They were out in front of their home and told us to drive in. We did. Just had time to take teams out when the storm struck and how it did hail & rain. Mrs. Springer lost a lot of her fryers. So she and Sallie fixed them for supper. All ate heartily of them. Gordon & Warren & I did not know they were drowned. But they were good.

· SAT 5.   We could not leave early. Too much muddy roads and high water. Mr. Springer did not want to charge me anything for the over night stop, but I payed him $2.00 for the feed I fed to my stock. They were nice to us. Fixed beds for all of us. We drove to Creta and that is as far as we could go. Boggy Creek is all over the low lands. Sallie & little ones went over to a Mrs. Coy's home. Ate dinner. Me & boys stopped in Ben Porter's house. We will have to stay here till the creeks run down.

· SUN 6. Well the creeks had run down enough that we could cross Boggy
Creek, but we could not follow the main Olustee road. Had to go
north from Creta then east to Olustee, arriving Frank Drake's [*Sallie's
brother-in-law*] home about 11 A.M. We were all wet, tired and played
out. May and Jim Melton fixed dinner and we all ate dinner at May's
[*Sallie's sister*].

Upon arrival they learned the storm that made their trip difficult also
spawned a tornado that damaged many homes in Olustee, Oklahoma. Nevertheless, the family found a house to rent for $10.00 a month, and as soon as the
weather cleared, DeLoach, his sons, and the two hired men began cutting and
threshing wheat. On a good day they could cut twenty to thirty acres, and on
one occasion they received as much as a third of the total crop as payment for
cutting it. According to the *Yearbook of Agriculture, 1915* (p. 421), the average
price per bushel was $1.17, so DeLoach received approximately $10.00 for that
day's work. They worked until about the middle of August. Diary entries stop
after August 11, and it is very likely that the DeLoach family spent the remaining days settling accounts and enjoying one last round of visits with family and
friends before packing their wagon for the trip back to Crosby County.

S·E·P·T·E·M·B·E·R

· WED 1. We came in yesterday. Sure was glad to get home. Don't seem like
we were gone 3 months. Things are sure shot up. My heifers look good
and my feed is good. My cane don't look good at all. Did not get a
good stand. Will go for my hogs & cows tomorrow.

Neighbors looked after the place and cared for the livestock while the De-
Loach family was gone. The cane DeLoach planted was a sorgo, or sweet sorghum, that produced sweet, juicy stalks ranging from five to ten feet in height.
The heads had only small seeds. The high sugar content of the stalks made
them excellent for forage and, to a lesser degree, for the manufacture of syrup
(See Martin, "Sorghum Improvement," p. 528; Paul D. Hutchinson, *Grain Sorghum in the United States*, p. 5).

· SUN 19. This night I decided I would not milk any more. I can't milk
and do my other work, so we will teach the boys to milk.

DeLoach had a good feed crop, but rains hampered the harvest just as the
year before. The maize started sprouting in the stalk and the market dropped,
so he decided to hold as many of his pigs as possible and feed them out. He tried

Sorghum   Wheat

to hire help, but decided the going rate for heading maize, $1.00 per load, was too high.

N·O·V·E·M·B·E·R

· Tues 9. I finished thrashing today. Got my car loaded. 37960#. Sold to Evans for $.65 per cwt. My check called for $244.98.

Farmers hauled marketable maize to town in a wagon that held about four thousand pounds and then loaded it into a boxcar. This was a hot, dusty job because maize was harvested in September, one of the warmest months of the year (See Charles C. Sherrod, interview with Jeff Townsend, Apr. 11, 1974, Oral History Files, SWC).

1915

D·E·C·E·M·B·E·R

· FRI 31.   The last day in the 1915. The year has been very prosperous for
me. I have payed, or have the stuff to sell to pay, the most of my obligations. Raining all day. Warren came out. He & I had a settlement. I
owe him $34.95, which I will pay tomorrow. He was a good hand and is
a good man. I think I will get me a new ledger as this one is all used up.

1·9·1·6

Because improved land rose in price, farms changed hands often, and therefore renters moved frequently. DeLoach was never happy renting land; he believed he could improve his lot in life by owning a farm. In 1916 he decided to commit his earnings to a mortgage on 320 acres. Despite problems at the beginning of World War I, the price of cotton stabilized then rose during the remaining years of the war as the demand for uniforms and other supplies increased. During a good year the rent could nearly pay for a place.

F·e·b·r·u·a·r·y

· Thurs 3.   . . . The Spawlding man came along. I bought a hack, $150.00. Lots of money for a way to go.

· Tues 8.   Rigged up the "Success." Broke the garden & go deviled it. Then harrowed it. I have the garden in fine shape.

The "Success" was a riding plow with a moldboard for deep breaking. Middle breakers could replace the moldboard, for planting. Average cost was fifty dollars. A harrow is an implement used after a breaking plow to work the soil to a smooth surface. Spike-tooth harrows were used to rough up the surface after a rain (See Hayter, "South Plains Agriculture," p. 43).

· Thurs 10.   . . . Used my Georgia stock & "Mother." She is a fine plow nag. Took the 3 mules and started in to break sod. The ground is getting dry. Had to put on 4. . . .

"Georgia stock" is a mule and double shovel, a popular combination throughout the south during this time. The double shovel had about half the plowing capacity of a cultivator and could handle about four acres per day (See Gordon, "The History and Development of Irrigated Cotton," p. 126).

· Fri 11.   Started out with the sulkey. Did not do but 2 or 3 rounds. Rigged
       up my walking plow. Sure did fine. Pulls a little heavy.

The sulky is the "Success" DeLoach referred to on Feb. 8. A sulky was a two bottom moldboard plow with steel shares. It was a heavy riding plow that required four draft animals to pull it. In contrast, the walking plow required only two animals, but it neither cut a wide furrow nor plowed very deep (See Hayter, "South Plains Agriculture," p. 42).

· Sat 12.   Plowed till a little after noon. Took team and plow and went to
       help put out a prairie fire that started in the "06" Pasture. Cause of fire
       unknown. Some cowboy threw down a match I suppose.

Even though a prairie fire was nature's way of cleaning up the range, it was the terror of cattlemen and settlers. The worst time was late fall and early winter, when the grass was dry. Often started from a match or a carelessly tended camp fire, it could destroy everything for miles as winds whipped the flames along. Men fought a prairie fire by backfiring—burning a strip along a road or furrow that had been plowed as a fire guard. They also beat a fire with brooms or wet sacks filled with dirt, or they dragged along the leading edge of the flame the bloody carcass of a beef that had been cut in half. When a fire could not be brought under control quickly, women gathered their children near a water tank for protection and helped the firefighters with supplies of water and food (See Spikes and Ellis, *Through the Years*, pp. 126, 249–50; J. Evetts Haley, *The XIT Ranch of Texas and the Early Days of the Llano Estacado*, pp. 169–81).

M·A·R·C·H

· Sun 19.   Stinson came up and helped me lower the pipe in the well but
       she would not pump. Sallie & I worked on the da—— thing all day.
       Would not pull a drop of water.

In 1916, DeLoach had more problems than usual with his windmill. When it was broken he had to take his animals to a nearby wet-weather lake each day for water. In addition to providing water for livestock, windmills were a household convenience, bringing water close to the house. Usually piped into a bar-

rel in the corner of the milk house, water could be stored for household and drinking purposes. The overflow ran through a milk trough to cool the milk and butter, then on out to irrigate the garden, and finally into a tank to water the livestock. Introduced by ranchers, the windmill received its greatest use from farmers, who made it the mark of human habitation on the Plains.

> · Mon 20.   Sallie & I pulled the sucker rods and pulled lower check. Tightened up upper check, put them back and she went to pulling water. Ha! Ha! I am sure glad. I did not have to take the stock to the lake tonight. They filled up on good cold well water. We watered the onion patch.

Wind blowing through the vanes of a windmill caused an up and down motion of the sucker rod within the cylinder that descended below the water level of the well. Water flowed into the cylinder during an up stroke of the sucker rod. It was held by the lower check until the sucker rod descended to the bottom of the well on a down stroke. The water was then held by the upper check attached to the sucker rod and lifted aboveground on the up stroke of the sucker rod (See Green, *Land of the Underground Rain*, p. 41).

> · Tues 21.   Sure was windy and the sand was walking about. Looks like rain tonight. I came back from town by Fred Lea's. He was in bed. Layed up from his horse falling with him.
> · Fri 31.   Rain! Rain! Woke up this morning about 5 a.m. Lightening & thunder. A bad cloud was in southwest. We hustled out to the cellar. It started raining. Now 10 p.m. Still raining. A good season now. The work will start now. . . .

A·p·r·i·l

> · Tues 11.   Finished planting sod cotton [*cotton planted on land that was prairie sod the year before*] about noon. Planted some cane around the edge. Then went to planting Kaffir corn. Mr. Newton filley found a fine mule colt last night. It measured 39 in. tall. Not bad. Windy and dry.

DeLoach often named his animals after their previous owner. Sallie's father, C. C. Newton, had owned this filly.

> · Mon 24.   . . . Sherman came over for my two row planter. I can't keep it at home. There is a little cloud in the N.E. tonight. Hope it will rain soon.

1916

M·A·Y

· Sun 28.   Sallie & I walked over the field. It don't look good to me. Near
the first of June and not much of my crop up. Hardy & Curtie came
over and stayed all day. I sure love for them to come. Curtie seems to
be falling off. She is taking some kind of antafat [*diet pills*].

· Tues 30.   Lord God! The wind has been raging all day. Fixed up a weed
knife and Harold tried to knife a few weeds, but the wind blew so hard
that the dust covered him up, and I told him to quit. . . .

· Wed 31.   . . . I dipped my hogs & one calf. The calf was the lousiest thing
I ever saw. He would have been dead in a few days if I had not dipped
him. The wind mill men came in just at night. No rain yet. Clear.

Livestock had to be dipped regularly to rid them of ticks and vermin. They
were run through a vat or a hole in the ground that was filled with an arsenical solution. The container had to be large enough for the stock to swim at least
two minutes in the solution. The procedure should have been repeated in
twenty-one days to kill the pupae, but ranchers and stockmen did not consider
this practical. In addition to spreading Texas fever, ticks consumed blood that
would otherwise produce milk or flesh (See J. H. McClain, *Eradication of the Cattle Tick Necessary for Profitable Dairying*; Robert M. Chapin, *Arsenical Cattle
Dips*).

J·U·N·E

Despite scant summer rainfall, the cotton crop fared better than expected.
Livestock feed suffered, however, and DeLoach had to sell some of his stock.

· Thurs 8.   Started in to plant Chaney's [*DeLoach's landlord*] feed, but
could not get my planter to work. The ground is so dry that you can't
get a sod planter to take it without lots of weight. Then when I strike
a sod place I break my planter so I guess I'll have to wait till it rains.
Sure is some dry. . . .

J·U·L·Y

· Tues 4.   We fixed up and looked for Hardy & Curtie to come and we
would go to the canyon, but they did not come so we stayed home all
day. Sure was a lonesome day. Hot & dry.

DeLoach was referring to nearby Blanco Canyon which was a popular place for fishing and swimming. Cottonwood and hackberry trees growing near the water provided shade for picnicking. Early settlers on the flat, treeless Plains especially enjoyed the canyon because it reminded them of the terrain where they previously lived. Blanco Canyon, and the streams that feed into it, is a major drainage course for rainfall on the Llano Estacado.

· Sat 8.   Poisoned a few dogs [*prairie dogs*] in the field. . . .
· Fri 14.   . . . Loaded 6 head of hogs. Took them to Ralls, leaving home about dark. Got back about 12 o'clock. The 6 weighed 985 @ $8.60 per cwt. or $84.71. Not bad. The 4 that I got to-boot in the mule & mare trade brought me nearly $70.00. Near the price of the mule.
· Tues 25.   . . . I boiled the buggy wheels in linseed oil & painted it. She looks like a new buggy now. Sure wish would rain a little jag.
· Fri 28.   The long-looked-for-rain came up about 10:30 A.M. Sure did rain some. The ground is soaked.

S·E·P·T·E·M·B·E·R

· Thurs 14.   Our first norther came today. Was quite chilly. Went to Ralls. Took first degree in I.O.O.F. Was rather cool coming home. The Lorenzo team came over to Ralls with one of their candidates and three of us went through together. . . .

Old-timers believed the first freeze of the fall would come ninety days after the first norther. The Independent Order of Odd Fellows, I.O.O.F., was founded by Thomas Wildey at Baltimore, Maryland, in 1819. It was organized primarily for fellowship, but also provided small insurance benefits intended to defray the cost of interment (See Ferguson, *Fifty Million Brothers*, pp. 217–33).

· Wed 27.   We went and picked cotton for Butler. Sure did work hard. He will have to do something with his cows now. The stock law went into effect the 25th inst.

Approved on Mar. 1, 1915, Senate Bill No. 69 granted each county authority, upon petition of fifty freeholders, to hold an election to determine whether livestock should be allowed to run at large. Apparently Crosby County voted in favor of requiring livestock to be penned (See Texas, *General Laws of the State of Texas*, pp. 45–46).

O·c·t·o·b·e·r

· Mon 9.   Sherman & I went to Crosbyton to see the Bassett Land. Saw
Mr. Bassett. He sent us out to see the land. Can't say that the proposi-
tion appealed to me. Came up a cold wind. We got cold coming home.
Hope won't frost yet a while. We ate dinner at the Bassett Hotel. They
would not take a thing for our dinners. Good feed. Will go and load
up again.

Until 1918, Julian M. Bassett headed one of the more successful land development companies in Crosby County. He was the general manager of the C-B
Livestock Company that owned the ninety thousand-acre Bar–N–Bar Ranch.
Bassett laid out the town of Crosbyton, Texas, supervised the building of a railroad spur from the nearest Santa Fe line, and began breaking land for sale to
immigrants. By 1911 about forty thousand acres had been sold at prices ranging from twenty to thirty dollars per acre, depending on the distance from
Crosbyton. Buyers were brought in on special trains, were guests at the Bassett
Hotel, and were entertained with a banquet and speeches extolling the virtues
of Crosby County. Land promoters usually tried to prevent prospective buyers from mingling too closely with the local folk, because stories about the extreme weather of the Plains, hail, drought, and blizzards would not help land
sales. Neither did they want them to hear stories about cheaper land. Other
developers used a similar approach in the settlement of the Plains (See Gordon, "The History and Development of Irrigated Cotton on the High Plains
of Texas," pp. 53–59; Crosby County Pioneer Memorial Museum, *A History of
Crosby County, 1876–1977*, p. 27).

· Mon 16.   Jim Orr [*a brother-in-law*] & I went to Lorenzo. Saw James Gray
and he took us out to see some land of Uncle Don James. I guess I'll
buy ½ section at $25.00 per acre. Will be in debt some, but I can't rent,
so will have to buy.
· Thurs 19.   Woke up this morning. The damnedest norther I ever saw.
Freezing. Good-by young feed & cotton. Will not make enough feed to
do me now. Sure do hate to see this freeze come so soon. Nearly 30
days earlier than last year.

Despite DeLoach's laments about the damage of the early freeze, Crosby
County ginned 11,879 bales of cotton in 1916, compared to 3,425 in 1915.
Droughty weather caused a small harvest in 1917 and 1918, but the number of
bales ginned grew each following year, establishing the cotton industry in West

Texas (See *Texas Almanac and State Industrial Guide*, 1927, p. 152; Spikes and Ellis, *Through the Years*, p. 81).

· Fri 27. Sold cotton for 18.30 [*cents per pound*]. The most I ever sold a bale of cotton for in my life. Bale weighed 489 lbs.

· Mon 30. Went to Crosbyton to see Evers [*County Clerk and Surveyor*] about some land. He could not get off to show me. So had to stay all night.

· Tues 31. We went and took a look at land. I bought ½ section at $10.00 [*per acre*], 9 mi N.E. of Crosbyton. Put up $50.00 forfeit money. . . .

Land near the town of Crosbyton sold for twenty-five to fifty dollars per acre, but unbroken land several miles away from town sold for much less (See *Crosbyton Review*, Feb. 29, 1912, p. 13).

D·E·C·E·M·B·E·R

· Sun 17. We stayed home all day. Gordon went to see his brother. Will move tomorrow.

· Mon 18. I brought Sallie & kids over. She dreaded the canyon. Ellison's boy came for a load.

Sallie was frightened of crossing the canyon with young children in the wagon. It was very difficult to control wagons, especially loaded ones, during the steep descent into Blanco Canyon, and getting up the incline on the other side was equally difficult. Often, everyone had to get out and walk or push (Robert E. DeLoach, interview with Janet Neugebauer, Sudan, Tex., Mar. 16, 1987).

· Sun 24. Christmas eve. Nice day. We went up to Mr. Ellison's in P.M. They made Kodak pictures. The old jent & I had ours made together.

· Mon 25. Dull Xmas. We did not have the money to spend. That is what makes a Merry Xmas. The Ellisons took dinner with us. Nice day.

1·9·1·7

DeLoach's 1917 entries describe the well-known signs of drought for the first time. He wrote about hot, dry winds, clouds that disappeared before dropping rain, crop failures, the "blues," and, finally, selling out. Sooner or later, these signs become familiar to everyone who lives on the Plains.

J·A·N·U·A·R·Y

· Wed 10. Gordon & I went to Crosbyton. I made a deal for $300.00. Paid balance on down payment on land.
· Fri 12. Sent Gordon to Woodson's for a load of feed. He got a ton and ½, $37.50 worth. Sure is high. We put it in house. Too high to waste.
· Tues 16. The same old thing as Monday. Set by stove. Made fire out of "cow chips." We have no coal. They save the coal bill. Coal is $12.00 per ton and a ton would last about 20 days. The "sap" will come up in this wood as soon as this snow melts.

Dried cow manure, called prairie coal, was commonly used as fuel on the treeless Plains. The cow chips were gathered in a burlap sack and stored near the stove to keep them dry. Women speared the chips with a pointed stick and dropped them into the fire, never touching them with their hands while working in the kitchen. Though very economical, they left a lot of ash, which was a source of irritation to children assigned the task of taking it outdoors (See

Harry H. Hewlett, interview with Richard Mason, Mar. 31, 1982, Oral History File, SWC).

- Fri 19. Some warmer this morning. Loaded up the chickens, took them to Crosbyton. Sold 216 lbs. at 12½ cents per lb. $27.00 in all. Bought some Gro. Bought a gobbler for $3.00. Nice bird. Two cocks one $ each. Fine R. I. [*Rhode Island*] Reds. . . .
- Wed 31. Old "Mother" was completely knocked out. Had to hitch up my Newton filley. She did fine after I got started. I drove her around the land. Taught her to turn at the corners. Then I hitched her traces [*harness*] to a single tree [*a bar to keep draft chains apart*]. Tied a catch rope to single tree and let her drag it around the land. Then I put the 3 horse eavener [*equipment used to make a team of draft animals pull in tandem*] to them and let them all drag it a while. Then I hitched on to the plow. Started out and took land little at a time till finely was cutting 15 in[*ches*]. She never knew when the full load came on her. I worked with her kind so she is well broke and gentle. Plowed till noon. Came up a cold N.E. wind. Awful cold. I grubbed out some land. Want to take out all the grubs on it. I think I have some fine land.

The mesquite tree has roots spreading out ten or more feet, in addition to a large tap root. Pioneers had to remove this root system with a grubbing hoe and axe before the ground could be broken. The hardy mesquite is so well-adapted to arid and semi-arid regions that it not only survives but continues to spread during a drought. Livestock find the beans palatable, but they are not easily digested. Through livestock droppings, mesquite trees spread rapidly over the grasslands.

M·A·R·C·H

- Sun 11. We stayed home all day. Mr. Cannon & family came over in p.m. He & I went to the mail box. Came back, left the buggy and team standing. They took a notion they wanted to run a while. They made a 4 or 5 mile heat. Went over one fence, through one gate and never hurt a thing. Lost one paper. Lucky run.

A mail carrier left Floydada, Texas, every other day to travel a thirty-five-mile route to Dickens, Texas, where he spent the night before traveling the route in reverse. Thirty-five miles was considered a good day's journey.

A·P·R·I·L

· Fri 6. Our Uncle Sam declared war on Germany this day. . . .

· Sat 7. Sure did come some sand storm. Cold. Some ice. Easter spell I guess. Helped dig a grave for an infant of a Mr. Parker living east of me. His wife had twins.

Many old-timers in West Texas refer to any cold weather that occurs near Easter as the Easter Spell. This is presumed to be the last cold spell of the winter.

· Sun 8. Cannon and folks came over and we all went down in the canyon to have an Easter egg hunt for kids. Heard the other twin baby died.

M·A·Y

· Tues 29. Mr. Cannon came over and brought a horse and he & I went to Crosbyton. The school boards of Wake & Leatherwood Dis. came over and we got together and went to the Courthouse to see the Dis. maps. We could not, or did not, do anything. I feel a little down and out. Guess will have to move. Can't have a school closer than 4 or 5 miles. Looks a little like rain tonight.

Four or five miles was the maximum distance most parents wanted their children to travel for schooling, because they had to either walk or ride horseback.

· Wed 30. We did not do anything till afternoon. Then all went on the creek fishing. Caught 7 fish and a young cotton tail hare. Will have to get them. Things are so high and don't look as though we will make anything.

Before the onset of irrigation, the White River received enough water from the springs flowing into it to sustain a fair amount of catfish. Harold and Robert (Bud) remembered going fishing whenever they got a chance. They had twenty-four hooks that were set out in the morning and when checked in mid-afternoon they usually had enough fish for supper. Twisting cottontail rabbits out of prairie dog holes was also considered great sport. They twisted the end of a piece of barbed wire, put it in the hole, and started turning it. If a rabbit was in the hole, the wire would hook into its fur, and sometimes flesh, and the boys pulled it out. Fish and cottontail rabbits were considered delicacies dur-

ing these years, as the steady diet of beef and pork became monotonous. During the Great Depression, rabbits were a source of protein for many families in West Texas (Robert E. DeLoach, interview with Janet Neugebauer, Sudan, Tex., Mar. 16, 1987; DeLoach family to David Murrah, Mar. 18, 1975, Oral History Files, SWC).

J·u·n·e

· Tues 5.   This is the day the President of our U.S.A. has ordered all men between the ages of 21 and 30 years to register for military service. I am not in that age limit. . . .

· Thurs 7.   The hot dry wind. Lord! It sure has howled. I went over the pasture. The grass is good yet, but can't stay good long if it don't rain. I get awful tired of wind.

· Fri 15.   Mr. Cannon came over and we went to Crosbyton. He sold his place for $27.50 per acre. If I could sell out I would move closer to school. Came up a nice cloud, but the sand got in it and she scattered. Cool tonight.

· Fri 29.   My God! Nothing to write about, but the same old thing. Set around and dry up. Nothing doing of any kind. Went down to mail box.

J·u·l·y

· Fri 6.   No use to try to raise cattle. They will all die. My dogie cow is no better. In fact, I do not see how she is alive. Went to town to see my banker about taking my stock out of this county and hunting some grass. Sure is awful dry. I listed my land with a land agent for $17.00 per acre. Cannon came over to see how cow was.

A dogie calf is a motherless calf. Apparently DeLoach raised this one to adulthood and continued using "dogie" to identify it.

· Fri 13.   Lay around all day. Sure was hot. My God! If it would only rain. This is awful "blue" times. . . .

· Sat 28.   Gathered up the chickens. Took them to the −N− Ranch for Jim McDonald. $12.25. They were starving to death. I could not buy feed for them to keep them going. Too high. Lord, things are getting out of sight. I don't see what people are going to do. They are shipping all the food out of the U.S. Sinking it, when people here will be starving to death in 60 days if things don't loosen up. You must be contented. Can't express yourself. Matters not what one thinks. If one don't like the way things are, he has to hold his tongue anyway.

The Bar–N–Bar Ranch was owned by the C. B. Livestock Company and managed by Julian Bassett (See comments for Oct. 9, 1916). The Food Administration, under the direction of Herbert Hoover, implemented a systematic program to persuade the American people to eliminate waste and reduce consumption of food in order to send more to the European allies during World War I. "Wheatless Mondays, Meatless Tuesdays, and Porkless Thursdays" were part of the regimen. As a result, the United States was able to export in 1918 approximately three times its normal amount of meat, sugar, and wheat. Many people, including DeLoach, had difficulty accepting restrictions on food that was often sunk during shipment to Europe. World War I was different from any previous military conflict involving the United States. It required the mobilization of every element of life: commercial, social, scientific, and educational. Legislation was enacted to direct all of these resources toward winning the war. When the powers of the government were extended over the lives of the people, Americans experienced censorship. The Espionage Act of June 15, 1917, authorized prison sentences for people who made false statements or reports that caused dissatisfaction or interference with U.S. military operations. The Sedition Act of 1918 provided additional force by making it a crime to write or say anything against the United States (See Zechariah Chafee, Jr., *Free Speech in the United States*, p. 39; William Franklin Willoughby, *Government Organization in War Time and After*, pp. v–vi).

O·c·t·o·b·e·r

· Thurs 4.   . . . My Lord, sure is lonesome here. Seems like Sallie has been
    gone a month. The boys did not cook but one meal today, breakfast. . . .
· Thurs 11.   Set around looking down my nose till afternoon. We rigged up
    a sled and cut rows of cane. The first time had cut any feed with a sled
    in a long time, 17 years.

A sled was a low platform on runners used to convey a load and usually pulled by draft animals. The person harvesting cane rode on the sled, cut the cane by hand, and tied it in bundles, which were thrown on the ground. The bundles were shocked to dry before stacking them for winter feeding.

N·O·V·E·M·B·E·R

· Fri 9. We finished my feed. Two stacks. A great crop for 1917. Will long
   be remembered. Harold went over to help Richmond stack feed. Brother
   & I did the family work today. Now I don't blame no woman for saying "washing is a hard job." We have not cooked but one meal today.
   Cooked enough to last them all day.

Total precipitation in 1917 was twelve and one-half inches, approximately
eight inches below normal. Most importantly though, seven inches of this fell
in August and September, too late to plant anything but feed crops or winter
wheat. DeLoach's oldest son, Harold, remembered that most of the cotton seed
planted in May had not germinated by October. It was just lying in the ground.
The comment about two stacks of feed being a great crop is sarcasm — several
large stacks of forage crops were needed to carry the livestock through the winter (See *Climatological Data, 1917*; DeLoach family, interview with David Murrah, Feb. 21, 1975, Oral History Files, SWC).

· Fri 23. . . . Had letter from Sallie stating the birth of a boy baby. Born
   Wednesday 21, 1917. She was doing well. Sure glad that much of the
   ordeal is over (Billy Roland DeLoach).

Because the DeLoaches lived so far away from a doctor, Sallie returned to
Oklahoma to receive the care of her sisters and the local doctor at the time of
delivery. DeLoach's failure even to mention her pregnancy in the privacy of his
diary sheds light on the culture of his time that considered any mention of sex
taboo. It also indicates the diary was intended for his eyes only. He knew she
was pregnant and needed only a reminder about the day Sallie left and how
lonesome he was without her.

D·E·C·E·M·B·E·R

· Mon 3. I went to Crosbyton. Sold my place. Had to pay the interest
   which amounted to $261.00. Did not like to do it for my trade with
   Paxton was "to-wit." I was to get $7.50 [*per acre*] clear, or $2600.00.
   Hated to sell out, but did not make anything to pay up my debts and I
   want to get out of debt. Mr. Dykes came over. We traded saddles. I gave
   him a sow pig to-boot. Think maybe I can sell him my two row planter.
   Sent deed to Sallie for her signature and acknowledgement. She can
   send them in before she gets home.

Texas practices the community system of property rights, in which assets acquired after marriage become the property of the couple. DeLoach needed Sallie's signature on the document of sale (See Walter Prescott Webb and H. Bailey Carroll, eds., *The Handbook of Texas* 1, p. 388).

- Mon 17.   Went to town. Had my wagon worked on. Sallie and little ones came in. Columbus [*Sallie's nephew from Oklahoma*] came home with them. Was glad to see them coming home. Gone near 3 months.
- Tues 18.   We stayed here all day and cleaned. Takes one hand to tend this new boy. We have been here one year today. Columbus and the boys went to the Mount Blanco Canyon. They reported a great time.

1·9·1·8

DeLoach returned to Oklahoma to raise wheat that was averaging two dollars a bushel due to wartime inflation. When he arrived, the current crop was already four months old, so he tried cotton until it was time to plant wheat in September.

J·A·N·U·A·R·Y

· Tues 1.   Another New Year. I am not worth as much by $500.00 as I was this day one year ago. Did not make any crop to speak of. Lost some stock.
· Sun 6.   Cold wind from North. . . . We took cattle & stock and started for Roaring Springs [*railhead for Quanah, Acme & Pacific Railway*]. Sold three steers to Jim Warner for $75.00. Hated to see them sell so cheap, but could not take them without paying excess on them.
· Mon 7.   We finished loading car. I gave the old brown mare and the Kirby mare to a fellow at Roaring Springs. Could not sell them. Did not want to pay excess on them. We shipped out of Roaring Springs about 3 o'clock, getting to Quanah 8 or 9 P.M. Unloaded stock. Cold as the devil. Hid the boys in the car. Saved $7.50 by doing so.

Farmers moved in railroad boxcars that were rented at reduced rates from the freight agent. They were called immigrant, or Zulu, cars. Household goods and farm equipment were secured at opposite ends of the car, and animals rode in the middle section. A maximum of ten head of livestock, only work stock and milk cows, was allowed. Other family members rode with the passengers while one member—usually the husband—stayed in the boxcar to care for the animals. This was an uncomfortable ride, as most farmers moved in December or January when their leases expired, and fires were not permitted in the immigrant cars. Some trips lasted several days and the person riding in the car had to carry his food along. Hot coffee was said to be missed more than anything else, including lavatory facilities. The trip was hard on the animals, but the trains did stop periodically at watering places. Cars were leased for a specified period of time, and the price rose considerably for overtime. This was a problem because bad weather could delay loading or unloading. Unloading was the hardest of all because there were no friends or family in a new place. Stock was unloaded first and taken to a wagon yard near the depot. Confused stock sometimes refused to leave the boxcar, or might bound out over the head of the owner. Moving in an immigrant car often remained a nightmare in the mind of the farmer as long as he lived (See Claude W. Medlock, interview with Sylva Wesendonk, July 26, 1976, Oral History Files, SWC; Harry H. Hewlett, interview with Richard Mason, Mar. 31, 1982, Oral History Files, SWC).

· WED 9.   Started boys out with horses & cows. I loaded up what I could put on wagon. Stored balance at section house. Left Quanah about 11 A.M. Came a cold west wind. Had to walk near all the way. Stuck on a hill near Frank Drake's. Had to leave wagon & buggy.
· THURS 10.   My God! Such a spell. The worst since Feb, 1899. Had to leave cows in lane and I guess they are all froze to death.

January was unusually cold, with severe changes in temperature and excessive snowfall. The cold wave of the tenth through the twelfth swept in as a blizzard and was the worst since February, 1899. Many livestock froze to death during the blizzard, as temperatures dropped below zero with winds ranging from forty to fifty miles per hour. Harold recalled driving the livestock behind the wagon in which the family was riding. They had crossed the Red River, on their way to C. C. Newton's ranch (Sallie's father) near Elmer, Oklahoma, and were about five miles away when the storm hit. It got so bad the boys had to leave the livestock and catch up with the wagon. The family made it to the ranch, and the animals drifted back to the Red River where they found some protection along the banks (See *Climatological Data, 1918*, p. 3; DeLoach family, interviews with David Murrah, Feb. 21, 1975, and Mar. 18, 1975, Oral History Files, SWC).

· FRI 11.   Went out on foot to look for Cows. Could hardly walk. Found
cows near Bob Drake's [*a relative*] place. They drifted south. They
seemed to stand the cold well enough.

· WED 16.   We got moved in. Straightened up some. Snowed some today.
Will start kids to school soon. They are behind in their books. We did
not have much school advantages on the "cap rock."

The DeLoaches rented a house in Olustee, Oklahoma, approximately ten
miles northwest of C. C. Newton's ranch. They lived in town until Will found
a farm to rent. The Caprock is a mineral layer underlying the Llano Estacado
that protects the sediments beneath it from erosion. It is not a rock in the usual
sense of the word; it is a "hard-pan" layer that developed a few feet below the
ground surface as mineral subsoil particles cemented together to form the rock-
like layer. Although the term *Caprock* applies only to the formation itself, the
expression is loosely used to mean the whole Llano Estacado (Webb and Carroll, eds., *Handbook of Texas* 1, p. 292).

· THURS 31.   No warmer. Sallie is down. Under the weather. Some LaGrip,
I guess. Awful bad weather. Good for grip and "pheunuonia." I guess
that is the way to spell it.

F·E·B·R·U·A·R·Y

· SAT 2.   I settled up with Frank & Jim [*brothers-in-law*]. I owed them
$25.45. That is an awful price to pay for getting a load of freight hauled
to Olustee from Quanah [*twenty-eight miles*], but I paid it. Hope I will
not have to do that any more.

· THURS 14.   Scott Olson & I went to a sale over at Glenn Thrash's. The
sand was something awful. I bought a writing desk, two saws & a
square.

· TUES 26.   Went to Duke with Bob Tipton. Looked at the place. I don't
much like to move in to such a shack, but is the best we can do this
time of year. Some good pasture land and plenty of water.

After moving, DeLoach discovered that the well was not a good one, and
creek water had to be used for drinking.

M·A·R·C·H

· MON 4.   Went to Altus [*regional shopping center*]. Thought I might get a
lister planter. None offered. Ordered a new one. . . . Went and looked

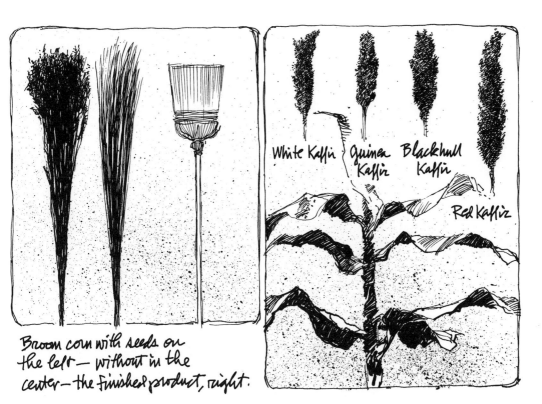

Broom corn with seeds on
the left — without in the
center — the finished product, right.

White Kaffir Guinea Kaffir Blackhull Kaffir Red Kaffir

at Jim Melton's feed. Guess I will buy 500 binds of Kaffir corn and
what headed maize he has at $42.50 per ton and 10¢ per bind for
Kaffir.

A lister planter is a drill planter designed to place seeds in the bottom of a
deep furrow made by a lister plow, which is a double moldboard plow used to
open a furrow and throw the soil in opposite directions (See Arthur W. Farrall
and Carl F. Albrecht, *Agricultural Engineering*, pp. 196–97).

· Fri 8.   Took two loads up to place. . . .
· Sun 10.   Feeling bad all day. Little cold. We went down on creek to see
the "Gipsys." Sallie & Mae had their fortunes (or misfortunes) told, as
did Frank and Jim. 50¢ per dose. I think the whole lot expected something they didn't get or got something they didn't expect. They all
seemed down in the mouth. God!, but I feel bad. Throat all swelled up
so I can't hardly talk.
· Mon 11.   . . . Mildred died 5 yrs today.

45

One of the reasons DeLoach left Oklahoma in 1913 was to get away from the scene of his daughter's death—she ignited her clothes while playing with matches she found in "the big rocking chair." When the family returned, the memories of that tragedy also returned to haunt them, and he wrote about it on each anniversary of her death. In one entry he wrote, "we lost a sweet little girl. Mildred was 4 yrs, 1 mo., 2 days old when she died."

· SAT 16.   Sallie & Harold went to Duke. Newton and Dick [*Sallie's father and brother*] came up. Ate dinner. Mr. Newton cooked. I liked to have choked up at night. Sent for Mr. Carley to come and take me to Olustee. I phoned for Craig to come to the barber shop and lance my throat, but he did not come. He had a "greasy" case on Red River, so did not come till after my throat had burst. I sure did get some relief then. Went to eating and drinking water. . . . Slept good for first time in a week.

· FRI 22.   Went to Olustee. Paid $50.00 on my planter. Brought it out. Bought 12 hens off Mr. Crane. They cost me $2.70. Can sure spend money when one has it.

· SAT 30.   . . . Went up to Duke. Bought Wes Lockett's Ford Car, $500.00. Lots to pay for a way to go.

· SUN 31.   Went over to Altus, Olustee. Some quick way to go.

A·P·R·I·L

· THURS 11.   Took $50.00 Liberty Bonds.

Liberty Bonds were public loans to the U.S. government to finance World War I. Beginning in May, 1917, five series were sold to more than twenty-five million people. The drives raised over $24 billion and encouraged nearly as many enlistments as did recruiting agencies. The Third Liberty Loan, issued in April, 1918, called for $3 billion at 4.25 percent interest. Over $4 billion was raised.

· MON 15.   . . . This is the day that all saloons close in 10 miles of an army camp. . . .

· WED 17.   Kline came down and I sold him the old Red cow. Hated to sell her for she was the first cow that I bought when I went to the plains in 1913, but she was getting too old to keep for profit. I got $50.00 for her. Gave $60.00 for her & calf.

Kline was probably the owner of the local meat market. If a cow was too old to be a productive milker, it could be slaughtered for human consumption.

· Mon 22. . . . I went to Eldorado to get some cotton seed. Bought 19 bu. $2.00 per bu. Put them in my car. Came home flying.

M·A·Y

· Wed 1. I applied for my car number and license, which cost me $11.25.
· Fri 3. . . . We went to the show. Saw the "Kaiser of the Beast of Berlin." Enough to make the hair stand on ends.

After the United States entered World War I, the country was flooded with anti-German propaganda films, such as "To Hell with the Kaiser," "The Kaiser, the Beast of Berlin," and a parody of it called "The Geezer of Berlin." The most popular of all these pictures was "The Kaiser, the Beast of Berlin," which stopped traffic on Broadway when it showed in New York (See Daniel Blum, *A Pictorial History of the Silent Screen*, pp. 152–53; James R. Mock and Cedric Larson, *Words That Won The War*, pp. 149–52).

· Wed 8. We took Dorothy to Mangum. Had her tonsils removed. Also adnoids took out. Maybe she can hear better now. Cost me $50.00. I do not mind what it cost if she can gain her hearing back. My God! The wind from the southwest was hot and sandy.

J·U·N·E

· Tues 11. Plowed till noon with one team. Planted some broomcorn, then rigged up a four mule outfit for the harrow. Can get over the ground so much faster. Went up to Duke for some "eats" and some oats. Sure has been some of the hot the last two days.

Broomcorn is a sorghum with fibrous branches, twelve to thirty-six inches long, that were used to make brooms and whisk brooms (See Martin, "Sorghum Improvement," in *Yearbook of Agriculture, 1936*, p. 529).

· Mon 17. . . . Took Red cow to Carley's. Bred her to his Durham Bull. (due March 17, 1919).

J·U·L·Y

· Wed 17. We went down to Olustee for Moley Baylie's show. Hot & dry. That is all that I can write about in the last three summers.

Tues 11 ... rigged up a four mule
outfit for the harrow.
Can get over the ground
so much faster.

Mollie Bailey's Circus, a southwestern institution, conjured up visions of the trapeze, clowns, and nasal-voiced vendors calling out "peanuts–popcorn–cotton candy–crackerjacks–a prize in every box." The Circus Queen, known as "Aunt Mollie," was stunning in her long black taffeta dress and jewels as she welcomed the crowds at the entrance. People traveled for miles to enjoy the performances and the circus's exotic atmosphere of charm and mystery. Mollie Bailey died in 1918, but her sons kept the show on the road two more years (See Olga Bailey, *Mollie Bailey: The Circus Queen of the Southwest*, ed. Bess Samuel Ayres; Eleanor Mitchell Traweek, *Of Such as These: A History of Motley County and Its Families*, p. 138).

A·U·G·U·S·T

· TUES 6.   . . . Cut feed till noon. Can't cut in P.M. Too dry. All shatters up.
· FRI 9.   . . . Have a nice little batch of bundles up now. Want to put up 4 or 5 thousand binds. Am tieing it with bailing wire. Much better than twine.
· THURS 15.   We all went down to Mr. Newton's. Was his birthday. Had a fine dinner. Large crowd. Went up to Olustee. Got the photo man. Had picture made of the crowd.
· MON 19.   Went down to Newton's to meet Hershey, but he did not come home till near noon. I went over his crop. Made him a price. Saved $50.00 by staying with him. Paid him $100.00 in money. Took up $225.00 of his debts. . . .

It was common practice to buy a crop in the field. The purchaser, who then became responsible for its care and harvesting, hoped to realize a profit when the crop was marketed.

· SUN 25.   We all went down to Jim Melton's. Went down to see the cotton I bought. It looked O.K. . . .
· TUES 27.   . . . I went down to Olustee to rent a house. Rented one from Frank Kidd.
· FRI 30.   We moved to Olustee.

S·E·P·T·E·M·B·E·R

· TUES 3.   Came a very good rain. Nice season for wheat. Will sow soon. Went out and traded red bull calf and $5.00 for a patch of maize. . . .

· THURS 12. We, or I, pulled cotton all day. Came up in P.M. to register. I
am now subject to be called out for military service. . . .

The draft age had been extended to cover men between eighteen and forty-
five. This move was designed to register nearly thirteen million men for military duty compared to only ten million when the draft age of twenty-one to
thirty-one was enacted in July, 1917 (See *Dallas Morning News*, Sept. 1, 1918,
p. 1).

· TUES 17. . . . I took a Sailor boy down to see his girl. Craig Burke was his
name. He employed me to take he & his girl to a dance. I made a 53
mile run for him. He paid me $7.00.

O·C·T·O·B·E·R

· THURS 17. Started to cotton patch, but met Mr. Newton. He and I went
back to the sale. . . . I bought a Library Set [*probably encyclopedias*]. Finished my 6th bale of cotton. . . .
· THURS 24. Sallie sold her hens, $10.52. Can't have chickens in town. . . .

N·O·V·E·M·B·E·R

· WED 13. Pulled cotton and drilled wheat all day. (Well I forgot to set
down that peace reigns now in the "war field." It being declared Monday, Nov. 11. We celebrated some here in Olustee). Finished drilling
wheat at sunset. Have between 90 and 100 acres. Looks rainy.

Wheat was planted with an implement (a drill) that deposited the seed at random, covered it, and packed the soil around it.

· THURS 14. Took bale cotton to Duke gin. Something over 2100 lbs. Bale
weight 530. Sold for 18.10 per cwt. . . .

D·E·C·E·M·B·E·R

· FRI 6. The Flu took me down today.
· MON 9. . . . Had letter from Slaton, Texas telling me of the death of
Eunice Orr, the next to my youngest sister. She died in Arizona. She
died on the 27th of last month.

· THURS 12. Stayed in bed near all day. Don't feel well as I would like to
feel. Quite a few people are dying now.

In the fall of 1918 the influenza reached epidemic proportions. Over five hundred thousand died in the United States, and an estimated twenty million were
killed worldwide. DeLoach's sister, Eunice, was one of the victims.

· SAT 28. . . . Harold is working for Forest Williams, $1.00 per day for him-
self, and 50¢ for the horse.

1·9·1·9

After the armistice in November, 1918, Allied demand for agricultural commodities declined only slightly before reaching even higher levels. United States' credit, extended to the war-torn countries, was used to continue purchases of American food and fiber throughout 1919. By the end of the year farmers thought that a new and higher level of prices had come to stay.

J·A·N·U·A·R·Y

· Tues 14.   Cotton is still going down. I have lost what I made on the cotton I bought. . . .

· Tues 28.   Took cotton samples to Altus. Could not get as much on it as I could at home. Sold for 18 3/4 cents. Not much and good too.

Altus, Oklahoma, was one of the largest cotton centers in the Southwest. Even though DeLoach believed his cotton was worth more money, cotton was bought in "hog round" lots, in which everyone from an area was paid about the same price regardless of grade. When cotton buyers sold the lint to the mills, they received the price differential (*Fort Worth Star-Telegram*, Dec. 14, 1913, p. 15).

· Wed 29.   . . . Guess will sell my car. I need money worse than a car. Hate to sell it, but will have to sell it or some thing.

F·E·B·R·U·A·R·Y

· Sat 1.   Sold my car to C. C. Quinn, $375.00. . . . If I miss a few more
  crops will be broke good and stout.
· Tues 18.   Started for Burkburnett. Did not get an early start. We traveled all day. . . . Was awful lonesome. I do not enjoy being away from
  home.

After several small flurries of oil activity in Burkburnett, Fowler's Folly blew
in on July 29, 1918. It was a twenty-two-hundred-barrel gusher and set off one
of the wildest oil booms ever seen in Texas. Soon more than fifty rigs were set
up within the town itself, and by the end of 1919 Burkburnett had produced
about forty million barrels of oil. It attracted people throughout north-central
Texas and southwestern Oklahoma who were looking for work (Carl Coke
Rister, *Oil! Titan of the Southwest*, pp. 115–17).

Hoping to find work in the booming oil fields, DeLoach and Harold started
out on mules for Burkburnett, Texas, about 70 miles away. Upon arrival they
discovered the town was overrun with other farmers who had the same idea.
Wheat farmers had their crop "laid by" until the harvest in June, and cotton
farmers had not yet planted. This illustrates one of the weak spots in cash-crop
farming. Farmers experienced a cash flow problem during the off-season without a sufficient amount of livestock and poultry to provide work and income.
Inflated prices of cotton and wheat during World War I enticed farmers to concentrate on cash crops at the expense of livestock and poultry.

A·P·R·I·L

· Thurs 3.   Did not do any thing all day. Could not find the fellow I
  worked for 22 hrs at 60¢ per hr., $13.20.
· Sun 6.   . . . Came up a cloud in night some time. The wind walked
  about. Blew down a number of rigs. Some say 150 to 300. Killed 15
  people last report. Things are shot up some.
· Fri 11.   Started home on the 8 A.M. o'clock train, but did not get home
  till night. Had to be transferred across R.R. bridge. High water.
· Sat 12.   Stayed home with Sallie all day. We had a good time together.
  Seems like had been 5 years since I had saw her, or that we had been
  married again, ha, ha. . . .

After returning to work, DeLoach had an attack of appendicitis and had to be taken back to Olustee. The attack subsided without surgery, but within the week he was down with smallpox, obviously contracted from the mob of workers swarming into Burkburnett. To protect Sallie and the younger children, DeLoach moved out to the farm. Harold and Bud went along to take care of their dad.

M·A·Y

· FRI 2. . . . My eyes are nearly swelled to and it feels like I could not put down a pin without putting it on a pimple. I guess I have what would be called a good case of small pox. I sleep in the barn. The boys sleep in the dug out. . . .

· SAT 10. The boys are both down. I will try to get up and take charge and wait on them. They were faithful to wait on me. Would do anything at once. . . .

· THURS 15. . . . Have not seen any body in 15 days nor a newspaper either. . . . Keith Bonner came down and told us that the folks at home had small pox and we decided we would go home. So we got ready and left just before sundown, getting home after 10 o'clock. Found Dorothy broke out, Sallie, Jim, & Billy yet to take them.

· MON 19. We sure are in jail. Only difference we can see the sun and run around on this particular lot. . . .

· TUES 20. . . . The same thing at this "pest house."

· FRI 23. . . . Shaved. Now that was some job. My face bled and I cryed. Those sores and tough beard. Newton saw Higgins and I got my twine. 400 lbs. Think that will be enough to cut and tie my wheat. . . .

· WED 28. The boys, Dorothy, and I went up to the place today. The army worms was there working on a night shift on my wheat. Now if they eat that up I will be a broke sucker and they have a good start to finish it.

Robert DeLoach recalled his father's disappointment when the army worms ruined his crop. He said the wheat was in the "dough" stage when the worms struck. The adult moth lays eggs at night in the folded blades or under the leaf sheaths of grains. The larvae consume increasing amounts of food as they grow, and when an outbreak occurs they move forward in a solid front, like an army, destroying everything in their path (See *Yearbook of Agriculture, 1908*, pp. 369–86; W. R. Walton, *The True Army Worm and Its Control*, pp. 1–12).

· FRI 30.   The worms are still eating. They don't eat in day time much, but give it the devil at night. . . .

J·U·N·E

· SUN 1.   Cold wind today from north that is bad on worms. They can't stay on wheat. Maybe that will stop them.
· WED 4.   Harold and I went up to place. He went on up to Duke. Got some sulphur to fumigate the dug out. Also some new work clothes. . . .
· FRI 6.   . . . We went up to Olustee in P.M. Harold came back home with one team. He can stay at home by changing clothes.
· SAT 14.   . . . The quarantine was lifted. . . .

By the time everyone had recovered from smallpox the wheat harvest was in full swing. The family moved from farm to farm with DeLoach as he did custom cutting and threshing. Each place had some sort of building they could live in while he harvested the crop. This arrangement allowed the boys to help their dad and made it possible for Sallie to prepare the meals they needed while working. Besides, after being quarantined for a month, everyone was ready for a change of scenery!

J·U·L·Y

· FRI 18.   Rained off and on all day. This is bad on wheat. I guess something will happen yet that the people will not get any thing out of their wheat. It will sprout in shock. Seems like one can't make any money.

A·U·G·U·S·T

· THURS 21.   . . . Mr. & Mrs. Springer came over from Eldorado. Took dinner with us. They took us in once when we were travelling. We were caught in a storm. Had to stay all night with them [*June, 1915*]. Good people. . . .
· TUES 26.   Went back down to thresher. Threshed off little jag of rye. Made 34 bu. and 45 lbs. I lost money on the deal. Sold for $1.15. Cost me $32.50, payed $9.75 for threshing. Lost my work and trouble and $2.20. . . .

Friday 18—...Rained
off and on all day. This is
bad on wheat....It will
sprout in shock.

S·E·P·T·E·M·B·E·R

· FRI 5.   Finished up in A.M. Moved. Made 1178 bu. No good. . . .
· MON 22.   . . . I bought 2 hogs from B. K. Hitt, cost $38.00, 1250 lbs maize, $16.00 per ton, $10.00. . . .
· TUES 30.   We got ready. Went up to place. Loaded up [*wheat*] and went to Altus. Sold for $1.91 per bu. Only had 67 bu. of wheat. Bad roads. . . .

O·C·T·O·B·E·R

· FRI 3.   Went back got the bal. of wheat. Took it to Altus. The check called for $579.00. Not much these high times.
· THURS 16.   . . . Had letter from Cannons out on Plains. God! but I am sick that I sold my place out there. But no use to cry over milk spilt. . . . If I had of kept my place I could have had something by now, but one has to live and learn.
· SUN 19.   . . . Cotton picking is now $2.50 per hundred. Cotton is selling around 40 cts, but as usual when stuff is high I have nothing to sell and everything to buy. That wheat deal is a huge joke. I could have made some money if I had put that place in cotton. I don't know what to do. No place. Guess it is down to a work proposition.

Middling cotton rose to 43.95¢ per pound on the Dallas Spot Market and to 46.25¢ per pound on the Galveston Spot Market (See *Semi-Weekly Farm News* [Dallas], Dec. 26, 1919, p. 7).

· THURS 23.   . . . We picked 733. Finished bale, sent it in town. . . . Ordered Talking machine [*a phonograph*], $87.00. Lots for a talker, but I and the rest enjoy it. . . .

N·O·V·E·M·B·E·R

· WED 5.   . . . Byron Milligan took up his note for mules, $307.00. Old Nig & Mike are gone now. . . .
· SAT 29.   . . . This old pen is the devil to write with.

D·E·C·E·M·B·E·R

· Sun 7. . . . Got Gramophone [*phonograph*]. The thing has been going since we put it up. . . .
· Wed 17. The world did not come to an end as some had planned. Nor did the sun fail to shine. Some had planned for 3 dark days, starting today. . . .
· Fri 19. We moved back to town.
· Thurs 25. Not much Xmas. No booze, no sugar, no cake. Don't seem like Christmas without some of those things. . . . Did intend to pick cotton, but was cloudy and foggy.

1·9·2·0

In January the cotton market opened at forty cents a pound, and by December it was down to ten. The price of other agricultural products also fell when European markets collapsed after World War I. Farmers formed cooperatives to bargain for better prices and even tried withholding cotton from the market. Overproduction, from wartime expansion, was the main problem, and marketing tactics could not offset the surplus.

J·A·N·U·A·R·Y

· THURS 1.   New Year! I began the new year by picking cotton all day. Cold.
I payed in full for my share in Farmer's Co. Assoc. $50.00 per share.
Can't say what it will amount to but will try it out.

The price relationship between farm and nonfarm goods was more important to commercial farmers than it had been on the self-sufficient farm. Hoping to bargain more effectively with other elements in the economy, farmers organized cooperatives to reduce the cost of supplies through bulk purchases from manufacturers and to market their products in bulk for better prices. Collective group action (self-help) was seen, by most farmers, as more desirable than government support (See Gilbert C. Fite, *Farm to Factory*, pp. 1–15).

· THURS 22.   . . . We exchanged some records with Lowreys. I am now taking dancing lessons. Sallie is my teacher, ha!

1920

· Sun 1. Another birthday. Am 40 yrs young. Sallie gave me a nice chain
and knife. She also gave a supper. Called in a few friends. . . .

Birthdays among farm people are often bigger celebrations than holidays.
This may be because two of the principal American holidays, Thanksgiving and
Christmas, fall during the harvest season, and taking off from work to celebrate
can be quite costly.

M·A·R·C·H

· Mon 29. . . . Got letter from Harold stating he had joined army for 3
years and would go to Phillippine Islands. Sure do hate to see the boy
go on such a chase. . . .
· Tues 30. . . . Think I will go to Ft. Sill to see Harold before he leaves on
his long journey. It hurts me for him to go so far away from home.

A·P·R·I·L

· Thurs 1. . . . got up, ate breakfast, caught car and went out to Ft. Sill.
Harold got his pass to San Francisco, Cal. We went over to depot.
I had to leave before his train run. Left him at depot at Ft. Sill. That
was the trying time of my life. Did not want to make him feel bad,
but I could not help it when he took my hand in both of his and
told me Good-bye. The last words he said to me "Now papa, don't
do that." I turned away and did not look at him again till I was on
car. . . . I did dread to tell Sallie about the parting. She stood up all
right till she went to bed and then poor girl. She could not stand it
any longer. . . .
· Thurs 8. Helped Logan in his shoe shop. Made $3.50 would not mind if
I had a shoe shop of my own. . . .

This was the same shoe store DeLoach worked in before moving to the Plains.
A grandson now has the last that DeLoach used as a cobbler.

· Sat 10. . . . The wind howled all day and sand how it did blow. . . .

M·A·Y

· SAT 1. . . . This day 30 yrs ago I went to a picnic at Millsap, Texas. We had a school picnic and I belonged to the Post Oak school in Parker County [*Texas*]. Lord, I sure did have a big time, but I had no money to spend like kids now days have to have. I took a fellow's horse to water and he gave me a nickle. I rode the flying jenny with the nickle. Went bare footed with long pants and only 10 years old.

· TUES 4. Planted cotton all day. 8 acres.

· SUN 9. . . . Fell an awful rain about 10 P.M. The planting is all off now for a while.

· THURS 13. Went out. Scratched cotton patch or some of it. . . .

After a rain the ground was plowed with a spiked tooth harrow to break the crust, allowing the young cotton stalk to come through. Failure to do this would cause the tender stalk to break, destroying the plant and requiring replanting.

· WED 26. Mr. Newton came up. He & I went up to old place for our binder. I found a $10.00 bill on way up. We had a wreck. A mule I was leading tried to get up in buggy seat with us and threw Mr. Newton out. . . .

J·U·N·E

· SAT 26. Did not do any thing. Rigged up to go out to thresher. I did not want to go with the thresher this year but I have nothing else to do and might as well make the money.

DeLoach had an International Harvester six-foot binder that he used to bind shocks of wheat for farmers who did not want to invest in equipment of their own (Robert E. DeLoach, interview with Janet Neugebauer, Sudan, Tex., Mar. 16, 1987).

J·U·L·Y

· SAT 17. Bud & I hoed till noon and was so hot that we came in afternoon. I believe that was the hottest day or afternoon I ever saw (to-day). We went to show. Came near having a stampede in the building. An electric fan burnt out and the whole house broke for the door. . . .

Boll Weevil   Pink Bollworm

A·U·G·U·S·T

· Mon 16. . . . We went to church. The Baptists are holding a revival
    meeting.
· Fri 20. . . . Came the hardest rain of the year. Something like 10 in. in
    last wk. . . .

S·E·P·T·E·M·B·E·R

· Tues 7. . . . The boll worms [*not boll weevils*] are eating on the cotton.
    Went out to see my cotton. The older cotton is O.K. yet, but the young
    cotton is being damaged some by the worms.

   The first pink bollworm in the United States was found in Robertson County,
Texas, in 1917. It migrated from southern Asia to Mexico and entered Texas
through imported cotton seed. The adult, similar in appearance to the common

63

clothes moth, lays as many as one hundred eggs during a lifetime. Each egg produces a tiny worm that bores into the cotton boll to feed upon the seed and remains there until the worm matures. Damage to the bolls reduces the yield, grade, and staple of the lint, in addition to destroying the germinating quality of the seed. Before insecticides, quarantines on cotton lint and seed were used to control the bollworm's spread (See W. D. Hunter, *The Pink Bollworm with Special Reference to Steps Taken by the Department of Agriculture to Prevent Its Establishment in the United States*).

·Mon 13. Went up to town. Bought Dr. Styles old Ford. Cost me $225.00. Will do me as well as a new one.

O·c·t·o·b·e·r

·Fri 1. . . . A whole lot more Mexicans came in tonight. They are getting thick around here.

The Southwest was part of Mexico in colonial times. During the nineteenth century large-scale ranching, financed by Anglos, displaced many small farmers and stockmen, forcing them into the economy as wage earners. When the labor-intensive cotton culture replaced ranching, it contained many jobs for unskilled laborers. This seasonal work demanded a mobile labor force, the workers living in temporary housing provided on site. Mexican Americans, more than blacks or Anglos, filled the demand. Migratory work, the only economic choice in many cases, retarded their development of a power base from which other gains could be achieved, hence their slow assimilation into the larger society. As machines replaced workers, Mexican Americans migrated to cities where they found social systems to aid the process of assimilation. However, as they reach for the opportunities enjoyed by the larger society they often realize there is a great discrepancy between promise and fulfillment (See Leo Grebler, Joan W. Moore, and Ralph C. Guzman, *The Mexican-American People: The Nation's Second Largest Minority*, pp. 575–95).

·Wed 27. . . . Went to a republican speech. Cold tonight. May frost. Would not care. Maybe the cotton would open up. The gins were ordered to close down and not gin any more until further orders. That may Bull the market.

Governor Parker of Louisiana issued an appeal to all gins in the South to close down for at least 30 days to drive up the price and allow producers a living wage for their cotton. This appeal was sent to the governor of every other southern state. Bankers and merchants were urged to cooperate with the movement by allowing farmers additional time to fulfill financial obligations. The movement was not effective because the 1920 cotton crop was quite large, and the number of bales already ginned exceeded the amount ginned by that time in 1919. Also, time proved that federal, rather than state and local, support was necessary to aid the ailing cotton industry, because only the federal government could pass regulations that were binding to all people involved (*Semi-Weekly Farm News* [Dallas], Oct. 29, 1920, p. 1).

N·o·v·e·m·b·e·r

· Tues 2.   . . . Came by town. Voted the Dem. ticket.
· Wed 3.   . . . Bought 3 head mares. Sold two. Made $23.20 on them. Will keep one. A brown mare that cost me $62.50.
· Sat 20.   Went up to cotton patch. Brought in two bales of cotton. Sold 3 bales at 10½¢ per lb. Sure is not much money. . . .

D·e·c·e·m·b·e·r

· Thurs 2.   Went out and planted wheat all day. Was a little tired. The first walking I have done since I broke sod on the Plains in 1917.
· Sat 11.   Sallie got a sow from her father for a Xmas gift. He gave her the sow in lieu of $25.00. She found 7 pigs [*DeLoach's animals "found" their newborn*]. Saved them all.

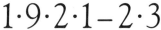

1·9·2·1–2·3

Not all Americans shared the prosperity of the twenties. Farmers were in distress. Especially hard hit were producers of cotton, wheat, and corn, many of whom were heavily in debt from wartime expansion. They had to sell their products on a dwindling foreign market. High tariffs added further injury by provoking retaliatory foreign tariffs against American agricultural exports. Farm distress encouraged a coalition of congressmen, known as the Farm Bloc, to begin developing an agricultural policy that would promote the farmers' interests in Washington. Some laws were passed, but it was soon apparent that legislation could not provide the rapid relief that was needed. As prices fell to an all-time low, family farmers, like DeLoach, could not generate enough income to cover the high cost of production in addition to taxes and mortgage payments. Many were forced to find nonfarm employment.

When the cotton market collapsed DeLoach moved his family to a smaller farm (forty acres) near Vernon, Texas, and hired on with a road construction crew out of Wichita Falls. Harold and Bud joined him. Sallie and the younger children stayed on the farm, trying to keep the work going until Will returned on the weekends.

The growth of automobile traffic after World War I had led to an interest in highway improvement and had increased appropriations for construction. In 1922, Texas spent over $54 million on highways, employing many people and building one of the better systems in the nation, but not without the specter of fraud (John David Huddleston, "Good Roads for Texas: A History of the Texas

Highway Department, 1917–1947," [Ph.D. diss., Texas A&M University, 1981], pp. 58–59).

Diary entries for 1921 through 1923, reflecting his work with the construction company more than farming, have been omitted in the interest of space.

By 1924 the cotton market was showing improvement, having recovered from its deflation in 1920 more quickly than any other commodity. The average price in December, 1923, was thirty-seven cents a pound, brought on partly because the world supply of American cotton was at its lowest ebb in twenty-five years. In contrast, the price of cattle recovered slowly after World War I, and West Texas ranchers took advantage of rising cotton prices to sell part of their ranches. Between 1920 and 1930 the number of farms in West Texas increased nearly 70 percent.

I asked Robert DeLoach how his father learned about the land boom on the South Plains and he replied, "Oh, my goodness, everyone knew about that land. That's all anyone could talk about." News articles of the time confirm his statement. Victor Schoffelmayer, agricultural editor of *The Semi-Weekly Farm News* (Dallas), wrote "Eyes of the Cotton World on Northwest Texas," a long article on February 12, 1924, touting the fertility of West Texas. Leo Potishman, Chairman of the Public Relations Committee for the Fort Worth Grain and Cotton Exchange, toured West Texas in October of 1924. W. G. Byrne wrote an article entitled "Prosperity of West Texas Amazing to Grain Man" for the *Fort Worth Star-Telegram* on October 16, 1924. In it, he quoted Potishman as saying, "The Panhandle has hardly been scratched in the search for wealth. . . . All classes have money in the bank or are in a position to borrow easily. . . . others are in a position to hold cotton and grain for better prices and some of them are doing that very thing." The boom was on!

Even after making allowances for the exaggerations of advertising, West Texas was truly on the leading edge of agricultural opportunities in the nation during the 1920s. The land still had to be broken for row crops, but it cost only about one-tenth as much as farms in older areas, and its yields were far better than land that had been farmed several years. More importantly, the boll weevil (not bollworm), the scourge of cotton growers in East and Central Texas, could not stand the cold winters of the Plains, and the physical features of the land were conducive to mechanized, large-scale farming. Two-row planters and cultivators were ideal for the flat land; adjustable planter boxes spaced seeds at proper intervals, eliminating the necessity of thinning plants with a hoe; and mechanical harvesters (i.e. cotton sleds) were being perfected. Even the sparse rainfall was advantageous—it reduced the need for weed control. These factors brought the cost of cotton production in West Texas below that required for other parts of the South and hastened the migration of farmers to the Plains. Studies of production costs in the eight cotton states revealed the Llano Estacado required 38.9 manhours per acre and could produce lint for ten cents per pound. In North Carolina, the highest of the group, cotton production required 154 manhours per acre and cost fifty-four cents per pound to produce (Karper and Jones, *Varieties of Cotton in Northwest Texas*, p. 7; production costs were studied in North Carolina, South Carolina, Georgia, Alabama, Mississippi, Arkansas, Oklahoma, and Texas).

The Cotton Belt was quietly shifting from the Southeast to the Southwest. By 1923 the shift was evident when 200,000 bales of cotton were harvested on the Llano Estacado, a 2,000 percent increase over 1909 (Jones, Hurst, and Scoates, *Mechanical Harvesting of Cotton in Northwest Texas*, pp. 24–25; Victor H. Schoffelmayer, "South Plains Section Makes 200,000 Bales of Cotton in 1924," *Semi-Weekly Farm News* [Dallas], Jan. 22, 1924, p. 4).

1·9·2·4

By 1924 DeLoach was tired of being separated from his family. Boarding house food, sloppy work from the men he supervised, and a dishonest boss did not fit his concept of a decent way to earn a living. He was ready to return to farming and rising cotton prices.

J·a·n·u·a·r·y

· TUES 1. Another New Year. Well, if the New Year is as prosperous as the old year, I can't complain. I have had plenty to eat, paid my note on my little home. Things could have been worse. At any rate I am thankful for the good health we have enjoyed. . . . Made nice little crop on the little place. Can't say that I feel any older than I did 10 years ago. However, I know that I can't stand the hard work I did then.

· WED 2. . . . It seems like it has been a month since I saw the folks. We left home a week ago today. Dear old Sallie, I guess, gets lonesome. I know I do. . . . Only go home every two or three weeks.

· MON 14. Well, another wedding anniversary. 21 years ago today Sallie & I were married. I sure do wish I could see her and not be gone all the time. I miss the companionship of my wife and children. Sometimes I think I will give up this work, and go home, but I know there is nothing to do there, and $182.00 is not to be turned down each month. 21 years ago today I felt like a fighting cock. Well, I do not feel old now.

69

Was married about 3 P.M. at Parson Blevins' near Duke, Okla. The day will long be remembered. I thought then and do yet, that I got one of the best and dearest girls in the world. She has always been just what a good wife & mother could be to her husband and children. It seems I never did do what a man ought to do for a good woman. But I want to live to see her enjoy life as she wants too. So much for "war contracts."

DeLoach always referred to a marriage license, or the marriage contract, as a war contract.

· Tues 15.   21 years ago today I did not feel like the fighting cock, only the cock that had been fighting. . . .

· Tues 22.   . . . Next Sat 26, I will be away 1 month. Well, maybe I will be fixed some time when I won't have to go away from home to work. I would not now if I had my place paid for.

F·E·B·R·U·A·R·Y

· Mon 11.   Raining when I awoke this A.M. Decided I would go home. Caught the 8:15 Interurban car. . . . Was home by eight P.M. The folks were reading when I came up. I scratched on the window. Bud came out. Was sure glad to see the children's Ma. We had a pleasant time.

· Tues 12.   We decided to rent the place out and move down to my work. . . .

M·A·R·C·H

· Fri 28.   10 years ago today I started this diary. My aim was to make accounts of each day, which I have done only about 90 days in 1915 while I was in Oklahoma, June, July and August. I now will start in for another 10 yrs. That will mean 1934. If I live to do that I will be 53 yrs old. This is the third ledger that I have written up, or I am writing.

M·A·Y

· Sat 24.   . . . Harold took to himself a wife. A widow with one child. Hope he will treat the child as he would his own because if he does they will be all O.K. . . .

Harold married Dellie Shipman McMahan, who was from McKinney, Texas. DeLoach was fond of Dellie's child, Walter McMahan, Jr., and often wrote about him in the diary.

J·U·L·Y

· Fri 25.   . . . Harold took wife & Dorothy & him to a K.K.K. meeting out in a pasture.

Although the Ku Klux Klan of the 1920s took its name and costume from the secretive, post–Civil War organization, it was more akin to nativist movements in America. It seemed to have a great appeal to men of rural origin who were frustrated by the rapid social changes following World War I. They identified easily with the group's professed principles of Protestant Christianity and Patriotic Americanism. Despite lofty ideals Klansmen, or persons posing as Klansmen, embarked on a campaign of intimidation and violence against those whom they considered moral lawbreakers. Most members did not participate in the violence, but they did join in the political activities of the Klan, electing a U.S. senator in 1922 and many city and county officials from 1922 to 1924. By 1922 resentment of the alleged violence was building, and anti-Klan groups began appearing around the state. Its decline was rapid in Texas after 1924, when members realized it was not what they expected it to be and attorneys general began vigorously attacking Klansmen charged with violence. Harold, Dorothy, and Harold's wife, Dellie, obviously went to watch the meeting, as women did not belong to the Klan. Seeing mysterious, torch-bearing riders in hooded sheets was exciting, and people often hid in the bushes to watch such a scene (See Seth Shepard McKay and Odie B. Faulk, *Texas after Spindletop*, pp. 72–92; Norman D. Brown, *Hood, Bonnet, and Little Brown Jug: Texas Politics, 1921–1928*, pp. 6–7, 49–89, 211–52; W. C. Wright, *Religious and Patriotic Ideals of the Ku Klux Klan*, pp. 1–2).

DeLoach's work took him to Mineral Wells, Texas, in July to work on the brick highway between Mineral Wells and Milsap, Texas. He rented three rooms at $25.00 per month for his family to live in. He did not like bricklaying and after discovering a second employer involved in graft, DeLoach quit. He moved his family back to Oklahoma.

O·c·t·o·b·e·r

· Mon 13.   We picked cotton all day. I picked 405 lbs. We all picked 927 lbs
@ $1.50 per hundred.

N·o·v·e·m·b·e·r

· Sat 8.   Had election returns. Coolidge was elected. Davis did not run at
all. "Ma" Ferguson was elected Governor of Texas. So much for "Farmer
Jim." Picked cotton till noon. We went to Altus in P.M., Sallie & I did.

In 1924 Miriam A. "MA" Ferguson ran successfully for governor of Texas as
a proxy for her husband, former governor James E. "Farmer Jim" Ferguson, who
was barred from holding a state office by the terms of his impeachment in 1917.
From 1914 to 1934, Jim Ferguson was an important and colorful figure in Texas
politics who successfully played on the frustrations and fears rural Texans were
experiencing during an era of change. In states with one-party politics, personalities often become more important than issues. In Texas this is known as "Fer-
gusonism" (See Brown, *Hood, Bonnet, and Little Brown Jug*, pp. 3–10, 253–96).

In November DeLoach and his father-in-law, C. C. Newton, made a trip to
Lamb County, Texas, where Newton bought a farm.

· Tues 18.   . . . The Thompson Land Company men took charge of us.
They took us to a resturant for dinner and then in P.M. took us out
to show us their land. Mr. Newton bought one Labor, 177.1 acres
@ $38.00 per acre. Out from Sudan. We came back to Littlefield, had
supper, and went to show. The Land people payed all expenses.

Explorers introduced the Spanish system of land measurement into the New
World, a system that is still recognized along the southern border of the United
States. A labor, 177.1 acres, was the quantity of land considered sufficient for
one family to work. It was a farm. This term is still widely used in Lamb County
(See Edwin P. Arneson, "The Early Art of Terrestrial Measurement and Its Prac-
tice in Texas," in *One League to Each Wind*, ed. Sue Watkins, p. 8). Sudan, Texas,
received its name from Sudan grass, one of the principal products of the area.
Due to the abundance of the grass grown around the town, a worldwide market developed for its hay and seed (See Joe Serratt, "My Home Town – Sudan,"
West Texas Today 16, no. 7 [Sept., 1935], p. 16).

1924

D·E·C·E·M·B·E·R

DeLoach, his father-in-law, and brother-in-law made a quick trip back to Sudan in December to look at the land Mr. Newton bought. Before returning to Oklahoma, Newton talked with a well man and hired someone to break the sod for $2.50 per acre.

· TUES 30.   We made a trip to Vernon. Sold our little place. Made the deed. Got the money and back home by 8 P.M. I did hate to sell it, but I made up my mind I could not promise myself anything more than a little home. Sold for $275.00 per acre. I payed $225.00. I did not make anything on it. Kids are going to school now.

1·9·2·5

"Come to the Wonderful New Cotton Country," broadcast land agents in Lamb County, and hundreds of farmers did just that. One real estate office boasted of selling twenty-nine farms in twenty-nine days during September, 1925. The DeLoach family was among the new settlers. Will bought a new Ford truck for the move and painted it "cold black." He and the two oldest boys came ahead of the family to get a house ready to live in. The first task was finding a lumber company and well driller. Demand was unusually high and so were prices.

F·E·B·R·U·A·R·Y

· Wed 25. . . . Came on back to Sudan. Made deal with Panhandle Lumber Co., also White the well man. Took out load of lumber. Started work on house. We slept out on ground. Also cold.

On Newton's farm, six and a half miles south of Sudan, DeLoach built a fourteen-by-sixteen-foot box-and-strip house that had two rooms. Widely used in West Texas, the box-and-strip house was simply a box constructed of boards nailed to a frame, without studs. The one-by-twelve-foot uprights were nailed vertically into place with their sides touching. A one-by-four-foot strip was then nailed over the cracks, leaving no room for insulation. DeLoach covered the inside walls with black tar paper, but during windstorms the walls moved in and out like a bellows. This simple design provided a maximum amount of interior space from a limited amount of lumber, a scarce and expensive item on the

Plains. The house had two doors, one in each room, and the windows, set flush with the outside, protruded into the rooms. Initially the house had a box car top for a roof. This was later replaced with a cone roof. DeLoach bought another building from his neighbor, Mr. Morton, and attached it to the new house. The second building was remodeled to serve as a kitchen, dining room, and bedroom (Robert E. DeLoach, interviews with Janet Neugebauer, Sudan, Tex., Mar. 16, 1987, and July 1, 1987).

· THURS 26. . . . We quit and moved camp over to a little shack. Was some better. Our neighbor, Mr. Morton, let us have a little stove.
· FRI 27. . . . Not so cold tonight. We pulled some Russian thistles, or tumbleweeds, for a bed. They act as mattress, springs, both.

M·A·R·C·H

· THURS 5. We were out early. I have been in a high tension today. The well is now down [to] 170 feet. No water to speak of yet. Just a seep. Will have to get some 3.5 inch caseing (steel) to lower in bottom. Mr. Newton will be dissappointed in the depth of well. He thought he could get water at 115 [feet]. Bought a lot of household goods. Kitchen C[abinet], oil stove, chairs, beds, springs and some other junk.
· SAT 7. I settled with well man. That is I OKed his statement to Newton for $196.00. We started on tower. Built it, had it raised, and two legs anchored down by sunset.

A typical windmill had a twelve-foot wheel on a tower approximately thirty feet high. In a fifteen-mile-an-hour wind, it would raise about thirty-five gallons of water per minute to a height of twenty-five feet. At that wind speed, it developed about one-sixth horsepower and cost about twenty-five cents a month to operate. DeLoach bought a Dempster mill for the tower. This brand was widely used on the Plains because the windmills could withstand severe winds yet still pump water in light breezes. Dempster mills are among the few still being manufactured (See *Lubbock Avalanche-Journal*, July 26, 1959, sec. 9, p. 3; T. Lindsay Baker, *A Field Guide to American Windmills*, pp. 194–95).

· MON 9. We finished every thing that we could see to do. Scrubbed the floors and walls of the shack. Made ready to start for Okla. tomorrow.

Final preparations for the move included buying Lady Cow for "$66.00, less 3% discount," then good-byes were said with joy and tears.

· SUN 15.   We were up by 4 A.M. Did not have a breakfast. Had a "smile out of Mr. Newton's fruit jar" [*a drink of homemade whiskey*]. Started for Sudan, Tex. a little before sun up. Had quite a lot of minor stops. Harold was a few miles out of Quanah with a broke down wheel when we passed him [*Harold moved the farm equipment in a wagon pulled by mules*]. Helped him get on the road again. Made it to Floydada by 6 P.M. Started for Littlefield and dark grabbed us near Hale Center. My lights got to cutting up and we got off the road, but we made home about 1 A.M. A tired bunch. We unloaded the cow. She was tired, too.

· FRI 20.   . . . Harold came in about eleven A.M. . . . We put the John Deere planter together. . . .

· WED 25.   . . . The wind blows like the devil in day time, but shuts off at night. . . .

A·P·R·I·L

· SUN 19.   We all had an early dinner, then we started for the old "yellow-house" head quarters. The high wind mill. I guess it is the highest wind mill in the world. In fact, I have read that it is. Not much doing about the old ranch headquarters now. One used to see lots of fun, but now it is all cars & tractors. No more cowboys lounging about the "dog house." This new bundle of would be cowboys—I doubt if they would know what a "dog house" is or what it was for. . . .

In 1901, Maj. George Littlefield bought the Yellow House Division of the XIT Ranch, a 312,175-acre spread that included the southwestern corner of Lamb County. In 1912, he founded the town of Littlefield and established the Littlefield Lands Company to sell part of his ranch to farmers. DeLoach's entry is reflective of his own life as he cowboyed on a ranch (the Two-Buckle Ranch in Crosby County) before becoming one of those who moved in with cars and tractors to farm the land (See David B. Gracy II, *Littlefield Lands: Colonization of the Texas Plains, 1912–1920*, pp. 1–42). Reputed to be the tallest windmill in the world, the Yellow House well was drilled in 1886. The 132-foot tower, referred to locally as "Old Daddy Long Legs," was necessary to catch the wind since the well was located in a canyon (See Evalyn Parrott Scott, *A History of Lamb County*, p. 84; "The Tallest Windmill," *Cross Section* 16, no. 9 [Sept., 1970], p. 3). The "doghouse," generally known as the bunkhouse, was the bachelor living quarters on a ranch. Located near the headquarters, the condition of the bunkhouse and its furnishings were considered an indication of the way ranchers treated their hands in other matters. Furnishings on the better ranches, though never elaborate, consisted of a bunk and mattress for each cowboy, and a table and chairs near a wood stove in the middle of the room. When bunks were not provided, cowboys just spread their bedrolls on the floor, if there was one. The turnover rate was high where bunkhouse conditions were poor (See David Dary, *Cowboy Culture: A Saga of Five Centuries*, pp. 284–85).

M·A·Y

· WED 6.   Well, the long looked for rain started falling some time from
   12 A.M. to 1 A.M. and rained on till about 7 A.M. The ground is wet—
   from 3½" to 4." I finished breaking up the garden. Disked and harrowed it. Rigged up the old John Deere lister and started Bud to listing
   up the old land. . . .

A lister was a double moldboard plow that was used to open a furrow and throw the soil in opposite directions, transforming the flat land into rows of small hills and valleys. This plowing technique made it possible to capture and save available moisture until planting time when a lister-type plow, with a planter attached, was used to break into the rows of small hills and open a furrow six or eight inches deep. Seed, from the planter, was then deposited in the moist subsoil. Listers reduced the time needed for plowing by at least 50 percent over the time required by a one-way plow like DeLoach used to break the prairie sod (See Farrall and Albrecht, *Agricultural Engineering*, p. 196).

· TUES 19.   . . . I made a milk box cooler. Put it up at wind mill. Keeps milk
   just like an ice box. . . .

A milk box cooler was a small building where milk and butter were kept. Water from the windmill ran through a trough in the milkhouse, and containers of milk and butter were placed in the trough to keep the contents cool. When possible, milkhouses were made of stone or adobe for added coolness.

· SAT 23.   I planted cotton all day. Bud took the folks up to Sudan to the
   opening of a new store. They had a blow out. Threw twelve hens from
   the top of the store building and several other things, among them the
   guessing at the amount of money in a show window. . . .

Diary entries indicate DeLoach planted Half and Half cotton seed, a variety developed in Georgia by H. H. Summerover in 1904. It had a short staple length, 5/6–7/8 inch, but its high lint yield (usually 50 percent, hence the name) and early maturity made it popular in West Texas. Prior to the 1940s, superior grades and staples received no recognition in the local markets; therefore, high lint yields greatly influenced a farmer's choice of seed. Consequently, West Texas developed a reputation for producing vast quantities of inferior grade cotton. Half and Half also carried a mutant gene for storm resistance from its parent stock, Cook cotton. This gene later played an important role in the development of storm resistant cotton, the ability of a mature boll to hold its lint during windy weather. Eventually, stormproof cotton made mechanical harvesting practical and profitable on the South Plains (See J. O. Ware, "Plant Breeding and the Cotton Industry," in *Yearbook of Agriculture, 1936*, p. 735; Richard Wilson Arnold, "The History of Adaptation of Cotton to the High Plains of Texas, 1890–1947," [Master's thesis, Texas Tech University, 1975], p. 20; Robert Hargrove Montgomery, *The Cooperative Pattern in Cotton*, p. 259).

J·U·N·E

· SAT 13.   We worked in field till noon. The kids wanted to go to Sudan to the first "Trade's Day." They had a real nice program. . . .

Trades Days, sponsored by the Chamber of Commerce, illustrate the cooperative spirit of West Texas businessmen. Merchants declared special sales and held drawings for free merchandise to lure farmers into town. They also organized stock judging contests and other entertainment. Initially Trades Days were held only two or three times a year, on Saturdays during the summer. As their popularity grew they were held every Monday, coinciding with cattle sale days (See *Lamb County Leader*, June 18, 1925, p. 1).

· SUN 28.   We made a slide go-devil. If we had bought it new would have cost $25.00. It is the go-devil I bought at Ralls, Tex. in 1914. We never did use it much. The runners were all that was wore out. . . .

J·U·L·Y

· TUES 7.   I started Bud to plowing. He plowed a strip of sod maize. . . .
Had to tell Bud a thing or two about letting the mules stand in the field. My motto is if they get to where they can't go, take them out and turn them in the pasture.
· THURS 30.   . . . I got 15# Sudan seed. Will plant a small patch. . . .

Sudan grass was brought into the United States from Khartum, Sudan, Africa. It is more desirable for hay than Johnson grass because it has no troublesome rootstocks. Average yield is five tons of hay per acre, and it can be grazed instead of harvested (See Lubbock Sudan Grass Seed Association, *Sudan Grass*).

A·U·G·U·S·T

· WED 26. . . . I had to punish Dorothy & Bill for going up to Morton's. They did not think I would whip them. I sure did hate to. I do not like to have to whip children. I do not believe in the whip, but it seems like they would not mind at all. Hope I will never have to repeat it. It makes me feel bad. . . .

The steady flow of settlers moving into Lamb County confirmed DeLoach's initial belief about the value of its land, and he began looking for a place to buy.

· MON 31. Bud and I went up town. Made trade for 177 1/10 A. of the Haddaway land at $30.00 per A. Bud & I went out to give it the once over. I think it is awful good dirt. . . .

In 1910, Haddaway bought eighteen thousand acres in Lamb County, part of which included the land on which the town of Sudan is now located. After the railroad arrived he sold his holdings to farmers, many of whom came from Greer County, Oklahoma (See *Lamb County Leader*, Oct. 1, 1925, p. 15).

S·E·P·T·E·M·B·E·R

· THURS 3. . . . Got my abstract to land I bought from the Haddaway Ranch. I believe I could sell that land now for a $5.00 [*per acre*] profit, but I want to keep it. Had to go over to Shuman's for my Nancy mule. Can't keep her in pen. . . .
· FRI 25. Harold took some cotton and Hegari, Sallie took some peppers, shirts, and some sheets, put them on display at the Lamb County Fair. . . . We all went up in the afternoon. They sure did have a fine collection of exhibits.

Hegari, a native of Sudan, was introduced into the United States in 1908, but did not become popular with grain producers until the mid-1920s. Dwarf hegari began replacing much of the acreage previously planted in milo because it was better adapted to machine harvesting with a header. Its early maturity and high yields on scant rainfall were also assets. Two or three pounds of seed planted per acre yielded nearly a ton of dry heads (See R. E. Karper, "Grain Sorghums: Facts You Want to Know about Hegari"; H. L. Atkins, Jr., "Hegari, an Adaptable Crop," *Progressive Farmer* 44, no. 3 [Jan. 19, 1929], pp. 8, 10). The third annual Lamb County Fair was held in Sudan. Agricultural exhibits reflected the wide range of crops grown in the county, and Home Demonstration displays paid homage to the skills that produced comfortable homes. The county nurse also held a baby clinic. Prizewinning exhibits, shown at the South Plains Fair in Lubbock and the State Fair in Dallas, advertised the county's agricultural potential (See *Lamb County Leader*, Sept. 24, 1925, p. 1).

O·c·t·o·b·e·r

The 1925 cotton crop was smaller than expected. A droughty summer delayed blooming, which in turn caused the cotton plant to set fruit late. The first freeze, on October 28, was only two days earlier than the average date, but that was too early for a late-maturing crop. Farmers who hoped to gather as much as a bale per acre found they had difficulty averaging half a bale, and those with late crops found the low yield did not even cover the cost of harvesting.

· Wed 14.   Bud took cotton to gin. 1350 seed cotton, made 525# bale. 808# seed, money over ginning & roping – $2.75.

This was picked cotton. Less poundage was required for a bale, making it easier to haul to the gin, and the bale usually brought a premium price because the lint was free of foreign matter.

· Thurs 22.   . . . I expect I ought to sell my cotton, am offered 22.25¢ per lb.
· Mon 26.   . . . Harold took load maize to Sudan. Sold for $17.00 per ton. They are determined to get this feed crop for nothing. Cotton fell $7.50 per bale. That is the devil on a man that is trying to pay out a place. I guess I will have to sell my truck. Better to sell it, than lose it outright.

Because of the publicity given the grain sorghum crop in West Texas, the market broke. Farmers were advised to store their grain, as it was predicted the demand for maize would improve before the next crop was harvested. However, very few could afford to store their crops for a year because land payments were due and most farmers needed operating cash by harvest time (See *Lamb County Leader*, Oct. 22, 1925, p. 7).

Tumbleweed   Hegari   bundled Maize

N·O·V·E·M·B·E·R

· Mon 16. I went up town to see Mr. Haddaway about my land note. He
agreed to cancel my contract and refund my note, due Nov 15, for the
$200.00 I payed on Nov 1, 1925. That means I lose $200, but it had better be that than for me to lose $400.00, for I can't make the grade for
the balance of $485.00, due Dec. 1, 1925. . . .

D·E·C·E·M·B·E·R

· Tues 8. . . . The Government report put the "damper down" some more.
The moneyed people have the poor devils spoke for. If one makes a
good crop of any thing, one can't sell it for only "Beans and corn
bread." It seems like there is a "leake" some where, but two or (two hun-

81

dred for matter) of farmers can't adjust the system. Just let a bunch of
farmers start some protective move and the first thing one knows,
some high collored "Gink" gets in and eats up the whole lot.

The price of cotton fell below twenty cents a pound following a report from
the Department of Agriculture estimating a large crop of 15,226,000 bales. Farmers objected to the release of estimates because they believed speculators used
this information to the detriment of the producer (See *Semi-Weekly Farm News*,
Dec. 3, 1925), p. 1).

· SAT 19.   The wind began to blow about sunup, by 9 o'clock the sand sure
was walking about. . . .

1·9·2·6

One of the worst sandstorms on record in the fall of 1926 topped off a year of erratic Plains weather. Despite problems, the cotton crop was the largest ever produced in West Texas and, as usual when there is a bumper crop, the price fell.

Early in the year, spokesmen for the cotton industry advocated production controls because a large carryover from 1925 drove the December futures below current prices. Farmers understood this foreshadowing, but as long as they had mortgages to pay off they planted as many acres as possible. They needed to make money and believed cotton was still the cash crop par excellence.

J·A·N·U·A·R·Y

·Thurs 21.   I went up town to pay my taxes . . . my poll tax and Sallie's
     were $3.50. . . .

The poll tax and the Terrell Election Laws worked in harmony to curtail the franchise of minorities in Texas. The adoption of a poll tax in 1902 discouraged all poor people from voting, but blacks were kept from the polls more effectively than any other group. Poll taxes had to be paid between between October and February, and many blacks either forgot to pay or lost their receipts. The 1905 law completed the process of disenfranchisement by setting forth in great detail who should be allowed to vote in the primary, which was tantamount to election in Texas. Only whites were permitted, hence the appellation "white primary." Blacks eventually gained a place at the polls; in 1944 the Supreme

Court ruled white primaries unconstitutional, and in 1968 it ruled the poll tax unconstitutional (See Rupert N. Richardson, Ernest Wallace, and Adrian N. Anderson. *Texas: the Lone Star State*, 3d ed., p. 302; V. O. Key, Jr., *Southern Politics in State and Nation*, pp. 533–618).

M·A·R·C·H

· Sun 28.   There was a crowd of young folks here all day playing croquet. Threatening rain all day. Mr. & Mrs. Newsom came in for a few games of 42 [*a domino game*] in the eve. Billy found a silver $ in the road. He sure was tickled.

A·P·R·I·L

· Wed 14.   . . . Bought a Queen Incubator. Will set turkey eggs in it. . . .
· Fri 16.   I am confined at home now. We put eggs in the incubator and it is up to me to look after it. The boys are plowing.

M·A·Y

· Sat 1.   . . . I did intend to go to town, but boys did not quit in time to go before night. Then Sallie was mad because I did not have money. My God! If I could get it I would, but I have everything tied up now. I would love to dress her in the kind of clothes she wants, but I can't. It takes all I can do to get something to eat. It makes me feel bad to be placed in such a shape. I will have to get out and see if I can't get a job, so I can have some money to put tires and license on the Ford, and for them to have some clothes. I can't stand this kind of life. She quarrels at me because the truck is all we have to go any place in. Oh! they look at me mad.

For the first time, Americans came face-to-face with an economy of abundance during the 1920s, but the prosperity was not distributed equitably among all groups. While farmers were struggling to make ends meet, urbanites were casually spending discretionary income for consumer items that gave them an image of power and style. Advertising persuaded people that a good life no longer meant food, clothing, shelter, independence, and righteousness; novel and stylish things had to be bought. In American society, money was becoming the measure of a man, which was a confusing concept for thousands like DeLoach. On the other hand, doing without tempting consumer items was frustrating for Sallie and the children. It was difficult for farm families to understand why they were not sharing in the national prosperity, and they often blamed each other for a situation that was beyond their control (See William E. Leuchtenburg, *The Perils of Prosperity, 1914–1932*, pp. 84–103; James H. Shideler, "Flappers and Philosophers, and Farmers: Rural-Urban Tensions of the Twenties," *Agricultural History* 47, no. 4 [Oct., 1973], pp. 283–99).

· Mon 10.   The most remarkable day I ever saw. Cold when we got up. Still cold at 10 a.m. Then began to get warmer. By noon it was real hot. Came up a rain about 4 p.m. Then followed up the da—— sand storm. Then cold again. By night it was cold. . . .

J·u·n·e

· Mon 7.   We took the incubator chickens out to chicken yard. 51. . . . Mrs. Fike let Sallie have a mother hen to put with the incubator chickens. . . .
· Sat 12.   . . . Came up cloud. Sallie & kids beat it for cellar. I to bed.

During the last week in June Will, Bud, and Harold went to White Deer, Texas, to work in the wheat harvest. By the middle of July DeLoach returned home with $180.

A·u·g·u·s·t

· Thurs 5.   Made a batch of home brew. . . .
· Sat 28.   I went up town and voted for "Ma" Ferguson for Gov. Don't think she will be elected, but voted for her any way. . . .

DeLoach's entry was quite perceptive. The runoff was short and quiet. Moody's enormous lead in the primary gave his friends a feeling that further work was unnecessary, and it apparently convinced Ferguson supporters that their cause was doomed. The final count was Moody 495,723; Ferguson, 270,595. The conservative administration of Texas' first woman governor ended on January 17, 1927, when Dan Moody, a thirty-three year old progressive, was inaugurated (See McKay and Faulk, *Texas After Spindletop*, pp. 104–11).

S·e·p·t·e·m·b·e·r

· Mon 6.   I made a sled to cut feed with. . . . I cut two rows feed with sled. Will have to move weeds off row before I can cut it.

· Mon 13. . . . I want to start picking cotton. Would love to get first bale.

It is still customary in West Texas for the merchants of each town to offer a cash bonus for the first cotton bale of the season. In 1926, the bonus averaged $130.00 in addition to a seven-cent bonus per pound when the bale was sold. DeLoach did not harvest the first bale (See *Lamb County Leader*, Sept. 16, 1926, p. 8).

· Sat 25. Rained all night. Fell about 4.5 or 5 in. during night. Drowned 10 near grown turkeys, one hen, and one large fryer.
· Sun 26. . . . A Mr. Foust, a near neighbor died Sat at 11:35 P.M. We did not know that he was sick. Mr. Fike, H. G., Bud and I went down to see if they needed any help. They did not need any company for the night. The undertaker had charge of the body. Embalming. H. G. & Bud could not stand to see him do it. . . .

O·C·T·O·B·E·R

· Sat 30. Fike came down to tell me about McNeece hogs having the cholera. Too bad, now that will get started over the country. . . .

Cholera, a highly contagious disease among swine, is characterized by vomiting, diarrhea, and general prostration. Once started, it often becomes an epidemic, and death in the herd is widespread. Cholera first appeared in the United States in 1833, but a vaccine was not perfected until 1913, after a serious outbreak the previous year. It reduced infection from 130 hogs per thousand to approximately 30 per thousand, and many farmers became negligent about vaccinating their herds. Consequently, by late 1926 the disease was more prevalent than any year since 1912 (See *Yearbook of Agriculture, 1926*, pp. 415–19).

N·O·V·E·M·B·E·R

· Wed 3. . . . One of the turkey hens died today. The Dr. said it was roup.

Roup, a highly infectious respiratory disease that attacks poultry fowl, can be controlled by vaccinating them when they are three to four months old (See William C. Miller and Geoffrey P. West, *Encyclopedia of Animal Care*, pp. 223, 791).

· Mon 15. Lots of ice this A.M. We pulled [*cotton*] all day. Sent one bale to Amherst, sold for 9¼¢. Harold brought 4 men to pull cotton. They pulled 129 lbs. They wanted to strip the stalks. I objected, payed them off.

Stripping the stalks would have mixed a lot of leaves and broken bits of stems with the lint and lowered the price. The large 1926 cotton crop was bringing lower prices than expected, and many farmers mechanically stripped the bolls from the stalks to save money, but apparently DeLoach was after the best possible price for this bale and wanted each boll pulled separately. Laborers, also trying to make as much money as possible, negotiated for the price of pulling the bolls, then tried to strip the stalks by hand because it was faster.

· Tues 23. We rigged up a cotton puller and pulled a bale of snaps. Harold took it to town to gin. . . .

Snaps were mature bolls that were snapped, or pulled, off the cotton stalk. A dry summer in 1926 retarded the cotton crop's growth and hastened its maturity. A low of 36° in September caused defoliation that made the bolls open several weeks earlier and over a much shorter period of time than usual. Scarcity of labor and high cost of picking low-priced cotton forced farmers to find a more economical method of harvesting. Cotton sleds had been used as early as 1914, but primitive ginning equipment made them impractical. By 1926 improved equipment that separated the burrs and trash from the lint allowed farmers to gather approximately 60 percent of the crop with mechanical harvesters. Most cotton sleds were homemade or made by a local blacksmith and showed little standardization of design. They cost about thirty dollars and could cover four to six acres a day, which was an average of two bales. Their approximate operating expense was $2.50 per bale compared to $15.00 per bale for hand harvesting (See Karper and Jones, *Varieties of Cotton in Northwest Texas*, pp. 10–14, 34–35).

· Thurs 25. The wind started blowing before we got up. By 10 A.M. one could not see 100 yds down the road. It blew all day. I thought the house would go. I do not understand how the windmill stayed intact. The cotton that the sand storm 8 days since left is all out and ruined. The yellow house mill blew down, it being the tallest wind mill in the world. I am conservative in saying the wind and sand today damaged me $500.00.

A deep area of low pressure passing over Texas caused fifty-mile-per-hour winds that started about 4 A.M., lasted until sundown, and destroyed thousands of bales of cotton. When A. H. Macha of Tahoka, Texas, surveyed the destruction in his field of Half & Half cotton, he discovered a plant with the lint so tightly compacted in the burr that it had escaped damage. He used the seed to start breeding plants with stormproof bolls. In 1934 he turned his work over to the agricultural experiment station in Lubbock and the first commercial variety of stormproof cotton, named Macha, was developed. According to D. L. Jones, an agronomist with the experiment station, this is the first known instance of cotton being developed for machine harvesting (D. L. Jones, "Cotton and the Texas High Plains," p. 5).

D·E·C·E·M·B·E·R

· SUN 12.   . . . Cotton down to 4¢ per #. How can a man pay debts and live at such prices. Things one has to have is as high as if cotton was 25 to 30¢ per lb. One can not pay his debts. I have nothing to show for my year's work. Only some new debts.

· FRI 24.   The whole face of the earth is covered in snow and is still snowing. Now 9:15 A.M. Sallie and kids did intend to go to Littlefield, but won't go. It will be dull Xmas since all this snow and short money. Mr. & Mrs. Fike went to Littlefield in afternoon. They sure had a cold & muddy ride. The snow thawed up a little. We had a Christmas tree up at Mr. Fike's. One of the negro cotton pickers acted as Santa. He made a good one. C. J., Billy, and Arnold Lee [*Fike children*] could not account who was the Santy. All of us men folks that they knew were in the room. One & all received some nice little gifts. The little boys air guns.

1·9·2·7

Rain came too late for the cotton, but the South Plains produced one of the largest grain crops in its history. Bankers were happy because most people farmed without going into debt. Farmers used poultry, cream, and egg money for living expenses, and used income from crops to cover land payments and farming expenses. Diversification got a lot of praise and attention.

J·A·N·U·A·R·Y

· Sat 1.   Another New Year. I have done nothing that amounts to much in the old year. Made lots of stuff of all kinds, but could not get it gathered, and no price for what I did get gathered. . . .

The average cost of raising cotton in Texas was almost eighteen cents per pound in 1926. Farmers who hired labor to help produce the crop actually lost money and those who did their own work had no profit (See *Semi-Weekly Farm News*, Feb. 8, 1927, p. 1).

· Fri 21.   . . . I bought a John Deere lister, cost $40.00. . . .
· Fri 28.   . . . Old Jack killed Slim Cow's calf. Mules like that ought to be worked all the time. . . .

Mules tend to abuse young calves by using their teeth to hold a calf in the middle of the back and then trotting around with it. A mule might also catch a calf by the back of the neck and throw it in the air. Unless stopped, mules often killed the young animals. Today, mules are not generally around calves (See Morton, *Snowstorms, Dust Storms and Horses' Tails*, p. 17).

F·E·B·R·U·A·R·Y

· WED 2.   . . . Bud got some Barred Rock eggs to set in incubator. Got my glasses.

Barred Rock, a variety of the Plymouth Rock breed, was a general-purpose chicken whose black and white plumage became synonymous with farm flocks. They were large enough to provide meat for the table in addition to being good layers. Because the general breeds had a quieter temperament than the egg breeds, they were more easily handled in confinement, but they were also good foragers, which meant they fattened readily when allowed to range. They made good mothers, an important consideration for farmers who did not want to invest in brooding and hatching equipment. Additionally, Barred Rocks were good layers during the winter (See Rob R. Slocum *Standard Varieties of Chickens: The American Class*, pp. 3–8).

· TUES 22.   . . . We decided to go over west of Circle back to see a cotton cleaner. Back by town. Got some lumber and chicken wire. Made one.

The cotton cleaner DeLoach made was an old threshing machine that was operated with a motor. After the sandstorm in November, 1926, lint that had been blown out of the bolls was gathered with rakes from the fields and fences where the wind had left it. The cotton was put through the machine to shake the dirt out of it and collected on a layer of chicken wire. Bud raked up enough lint to make four bales after it was cleaned and ginned (Robert E. DeLoach, interview with Janet Neugebauer, Sudan, Tex., July 1, 1987).

M·A·R·C·H

· WED 16.   I took bale cotton to town for boys. I know I have the finest cotton in the land. 425# seed, 435 lbs lint. Not that sure is good, if true. They stole more of the seed than they intended to or else they burnt them in the furnace. . . .

Cottonseed constitutes approximately 64 percent of seed cotton. It appears DeLoach took 1,200 pounds of seed cotton to the gin and should have had 765 pounds of seed and 435 pounds of lint. The dirt-laden cotton very likely clogged the ginning equipment, causing the missing seed to be sent to the burr-pit along with the burrs and other trash, where it was burned (See *Texas Almanac, 1958–1959*, p. 226).

· SAT 19. . . . My back is getting in bad order again. Seems like it will never get well. Won't as long as I stoop for this maize cutting.

M·A·Y

· FRI 6. . . . I signed Bureau cotton contract.

DeLoach signed a contract agreeing to market all of his cotton through the Texas Farm Bureau Cotton Association, a non-profit, non-capital stock organization. Extremely low cotton prices in 1920 encouraged the formation of co-operative cotton marketing associations that were designed to get the best possible price for large quantities of cotton of uniform character and staple length. The Oklahoma Cotton Growers Association and the Texas Farm Bureau Cotton Association, among the earliest groups formed, later joined a federation known as the American Cotton Growers' Exchange. DeLoach belonged to both associations. The federation wanted to stabilize cotton's price by marketing it steadily throughout the year instead of flooding the market during the harvest season (four or five months), which drove the price down (Montgomery, *The Cooperative Pattern in Cotton*, pp. 75–101; O. W. Herrmann and Chastina Gardner, *Early Developments in Cooperative Cotton Marketing*, pp. 23–38).

· MON 9. The sand storm did not ease up all night and it poured it on all day. Was up town for a while.
· SUN 15. . . . Bess cow had calf today. Heifer. She is only 18 mo. old. If the mules had not killed Slim's heifer I would have had 7 head of she Jerseys. No rain.
· TUES 17. I walked over the field. Things sure do need a good rain. I think I will start knifeing the lister beds. I did want to have a good rain before I did any work, then I could plant. Was over to Vernon's field. He has the "blues," too. . . . So hot and dry that chickens won't hatch out. Only 57 chicks out of a possible 160 eggs. About a third. That is no good.

Plowed ground was listed into beds to conserve moisture. Just before planting, long knives extending out from a center bar were dragged through the beds to loosen the dirt and kill any weeds. This practice, called knifing, is still used in West Texas. Total rainfall in Lamb County in 1927 was less than ten inches, or more than 50 percent below the average. Rainfall was not that low again until the Dust Bowl days of 1934. An interesting sidelight is the absence of the intense dust storms experienced during the 1930s; however, the 1927 drought only lasted one year, and a large portion of Lamb County was still covered with prairie sod (See *Climatological Data, 1927*, p. 100).

· Mon 23.   . . . Nearly all my home brew is gone. Sure was fine. . . .

J·u·n·e

· Sun 19.   Nesbitts & Templetons were quaranteened to day for small-
    pox. . . .

A doctor was called to verify smallpox, and a yellow flag was left to warn others. DeLoach, immune after his bout with the disease in 1919, took supplies to them.

J·u·l·y

· Sat 2.   . . . One of my old teeth got to hurting me and I had to quit and
    come to the house to pull it out. Sure did hurt, but I pulled it. We all
    went up town in P.M. . . .
· Sat 9.   We all worked till noon. Went to Littlefield in P.M. Sold cream &
    eggs and 7 fryers @ 20¢ per #. cream @ 31¢, eggs 13¢ per doz.

During the last week of June, 106 cans of cream were shipped from Littlefield, generating $1,272 for producers. Most of the cream was purchased for $.32 per pound. The grain sorghums that grew so abundantly brought a higher return when marketed through livestock, thus reducing the farmer's dependence on a single crop. This practice is generally known as the cow-sow-hen diversification (*Lamb County Leader*, June 30, 1927, p. 1).

· Sun 17.   The country is in bad shape. Lots of the people have gone. The
    land is not planted, and what is planted is all weeds.

Farmers who had difficulty making land payments due to a drought or low commodity prices often sold out and left before the situation worsened. DeLoach did this in 1917 when he left Crosby County. Previously there had always been cheap, unsettled land that appreciated in value after being broken, making it good business to move on. However, the western counties of Texas made up one of the last agricultural frontiers in the United States, and those farmers who remained discovered they owned the last of the cheap lands. More importantly, in developing areas boosterism was widely practiced. Newspapers purposely avoided any comments about people leaving for fear of starting a mass exodus that would hurt the business community and future land sales.

A·u·g·u·s·t

· WED 10. We did not do any thing today in the field. The boys & I went up town in P.M. and all of us went up to the street carnival at night. We played the "Bingo game." Sallie won a milk bucket and a lot of groceries. Had a good time.
· SUN 21. ... We went down to Jerry Wayne's. Was out in his cotton. The leaf worms are eating on his cotton. The folks are all gone to a singing at Vernon's.

Leaf worms are sometimes called army worms. Eggs, deposited on the underside of leaves, hatch in three to twenty days, producing a larva that feeds voraciously on young leaves. Prior to 1870, leaf worms ranked third among cotton insects with respect to destructiveness. Since that time paris green and other arsenical poisons have proven effective for controlling this insect. By the mid-1930s, farmers were dusting with calcium arsenate (See Harry Bates Brown, *Cotton*, 1927 edition, p. 313; *Progressive Farmer* 51, no. 7 [July, 1936], p. 35).

· THURS 25. I sent the truck over to Wayne's for them. They loaded up, came by, and we loaded our bedding and started for Tahoka to the Primitive Baptist Meeting. We got there about 4 P.M. Had supper and went to church.

In the early 1800s there was a division in the Baptist Church between those favoring missionary work, Sunday schools, seminaries, etc., and those opposed. The opposition group, known as Primitive or Hardshell Baptists, follows a strong Calvinistic doctrine that emphasizes salvation by grace, election, and predestination. Primitive Baptist congregations are found mostly in rural sections of the eastern, southern, and midwestern states. DeLoach belonged to a group called B.M.A. Baptists (Baptist Missionary Association Baptists), but he freely attended services and revivals held by other groups of Baptists. Like

Fri. 26... Sleep, eat, and go to
church. The eats were all free
and a hearty welcome for all.
Some fine preaching.

the Primitive Baptists, B.M.A. Baptists embrace local autonomy, but they also support missionary work. The primary purpose of a revival was saving souls, but it had social benefits as well. New friendships were formed, old ones renewed, and dinner on the grounds helped cement those relationships until the next big meeting. These people were drawn together by a common bond, that of striving to incorporate moral decency into the family and community life they were building (See W. J. Berry, "Primitive Baptists," in *Encyclopedia of Southern Baptists 2*, pp. 1114–15; C. E. Colton, "Baptist Missionary Association," in *Encyclopedia of Southern Baptists 1*, pp. 118–19; Dale, *Frontier Ways*, pp. 213–31).

· Fri 26. Up, had breakfast, went to church. Had dinner, back to church. Back to supper, then to church again. Sleep, eat, and go to church. The eats were all free and a hearty welcome for all. Some fine preaching.
· Sat 27. The same thing as Fri.
· Sun 28. The meeting broke up at 12 noon. We had dinner and started for home, arriving at sunset. . . .
· Mon 29. . . . Andy Newsom came by. He and I went to see about the bull we bought. Had to pay for him. $27.50 each. Seven in all, in the circle. They did not buy what we ordered, but we had to take him anyway, since the bank had honored the draft. . . .

DeLoach and six of his neighbors organized the Sudan Bull Circle #2 to improve the bloodline of their dairy cattle. The first cooperative bull association in the United States was organized in 1908 by Michigan Agricultural College. These associations were formed by farmers with small herds for the joint ownership and use of pure-bred bulls which were too costly for individuals. Purchase price and maintenance expense was shared by all members and, unlike most business ventures, the probability of loss was very small, due to increased butterfat production that remained noticeable for several generations. Cooperative bull associations encouraged members to begin studying pedigrees, confirmation, production records, and dairy problems. The associations also helped retard the spread of diseases because each member desiring service was required to maintain a disease-free herd through regular testing. An added dividend was the interest young boys developed in herd improvement and livestock exhibitions. County agents usually provided guidance in organizing associations and information about desirable bloodlines in bulls (See Joel G. Winkjer, "Cooperative Bull Associations," *Yearbook of Agriculture, 1916*, pp. 311–19).

S·E·P·T·E·M·B·E·R

· SAT 10. . . . We all went up town. Our bull calf came in. He is much better than I was expecting at 9 months old.

O·C·T·O·B·E·R

· SAT 29. Mr. Lynn called today for Harold and family about 6:30 A.M. . . .
I sure did hate to see the boy leave, but maybe he will do well. . . . Bud
left this P.M. I am sure lonesome. I did not want Bud to go back down
there, but he has a girlfriend, I think, that is pulling him back.

Harold and family moved to California looking for work, and Bud was working in McAdoo, Texas, approximately 100 miles southeast of Sudan. Harold's
move to California illustrates the growing exodus of young men from agriculture to industry. From 1920 to 1928 nearly half a million people left farming each
year mainly because farm income was depressed for the better part of the decade
while wage earners made more money than ever before in history. The Great
Depression forced many of these people back to the farm, but it did not stem
the tide permanently. Science and technology made it possible for one person
to farm more land and produce more per acre than ever before, thus reducing
the number of people needed in farming. Prior to 1940, the industrial phase of
Texas' economy did not develop as rapidly as it did in other states, hence the
move to California (See R. L. Skrabanek, *Characteristics and Changes in the Texas
Farm Population*, p. 4; Editorial Opinion, *Progressive Farmer* 44, no. 3 [Jan. 19,
1929], p. 4).

N·O·V·E·M·B·E·R

· MON 7. The Mexicans started picking cotton this A.M. . . .

People of Mexican heritage filled the heavy demand for harvest labor on the
Plains. Starting in the lower Rio Grande Valley, they followed the cotton harvest north and arrived on the High Plains in October. The area's remoteness
generally forced wages above that paid in other parts of the state. The average
worker pulled slightly more than a bale per five-day workweek. After the cotton harvest was mechanized in the 1950s many migrant workers settled on the
Llano Estacado, weaving their language and customs into the culture of the area

(See Joe R. Motheral, William H. Metzler, and Louis J. Ducoff, *Cotton and Manpower—Texas High Plains*, pp. 2, 12–13).

· Tues 8. Took off the first cotton, 1450#, Only put 1290# in the bale, it
     weighed 485#.
· Sat 12. . . . I shipped my three bales to Farm Bureau Association. . . .

In 1927, the Texas Farm Bureau Cotton Association advanced sixteen cents
per pound (eighty dollars per five hundred-pound bale) to farmers marketing
their cotton through this organization. More than half of Lamb County cotton growers signed contracts. Any additional money received when the cotton
was sold to the mills was returned to producers as a dividend.

· Mon 14. We loaded up the turkeys. I took them to town. . . . We sold for
     30¢ per lb. for #1 turkeys, 25¢ per # for old toms. Sold 9 that weighed
     116#. One old tom weighed 21#. Will keep 3 hens on one Tom, for
     herding stock. 4 turned down on being too light. . . .

Many farms on the South Plains produced Thanksgiving and Christmas turkeys for eastern markets. Seventy carloads were shipped from Lubbock in 1927,
generating over half a million dollars for South Plains farmers. Despite the
lucrative opportunities, unorganized farmers were at a disadvantage when trying
to sell perishable commodities through local buyers. The thirty cents per pound
that DeLoach received was the result of organized marketing led by the Sudan
Vocational Agriculture teacher. Farmers shipped a freight carload of three thousand turkeys to Kansas City and drove the local market nine cents per pound
higher. This single transaction brought ten thousand dollars of outside money
into the local economy (See *Sudan News*, Nov. 18, 1927, p. 1; *The Hub* 1, no. 1
[Nov., 1927], p. 5).

D·E·C·E·M·B·E·R

· Sat 3. . . . We all went up town in afternoon. Old Daddy Pierce (better
     known as "Popin Pierce") had the key to Sudan this P.M. He sure did
     pull a stunt. Tried to kill a Mexican. Would if he had found him. He
     punched the Mex. in the "Tummy" with his automatic. The Mex. took
     it from him. Pierce then got a rifle and went to the Mex. car. Then is
     when the scattering of women & kids started. He then jumped on another Mexican and hammered him with a shot gun. Some white fellow
     gave him (Pierce) an upper cut and the "war hoss" was down for the

count. He finally came to and secured another gun. He did not cease hostilities till about 11 P.M. The high Sheriff came and took him to jail.

· Fri 23. . . . I stayed in town near all day. The piano did not come. . . .

· Sat 24. . . . The kids are having a time shooting their fire works. . . . I bought C. J.'s shetland pony and saddle for Bill. That did tickle him.

· Mon 26. . . . Terry Newsom came by. Wanted me to go to town to have a Bull Circle meeting. We could not get quorum at town, so decided to meet at my place tonight. All members were present except Winston. The Circle bought out the two Burtons, $10.00 each. We also changed the breeding, $3.00 for outsiders, $1.50 for members.

· Tues 27. Fike and I went to town for our piano. He wants to buy the box. . . . I got home with the piano and Fike and I were thinking [of] some way to unload it when Bud and Buck Witt [a nephew] came in. The kids are sure playing that music box now.

This was a player piano and apparently one of the few in Lamb County. In January, 1928, the Sudan newspaper carried an article on the front page about a party in the home of Mrs. W. G. DeLoach, during which everyone enjoyed the new player piano she received for Christmas.

· Sat 31. This is the last of 1927 and believe me it is cold. Fike, Bud & I went up town in P.M. Was so cold one could not get away from the fire. Jim is at Walden's tonight, Dorothy at Vernon's. C. J. Fike down here. Two for one.

1·9·2·8

Poultry and dairy products became cash crops on the South Plains. Farmers used processing plants located within the region, and the rapidly growing population of area towns provided lucrative markets for all the milk, cream, and eggs they could produce.

J·A·N·U·A·R·Y

· MON 9. The Mexicans called me out for a conflab. They wanted $1.00 per cwt. Said they were offered that. I told them to go and get it. I would not pay but 75¢. They went on to work. I made trade with one of them to weigh and keep the weights. I went up town. . . .

· WED 11. . . . We had another "Bull Circle" meeting tonight. Newsom sold out to the circle. Only four now. His share cost each $3.71. I will get the $3.60 check back that I payed. . . . I am to take charge of the bull and books. I take up Newsom's contract, $1.00 per mo. for the care of bull. That is not to include feed. We are to have feed ground, and left with me. Each member to crush 3 or 4 hundred pounds as it comes his turn. Walden, Newsom, Winston, and myself being present.

Experiments conducted by Texas A&M College proved dairy cows preferred ground to whole grain sorghums. When they were fed whole grain, as much as 30 percent passed through their system undigested. Cows ate more when the grain was ground and produced more milk as result. The popularity of bull circles for herd improvement and a strong department of Dairy Manufacturers at Texas Technological College helped put the South Plains in the forefront of butter production for the state. Area farmers produced enough cream to support three butter plants in Lubbock that manufactured two million pounds annually (See A. L. Darnell and O. C. Copeland, *Ground versus Unground Grain for Lactating Dairy Cows*; R. D. Shinkle, "Tops for Texas—Lubbock Leads in Butter Manufacture, Egg Shipments," *West Texas Today* 21, no. 7 [Sept., 1940], p. 16).

F·E·B·R·U·A·R·Y

· Sun 12. . . . Mr. Max Walden brought one of Trent Walden's cows down to "Head Man." That is what I call the Company bull. . . .

· Wed 15. . . . I took Sallie to dentist in afternoon. She had four teeth pulled out. They did not hurt her. I could have pulled them myself. . . . We all went up to the school house. The P.T.A. had a very nice program. . . .

· Wed 29. I worked here at home in forenoon. Mr. Slagle [*an International Harvester dealer*] came down to look at a single row planter. I traded it to him on a new two row planter. I put mine in at $45.00. The new one cost $145.00.

M·A·R·C·H

· Fri 2. . . . The Singer Sewing Mch. Collector was out to see me. I gave him a check for $25.00, that being the first note due on our machine.

A·P·R·I·L

· Fri 13. . . . The folks have gone to the Style show at town. No one here, but Pal [*DeLoach's dog*] & I.

· Tues 17. . . . Heard at town the people near Mr. Derrick place were going to build a church. They did not say any thing to the folks up here about it, so we had a mass meeting at Jerry Wayne's place and decided to build one ½ mile south and two mi. west of me. A settlement church or union church.

The Friendship Union Church was made up of Baptist Missionary Association Baptists, Methodists, Holiness Pentecostals, and Primitive Baptists. Each took a turn conducting Sunday services during the month. Members attended every Sunday, readily accepting each other's doctrine. During months with five Sundays, everyone gathered for singing and dinner-on-the-grounds on the fifth Sunday (Jimmie DeLoach Moorhead, interview with Janet Neugebauer, Sudan, Tex., July 1, 1987).

- WED 18. Jed Wayne's call about noon for me to come to Jerry Wayne's place. He & I were appointed to solicit aid [*money to build the church*] in the Amherst country. We made a run, collected some better than $60.00. . . .

After another day of calls the men collected $129.50, and the building began.

- SAT 21. . . . The folks went to Sudan in P.M. I stayed home to look after Lady Cow. She found bull calf. Cold as the devil tonight.
- SUN 29. We fixed a basket lunch and went to Bulah to a Fifth Sunday Singing. They sure did "pour it on." Fine singing. The high west wind blew the sand something awful. All the dinner was "sanded down."

M·A·Y

- SAT 12. Bud took Sallie & Jimmie to Littlefield to get her (Jimmie) graduating dress. . . .
- MON 14. . . . Took out $150.00 Insurance. . . . Southwestern Life Insurance Co. . . .
- SAT 19. . . . I had my wheat insured for $10.00 per A., $550.00, cost $63.03.
- TUES 22. Took Harold's sow to Jerry Wayne's for service. He has a Poland China male. . . .

Apparently Jerry Wayne was keeping the registered male hog owned by a breeding circle. DeLoach paid $1.00 for breeding service.

J·U·N·E

- MON 4. Walked over field. Found things in bad shape [*after a severe hailstorm the previous afternoon*]. Went up to town to make my wheat report. Turned in 60% damage. Stayed in town till about 3 P.M. Came out with Ballard. He was writing cotton insurance. . . . I was in the north edge of the hail storm. South and southwest of me, and east, all crops were beat off the map.

· TUES 5. . . . Saw Mr. Cramer. Spoke for some cotton seed. Went over, got 21.5 bus. @ $1.25 per bu., $26.85. This is the third time I have bought planting seed. First planting the seed rotted in the ground, second planting the hail and water ruined it. I now wonder what will happen to the third planting? . . . planted 5 A. cotton for Sallie. She wanted a cotton patch.

· MON 11. . . . In forenoon started five scratchers on cotton. Bud started to harrow the little strip of cotton that I left. The S.W. wind started blowing and by noon a sure enough sand storm was blowing. Had to do any thing that would keep the sand from cutting down the crops. This kind of sand will kill a crop in 3 to 4 hours if one does not plow or harrow the land. Sure is bad.

· THURS 14. I dug up 4 little spots of Johnson grass. . . . Adjuster had come out to my place. . . . We looked the wheat over and I think he gave me a good adjustment, 24%. That is not much, but is better than a total loss. . . .

Initially considered a desirable plant for pasturage and hay, Johnson grass became an obnoxious weed to cotton farmers. Each mature stalk produced dozens of seeds of excellent germinating quality and a mass of vigorous rootstocks that often remained alive through the winter. The rootstock spread underground over a large area, and from every joint a new stem would sprout. Before widespread use of tractors during the 1930s the plant was difficult to control because excrement from horses and mules aided its spread. However, tractors allowed farmers to plow faster and deeper; this way they could "keep ahead" of it by destroying the rootstock and cropping the plant before it had time to produce seed (See H. N. Vinall, *Johnson Grass: Its Production for Hay and Pasturage*, pp. 1–2; M. W. Talbot, *Johnson Grass as a Weed*, p. ii). Historically, farmers have been skeptical of crop insurance, and this incident provides an insight into the reason. DeLoach's estimate of a 60 percent loss was very close to accurate. The undamaged wheat made 8 bushels per acre (35 bushels total). From this it can be assumed that approximately fifty-one of the original fifty-five acres sustained damage. Without hail approximately 408 bushels of wheat could have been harvested from this acreage. Sixty percent hail damage would have left approximately 163 bushels; DeLoach actually harvested 170 bushels. Payment for the 245 bushels that were lost should have amounted to at least $262.00 (figured at $1.07 per bushel, market price at the time of harvest). The adjuster used a per-acre yield of 5.33 bushels as a basis for figuring the loss and paid De-Loach for about a 25 percent loss. The check amounted to $68.47. Insurance companies were wise enough to see that farmers did not suffer a loss of premium in the event of severe hail damage.

- · Fri 15. . . . It makes me sick to get out of this hail district and see the nice crops, and I have no cotton up. I have spent to date $120.85 for cotton seed and no cotton yet. Feed is no good. Has been beat about with hard rains and sand. . . .
- · Sat 16. . . . I got my cotton returns from the cotton Bureau, $75.61. Not much. . . .

The length of time cotton growers had to wait for their money was a draw-back for cooperative marketing associations (See Herrmann and Gardner, *Early Developments in Cooperative Cotton Marketing*, pp. 32–35).

- · Sat 23. . . . My wheat insurance came in, $68.47. . . .
- · Tues 26. Took sample to Amherst. Was offered $1.20 per bu., #1 basis, my sample tested 57. The combine had finished up the ripe strip. It made about 8 bu. to A [*35 bu. total*].

J·u·l·y

- · Mon 9. The combine men came in and finished what wheat that would pay. Hauled 110 bu. to Amherst, sold for $1.07. Not quite enough to pay cutting and threshing expenses. I have some thing like 60 bu. in barn. Hot & dry.
- · Tues 24. . . . Bud has not come home yet. I look for him all the time. What is there to raising boys any way. One gets attached and then they leave just when they are lots of company. Oh! well, such is life. . . .

Bud had a girlfriend, living near Ralls, that he visited each weekend, and often he did not get back to work as soon as his father thought he should.

S·e·p·t·e·m·b·e·r

- · Sat 1. . . . We all went up town in afternoon. Jimmie & Dorothy called at Mrs. Day's for their music [*piano*] lesson. . . .

· FRI 7. ... Got my final settlement on Bureau cotton, a check for $34.42.
That is the devil. No more will I ship cotton in the outfit. . . .

· TUES 18. I cut corn tops all day and shocked them up. They make fine
cow feed. The first I have cut since I was 12 yrs. old in Parker Co.,
Tex. . . .

· MON 24. I cut hegari till about 3 P.M. Finished one strip. Came to house.
Made me a slide to cut stalks with. The same blade I used in 1918 near
Duke, Okla.

DeLoach was harvesting his hegari with a homemade sled that had long extending knives. He sat on the sled and as the mules slowly pulled it down the
row he grabbed the cut stalks, bundled them quickly with twine, and dropped
the bundles on the ground. They were later shocked to dry before stacking for
winter feed (Robert E. DeLoach, interview with Janet Neugebauer, Sudan, Tex.,
Mar. 16, 1987).

· SUN 30. ... We all went over to the church house in P.M. Old Sacred
Harp Singing. Had church at night. We did not go. . . .

Sacred Harp singing is the oldest form of gospel music in the United States.
The concept of solmization, which dates back to Elizabethan England, was
brought to America by the Pilgrims. Syllables are used to denote tones of the
musical scale. Singing a cappella, Sacred Harpers learn the sounds from four
shaped notes. The *mi* is a diamond, *fa* is a triangle, *sol* is round, and *la* is square.
The last three notes are repeated twice, making the full octave *fa, sol, la, fa, sol,
la, mi*, which is the predecessor of *do, re, mi* solmization. Songs are sung twice,
the first time in a chorus of *fas, sols, las,* and *mis,* the second time with the lyrics.
It is also known as *fasola* singing (Buell E. Cobb, Jr., *The Sacred Harp: A Tradition and Its Music*; Donald Davidson, *Still Rebels, Still Yankees, and Other Essays*,
pp. 137–51; Randy Mallory, "The Abiding Art of Sacred Harp," *Texas Highways*
34, no. 8 [Aug., 1987], pp. 30–33).

O·C·T·O·B·E·R

· FRI 12. I sent 3 mules up to Walden's to work on the push header.
Walden and I are partners on it. Bud stayed until they got started
up. . . .

A push header is an implement for harvesting wheat that cuts the heads
of grain from the straw instead of cutting the straw near the base of the plant

(Robert E. DeLoach, interview with Janet Neugebauer, Sudan, Tex., July 1, 1987).

N·O·V·E·M·B·E·R

· TUES 6.   Well today is the day that Smith or Hoover, one, will be ditched. We will go in the afternoon to vote and get a few other things. . . . We went up town. I voted for Smith. I could hardly do it, but I could not take that Hoover 'pill.' Sallie voted for Hoover. . . .

In the 1928 presidential election Texans voted Republican for the first time since Reconstruction. Rural, Protestant, prohibitionist Texans would not support an urban, Catholic, wet, with ties to New York City. An orphaned farmboy who worked his way through college, Hoover appealed to rural Texans. According to some historians, the election was a referendum on prohibition, prosperity (prosperous urbanites vs. economically depressed rural people), and prejudice (predominantly Protestant Texas was very sympathetic to the anti-Catholic propaganda of the Ku Klux Klan) (See Brown, *Hood, Bonnet, and Little Brown Jug*, pp. 3–10, 374–422; Seth Shepard McKay, *Texas Politics, 1906–1944*, pp. 158–85).

· FRI 9.   . . . Al Smith was snowed under.
· SAT 24.   . . . A Mr. Clemmons came and wanted to pull cotton. Wanted to move in today, but I had to do some work on shack. I am to pay him 75¢ per C.W.T. Cold all day.
· SUN 25.   . . . We scrubbed out the shack and fixed it up for the people. They came in about noon. Was proud to get in a house. I think from what they say, they had been living out doors. . . .

D·E·C·E·M·B·E·R

· SUN 23.   The people that live in my house will move to Templeton's place. They picked the best of my cotton and now they are going to leave. It seems that a man can't put any more trust in any body. They said when I let them move in that they would stay till the last boll was snapped. I hate to lose the confidence that I had in them. No use of one treating strangers any other way. Only as dead beats and grand rascals, then if they prove otherwise, one feels better and then, if they do not prove up to one's expectation one is not disappointed. . . .

1·9·2·9

Opportunity was the buzzword in Lamb County in 1929. Easy terms attracted home seekers, rapidly growing towns beckoned to businessmen, and heavy spring rains promised plentiful crops. Local newspaper editors cautioned readers against procrastination, warning that the door was already ajar as opportunity knocked. However, record-breaking surpluses of cotton and wheat cast a shadow over this rosy picture. Searching for a solution, President Hoover created the Federal Farm Board and charged it with the task of finding foreign markets for the surpluses. The distant tune of hard times was only faintly heard by West Texans.

J·A·N·U·A·R·Y

· Mon 14. . . . The little heifer found heifer calf. She being the great-great grand daughter of my Lady Cow. . . .

F·E·B·R·U·A·R·Y

· Thurs 7. A bitter day. . . . Took cream to station. One batch tested "24" and another "32" [*percent butterfat*] . . . cream $3.44. . . . The stock are all very well sheltered. . . .
· Sat 16. . . . I Dr. my pigs for mange! The little ones! . . . .

M·A·R·C·H

· Mon 4. Herbert Hoover stepped in to White House today. Weaned Red
   sow's pigs. Sold 3 of them for $4.50 each . . . cream $3.42. . . . Bought a
   radio from Milligan & Ballard, $126.50. . . .

DeLoach bought an Atwater Kent radio. This brand was popular because
it had a wide range and simple one-dial operation. In addition to entertainment,
the family received timely agricultural information from their radio. In 1926 the
Department of Agriculture, through the United States Radio Farm School, began targeting farm families with "Noonday Flashes" consisting of conversations
between a county agent and farmer about current problems, and five days a
week farm women could tune into "Housekeepers' Chat", a fifteen-minute program with the latest information about homemaking and food preparation.
Along with the automobile, telephone, and rural free delivery, the radio is
credited with removing the physical and cultural isolation of farm families.
Teachers reported that children from farm homes that had a radio were more
alert and better informed about current events (See *Yearbook of Agriculture, 1926*,
p. 56; Elsie Orr, "Radio—the Farmer's Liberator," *Progressive Farmer* 51, no. 2 [Feb.,
1936], p. 29).

· Tues 5. . . . The radio man came out and installed the radio. It has been
   going since. Mr. Bush's folks came down for a while. I guess we will lose
   a crop on this outfit.
· Thurs 7. . . . Bought a ½ Jersey off Archie the "Chevy" man. Traded
   for a "Chevy" car. Put my old Ford in at $100.00, put in Lady Cow
   @ $100.00, payed $135.00 cash. Bud put up $35.00 of the cash. Brought
   the Jersey-Hereford cow home. Will have to deliver Lady Cow to
   Archie. Hate to see her go. I bought her in Okla. at Jess Dickson's sale
   in March 1925 [*DeLoach paid $64.00 for her*]. She has been a faithful
   cow. . . .
· Wed 27. I think it rained near all night. Have been out of ink. Had to
   write with a pencil. . . .

A·P·R·I·L

· Fri 12. I went up to Earl Wyett for some Manco maize seed. Bud wanted
   to plant 3 or 4 A. of it. . . .

Manco maize was a dwarf, straight-necked Milo maize developed in Oklahoma. It was an early maturing cross between Blackhull Kaffir and Dwarf Milo. Yields of forty to eighty bushels per acre could be harvested with a row binder, or combine, because of the straight neck. Seed cost fifteen cents per pound (See *Sudan News*, Mar. 16, 1928, p. 3).

· Sat 13. . . . Had letter from Taft Ranch sending transfer blank on circle
   Bull from A. D. Newsom to Sudan Bull circle #2. . . .

The Taft Ranch was known throughout Texas for its Jersey herd sire, Masterman of the Oaklands. Young bulls from this sire were in demand for use in bull circles (See A. Ray Stephens, *The Taft Ranch: A Texas Principality*, p. 220; Paul Huey, "Best Bulls Only," *Progressive Farmer* 43, no. 22 [June 2, 1928], p. 615).

· Tues 30. . . . We found some Lamb's quarter greens on way home. Had a
   fine feed on them tonight. . . .

Young, tender leaves of lambs-quarters can be used in salads or cooked like spinach. Sallie canned them to use throughout the year. A popular item in the diet of early settlers who had fresh greens only during summer, lambs-quarters are still enjoyed by many West Texans (See H. D. Harrington, *Edible Native Plants of the Rocky Mountains*, pp. 69–71; Jimmie DeLoach Moorhead, interview with Janet Neugebauer, Sudan, Tex., July 1, 1987).

M·A·Y

· Tues 7. . . . A Mrs. Stacy called today, boosting for Littlefield for the
   county seat. . . .

Location of the county seat was an important matter. In addition to affecting property values and the growth of the business community, its location determined how far people had to drive over rough roads to take care of legal business. Many did not consider the matter closed even after a county seat was designated. The constitution provided that a county seat would become permanent after forty years, but until that time an election could be held every two years. Olton, situated in the northern part of Lamb County, was designated the county seat in 1908. "Relocation within a mile of the county's center required only a majority vote, but a two-thirds majority was needed to move the county seat elsewhere. Amherst, near the heart, could have won with a simple majority, while Littlefield had to have two-thirds of the ballots. Neither could muster sufficient strength" (See June Rayfield Welch and J. Larry Nance, *The Texas Courthouse*, pp. 4–11; June Rayfield Welch, *The Texas Courthouse Revisited*, p. 140).

· SUN 12. . . . Report is that the court house will stay in Olton for the next two yrs. Have not heard how the vote stands.

· TUES 14. . . . I went up to town for some coffee. Don't have any breakfast when I have no coffee. They put the hot chocolate to me, but I did not drink any of it. . . .

· WED 15. . . . The County Agent called to see the Circle Bull. . . .

· SAT 25. Caught a few fish out of the tank. Put them in the drinking trough. We all went up town in P.M.

Fish kept tanks and watering troughs clean. The DeLoach family had gold-fish, the most popular fish for this purpose, but catfish were also used and then eaten when mature (Robert E. DeLoach, interview with Janet Neugebauer, Sudan, Tex., July 1, 1987).

· MON 27. Took some plow points to Amherst to have extensions put on the points. They cost me $2.50. Gosh that was high. . . . Fike came down. He and I went up to Sudan. He had a pt. of red whiskey. A treat. We took a snort in the vault at the bank. Was good.

Prohibition, more than any other issue, illustrated the urban-rural conflict of the 1920s. Rural, Protestant forces held firm in their victory for over a decade, but the "noble experiment," as Hoover called it, was too extreme to achieve the desired results. Hypocrisy became commonplace as total abstinence drove moderates to violate a law that was impossible to enforce.

J·U·N·E

· SUN 2. We went to church and Sunday school. The preacher came home with us for dinner. Stayed till night services. Seems to be a fine man and a very good preacher. I do not belong to the church, but I thought it was as much my duty to pay him some as if I were a member, so I gave him a fine spotted pig. . . .

DeLoach is referring to the Church of Christ, where Sallie had her member-ship. He belonged to the Baptist Church.

· WED 5. . . . I circulated a petition for the protest of raising the school tax any higher [*tax rate was ten cents per one hundred dollars valuation*]. I made the west half of south half of the district. Only found one man that would not sign it. He was a new comer and wanted to talk it over with the school board, which is O.K.

The brunt of taxation in Texas fell upon the land; therefore, farmers were generally opposed to an increase.

J·U·L·Y

· SAT 13. . . . Meadow & Nolan came by. Wanted to buy my shotes. 5 of them. I sold to them for $14.00 per head. . . . Sallie's birthday. She was 45. . . .

· SUN 14. We all went to S. S. in forenoon. Back to singing in afternoon, back to B.Y.P.U. in evening. A young fellow will teach a singing school starting Wed 17th. He agreed to teach a school for a box supper, the proceeds at the end of the school. . . .

Dating back to the 1890s, the Baptist Young People's Union, the B.Y.P.U., was started to increase spirituality and Christian service, and to teach Baptist doctrine and history (See *Encyclopedia of Southern Baptists* 1, pp. 134–35). During the 1920s interest in gospel music was at an all-time high in southern rural communities. Hundreds of itinerant teachers traveled the countryside conducting singing schools. "Shape-note" singing, an expansion of "fasola" singing that uses all eight notes of the scale, was taught. Prior to the inclusion of music in the public school system, most church choir members received their training from singing schools (See footnote for Sept. 30, 1928; Virniel Joseph Lowrance, Jr., "Solmization: Historical Background and Contemporary Usage" [Master's thesis, Texas Tech University, 1969]).

· WED 24. . . . Bought a new ice cream freezer $6.00. Lots for a freezer, but can't do without one. Made cream in it. Sure was good.

· SAT 27. . . . The way the singing teacher did was a shame. He sure did work the people of this section. Oh! Well, we ought to be stung. We were looking for something for nothing and we got nothing for something.

A·U·G·U·S·T

· WED 14. Was up early. Bud and I started for Blanco Canyon to the Old Settler's Reunion which opens Aug 15. . . .

· THURS 15. . . . I met lots of people that I had not seen for a long time. One, a Mrs. Nell (Witt) Spikes. Had been 30 years this coming November since I saw her. I ate dinner with she and her husband and several old timers. Would love to have seen Walt Reynolds, my old friend of 1899. He and I went to Roswell in 1916. . . .

Nellie Witt Spikes was related to DeLoach's sisters, Fannie and Curtie, through marriage. Spikes' history of Crosby County, Texas, is an essential source for anyone researching the county's early years. DeLoach didn't realize at the time that he was compiling a similar record.

S·E·P·T·E·M·B·E·R

· FRI 6. . . . Dunlap & Holly came down this A.M. They wanted me to join the Sudan Chamber of Commerce, at 50 cts per month. We went up to the meeting at night. They gave away a few donations of the merchants. Dorothy drew a bed spread.

· TUES 17. . . . Talked with Gholson [*land agent for the Newsom Land Company*] about buying a little piece of land. ½ of a Labor or 90 A. at $27.50 per A.

· THURS 19. Mr. Gholson came out. He & I went over to the tract of land. I made him a "pass." He said he could not do that, $25.00 per A. He wants $27.50. . . .

· FRI 20. . . . I went up town. Saw Mr. Gholson. We dickered for quite a while. I finely took him up. I bought the ½ labor of land at $27.50 per A. . . .

· SAT 21. . . . The folks all went to Sudan this P.M. I did not want to go. We will have to cut out this town going now. I mean to pay for that land I bought if I live, and all we save is that much made.

O·C·T·O·B·E·R

· WED 30. Things are covered in water. Rained till about 10 A.M. Then began to snow. Fell till about 3 P.M. It is clear tonight. The first snow I ever saw in Oct. Maybe will clear up for a while now. Hope so, any way. . . .

N·O·V·E·M·B·E·R

· WED 13. Took cream to town. Only offered 33¢ per #. Did not sell it. Will churn and sell butter, it is 45¢. . . .

D·E·C·E·M·B·E·R

· SAT 14. Kids picked up some scattering heads of feed. I told them they could sell it for Xmas money. They gathered 500 or 600#, and there is quite a lot more. . . . Took 4 gal. cream to town, got 29¢ per # for it. That is no money. . . .

· MON 16. Bud & I went up town, took a load of cotton seed. Sold for $31.00 per ton, $45.26 worth. . . . Mr. Gholson told me the papers were ready for my inspection = $300.00.

· MON 23. . . . Billy took hegari to Sudan [*the heads gathered on Dec. 14*]. Sold for $13.50 per ton, $18.16 worth. That is to be cut 3 ways, Dorothy, Jimmie, and Billy, $6.05⅓ each. When I was 12 yrs. old I would have been scared to death with $6.00 for Christmas money.

· TUES 24. . . . Killed and dressed a Turkey. Killed a beef. Sent J. D. Wayne a ¼. Hind quarter. He is to pay me back as good meat as he got off me. Sure is fat and tender. The quarter I sent Wayne weighed 41 pounds. Fixing the Xmas tree.

· WED 25. We all went to Christmas Tree. Was up till 12 or 1 o'clock. A big crowd of young poeple have been here all day. Dorothy's & Jimmie's birthday dinner combined with Christmas. Dorothy's B. D. on the 26, and Jimmie's on the 24. The B.Y.P.U. had a social and a feed here to-night. We have had open house all day. Too many to name. . . .

In pioneer settlements Christmas celebrations tended to be community af-fairs. On Christmas Eve everyone gathered at the schoolhouse to enjoy each other's favorite candy or cake and to try to guess who was Santa Claus. A minister offered prayer, and school children often presented a play. The high-light of the evening was the gift exchange, when everyone received something (Dale, *Frontier Ways*, pp. 146–49; *Sudan News*, Dec. 27, 1928, p. 1).

· THURS 26. Sallie & I went over to Mrs. Buckner's place. She is the widow of the first preacher that preached in Friendship church. We made up a box for her at the Christmas Tree. She could not come, hence the trip to her place. . . .

Dec. 25... We all went to
Christmas Tree, Was up till 12 or 1 o'clock.
A big crowd of young people have been here all day.

1·9·3·0

Even though most journalists and their readers refused to acknowledge a depression until nearly a year after the stock market crashed, many farmers sensed that hard times were at hand. DeLoach's entries about tight money and dry weather foreshadowed the problems all West Texans faced in the coming decade.

J·A·N·U·A·R·Y

· WED 1. New Year. Will not make any new pledges, but will do my best to do better than I did in 1929. . . .

F·E·B·R·U·A·R·Y

· WED 5. . . . The little girl at Montgomery's died about 6 P.M. The father of the girl is in Montgomery's cotton picking house. . . .
· THURS 6. We buried the little girl that died at Montgomery's place. Was a sad funeral. The people did not have enough money to put her away. We made up about $51.00. . . .
· SAT 22. We took Bud to Clovis. [*Hoping to find work, he caught the train to California, where Harold was living.*] . . . Hated to see him go in one way, but he will do better I guess than on a farm. . . .

1930

M·A·R·C·H

· Mon 31. . . . We all went to box supper at Friendship [*Union Church*]. Had lots of fun. I won the jar of pickles for the ugliest man. Net proceeds $94.40 goes to pay one insurance note and will apply bal. on light note due next fall.

A·P·R·I·L

· Sat 5. . . . Some one stole all our hens but 9.

A group of chicken thieves was caught selling stolen chickens to a processing plant in a nearby town, indicating the declining economy of West Texas during the depression (See *Sudan News*, Apr. 10, 1930, p. 1).

· Thurs 10. . . . I attended a meeting of the trustees of Friendship Church, was elected Sec. & Treasurer. Took charge of books today. . . .

By mid-April Bud was back home. He couldn't find a job in California and realized if he spent any more time looking it would be too late to farm. He didn't like to work for the low prices that crops were bringing, but it was better than no income at all.

· Tues 22. Took Sallie over to Boyce's to meet the lady delegates of her club [*Home Demonstration Club*]. Sallie, Mrs. Rogers, and 4 or 5 others will represent Friendship at the state meeting at Canyon. . . .

Meetings of this type provided an opportunity to receive the latest information in homemaking and food preparation from the Extension Service of Texas A&M College. They also encouraged the interchange of ideas between the delegates, thus reducing the isolation of farm women. The overall goal of Extension work was developing a self-reliant, independent, and thinking rural population capable of its own leadership (See Lilla Graham Bryan, *The Story of the Demonstration Work in Texas*, pp. 8–19).

M·A·Y

· Mon 12. . . . I made a trade with Bud. I gave him 15 A. for cotton on this place and 20 A. sod on my place. That is if he can get the sod broke out. He is to help do any thing I want done on the place with out me having to pay him. . . .

J·U·N·E

· FRI 13. . . . Sallie and girls went to the church to quilt out a friendship quilt for Rick Trotter. He gets married Sunday. Then next Monday night he is to be "showered." Then in a short time *another* shower. Next week some time Mrs. Whitfield is to be showered. Then won't be long till Mrs. Trotter will have to be "rained on." I think I need a shower, but guess we will never get wet. Showers were not in style when we were married and I think the other rainy day is passed.

· SAT 14. . . . Mr. Green payed me $10.00 for bundles. I wrote the check and signed it for him. He can't sign his name, nor read. That is bad on a man. . . .

· FRI 20. . . . Sallie went to the Whitfield shower. These showers are get-ting some awful. I think maybe it will have a tendency to increase the birth rate. A. L. Bushell and Eugene Townsend are running neck to neck to see which one can be showered next. Is bad for Mr. Bushell & I to think we are in the showering class. Well it can't be helped.

· SAT 21. . . . The ice man made his first round this A.M. I bought 50 # at 40¢ per hundred. . . .

· FRI 27. . . . The girls joined the 4H Club that was organized at Friend-ship this A.M.

In 1914 Congress passed the Smith-Lever Act, making extension work a divi-sion of the land-grant colleges of the states. Under the direction of county agents and home demonstration agents, 4-H clubs were organized. The clubs' name is taken from the emblem, which is a four-leaf clover with an *H* on each leaf. These letters represent the training of the *head* to think clearly, the *hands* to execute the thoughts of the head, the *heart* to sympathize and feel for others, and *health* for better living. Their motto is "To make the best better." The clubs offered information about improved farm and home activities to farm boys and girls between the ages of ten and twenty. It was believed that training received during these critical years remained throughout a lifetime. Girls' activities largely consisted of homemaking, canning, sewing, home beautification, and better nu-trition; boys' activities included improved crop and livestock production (See I. W. Hill, "Boys and Girls' Clubs Do Pioneer Work in Improving Farm Life," in *Yearbook of Agriculture, 1927*, pp. 142–47; Bryan, *The Story of the Demonstration Work in Texas*, pp. 11–22).

J·U·L·Y

· Tues 8. I sent Bud and a cultivator and team over to Mr. Boyce's to help
work out his crop. Some 20 teams and a number of hoe hands came.
They cleaned his crop out by 12 noon. . . .

Boyce was a neighbor who was hospitalized after a stroke. It is still customary for farmers in West Texas to join forces and tend the crops of an incapacitated neighbor.

A·U·G·U·S·T

· Sat 9. . . . We all went up town in the afternoon. We do not need to go
to town only to set in the car. We have no money to spend. Things are
sure some tight.
· Tues 12. Jerry Wayne came by early. Wanted me to go to Portales, N.M.
Things look good over in the valley. They irrigate that land. . . .

Pump irrigation began in the Portales, New Mexico, region as early as 1905,
when a six-inch test pump in a shallow well delivered a six-hundred-gallon-per-
minute stream of water. Irrigated truck farms in the Portales Valley attracted the
attention of many West Texas farmers, especially after the dry year of 1927 (See
Green, *Land of the Underground Rain*, pp. 62–100, 122).

· Fri 15. Finished hoeing weeds out of the cotton. No heart to do any
thing. So dry. This is the first year since 1918 that we just set and wait
for a rain. 1916, 1917, and 1918 we did, and we did not make any
thing. . . .
· Sat 16. . . . I told J. M. Gholson if he could sell my land for $35.00 per
A. to do so. I think I could fix up better on a watered place.
· Sat 23. Came a little rain. Cooled. Helped in the election "MA" Ferguson vrs. Stearling, Gov. . . .

Twelve people filed for office in 1930. Only "MA" Ferguson and businessman
Ross Sterling made it to the second primary. It was a bitter contest in which
Sterling's promise of "a business administration to meet the demands of a grow-

ing State" gave him a hundred-thousand-vote edge. In times of economic distress, it appeared Texans were looking for more than a demagogue (See Rupert Norval Richardson, *Texas: The Lone Star State*, pp. 462–69).

N·O·V·E·M·B·E·R

· THURS 6. . . . Bud & I went to Littlefield. I wanted to see if I could get a sale for the Company Bull. I could not get a bid on him. Curtis Robbins offered $37.50. That seems like nothing for a bull that cost near $200.00. But we will have to sell him on the market, take our loss and forget it.

The circle bull would have sired heifers that were large enough to breed, and a new bull was necessary to avoid inbreeding. When several bull circles operated in an area, the bulls were rotated every two years, but apparently this was not an option for DeLoach's group. In addition, hard times prevented other farmers from paying a good price, regardless of the animal's heritage. Diary entries do not indicate that DeLoach ever participated in another breeding circle (See "Bull Circles," *The Cattleman* 16, no. 8 [Jan., 1930], pp. 43–44).

· TUES 18. . . . I had a check for $3.00 from C. C. Proctor. Pay for helping hold the general election Nov 3. . . . Did intend to get me some long handle drawers with the $3.00, but I had to let Jim [*daughter Jimmie*] have it to pay for a school book. Oh well!
· SUN 30. The cow is doing fine. I milked her this morning. We took a car pump and filled her bag with wind. That is a sure cure for milk fever. . . .

1·9·3·1

During the 1920s farmers learned to live with roller-coaster price cycles and knew it would take more than slogans to end the economic crisis. They stopped looking for help from politicians. Instead, they joined hands with their neighbors to solve the problems that arose.

J·A·N·U·A·R·Y

· WED 14. . . . Jake Parr and his wife called early. He told me he would give me the $1.00 per acre for the 50 A. He made it a loan. I gave him a note for $50.00 due Nov. 1, 1931 [*a forerunner of cash leasing land*]. . . .

· WED 28. . . . Have not bought anything on credit this month.

F·E·B·R·U·A·R·Y

· SAT 7. We took some cream up town in P.M. Only got 17¢ per lb. for it. One can't fool with cows for that price [*another reason for selling the circle bull*].

· WED 25. I had to go to Olton. On petty jury. Traylor came by. We were going in my car. Had to go in Traylor's car. The court excused us till Thur morning at 10 A.M. The courts sure do want the tax payer's money. . . .

Olton was fifty miles from Sudan, and Robert (Bud) remembered his dad complaining about jury duty. He had to spend the night in Olton or travel fifty miles each way when court lasted more than one day. Driving on dirt roads made the trip very difficult. If neighbors were called to serve at the same time, they usually traveled together (Robert E. DeLoach, interview with Janet Neugebauer, Sudan, Tex., July 1, 1987).

M·A·R·C·H

· SUN 1. . . . Earl Rogers came by for me to go to the Red Cross meeting at Sudan. We organized a chapter at Sudan. We went down to Ollie Wilmon's. He was appointed as one of the investigators of the chapter, to work the S. E. corner of the Sudan school district. We, Rogers & I, took his papers to him. The Lady that was sick near Wilmon's died this P.M. The baby died a few days since. Those people are on starvation. The cause of the baby's death is called Mal-Nutrition, or in other words starved to death before it came into the world. Too bad. A surplus of all commodities and people on the Red Cross and some starve to death. . . .

A policy shift pumped new life into the American Red Cross during the Great Depression. Initially chartered for aid during time of war and national calamities, its role broadened to include general relief regardless of the cause of suffering. Remaining steadfast in its philosophy of private philanthropy instead of government subsidy, the Red Cross did, however, cooperate with agencies of the federal government in providing aid for the drought-stricken and unemployed (See Foster Rhea Dulles, *The American Red Cross: A History*, pp. 276–94).

· THURS 12. . . . Mother saw her first "movie" and she is 77 yrs old, also my first "talkie." Well that was my first talking picture.
· MON 16. I went up to Sudan in forenoon. Sallie was out of "joy dust" [*snuff*]. We washed a pile of turnips. Took them to town. Traded them for onion sets. I had 38# turnips. The M System [*local supermarket*] man said he would give me 2¢ per # for them and sold me onion sets for 35¢ per gal. He set the price both ways. . . .

DeLoach recognized one of the farmer's greatest problems. Lacking bargaining power because of their independence, farmers were the only people in the business world who accepted what was offered for the products they sold and paid what was asked for the goods they purchased.

· THURS 19. The wind started blowing early and sure did get its sandy clothes on. The dirt and sand walked about all day. . . .

A · P · R · I · L

· TUES 21. . . . we went to Littlefield to hear the Great Evangelist Crimm preach. He is another Culpepper or Sam Jones. He poured it on picture shows and dancing. Also, women came in for a bawling out about bridge parties and going bare legged. . . .

Sam Jones was a popular Dallas evangelist who used the pulpit in the 1890s to preach against urban degradation, which he termed the "stinking now-and-now." He did not hesitate to tackle local political questions, although he usually stuck to the "triumvirate of evils embodied in drink, ballroom dancing, and card playing." Crimm would have been popular in a rural community where traditional agrarians regarded the city as alien and its vice threatening. Moreover, many rural Texans blamed the Wall Street financiers for the economic problems of the depression and would have been pleased to have "a man of the cloth" on their side (See Sam Acheson, *Dallas Yesterday*, ed. Lee Milazzo, pp. 255–56).

· MON 27. . . . The Singing School started at 8 P.M. tonight. The community will have to dig up $100.00 for the teacher, Stamps, by name. He knows his "singing." Think will be O.K. for the kids. . . .

The teacher was Frank Stamps of the Stamps-Baxter Music School, Dallas, Texas. The company published gospel music, sponsored daily radio programs, and taught itinerant teachers the basic rudiments of music, including methods of teaching "shape-note" singing schools. Advertising was done principally through quartets, and every sizeable city had a Stamps Quartet that traveled through surrounding communities, performing in churches and at singing conventions. Using these ready-made crowds, they organized singing schools throughout West Texas from the mid-1920s through the 1940s. During the hard times of the depression they accepted whatever they could get in the way of compensation. Proceeds from a box supper were normally used to pay teachers; however, Homer Garrison, a former teacher and member of the Stamps Quartet from Lubbock, recalled that during an unusually tight year, when no one would volunteer money to start a school, a fellow member of the quartet shouted out from the back of the room, "Who will give a hen?" A volunteer came forth, and others joined in until enough chickens and eggs were collected to pay for two weeks instruction. His comment was, "Teachers needed to teach, they had families to support, and the people needed to sing, it was their favorite social activity and brought a lot of joy during hard times." Interviews with people who attended Singing Schools for many years, indicate a high regard for the quality of Stamps teachers, and the song books published by the Stamps-Baxter Music Company were still widely used in 1987 (See M. Lynwood Smith, comp., *Give the World a Smile: A Compilation of Songs by Frank Stamps with a Story of His Life by Mrs. Frank Stamps*, pp. 2–11; Homer Garrison, interview with Janet Neugebauer and Richard Mason, July 18, 1987, Oral History Files, SWC).

M·A·Y

· Mon 4.   I set in to dry and restack my feed, but when I tore into the stacks I found that most of the feed was damaged and a bit of it was rotten. Too bad. No feed. No money and no credit. What the hell will people do. . . .

· Tues 5.   . . . The folks and Bushell's folks have gone to the Singing School. Mr. Bushell did not go. I did not want to go. Had rather read. This old pen is a free giver. The kids take my pen to school and I have to write with any thing that will write. In fact, I hardly ever have the same pen to write with twice. . . .

· Fri 8.   . . .We went to the last night of the Singing School. They sure did act nice (Mr. & Mrs. Stamps, the teachers). They did not get only ½ of the money that was promised. $53.50 to be exact, but he said was O.K. The crowd sure did enjoy the little program.

· Sat 16.   We went up town in P.M. I taken some cotton seed up town for Mr. Bushell. Exchanged them for some Qualla cotton. Two bu. for one of the Qualla.

Qualla cotton had a longer staple length (15/16 inches) and matured faster than the Half and Half (7/8 inches) that DeLoach normally planted. Later experiments indicated, however, that this strain of Mebane Triumph cotton performed best in central and south Texas (See *Texas Almanac and State Industrial Guide, 1954–55*, p. 193).

· Mon 18.   . . . Was out of smoking tobacco. Jimmie forgot to get it. . . .

· Tues 19.   Jim got the tobacco. Took it to school, put it in her locker. Some one stole both cans. I got in my car and went to town for it myself. . . .

One of the older boys at school took the tobacco for his own use, and De-Loach was very angry about it (Jimmie DeLoach Moorhead, interview with Janet Neugebauer, Sudan, Tex., July 1, 1987).

· Fri 22. . . . I finished planting cotton today. Except the "Triumph 44" I bought. . . .

Seed that ultimately became Oklahoma Triumph 44 was selected in 1914 from a patch of Mebane. It differs from the parent variety in its earliness, prolificness, and good character sample. This variety requires 70–90 bolls to make a pound, has a staple length of 29/32 inches, has a 34–36 percent lint turnout, and is disease resistant (See Basil G. Christidis and George J. Harrison, *Cotton Growing Problems*, p. 113; Gilbert R. Merrill, Alfred R. Macormac, and Herbert R. Mauersberger, *American Cotton Handbook*, p. 111).

J·U·N·E

· Tues 23. . . . One of Catt's horses was sick. We drenched her on harlem oil [*a standard remedy for kidney, liver, bladder, and uric acid problems*] & Watkins colic dope. . . .

J·U·L·Y

· Thurs 9. . . . Mrs. Wallace came by today. She is going to paper the two rooms in front. She told us that we could have this place if she did not sell or trade it. I do not want to move on my place till the kids finish school. I want to stay in this school till then. I do not like this blue weed place but if I can keep them in the Sudan school I will. Plowed cotton all day.

Low prices for agricultural commodities reduced the amount of rent Newton received and the amount of money that could be applied to land payments. Therefore, he decided to sell the Lamb County farm in order to concentrate his resources in his Oklahoma ranch (Robert E. DeLoach, interview with Janet Neugebauer, Sudan, Tex., July 1, 1987).

· Mon 27. I sent Bud over to Winston's for his two wheel trailer. Loaded two of my meat hogs. . . . Sold to Kent for Boyer @ 7¢ per #. They weighed 185 #. . . .

· THURS 30. They had two additions to the church last night. Jim and one of the Crain girls. . . . Was not much of a crowd out to Church tonight. We would have asked the preacher home with us, but we were out of sugar and Sallie said wait till tomorrow night.

A·U·G·U·S·T

· SUN 2. . . . We had dinner then went to the baptizing. The candidates were Alma Fae Higgins, Ida Crain, Jimmie DeLoach, and Alex Bushell. . . . The baptizing was in Mr. Boyce's tank near the church. . . .

Revivals, usually lasting several days, were held in late summer when the crops were "laid by" and everyone had free time. The Baptist doctrine of salvation is a personal experience, a covenant between man and God, that does not need an intermediary. Rejecting infant baptism, the denomination relies on revivals to gain converts. On the last day, converts were baptised into the church. The minister conducting this revival came from the next county (Hockley County) and stayed in the home of a church member. Ida Rene Crain (Bud DeLoach's future wife) and Jimmie DeLoach were among those converted and baptised. The three girls were about sixteen years old and all in the same grade at school; Alex Bushell was an older man with a family. Candidates wore ordinary clothing for the ceremony that was held in a neighbor's earthen tank containing four or five feet of water. Each girl's mother had a sheet to wrap around her daughter—to dry off with and to provide privacy when changing clothes—when she came out of the tank. That night the four newly baptized people stood at the front of the church to receive the "right hand of Christian fellowship" from the membership (See John Lee Eighmy, *Churches in Cultural Captivity: A History of the Social Attitudes of Southern Baptists*, p. 9; Jimmie DeLoach Moorhead, interview with Janet Neugebauer, Sudan, Tex., July 1, 1987).

· TUES 18. Billy and I went over and plowed Bud's young cotton. We finished about 2:30 P.M. We then went down to Roger's swimming pool and took a good swim. The first time I had been in swimming water since 1924 on the Brazos River west of Mineral Wells. That was Aug. 24, 1924.
· SAT 29. I went up town early. . . . a mass meeting of the cotton planters was called at 2 P.M. The "Long Plan" of cotton cutting acreage was adopted.

DeLoach is referring to approval by Sudan farmers of Louisiana governor Huey Long's request for a one-year moratorium on cotton production to raise

its price. Long called on other cotton-producing states to follow his lead in se-
curing legislation to remove the commodity from production for a year. He could
not convince all of them to agree, and the idea died. Strong opposition came
from the business community (gins, cotton oil mills, and bankers), which supported increased production in order to have increased business. Failure to get
the necessary consensus was another example of the futility of trying to handle
this problem at the state level (See *Semi-Weekly Farm News*, Aug. 21, 1931, p. 1
and Aug. 28, 1931, p. 1).

S·E·P·T·E·M·B·E·R

· WED 9.   . . . The oil man came out with the oil, but he would not leave it
without the cash and I did not have it. I did not think that times
would ever get so hard that I could not get 50 ga. of oil with out the
cash, but things are sure getting tight.
· THURS 10.   . . . Caught two hens, went to town for some coal oil. Have to
buy it in a 5 gal. can now. Sold hens for 50¢ apiece, $1.00. Sold some
cream, $1.02. Had plenty of money. Had 15¢ when I got back home.
· THURS 17.   I have to use a common pencil now. The kids take my pen to
school and leave it. . . . We took cream to Amherst, also 3 hens. Sold
hens for $1.70, cream 21¢, $1.20. (The kids fixed up a pen on a 5″ bolt
and I will try to use it.) . . .
· SUN 20.   I did not go to the B.Y.P.U. Am afraid to go. That is all of us go
away at night. Some people are losing their canned goods. We have
quite a lot of foods of different kinds canned up, can't afford to take a
chance on some road tramp coming here and getting it, so I stayed
home.
· MON 21.   Billy and I went over to Mr. Henry's. Stripped a load of sugar
cane, took it to the syrup mill at Sudan. . . .

DeLoach was referring to a sweet cane sorghum, probably ribbon cane, from
which sorghum syrup was made. An average of eighty gallons of high-grade
syrup could be made from one acre of cane, and many farmers sold what was
not used by the family (See *The Earth*, May, 1933, p. 4).

· SAT 26.   . . . I went up to Sudan for some twine. Went to the bank, got
$6.00. Bought 2 balls of twine, $1.90. All one hears is hard times. Well,
things are in an awful shape. Cotton down to 5¢ per lb., maize $3.00
per ton. One can't pay any thing with such prices for what one raises.

· Tues 29. We finished the bale by noon. Field wt. 1790#, gin wt 1782. That is close enough. Bale wt. 515, seed wt 880. $2.83 due gin. That is awful. The seed won't pay the ginning. Was offered 4.70¢ per #.

This price was per pound of lint. Cotton seed was selling for $10 per ton.

N·O·V·E·M·B·E·R

· Thurs 26. . . . This Thanksgiving was passed without a turkey dinner.

D·E·C·E·M·B·E·R

· Wed 2. . . . Bud went to town in P.M. for Molly Hamilton. He is the cow & horse Dr. My Slim Cow was sick all day. We gave her all the home remedys we knew. She got worse in afternoon. Molly came down and punctured her. She had eaten a bunch of grain that had soured on her "tummy." She is resting well now, 10 P.M. Awful cold all day.

A former bronc-buster and all-around ranch hand, Molly (L. P.) Hamilton, helped many settlers break horses or doctor sick livestock. Drawing on the knowledge gained from years of handling cattle, Molly worked as a veterinarian during the last years of his life. He punctured the animal's stomach with a sharp instrument, to reduce the bloating that was making the cow sick.

· Thurs 24. . . . The folks have gone to Friendship to the Xmas tree. I did not want to go. Was a little afraid to go away and leave meat hung all over the wind mill. . . .

Before refrigeration, meat was wrapped in a clean cloth and hung from the windmill to prevent spoilage.

Diary entries for 1931 contain more financial information than other years, making it easier to get an overall picture of annual income and expenses. Rainfall was above normal in Lamb County during 1931, and the 79,470-bale cotton crop was the largest since 1926. DeLoach produced 54 bales that averaged $.05 per pound on the market. After paying rent, his income was approximately $1013.00, plus $87.95 from grain. Rent received from the Bailey County land was $188.00. This was enough to pay all of his debts at the bank and start the next year in the black.

Wednesday, December 2 ... My Slim cow
was sick all day ... worse in afternoon ....
Molly came down and punctured
her .... resting well now.

This year, combined with 1926, illustrates the dilemma that farmers often faced. When the weather cooperated, the market didn't, and vice versa. The 1931 crop would have brought DeLoach $2026.00 at $.10 per pound, which was deemed a fair price for cotton in 1933 by the Agricultural Adjustment Administration.

1·9·3·2

The depression magnified the difference between the prices farmers received for products they sold and the cost of goods they had to buy. By the end of 1932, farm prices were less than half what they had been in 1929, according to the *Yearbook of Agriculture, 1934* (pp. 1–27). Cotton had not been so low since 1914, when fear of an embargo destroyed the market. While these prices were falling, farmers' fixed expenses—mortgage payments, interest rates, and taxes—remained at their pre-depression level, catching farmers in a deadly cost-price squeeze.

J·A·N·U·A·R·Y

· Thurs 7. . . . Jim & Billy went to the basket ball game at the Sudan High gym. I did not like for them to take the car out on a night like this, but I hated for them not to go as Jim is in the "glee squad." That is the bunch that does the screaming & raving. . . .

· Sat 16. . . . I wanted to see about bro J. P.'s sudan. A Mr. Ramsey [*the man renting J. P. DeLoach's farm*] has the sudan stacked at his place but has not threshed it yet on account of the seed being so cheap. Only 40¢ per hundred lbs. That is low for any money. I have paid 14¢ per lb in 1927. . . .

· Wed 20. . . . I find the letter 'T' is the most used letter in the alphabet.

F·E·B·R·U·A·R·Y

· SUN 28. . . . Bud came in from Lubbock with a Model A Ford. She sure does "scatt."

M·A·R·C·H

· MON 28. Eighteen years ago I started this diary. This is the sixth ledger I am on. Things have changed since then. . . .

A·P·R·I·L

· FRI 15. Bud hauled the last of the feed [*maize*] today except the clean up. Took 3700 # to Moffitt. He is to pay me 5¢ above the market which would be 46¢. I settled with elevator. Had a check for $131.56.

M·A·Y

· SUN 1. 41 years ago today I went to a school picnic at Millsap, Tex. I had to go barefooted. I was 11 years old, but thought that was all O.K. All the boys my age went that way. . . .

· WED 4. . . . Bought two new plow shears, $4.75. Gave Jimmie $3.00 I drew last Sat. Tonight I have $1.03. I can't keep money and that is what it is for, to spend.

· SUN 8. We did not go to church, or I did not. Sallie and kids did. Was Hard Shell [*Primitive Baptist*] day. They washed feet.

Some Hard-shell, or Primitive, Baptist groups practice foot washing. It symbolizes the willingness to serve and is patterned after Jesus' assuming the role of a servant when washing his disciples' feet at the Last Supper.

· FRI 13. . . . I fixed up some coops for the incubator chicks. I went to town for them. We set 208 eggs [*purchased for two cents each*] at town, got 140 baby chicks. Six were cripples. The balance were frisky. Gave them to hens [*hens raised the cripples; the others were put in a brooder*].

· SUN 15. . . . We attended the Baccalurate Sermon at Sudan High School. Sure was a large crowd. A preacher from Littlefield had charge, assisted by a local minister. Jimmie and 26 others were in the class. The Friend-

ship girls and boys that were in the class came by and they all went
some where to make pictures. . . . Have been reading about the murder
of the Lindbergh baby. The cold bloody bunch ought to be (Oh! I
don't believe in Capitol punishment) put in a dungeon for the balance
of their days. 'Tis too awful to think about.

DeLoach is referring to the kidnapping and murder of the firstborn son of
Charles A. Lindbergh.

· SAT 28. We started a 1 row knife and a two row. They sure do a two fold
job. They kill the weeds and also cultivate. . . .

Long knife blades extending out from a center bar can be dragged through
planted beds to loosen the dirt and kill weeds. The knives are set to enter only
the outer third on each side of the bed, thus avoiding contact with plants. This
method of cultivation is still practiced in West Texas.

J·U·L·Y

· SUN 17. . . . Was an awful hot day. No wind. No water. The mill does
not run enough for plenty of stock water. We need some of that hard
wind we had in the spring.
· SUN 24. Did not get home till near sun up from the [*primary*] election.
Worked all night or till 5 A.M. . . .

DeLoach helped in the Democratic primary. More interest was shown in the
1932 primary than in any previous election in Lamb County. The depression
was causing severe problems for Lamb County farmers, and they turned out
in record numbers to support 'MA' Ferguson for governor and A. P. Duggan,
of Littlefield, for state senator, 30th senatorial district. They hoped to fill the
positions of power with people who understood the plight of the "little man"
(See *Lamb County Leader*, July 28, 1932, p. 1).

A·U·G·U·S·T

· FRI 5. We canned peas all day. That is some job shelling peas by hand.
One's thumb gets sore.
· FRI 12. . . . Billy went to the annual encampment of the 4H boys & girls
that convened in Amherst.

· Sat 13. . . . Billy came in at noon. He reported a great time. Said he had signed up for two baby beeves. They camped out. . . .

· Mon 22. . . . Gholson came by at noon and wanted me to sign a rental contract for the ⅓ and ¼ of the crop I get off my place. I told him that Bud had borrowed $100.00 of the Government seed & feed money for me and that the whole crop stood for that. "He said he knew that if it taken all the crop to pay it, it would have to be payed."

With low depression prices, DeLoach was having trouble making land payments, and apparently the company holding his mortgage was trying to rent the land to him, which would guarantee the company some income. Details are not available, but later entries indicate the rental income was applied to land notes. This type of maneuver assured the mortgage holders a first call on any income from the farm, before the money could be used for farming or living expenses.

· Tues 30. Rained about 1 inch to day. We went up town in P.M. We went in the trailer with two hay burners. "Two Cylinder Jackson."

S·E·P·T·E·M·B·E·R

· Sat 3. . . . Billy is busy as a hen with one chick fixing his lot and shed for the baby beeves he is taking. He will have to go for them next Thursday. I cut a load of heads [*maize*] before noon. The girls cut a load in P.M. . . . They liked to have throwed a fit because I had them work. They think they ought to go to town Sat P.M. I am in a place where I will have to declare my self or just put up with the way things are going. Those boys have to go to town no matter what they have to do. All they study about is to get the money out of each load of feed. I gave it to them thinking they would cut it, but no.

· Thurs 8. Think must have rained all last night. We did not think we could hardly go to the Mashed O headquarters for the baby calves that Billy will feed out, but went in this afternoon. . . . The calves weighed 825 lbs. at the headquarters scales. They are very good calves. A little bit 'salty.' . . .

Mashed O was the brand used by William E. Halsell on his 184,155-acre ranch located in Lamb County. When Halsell reduced the size of his ranch during the 1920s, he established the town of Amherst and sold land to settlers moving into the area. Thereafter, the family's philanthropic donations contributed greatly to the development of the county. Furnishing calves that would be entered in regional stock shows, and possibly win awards, was also very good advertising for the sale of breeding stock to area farmers (See William Curry Holden, *A Ranching Saga: The Lives of William Electious Halsell and Ewing Halsell*, pp. 240–56; Scott, *A History of Lamb County*, pp. 34–36).

· SAT 10. . . . We necked the baby beeves to the milch cows. They will tame them.

O·C·T·O·B·E·R

· WED 5.   Some frost this A.M. but not enough to kill things. . . . Started pulling cotton. . . .
· FRI 7.   . . . Took my first bale of cotton to the Beall gin 2 mi south of me. 2300 # field and gin wt, bale wt. 640#. Sold for 6¢ per lb. Caught seed. Ginning and wrapping $8.25. Beall ginned the bale free. I pulled his car out of a bog some time since and he said he would not let me do it for nothing, hence the free ginning.

In 1932, DeLoach harvested 14 bales of cotton that he sold for $378.30. The lowest amount he received was $.0475 per pound.

· SAT 8.   . . . This blueing makes very good writing fluid. Am out of ink.
· WED 26.   . . . County Agent Algood called today to have a look at Billy's baby beeves. He was well pleased.

N·O·V·E·M·B·E·R

· WED 9.   . . . Heard that Albert Mittle killed himself this forenoon. He took the strychnine route. Do not know what it was all about. Heard we had another Democrat President, Franklin Roosevelt and a Texan for Vice-President, John N. Garner. Also Ma & Jim were elected Governor of Tex. . . .
· THURS 10.   I had to go to Amherst to pay bank $16.75. I walked about ½ the way, rode balance of way with Thompsons. They were going to the Mittle funeral. I stayed for it myself. A large crowd. . . .

D·E·C·E·M·B·E·R

· Fri 2. ... Bought a hog at 3¢ per lb. ...

· Wed 7. I went down to the meat demonstration. County Agent Algood showed us how to butcher a hog and beef. That is, the easy way. Well worth the time. ...

· Sat 24. Bud & I went up town early as Jimmie wanted to work at the Saunders Notion Store. We did not buy very much Christmas. Did not have much money.

· Wed 28. Sallie, Jimmie and I went up town to see the Whittlesworth girl about the John Tarlington school at Stephenville, Tex. I will try to send her there to school. It will be a tight game. If I could sell "any thing for any thing" it would not be so hard, but will do the best I can. ... The sow I traded from Manley found 10 pigs. Two froze to death.

1·9·3·3

· Sun 15.   Well, this is the first time I ever used red ink in my diary. . . .

Red ink was appropriate for the beginning of 1933. In many cases cotton produced a negative income and livestock generated West Texas farmers' only cash for their year's work. The situation was equally critical for other farmers in the nation. In January, 1933, the president of the American Farm Bureau Federation warned that unless something was done a revolution in the countryside would likely occur within the year. (Gladys L. Baker, Wayne D. Rasmussen, Vivian Wiser, and Jane M. Porter, *Century of Service: The First 100 Years of the United States Department of Agriculture*, p. 143).

Even though money was tight, DeLoach met his family obligations remarkably well. Only his diary knew the extent of his struggle.

· Wed 18.   Jimmie is making ready to go to school down in Stephenville, Tex. John Tarlton College [*a coeducational branch of Texas A&M University*]. It is a sacrifice to send her, but I always did say if I had one that wanted an education I would do all I could to sent them to school. . . .

F·E·B·R·U·A·R·Y

· Tues 7.   . . . This has been a bitter day. Not so bad now, 9 p.m., since the wind calmed down. We lost one hen, froze, up to now and several more

137

that were in bad shape. The piano box blew over. Some 15 or 20 hens parked in it. The whole lot were near frozen. We have burned 3 tubs of corn and 2 tubs of Kaffir corn today. The feed makes good fire, but does not last long. Have burned corn and feed heads all winter. A reading of from 20° below to 25° below 0. A low 28° below. The school bus did not run today.

· Thurs 9.   About the same as yesterday. Just sit by the stove and burn corn, maize and hegari. That will keep us warm and does not cost any thing and it is not worth but $2.00 per ton and coal is from $9.00 to $10.50 per ton. . . .

M·a·r·c·h

· Thurs 2.   . . . Bud and wife came in forenoon. I went over, rented my place to Mr. Montgomery. I reserved 25 A. We all went down to Hal Higgins to the shower given for Bud and Ida R. They received several nice things. Shower #1. Fike and I came back home soon after arriving at Higgins. Too much stealing going on. If we were to lose our meat, lard and canned stuff we would have to go on a soup line.

Bud married Ida Rene Crain. Her family moved into Lamb County during the land boom of the 1920s. During the depression, soup kitchens were set up for people who had no food. Even though cash was extremely short, chickens, cows, hogs, and a small garden watered by the windmill provided a nutritious diet for farm families on the South Plains.

· Sat 11.   . . . Went up town in P.M. Broke my last $1.00 bill. No money and lots to buy. . . .

· Tues 14.   Bud & I went over to Amherst. Could do no business. The banks have not opened up yet. . . .

During the Great Depression many banks in the nation teetered on the brink of bankruptcy, and in February, 1933, frightened depositors started a "run" on the banks to withdraw their money. To avoid a panic, the governors of most states (including Texas) declared a bank holiday, and on March 6, 1933, newly inaugurated president Roosevelt suspended all banking operations temporarily. He went on the air with the first of his fireside chats to reassure the nation that a sound banking system would emerge from the reorganization taking place. Funds from the Reconstruction Finance Corporation (R.F.C.) sped up reorganization. By the end of March, financially sound banks were opened, while others were closed permanently. Banking reforms included establishing the Federal Deposit Insurance Corporation to guarantee bank deposits up to five thousand dollars per depositor. Ninety-five percent of the Federal Reserve banks in Texas reopened, and 100 percent of the banks in West Texas reopened; however, five banks operated under restrictions (See Jesse H. Jones with Edward Angly, *Fifty Billion Dollars: My Thirteen Years with the RFC, 1932–1945*, pp. 13–53 and *Lamb County Leader*, Mar. 9, 1933, p. 1; Mar. 16, 1933, p. 1; and Mar. 30, 1933, p. 5).

· WED 15. . . . Could not do anything at bank yet. Told me to come back Friday. . . .

· THURS 16. Algood came out this early A.M. Cut the hair of the 4H calves and gave Bill some dope on giving them the Permanent wave. We will have to fix up the two wheel trailer to take them to Amherst. And when the show is over at Amherst we will take them on to Lubbock. The Lubbock trip is more than I expected to do.

Show animals are always washed and groomed to look their best in the judging ring. The hair on a calf's body is combed, usually in a zigzag manner to give it a curly appearance, and the switch on the tail is dressed. During the 1930s it was popular to wet the switch and comb it into waves (Stanley Young, county extension agent–agriculture, Lubbock County, interview with Janet Neugebauer, Apr. 8, 1988).

· MON 20. I went up to Sudan. Put in an application for $150.00 of the R. F. C. Money. Lots of red tape. How many kids, how old, color of hair, eyes, length of toe nails, and a lot of other junk. Came home. Billy and I took his calves to Amherst. I fixed a bed for Billy in the Legion Hall where the Club boys are camped, then I came home. Lots of nice fat calves. Some 106 head of 4H Club calves.

Reconstruction Finance Corporation (R.F.C.) loans were general-purpose farm loans that could be used for anything farmers might need, provided the applicant had sufficient collateral (implements, livestock, crops). Landlords were not required to waive their lien on crops before a tenant could obtain feed and seed loans. On the average, 5 percent was cut from the amount each applicant asked for. In Lamb County approximately two hundred fifty applicants received over $62,000, a welcome boost to the local economy (See *Lamb County Leader*, Mar. 16, 1933, p. 1 and Mar. 30, 1933, p. 1). After Amherst, the calves mentioned were taken to Lubbock for the Quality Meat Show, the largest of its kind in the Southwest. People from Texas Tech's agricultural school and the extension

Thurs. March 23 — Judging of all the Calves came off today...

service of Texas A&M College worked with show entrants, teaching them to use home-grown feed grains to finish beef for marketing. A bonus price for the show animals was an added incentive to participate. The show also included a section for judging cured meat which encouraged top quality home-cured meats. This helped farm families to "live-at-home" and generate cash through the sale of anything extra.

· Tues 21. . . . We got to the Fair Grounds about 5:30 P.M. Unloaded, bedded the calves down, cooked a bite of supper and went to bed. Could not sleep. Too much fuss and racket. We all slept in the stock sheds. Lots of kids.

· Wed 22. I did not sleep any at all. Billy and the boy that is with us, they had a fine night's sleep. . . . The boys did not do anything, but rub and wash the calves today. They would not drink or eat to do any good. Some fine calves here. The "Mashed O" stuff has no chance here for any of the show ring money.

· Thurs 23. About the same thing as yesterday. Only the judging of all the calves came off today. . . . Billie's two were thrown in a bunch of 105 head to be sold in car lots. . . . The boys and their dads had a feed at the Hilton Hotel and a dance at the Lubbock Hotel. . . . The kids were royally entertained.

· Fri 24. The kids and dads were treated to a free show at the Lindsey Play House. . . . At 1 P.M. the auction sale started. . . . [Billy received $34.50 for his calves.] After the car lots had been properly tagged we, or each owner, had to take them to the McDonald Packing Plant to be weighed. That was another grand rush to lead those semi-wild calves ¾ mi. . . .

A · P · R · I · L

· Sat 29. . . . The wind was blowing hard when I woke up and by noon one could hardly see any where for the sand. It howled and blew sand all day. Now 11:10 P.M. is doing the same. All the good soil will blow off this land if these sand storms continue to blow. . . .

Much of the soil did, in fact, blow off the Great Plains during the Dust Bowl years. Farmers had been accused of not understanding how wind erosion would damage their land, but DeLoach's entry indicates they understood and were concerned. The absence of tractors and irrigation made it impossible either to plow as much as necessary to prevent blowing or to grow cover crops when moisture was insufficient. The land that lay fallow from the end of the harvest season (December) until spring planting (April or early May) was especially subject to wind erosion. Plains farmers knew a winter cover crop would protect the topsoil from windstorms, but they also knew it would exhaust the subsoil moisture and leave no reserve for starting cotton or grain crops.

M·A·Y

· FRI 5. . . . Had notice from Littlefield that my R.F.C. loan check had been sent to First Nat. Bank at Sudan. I went up to see about it. Got $75.00. . . . Payed the charges for release of mortgages $1.75, also $1.25 for making out of note and mortgage to R.F.C. That is a lot of expense to get a loan, but the money class has the poor devil by the tail. . . .

· TUES 16. . . . The Whaley man, a Mr. Scofield, came out and wanted to know if I owed Whaley Lber Co a note for $13.00 I told him sure not, that I had a record of where I had payed it with feed that Monroe (a former Whaley man) had bought. I got this Ledger. [*See Apr. 15, 1932.*] He would not give me time to find all the dope. He looked at what I did find and said he was satisfied that I had payed Monroe and I would hear no more about it. Thanks for this diary.

· SUN 21. Some time around 12 o'clock last night a rain started and fell 1½ in. rain and some hail. A very good season now, I think. If I had known the rain was coming I could have saved a ½ cup of lather by waiting till this morning to shave. I shaved Sat. afternoon and my face was so long it took more soap to shave. Things sure do change after a rain when we were as dry as this. . . .

Total rainfall recorded in Lamb County during 1933 was 13.57 inches, 30 percent below average (See *Climatological Data, 1933*, p. 100).

J·U·N·E

· SAT 10. . . . Hot today. 100 in shade.

· FRI 16. . . . Only a mare's tail of a cloud in the N.W. It is beginning to get serious. Things are going to burn up. . . .

A mare's tail cloud is a feathery, spreading cirrus cloud indicating fair weather ahead (See Thomas C. Gillmer and H. Erich Nietsch, *Clouds, Weather, and Flight*, p. 132).

In May, 1933, Congress passed the first Agricultural Adjustment Act, which attacked the problem of surplus farm products with production controls. It was reasoned that eliminating the surplus would raise commodity prices, allowing farmers, nearly 25 percent of the national population, to become purchasers again. This in turn would stimulate sales for retailers, wholesalers, and manufacturers. This was believed to be the fastest way to relieve the existing national economic emergency. Cotton farmers were asked to plow up already planted acreage for which they would receive cash payments funded by a processing tax levied on initial processors, textile mills. Ultimately the tax was to be passed on to the consumer.

Cotton producers were paid to destroy 25–40 percent of their crop at a rate of seven to twenty dollars per acre. Although most West Texas farmers were reluctant to accept money from the government, all needed the payments. The depression and the drought were causing severe hardships.

· TUES 27.   . . . I went up town to sign up in the cotton reduction plan, but did not. It seems that the land owners want to share 50–50 with tenant. I never did expect to get only the regular ¼ off my place, but the W. & F. [*mortgage holders*] people, they want ½ of the pay for each acre of cotton that the government pays the farmer to take out of production. That is not right. The money class wants the lion's share.

· WED 28.   . . . The renters are all up in the air about the land owners wanting more than the ¼ of the cotton acreage reduction money. . . .

At the outset, some landlords demanded 40–50 percent of the cash rentals in exchange for allowing tenants to sign up for the acreage reduction program. Normally the landlord received a fourth of the money generated by the cotton crop. They argued that the farmers had not put out much effort to get the cash they were receiving and therefore weren't entitled to their usual three fourths. Area newspaper editors took the landlords to task for their greed, reminding them that undermining the recovery measure would have serious repercussions throughout the cotton industry. The landlords' movement was not successful. According to the Department of Agriculture, legal ownership of the crop was the basis for eligibility to enter a plow-up contract, therefore the landowner received the same portion as if the cotton was produced and sold through regular methods (See *Lubbock Avalanche-Journal*, June 30, 1933, sec. 1, p. 12; USDA, *Agricultural Adjustment: A Report of Administration of the Agricultural Adjustment Act, May 1933 to February, 1934*, p. 26).

1933

J·U·L·Y

In July DeLoach went to Los Angeles, California, to visit a sister, Fannie Witt (married to an uncle of Nellie Witt Spikes), who had lived in Emma, Texas, when DeLoach moved there in 1913 (see diary entries for March–November, 1914). He earned his train fare by attending two cars of cattle being shipped to Los Angeles. After going to an amusement park and seeing the sights around town he made the following entries, which shed light on the widening gap between urban and rural lifestyles.

· Sun 9. . . . All kinds of people gather there [*at an ocean-side amusement park*] to spend Sunday. The tall, the short, the fat, and the lean. Big, old, fat women will pull off everything but a smile and play in the sand. . . .

· Tues 11. . . . I went with a Mr. Alan Jensen, a man that is working for Fannie & Geo. He showed me up in the city hall, 32 stories. Also down in China Town and through the Spanish or Mexican Town. Through some of the largest markets and departments and several places that was an eye opener to me. [*He arrived back in Sudan on Thurs., July 14.*]

· Sun 16. We all went to Friendship. The Reunion for the 1928 Organizers of the Friendship Church. Was a success for no one to push it, no move. We had the song books that were used then. Had a big spread of good eats. Afternoon, a business meeting. I being elected President. . . .

· Tues 18. Went in town for some seed, hegari and cane. Drew my bal. out of bank, $38.70. The cotton committee came out. Gave me a fair stand.

· Thurs 20. . . . Bought a cream separator [*Baltic*], $42.50, $6.10 per mo. I guess cream will go down now, 22¢ this date. . . .

· Fri 28. I was not satisfied with the inspection the committee gave me. My neighbor got $17.00 on his cotton and I only got $14.00 on my cotton, and I have a perfect stand other than some blue weeds. He had a very poor stand.

Seventeen dollars per acre was the average amount received for plow-ups in Lamb County. This dollar figure indicated an average production of 225–275 pounds of lint per acre for the previous five years (1928–32) in addition to a 1933 crop that was up to a fair stand. The county average was 239 pounds of lint per acre. The fourteen dollars per acre DeLoach received indicates his lint yield history was 175–224 pounds per acre for the previous five years. His diary entry reflects the confusion of many farmers about how the amount of their plow-up money was determined. At first, they thought it was based only on the condition of the current crop and didn't include lint yield history (See USDA, *Agricultural Adjustment: A Report of Administration*, p. 23; *Lamb County Leader*, June 22, 1933, p. 1 and June 29, 1933, p. 8).

> · Sat 29. I could not get any thing done about it, or I did not do any thing. I could have taken it up with the Federal people and could have had some people cut down, but they took what they gave them and I would have done the same thing and I would have felt sore at any one that would have caused me a loss. . . .

A·u·g·u·s·t

> · Fri 4. . . . The crop is badly below normal at this time of year.
> · Wed 16. . . . Bud finished plowing up the 15 rows of cotton I sold to the U.S. Government at $14.00 per a. 55 A in all. . . .

Two thousand Lamb County farmers pledged 94,426 acres of cotton to the government in the acreage reduction campaign. They received over $1,371,423 in return, placing the county first in the state for acreage pledged and money received. Nearly tripling the 32,000-acre quota, many farmers pledged 50 percent of their acres already planted to cotton. This was wise, considering the shortage of moisture and the size of their lint yield history (See USDA, *Agricultural Adjustment: A Report of Administration*, pp. 313–16; *Lamb County Leader*, July 20, 1933, p. 1).

> · Sat 19. . . . Sallie payed to Foxworth & Galbraith Lber Co. $3.18 on seperator, Cream is down to 12 & 13¢. I might have known when I bought the thing cream would go down.
> · Sat 26. . . . Election to repeal the 18th Amendment. (Rain) I did not go and vote.

The twenty-first amendment, ratified by the end of 1933, abolished the eighteenth amendment and returned control of liquor to the states. State prohibition in Texas ended in 1935, but local option was permitted, and Lamb County remains dry to the present time. Some voting precincts within the county voted to legalize 3.2 beer in Sept., 1933 (See Richardson, *Texas: The Lone Star State*, pp. 465–66).

S·E·P·T·E·M·B·E·R

· Mon 11. . . . We will send Jim to Texas Tech. I saw Mr. Motley, the man I
was on the road with to California and made plans for a room for light
house keeping at $10.00 per mo. $5.00 for she and room mate.
· Thurs 14. . . . The 3.2 beer is being put to the boys in all wet towns in
Texas today. . . .

People in the county who were opposed to repealing the eighteenth amendment organized a committee to speak for its retention and to fight against legal-
izing beer in Texas (See *Lamb County Leader*, June 29, 1933, p. 8).

· Sat 23. . . . Mr. Montgomery got his check from the government for the
cotton he plowed up on my place, $336.00, $84.00 to my part, ¼. I
signed the check for him.

O·C·T·O·B·E·R

· Wed 11. . . . Two men came this a.m. Wanted to pull cotton, or snap it.
I gave them a job at 40¢ per 100#. . . .
· Fri 27. . . . Got my Government plow check back from Ft. Worth,
$615.65 [*rent was $153.91*]. Has been a long time coming.

Favorable weather in the Southeast led to a bumper cotton crop. To protect
the price, the Agricultural Adjustment Administration established non-recourse
loans that were handled through the Commodity Credit Corporation. Producers who agreed to participate in the 1934 acreage reduction program could
receive an advance of ten cents per pound on their 1933 cotton (USDA, *Agricultural Adjustment: A Report of Administration*, pp. 34–35). If the market price
rose above the loan price, farmers could sell their cotton on the open market
and repay the loan. If the loan rate remained above the market, farmers could
turn in the commodity as full payment for the loan (Luther Tweeten, *Foundations of Farm Policy*, p. 302). DeLoach put some of his cotton in government loan.
It cost him thirty cents per bale to have it hauled to Littlefield, where it was
classed and stored.

D·E·C·E·M·B·E·R

· Wed 6. Bud & I went over to Bert Tyler for his scalding vat. Made ready,
killed 5 hogs. . . .

During the butchering process, hog carcasses were dipped in a vat of scalding water to remove the hair from the outer skin. There was a skill to this — the water had to be just barely below boiling to avoid damaging the meat, and the hog had to be removed from the water just as soon as the hair started to "slip" from the skin (Robert E. DeLoach, interview with Janet Neugebauer, Sudan, Tex., July 1, 1987).

> · THURS 7.   We cut up the lard and rendered it out today. I am tired tonight. Cut up the meat and "sugar cured" it. . . .
> · FRI 15.   I took the last bale of cotton that I will hire picked. Gin wt 2290#, bale wt 606#, seed 860#. I had it ginned on the Farmer's Gin Co ticket I bought at the Sudan School meet. It cost me $5.00, the ginning at 30¢ per hundred = $7.85. I saved $2.85. . . .

Local ginners signed the National Cotton Ginner's Code, part of Roosevelt's National Recovery Act, that established maximum and minimum amounts gins could charge farmers. Picked cotton cost thirty cents per hundred pounds for ginning, and snapped cotton cost forty cents per hundred (See *Sudan News*, Sept. 14, 1933, p. 3).

Figures from the Crop Reporting Board of the Department of Agriculture indicate income for cotton producers doubled between 1932 and 1933. Without government intervention, the world carryover would have exceeded twenty-nine million bales. This would have kept the price of cotton near five cents per pound, with little or no market, and caused complete economic destruction for the southern states. Many government and agricultural leaders believed the Agricultural Adjustment Act prevented a major disaster.

1·9·3·4

Drought crept in gradually, showing only small telltale signs at first, such as clouds that did not rain and more sandstorms than usual. Finally, when crops began to wither in the field, everyone knew it was present. Government programs relieved some farmers from the financial stress, but nothing helped the land as nature went through its recurring cycle of travail.

J·A·N·U·A·R·Y

· SAT 13. . . . We went up to Sudan, on out to Lymon's place. Bud bought the tractor, $575.00. $262.50 cash. I let Bud have $112.50 to pay on it. . . .

Federal plow-up money set off the biggest business revival since 1929, with farmers' purchases on the South Plains showing a 28 percent gain. Farmers spent nearly a million dollars for new tractors. Politicians reasoned that money spent locally would flow to the industrial centers of the nation when orders were placed to replenish inventories. A survey conducted by the Agricultural Adjustment Administration revealed that for the first time in four years, many farmers were able to buy back their own cotton in the form of cloth and articles of clothing (See *Semi-Weekly Farm News*, Nov. 24, 1933, p. 2 and Nov. 28, 1933, p. 2; USDA, *Agricultural Adjustment: A Report of Administration*, pp. 261–70; *The Earth*, July, 1935, p. 7).

· WED 17. . . . I took, or went with, Billy to the Future Farmers of America meeting at Sudan. He was elected Sec.

Future Farmers of America, an organization for students of vocational agriculture in secondary schools, was organized in Kansas City in 1928. Classroom study was supplemented with hands-on experience in judging farm products, public speaking, cooperative marketing, and financing their activities. Local chapters and state associations are part of a national organization which provides leadership training and news publications.

· SAT 20.   . . . The vocational teacher came out and run a line for some
        terraces. I do not like it so well. Too many short rows. . . .

Terracing is building up ridges of soil across sloping fields to slow down run-off water after rainfall. In addition to preventing water erosion, it is effective for water conservation. Experiments indicated terraced land often yielded a bale of cotton to the acre, considerably above the normal yield of a third to half of a bale. The government helped farmers combat wind erosion by providing technical assistance and lending equipment. Restoration of native grasses, strip planting, and terracing were some of the techniques taught. These efforts to restore the damaged land marked the beginning of a new era in Plains farming (See Hugh H. Bennett, *Our American Land: The Story of Its Abuse and Its Conservation*, p. 22; *Semi-Weekly Farm News*, Oct. 16, 1934, p. 4; *The Earth*, Mar., 1934, p. 2).

· FRI 26.   . . . I went up and signed up the cotton reduction contract on
        this place. I will have 36 A. if the plan goes over.

Producers operating a farm that grew cotton at least three out of the five base years (1928–32), one of which was either 1931 or 1932, were eligible to enter a contract. Only farms that grew cotton in 1934 or 1935 were elegible. Contracting producers were required to reduce cotton acreage in 1934 by 35–45 percent of the acreage planted to cotton on the farm in the 1928–32 period. The 1935 reduction was not to exceed 25 percent of the 1928–32 period acreage. Cotton land rented to the secretary of agriculture under the program could be planted in soil-improving crops, feed or food crops for home consumption, or left idle, but it could not produce income (See 48 U.S. Statues at Large 31).

· TUES 30.   I went to Muleshoe to pay my tax on my Bailey Co. land,
        $43.80 for 1932–33. I sent Jim $43.50 for the next semester at Lubbock
        Tech. When I got home from Muleshoe found letter from her stating
        she would be married at 2 P.M., Sat, Feb 3rd. I was somewhat surprised,
        but such is life.

1934

F·E·B·R·U·A·R·Y

· SAT 3.   I worked on a six up evener. Had a bunch of rent maize loaded up, took it to town. Sold it at elevator for $10.00 per ton. Had $9.50 worth. . . .

· SAT 24.   The sand started blowing out of S.W. and sure did cover things up. All day long. We went up town in P.M. All the old regulars went. If it was raining fire they would go. OK, well, staying at home would not keep the sand out.

J·U·N·E

· TUES 19.   Hoed and knifed all day. Harvey Darnell & Thad Nesbitt came by. Took my application for Membership in the Mason Lodge. . . .

DeLoach applied for membership in the Masons when he lived at Ralls in 1916. He was accepted, but did not join because he moved. Records of the Sudan lodge indicate he joined August 21, 1934. The history of social order and education parallels that of Freemasonry in Texas. Prior to the establishment of a system of free public education, schools were organized under the auspices of the Masons. In more recent years, Masonic lodges have been the silent partners and promoters of local school systems (See Webb and Carroll, *The Handbook of Texas* 1, p. 645; Joseph W. Hale, "Masonry in the Early Days of Texas," *Southwestern Historical Quarterly* 49, no. 3 [Jan., 1946], pp. 374–83; Robert Edwin DeLoach, interview with Janet Neugebauer, Sudan, Tex., Mar. 16, 1988).

J·U·L·Y

· MON 16.   . . . One weather man said would rain before Friday. All the cocks in Sudan were crowing at high noon. An old sign he said. Hope he hits. We can't stand much more of this.

Total rainfall recorded in Littlefield, Texas, during 1934 was approximately twelve inches, eight below normal. There was no winter moisture to sustain a deep root system, and there were only scant summer rains (See *Climatological Data*, 1934, p. 100).

· WED 18.   Worked in A.M. I went up to the cotton meeting at school house at Sudan in P.M. So much red tape to what one has to do that one can't understand it all.

· Mon 30. Bud & I went to Circleback to get our exemption papers for
cotton tags for Bailey Co. Signed up. I could not get mine. They did
not have it. We came by Sudan. I signed up for the tags on this place.
Will get some where between 10 and 15 tags. Will not need but 2 or 3 if
we do not get a good rain soon.

On April 21, 1934, the Bankhead Cotton Act was accepted in a referendum
by a two-thirds majority of the voting cotton producers. This type of production control prevented non-cooperating farmers from increasing their acreage
in order to capitalize on improved prices resulting from the reductions made by
farmers in the government program. Each producer received tax exemptions
(tags) for two-thirds of his established per-acre production for the base years,
1928–32. Cotton produced in excess of the quota was taxed at 50 percent of the
average central market price of 7/8 Middling spot cotton, but in no event less
than five cents per pound. Texas was allowed to produce and sell 3,237,530 bales
tax-free under this act. The tax-free certificates were transferable, which was a
boon to farmers in the Southwest since their production was severely limited
by a drought. Marketed through a national pool organized by the secretary of
agriculture, these certificates brought four cents per pound of lint (twenty dollars per bale), which was approximately 70 percent of the tax on excess cotton.
Texas farmers sold certificates for more than thirty-eight million pounds of lint—
primarily to farmers in the Southeast, who were harvesting a bumper crop.
Often this method of production control worked a hardship on small tenants
and sharecroppers, who lost their farms because landlords kept the certificates
and idled land that had formerly been rented out (See *Semi-Weekly Farm News*,
May 18, 1934, p. 1; USDA, *Agricultural Adjustment in 1934: A Report of Administration*, pp. 50–55).

· Tues 31. Plenty of wind today. That means plenty of water. Things are
going to bad fast. Can't hold up much longer with out rain. The hot
wind has blown all day and when I say hot I mean it was hot. I went
up to Sudan in P.M. People are beginning to look at this drouth with a
dark and rolling eye. Only for the cool nights one would suffer and
crops would have been burnt up long ago.

A·u·g·u·s·t

· Fri 17. . . . Another meeting [*revival*] started at Friendship tonight. A
preacher from Teague, Tex, named Hartsell. This ought to be an awful

good place. As fast as one is over another starts. Have had one Christian meeting before this, Rev. Spade from Sudan, then the Baptists had their meeting. Now Hartsell for two weeks. If one goes to all and takes in what they all say, one would be as "nutty" as a peanut stand. One of them tells one that unless one believes his way one is hell bound, then up jumps an other and says one is wrong and one had better catch a hand full of his shirt tail or you will go to hell. So the Negro preacher, he sandwiches between with his line.

· WED 22. . . . I have not received any check in this county or Bailey County either. Would love to get my checks as I sure do need the money.

Late rains renewed hope for a "top-crop," bolls grown at the top of the stalk after a dry spell. But the return of droughty conditions forced the bolls to open prematurely, producing low-grade lint. Additional damage from insect activity spawned predictions of the smallest cotton crop in Texas since 1921.

S·E·P·T·E·M·B·E·R

· TUES 11. . . . I took out membership in the Lamb Co. Funeral Association [*a mutual aid burial association*]. . . .

· MON 17. . . . The fellows came to measure my Government rented cotton land. Will plow it up tomorrow.

USDA employees, hired at the county level, measured and certified the number of acres farmers removed from production before checks were issued to the farmers.

· WED 19. I took my bale of cotton to Sudan. Sold for 12¢ per pound. Went to Amherst to sell my contract cotton, but did not sell. Was offered $7.50 per bale. I may take less, but will not take that now. I want to get some pullers in my cotton again.

The average price for picking cotton in 1934 was $.60 per hundred pounds of seed cotton. This was the best price since 1930, but less than half the 1924–28 average of $1.29 (See *Semi-Weekly Farm News*, Nov. 23, 1934, p. 1).

O·C·T·O·B·E·R

· MON 1. I had to go to Amherst to get my cotton tax exemption certificates. They have cut me down till now I can't gin but 8 bales to my post tax free. . . .

Farmers across the Cotton Belt complained because quotas were not established before crops were planted, thus they ran the risk of either having to plow up acres or pay the penalty tax. Because tax-exempt certificates were measured in pounds rather than bales, South Plains farmers were not affected; the drought made the necessary reductions. However, those in the southeastern states either had to scramble to buy certificates or pay the penalty when their crop was marketed. Quota announcements were made earlier in future years.

N·O·V·E·M·B·E·R

· SUN 11. . . . Curtis Robbins told me to bring the cattle I want to sell the government in Wednesday.
· WED 14. I took the two bulls and the heifer calf up town. Sold them to "Uncle Sam." $14.00 for one, $11.00 for one, $7.00 for one. I hated to sell them, but I did not want to feed them. . . .

A congressional appropriation ($525 million) and funds from the Jones-Connally Act were used to purchase cattle, sheep, and goats in drought-stricken areas during 1934 and 1935. Animals considered fit for food were turned over for relief distribution; others were shot. Accredited veterinarians, or specially appointed local committees, purchased the animals. A uniform pricing schedule, followed in all states, allowed an average of $13.50 per animal throughout the program. The government bought 14,369 head of cattle in Lamb County for over $163,000. The cattle industry was experiencing a peak year, and this program limited farmer's losses by keeping thin cattle off an already glutted market (See *Lamb County Leader*, Jan. 10, 1935, p. 1; *Yearbook of Agriculture, 1935*, pp. 18–19).

· FRI 23. I had notice to come to Amherst and sign up for the extra exemption certificates that was issued under the 10% reserved. I did not apply for any of it, but got 965# lint tickets. I posted them as tomorrow is the last day that they can be pooled for sale. . . .

An additional 4,430,225 pounds of Tax-Exemption Certificates, from the Bankhead Act Ten Percent Reserve, were allotted to 2,215 Lamb County farmers. This reserve was allotted to farmers who historically planted less than a third of their cultivated acres in cotton or who during some years of the base period (1928–32) had exceptionally low yields due to drought, hail, or other natural causes. Unused certificates for 30,000 bales, placed in the National Pool, yielded $570,000 ($19 per bale) to Lamb County farmers. The entire state sold certificates equivalent to 847,530 bales (See *Lamb County Leader,* Nov. 22, 1934, p. 7; *Semi-Weekly Farm News,* Nov. 20, 1934, pp. 1–2).

D·E·C·E·M·B·E·R

· WED 12.   . . . Fike called by on way to Ollie Wilmon's farm sale. I went with him. I bought a 2 row cultivator for $20.00. Things sold O.K. Some one wanted what ever was offered. . . .
· FRI 14.   . . . I went up to vote on the "Bankhead Bill." I do not know just how it will go.

Texas farmers voted 4–1 in favor of retaining the Bankhead Cotton Control Act for 1935. Chief opposition to the bill came from the South Plains. Opponents believed the act penalized farmers who had reduced their cotton acreage, and increased that of food or soil-building crops, before the beginning of government programs. Allotments, based on production during the 1928–32 base years, reduced their cotton quotas so low they were having difficulty making land payments. For example, DeLoach's cotton acreage varied, but it seldom went above 50 acres. According to his entry on Oct. 1, 1934, he was allowed to gin only eight bales tax free. If he had had a history of planting his full 177 acres in cotton, the quota would have been closer to twenty-five bales. By comparison large cotton producers, located primarily in the southeastern part of the Cotton Belt, had no history of diversification and received greater benefit from government price-support programs. Many West Texans feared this act would restrict further development of the area (See *Semi-Weekly Farm News,* Dec. 18, 1934, p. 1; *Lubbock Avalanche-Journal,* Jan. 6, 1935, p. 4 and Jan. 8, 1935, p. 6).

· SAT 15.   Bud and I went up town in forenoon. The Government cattle buyers were at Sudan today. They sure were slaying the cattle. They killed some fat calves. I got one and gave the hide to have it skinned.
· MON 31.   The last day of 1934. Was up town to grind some chili meat and to get some things for hot tamales. We made quite a few tamales and canned several pint jars of chili.

Wednesday, December 12 ... Fike called by
on way to the Ollie Wilmon's farm sale.
I went with him.

1·9·3·5

As drought reached its peak of intensity in 1935, high winds often moved more dirt in a single day than realtors could move in a month. The picture was grim, but West Texans clung to memories of how the land could produce "when it rained."

J·A·N·U·A·R·Y

· SUN 6.   . . . We all went to the show this afternoon. Will Rodgers in "Judge Priest." I did not think the picture was so "hot." Only the name Will Rodgers sells it. Nice day.

A frequent visitor to the Halsell's Mashed O Ranch, Will Rogers became the favorite humorist and "philosopher" of Lamb County.

· TUES 15.   . . . This morning at 4 A.M. Bud called us. He and his mother took Ida to Mr. Crain's. I went to Sudan to call Dr. Mills of Amherst. A girl baby [*Wanda Lee DeLoach*] was born to them at 9 A.M. . . .
· SUN 20.   . . . Sallie & I went over to Crain's to see the new grand-daughter. While there a blizzard out of N.W. struck, freezing. . . .The Black blizzard moved in. Had to light lamps. Dark as night.

Like the winter blizzards to which they were compared, black blizzards were caused by the arrival of a polar air mass. The atmospheric electricity it gener- ated helped lift the dirt as high as seven or eight thousand feet in a dramatic rolling turbulence. Sometimes they were accompanied by thunder and lightning, other times by an eerie silence. Such storms were not only terrifying to observers but also immensely destructive to the soil (See Donald Worster, *Dust Bowl: The Southern Plains in the 1930s*, pp. 14–15).

· Tues 22. . . . Hallman brought out the Maytag washing machine. Bud & Ida came home this P.M. The new baby sleeps all the time.

F. L. Maytag, who knew how to sell his rural heritage as well as washing machines, developed the Maytag gasoline, multi-motor washer for the farm housewife. According to advertisements, Maytags were the most common washers on farms in 1935. Advantages such as "the roomy, heat-retaining cast-aluminum tub, the fast, thorough-washing Gyratator water action, and the Roller Water Remover" were reputed to make quick work of a big farm washing (See *Lamb County Leader*, Sept. 5, 1935, p. 3).

· Thurs 24. We washed in the new Maytag. One can put out a big washing quick. We were through about 1 hour after we got started. . . .

F·E·B·R·U·A·R·Y

· Sat 2. . . . Wes Greer came by with a telegram from Snyder stating that Father was dead. Sallie & I made ready. Caught the 10:40 train for Snyder, arriving there at 2:50 P.M. I phoned from the Harvey House at Slaton to Mother's home for someone to meet the train. . . . The undertaker came out just about 7 P.M. Took the body to Snyder and prepared it for burial, so this morning about 10 o'clock he brought it back out to Mother's home. . . .

Fred Harvey operated a chain of restaurants, called Harvey Houses, along the Santa Fe route. From small beginnings at Topeka, Kansas, in 1876, this joint venture between Harvey and the railroad spread throughout the West and grew to include hotels. During a twenty-minute stop, fifty to sixty passengers were served a hot meal by efficient, well-groomed waitresses known as Harvey Girls. Initially, Harvey Houses were available only for travelers, but popular demand forced Harvey to open his doors to the townspeople. Owners of local restaurants objected to the excellent food and service that had already won a reputation for "civilizing the West." By 1940, automobile traffic needed facilities along highways, and an era ended with the closing of these restaurants. (See James Marshall, *Santa Fe: The Railroad That Built an Empire*, pp. 97-113; Keith L.

Tuesday, Jan 22... Hallman brought out
the Maytag washing machine.

Bryant, Jr., *History of the Atchison, Topeka, and Santa Fe Railway*, pp. 331–34; Fannie Teague, interview with David Murrah, July 1, 1975, Oral History Files, SWC. Fannie Teague was a Harvey Girl in Slaton, Texas, where DeLoach stopped.)

· MON 4. After all the family got back to Mother's [*from the funeral*] we called a business meeting to settle up the expense of the funeral. The undertaking expense was about $300.00. . . .
· THURS 7. I went to Muleshoe to get my parity check, $31.31. The Nugent people are due ¼ of it. The ¼ is to be applied on my land notes. . . .

DeLoach received 3.5¢ per pound on the average yield of lint cotton for the acres he rented to the government in 1934 (See USDA, *Agricultural Adjustment, 1933–1935: A Report of Administration of the Agricultural Adjustment Act, May 12, 1933, to December 31, 1935,* p. 125).

· SUN 24. The wind started early out of the west. Hard sand storm. . . .

After going six months with barely over two and a half inches of rain, the topsoil was dry enough to take to the air with the slightest breeze, and the breezes in March and April were not slight. High winds blew forty-seven days in those two months. During most of these dust storms, visibility was limited to a mile or less, and during six of them it was less than five hundred feet. At these times such darkness prevailed that artificial light was necessary in homes, businesses, and on vehicles, according to Arthur H. Joel (*Soil Conservation Reconnaissance Survey of the Southern Great Plains Wind-Erosion Area,* p. 2).

M·A·R·C·H

· SUN 3. The folks went to church at Friendship in forenoon. We went down to Stan's in P.M., but they were gone. On over to Crain's. A sand storm struck where they had to light the lamps. Bad. Oh, bad.
· MON 4. Was nice and pleasant up to about 10 A.M., then the wind and sand began to move east. By noon it was equal to the Thanksgiving sand storm of 1926, but calmed down before night. Nice now, 8:25 P.M. Of my 37 years on the Plains and Western Okla, the sand storm of yesterday was the worst I ever saw and I have seen lots of them, but never before had to light lamps as on a dark night. We have stayed inside all day. Hope will not blow tomorrow.

See R. Douglas Hurt, *The Dust Bowl: An Agricultural and Social History*, pp. 36–37. During research for his book, Hurt read DeLoach's diary and further supported the entry describing the intensity of this sandstorm by noting that it broke glass windows, interrupted railroad communications, and turned day into night in the Texas Panhandle.

· Tues 12.   I worked all day on the milk house I am building. The lumber I bought at Littlefield Saturday cost me $2.25. I will make one door and two windows. I use "doby mud."

The correct name is adobe, but DeLoach shortened it to *dobe*. Its insulating properties made it an excellent building material in an area of extreme weather changes. Prior to widespread refrigeration, an adobe building made an ideal milkhouse. The necessary ingredients and tools were readily available on every farm, and adobe buildings cost about a third less than wooden ones. DeLoach and Bud worked on this building in their spare time and finished it in about four months. (Robert Edwin DeLoach, interview with Janet Neugebauer, Sudan, Tex., Mar. 16, 1988; see W. C. Holden, *Why Use Dobe?* pp. 3–18).

· Wed 13.   I went up town to the Cotton Meeting. A lotta bull.
· Fri 29.   . . . We did not have any local sand today, but dust. Oh! my, that comes from some other state, Colorado, I guess.

Extremely high-level winds captured dirt and blew it many miles eastward. In May, 1933, dirt sucked into a high-level airstream was carried from Montana and Wyoming eastward to ships in the Atlantic Ocean, some three hundred miles off the coast. Portions of the estimated 350 million tons picked up in that wind storm were deposited all the way across the United States (See Worster, *Dust Bowl*, pp. 13–14).

· Sat 30.   Boy. Oh! boy. Did we have dust! No hard wind, but dust that was awful. Visibility some 100 to 150 yards, and was that way all day. . . .

A·p·r·i·l

· Mon 8.   The day came in blowing hard and the dust and sand is bad. Has been all day. Can't see over ½ mile, at times not so far. . . . I did not do any thing today. Stayed in house all day. I can't stand this dust and sand.
· Tues 9.   I started in to set the forms around the milk house I am building, but the wind and sand began to blow so hard I quit and came in the house and have been in all day, now 4 p.m. One can't see over 2 or 3 hundred yards at all. This sand and dust is getting to be awful. The

dirt is sure blowing in the orchard. Looks to me like the stock would get so much sand it would kill them.

The death of man or beast from dust storms, while not common, did happen during the Dust Bowl days of the 1930s. Hurt recounted that on February 21, 1935, "during the height of the storm, a western Kansas farmer drove his car off the road and began to walk the two miles home. Searchers found him the next day suffocated after having walked half way home." During that same year, livestock in eastern Colorado died in considerable numbers after ingesting dust that was several inches deep in pastures (See Hurt, *The Dust Bowl*, pp. 36–47).

- WED 10.   Stayed in house all day. The sand storm was bad all day.
- THURS 11.   About the same kind of a day. Bad sand storm.
- SAT 13.   Another sandy day. . . .
- SUN 14.   All gone to church but me. I did not feel like going. The sand storm is getting bad from S.W., now 9:10 A.M. Sunday night, 8:40 P.M. While reading a sand storm struck from the north and one could hardly get breath. I thought I would choke when I went to bed. We went over to Bud's after church. They had a good dinner. The sand storm raged from S.W.

The black blizzard of April 14, 1935, is the most notorious of all the sandstorms during the Dust Bowl years. The day dawned clear and fresh. By noon the blue skies and balmy temperature were too tempting to resist, and people rushed outdoors to do all the things they had postponed during the first three dust-ridden months of the year. About 6 P.M. that evening "the menacing great-granddaddy of all Panhandle dust storms engulfed the area," according to the *Dalhart Texan*. After it struck, visibility was reduced to zero. In Dalhart, approximately a hundred and fifty miles north of Sudan, one man was within forty-five feet of his barn when the dust struck, and it took him more than an hour to find his way to it. Automobiles and trains had to stop where the storm struck them. People feared for their lives, and this fear did not quickly fade. Teachers and superintendents demanded frequent weather reports during the remainder of the school year, in order that every precaution might be taken for their pupils (See *Amarillo Daily News*, Apr. 15, 1935, p. 1; *Dalhart Texan*, Apr. 15, 1935, p. 1).

- MON 15.   More sand. . . .
- TUES 16.   . . . A hard sand and dust storm came up from S.W. in P.M. and one could not see his team a head of him.

· Wed 17.   The wind and sand blew till 10 or 11 o'clock, then was a fine
     day after that. . . .
· Thurs 18.   The wind and sand was too bad to be out much. . . . Bud
     came over and helped me set the forms for the last batch of doby mud
     on my milk house. . . .

M·a·y

· Sat 18.   Came another good rain in forenoon and another in P.M. while
     we were at town. I think we have a fine planting season now. . . .

J·u·n·e

· Mon 17.   . . . I worked all day with one mule, walked. Sure am tired.
· Sat 29.   . . . We went up to Sudan in P.M. The first time I have been up
     there on a Sat. in 5 wks.

J·u·l·y

· Wed 3.   . . . Bill & Dot have gone to show. $600.00 is the show money to
     be given away. The name was called out, but no one answered to the
     name, so the show man will try again tomorrow night.

A drawing for money was a gimmick used during those money-scarce years
to get people into town and into the movie theater. Every family that could
possibly do so sent a member to the show. Six hundred dollars was equivalent
to a year's income for most families.

· Thurs 4.   . . . The money was given away tonight. I do not know who
     was the lucky one. A woman. . . .
· Thurs 11.   Our first north wind. According to old timers, 90 days from
     now we will have our first frost. . . .
· Mon 15.   We started in to put in a week's plowing, but a cloud formed
     over head and began to hail and rain about 3:30 P.M. and the hail did
     clean up. I think maybe I will have my cotton left, that is the main
     stalk. All leaves and squares are beat off. Feed is in bad shape. In fact,
     all growing crops are damaged badly, but could have been worse.
· Tues 16.   . . . The cotton looks like the leaf worm had just finished it. I

am afraid the hail has ruined the cotton. Feed has a chance to come
out and do O.K.

· Thurs 18. . . . Had Bill harrowing young field. Anything to break the
crust [*roughening the surface prevents blowing dirt*]. Too wet to plow.

· Sat 20. I hoed all day. Sallie and Bill plowed. . . . Is raining now, 9 P.M.
Not very hard.

· Tues 23. Planted hegari and some milo, "50 days milo" they call it. . . .
We planted where the hail had completely killed out the cotton. . . .

A·u·g·u·s·t

· Wed 7. I worked all forenoon cutting weeds out of feed and cotton. The
measuring men called this P.M. to measure the cotton land the U.S.
rented. He did not have my contract. . . .

Before federal payments were mailed to producers, farms had to be inspected
to certify acreage reduction and authorized use of land formally planted in cotton (See USDA, *Agricultural Adjustment 1933–1935: A Report*, pp. 124–31).

· Fri 9. . . . I did intend to plow the hail beaten cotton up, but it has come
out to the extent I will work it out and maybe it will make something.

· Fri 16. . . . Heard Will Rogers and Wiley Post were killed.

Humorist Will Rogers and Wiley Post were killed when the plane Post was
piloting crashed fifteen miles south of Point Barrow, Alaska. Extensive front-
page news coverage indicates Lamb County residents mourned Rogers's death
as they would that of a civic leader (See *Lamb County Leader*, Aug. 22, 1935,
p. 1).

· Wed 28. Two weeks since Sallie went to stay with Jimmie in her sickness
[*pregnancy*]. Seems like she has been gone two months. Had card from
her today. She said she did not know just when she would be at home.
Jim is still up. I am about played out. I have been in the field on a hoe
handle almost all the time since I came home on the 17th and I am
sure played out. I hoed most all day. . . . Dot does well in her house
work, but not like Sallie at home. I sure do get lonesome. The young
ones do not have things in common with me. . . .

· Fri 30. . . . I sure am getting lonesome for Sallie to come home. Bill has
gone to a party somewhere. Dot has gone to bed and I am here reading
(or have already read all the papers) and am lonesome. I wish Jim had

come up here for her confinement, or kept a better record. I came in tonight tired, ate supper and no one to talk to.

Jimmie DeLoach Moorhead recalled that her dad teased her for a long time after the birth of her first child, telling her, "If you can't keep a better record, I'm going to keep the 'notching stick' the next time" (Jimmie DeLoach Moorhead, interview with Janet Neugebauer, Oct. 23, 1987).

· SAT 31. . . . Cream check this wk was $5.25. Payed most of it for groceries. I gave Bill the young gilt for the Lady cow's heifer. He is to give me the first litter of pigs up to six. The gilt is a picture of a hog.

DeLoach averaged slightly over one dollar per week for the cream each cow produced. Compared to cotton that was yielding about a third of a bale per acre and selling for sixty dollars per bale, DeLoach's five dairy cows produced as much income as an additional fifteen acres of cotton. Moreover, during a drought they were more dependable. Year after year they dropped a calf that was sold, and they ate homegrown feed grains that matured quickly on minimal rainfall. In contrast, cotton's long growing season subjected its yield to the dry spells that were characteristic of the Plains.

S·E·P·T·E·M·B·E·R

· THURS 5. . . . Worms in the cotton. Too bad now if they eat it up. . . .
· MON 9. . . . Had letter from Sallie. Things are all O.K. . . . She seems to be enjoying herself. Heard that Huey P. Long of Louisiana was shot yesterday. Too bad for him to champion the cause of the poor masses. Any man that does that will be killed. The grafters killed Christ. Wish she [Sallie] was at home. We need her at home.

The assassination of Louisiana senator Huey P. Long disturbed many rural people, especially older ones. George H. Mahon was the congressman from De-Loach's district, and his incoming correspondence for the early months of 1935 is heavy with pleas for Mahon's support of an old-age pension program. Most of these constituents were jobless because of the depression and would have been attracted to Long, who claimed to be a champion of the underdog. Initially a Roosevelt supporter, Long broke with FDR in the early months of 1934. He was convinced New Deal programs were not redistributing America's wealth fast enough to really help the ever-increasing number of poor people whose situation needed immediate attention. Long's solution was a vague program named Share Our Wealth, consisting of heavily taxing the incomes and inheritances of the wealthy. Fearing the growth of Long's national reputation and his possible presidential candidacy in 1936, Roosevelt tried to "steal some of Long's thunder" with the passage of the Wealth Tax (a sharply graduated increase in income and inheritance taxes) and the Social Security Act in August, 1935. This legislation had the unmistakable stamp of Huey Long on it, and in the Senate Long responded with "Amen." In public Will Rogers quipped, "I would sure liked to have seen Huey's face when he was woke up in the middle of the night by the President, who said, 'Lay over, Huey. I want to get in bed with you.'" Long did not remain satisfied, however, and he continued to expose the shortcomings of New Deal legislation until his death (See T. Harry Williams, *Huey Long*, pp. 819–47; Alan Brinkley, *Voices of Protest: Huey Long, Father Coughlin, and the Great Depression*, pp. 3–81; and George Mahon Papers, 1918–1981, SWC).

· SAT 14. I went up town to trade or buy a car of some kind. Am tired of bumming rides off other people. I was there near all day. I decided on a "Chevy" of the 1930 model. Will cost me $319.00. That is too much, but the best I could do. I borrowed $50.00 to pay down on it. Well any way I have a car that we can go places. . . .

· TUES 17. . . . We had card from the new arrival stating she arrived at Sept. 14, 1935 [*a granddaughter, Kalah Yvonne, who was called Kay*]. Well, I guess Sallie will be coming home soon.

· SAT 21. . . . Sallie came in about 7:30 P.M. She sure did look good. Gone nearly 6 wks. Left Jim and baby doing well. . . .

N·O·V·E·M·B·E·R

· TUES 5. Sure enough, the white frost came last night. I think all green things are killed. I cut one load of heads. A combine man called to get some feed to combine. . . .

· THURS 7. I loaded trailer with maize & Kaffir heads. Took them up to the Boles Orphan Home car they were loading. I had 950#. . . .

· TUES 12. I took the bundles to the mill, but they were too wet to grind. They would not keep and I did not want them to get hot. Only ground about 500#. Shocked the balance up and will go and have them crushed when they get dryed out. 1500# in all. I payed $1.95 or 12½¢ per hundred. . . .

Grain that had not completely dried out (matured) would mold or ferment if stored where air could not circulate freely.

· TUES 19.   . . . Ida Rene was here to day. She and Sallie went to town. They had some business with the hair dresser. Permanent, two for $1.99.

· THURS 28.   An other Thanksgiving day. Not like the one in 1926. An account in Ledger #4. Sallie, Dot and I went up town. Ate turkey dinner at White Rose Cafe. They sure did put the feed bag on, 50¢ per plate. I guess that included cover charge for we covered up in "grub." We came back home, milked and attended the things and stock then went over to Guy Noble's to a farewell party given for Robert Hood. He is leaving for Calif. soon. . . .

D·E·C·E·M·B·E·R

· MON 2.   . . . Sold 2200+ lbs. cotton tax coupons, $54.00. . . . I bought me a suit of clothes, $24.00 suit and shoes.

· TUES 3.   The feed man called. I sold him the white feed, Kaffir, hegari at $9.50 per ton on [the] ground. . . .

· FRI 13.   . . . Sent the third payment to the Commercial Credit Co. Inc., Amarillo, Tex at $16.00 on the Chev.

· TUES 31.   . . . I took cotton sampler to Littlefield. Was offered 10.75¢ per lb. on press at Littlefield. Did not sell. . . . I am going . . . to look at some mares tomorrow. Do not know whether I will get another team or a tractor. Will know by last of week.

1·9·3·6

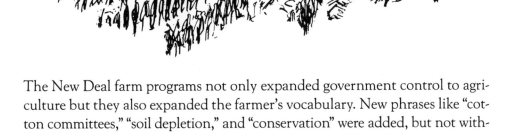

The New Deal farm programs not only expanded government control to agriculture but they also expanded the farmer's vocabulary. New phrases like "cotton committees," "soil depletion," and "conservation" were added, but not without a few moments of anxiety.

J·A·N·U·A·R·Y

· TUES 7. . . . The A.A.A., the Supreme Court ruled it unconstitutional. . . .
I am about ½ sick tonight.

Based on a case filed by Hoosac Mills Corporation of Massachusetts, the Supreme Court ruled the Agricultural Adjustment Act of 1933 unconstitutional for the following reasons: (1) taxes cannot be levied on one class of people (processors) for the benefit of another class (farmers); (2) taxes cannot be levied to help a particular class of people (farmers) rather than promoting the general welfare; (3) regulating crop production is a local prerogative and not given to Congress (See *United States v. Butler et al., Receivers of Hoosac Mills Corp.* 297 U.S. Reports 1).

· TUES 14. . . . They [*DeLoach's children and their spouses*] all had made medicine to suprise wife & I with a 33rd wedding anniversary supper. They had lots of eats and a big cake with 33 candles on it. . . . No kidding, I am not what I used to be. . . .

169

· Fri 17. . . . The old man Morin took carbolic acid. Died about noon. One of his boys told me about it. They pulled cotton for me.

· Sat 25. . . . Mr. Gholson came by this A.M. and wanted to know what I was going to do about my land notes. I told him I could do nothing, only let them have the land back. . . . I told him I had payed the school tax for 1934. Owed the state and county for 1935, also the state for 1934. All tole about $37.50. He said he would pay that and we (wife & I) could deed the land back to the Nugent people. I hate to lose the land and what I have payed on it, but I can't do any thing else. "Big fish eat the little ones." The law is take from the poor devil that wants a home, give to the rich. I have lost about $1000.00 on the land. . . .

F·E·B·R·U·A·R·Y

· Thurs 6. . . . Mr. Gholson came by. Told me about the deed he had drawn in Dallas. I could not read it for I did not have my glasses along. He said if I would pay for the deed and stamps, which would be $5.00, the deal would be closed. I asked him if that meant just as the land stood now. He said yes. He said they would pay the balance of taxes. Well, they ought to. I have payed $800.00 or better on the land, but got behind and could not do any thing else. Any way my mind is at ease. I do not think Gholson or any of the cold blooded land grafters would lose any sleep on account of taking a home away from any poor devil.

Loss of government price supports and the absence of moisture made the future look pretty dismal to DeLoach. Other oldtimers in West Texas remember turning land back to mortgage holders during the 1930s to find relief from the pressure of payments that couldn't be made with meager crops. One man tried to make the Federal Land Bank take his land back, but the office manager refused. Years later, after the land was paid for, the story was repeated many times to convince young people that federal farm credit institutions were often more dependable than private financiers, who made an additional profit from the sale of repossessed property.

In February, 1936, the Soil Conservation and Domestic Allotment Act was signed into law. It was worded to circumvent the Supreme Court by making its main purpose soil conservation, which promotes the general welfare. Farmers were sent invitations, instead of contracts, to reduce their acreage of designated crops. Reduced acres were to be planted in soil-building crops for which they would be paid out of the general treasury. It clearly stated that no taxes would be levied to cover this expense. The Act was not effective, because payments were not large enough to attract farmers. Farm leaders began to plead with cotton producers to remember the ruinous prices that accompanied overproduction. The speed with which the new act was drawn up and DeLoach's entry of January 7 testify to the dire need for agricultural relief during the 1930s.

M·A·R·C·H

· Sun 22. . . . Hard sand storm all day. The car stopped. The sand had
   formed glass on the points of the distributor. A man fixed it for me. . . .

A·P·R·I·L

· Wed 1. We worked on the model near all day.

In April, 1936, DeLoach, his two oldest sons, and his son-in-law drove to Washington, D.C. seeking a patent for his collapsible chicken coop. This was put on the back of a truck and extended to form two large cages for transporting chickens to market. After the chickens were sold, the coops could be collapsed, making a flat bed to haul other merchandise back home. Discovering that about a hundred similar inventions were awaiting a patent, the group returned home to make some modifications and find financial backing. After getting home, most of his spare time was taken up with the local cotton committee, to which he had been elected, and not much more was done with his collapsible chicken coop. His model is now housed in the Southwest Collection.

· Fri 3. . . . We finished the Model, up to the door and fasteners that
   clamp it together. At 7:46½ o'clock C.S.T. they electrocuted Hauptman.
   He was charged with the kidnaping and murder of the Lindberg baby.
   I call it legalized murder. . . .
· Sun 5. . . . They [DeLoach's family] seem awful indifferent about the deal
   I am trying to put through. . . . I am not having much cooperation. I
   guess I would have to have the money in hand before they would be
   interested.
· Tues 7. We went up to Sudan. Made ready to start on the Washington
   trip. H. G. & Bud came in about noon. We left at 1 P.M. by north road
   out of Sudan. . . .

Friday, April 3 ... We finished the Model, up to
the door and fasteners that clamp it together.

· Sun 12. . . . We arrived Washington about 11 A.M. We did lots of sight seeing all A.M.

· Mon 13. H. G. & I went down to Patent Office. They showed us all the dope we were looking for. Found lots of ideas but none like mine. A fine building and a fine personnel. They would show and tell one all they could to help him out. . . . Went and employed the James R. Eavins, Patent Atty. to put my model through the Patent Office. Payed them $25.00 to start in. All will cost $140.00. . . .

· Tues 14. Had an early breakfast and left for home. . . .

· Thurs 16. . . . Ft. Worth, Weatherford, out to Greenwood, 3½ mi west of Weatherford we cooked supper. I used to go to school at Greenwood when a kid. I did not see any one I knew. Heard of a few. The first girl I ever went with was buried there. I looked at her grave and tomb stone. She died Aug 12, 1899. Does not seem could be that long ago. . . .

· Fri 17. . . . On home about seven A.M. We were all tired out. I went to bed. Slept till noon and some afternoon.

M·A·Y

· Fri 8. I knifed most of the day. Prof. Whit came out this P.M. to tell me that I had been elected on the local cotton committee. I told him that I did not want the place, but would serve.

State and local committees made up of farmers were authorized by the Agricultural Adjustment Act of 1936. Under the administration of the county extension agents, these close-to-the-soil committees were charged with the task of making the program work. They encouraged the farmers in their area to sign agreements for specified production allotments and checked to determine whether each man was fulfilling his agreement (49 U.S. Statutes at Large 1148; Richard S. Kirkendall, *Social Scientists and Farm Politics in the Age of Roosevelt*, pp. 90–93).

· Sat 9. I went up town. Then Whit took the 3 of us, King, Proctor, and my self to Amherst for a little drill in the work. We worked out a plan by which the little cotton man could sign up with out being penalized as he has been in the life of the A.A.A.

· Sun 10. . . . We, Sallie & Dot & I, went back to the Commencement exercises, Bill's class graduation. He is the last to go through it. Only two out of the five to finish high school. In a way it is a sad time. The school bus has been stopping here 9 months out of the year for 11 years, but will stop no more for ours.

- MON 11.   I went up town early. Worked on the new cotton plan. We did not do much. We did not under stand all the dope on the work sheets, hence we did not sign up very many. No rain yet.
- TUES 12.   We did some better as for speed, but for correctness I do not know. The whole set up is "dutch" for a bunch of men picked off the farm with out any "dope" to go by.
- THURS 14.   We just started work when the County Agent came over and said the 37% basis we were working under would not stand up, so Mr. King and I quit. If I could not help the fellow that had no cotton acreage, I did not want to be a party to help the big dog or "hog." They have fattened off the Government for the last 3 or 4 years and want to keep it up. . . . I came home. Knifed the balance of day. . . .

Farmers whose lint yield history was low because of diversification were in favor of cotton acreage allotments based on a percentage of the total acres under cultivation. This arrangement would have given small farmers a greater number of cotton acres, hence a larger gross income.

- FRI 15.   Prof. Whit and Mr. Proctor and Traylor came out to see me. They wanted me to come back and help finish the cotton committee job. I told them I would. . . .
- SAT 23.   I went up town. Hit the bank up for a $100.00 Did intend to send $35.00 to James R. Eavins Patent Atty's, Washington, D.C., but did not. The boys seem to want to wait for a while. . . .
- TUES 26.   I went up town. We worked on the "new deal cotton set up." The big fellow will be glad. One [DeLoach] is in place where he does not like to be on this cotton committee. I just want to see every fellow treated alike.

J·U·N·E

- SUN 7.   . . . We went to a ball game at Amherst. Amherst v. Morton. Amherst beat.
- TUES 16.   . . . I went up to the cotton meeting. The old committee resigned. We could not do the fair thing with the people, so all we could do was quit. The most unfair thing that the Democrat Add. ever put

over. An other instance where it is same. The rich richer and the poor poorer. . . .

S·E·P·T·E·M·B·E·R

· THURS 24. . . . I saw Mr. Bosen and made arrangements for the money to swing the deal for the 68+ A. of the Halsell land, through Mr. James Blankenship. I am to pay $200.00 now. On, or before, Dec. 25, 1936 I am to pay $250.00 more. Bal. in 15 notes of even money at 6% interest.

With the reestablishment of government farm programs, which provided a guaranteed income from farming, DeLoach was ready to try again to buy a farm of his own.

· FRI 25. . . . Sallie and Dot went out and looked over the land. Sallie is sold on it. . . .

O·C·T·O·B·E·R

· WED 21. . . . I made reservations for 4 to Dallas on train, $4.10 each. . . .
· FRI 23. . . . Mr. Hess took us to train in his car. The train ran late. Did not get going till 4 P.M. We could not see anything after we left Lubbock. Dark came on us. Think was about 12 o'clock when we arrived Brownwood, Tex.
· SAT 24. The Santa Fe took us by way of Temple. In to Ft. Worth about day light. On to Dallas, arriving about 9 A.M. All played out. No sleep. No rest. We had breakfast and all went to Cen[tennial] ground. Mr. James Blankenship was with us. We could not, or did not, enjoy the trip, not any thing we saw in Dallas for all were tired out.

The Texas Centennial, celebrated in 1936, officially marked one hundred years of independence from Mexico and at the same time advertised Texas to the world. The main celebration was held in fifty buildings at the State Fair Park in Dallas. A principal feature was the "Cavalcade of Texas," a historical spectacle presenting four centuries of Texas history. Agricultural exhibits, advertising one of Texas' major industries, were also prominent. Poultry shows, featured during October, would have been especially interesting to DeLoach since the poultry industry was quite prominent in Lamb County. The exposition was open in 1936 from June through November and in 1937 from June through October. Nearly thirteen million visitors attended this two-year run (See *Semi-Weekly Farm News*, Oct. 2, 1936, p. 6; Webb and Carroll, *Handbook of Texas 2*, pp. 733–34).

N·O·V·E·M·B·E·R

· Fri 13. . . . I went up town in P.M. Payed land note at bank, $205.00. . . .

· Thurs 26. We all went to Bud's for Thanksgiving feed. Ida had a fine dinner. All eats this writer ate were good. . . .

D·E·C·E·M·B·E·R

· Thurs 3. Bad weather. Cold, foggy and raining. Bill & I shocked up some feed in P.M. Sure would love to see a few days of pretty weather so I could get balance of cotton out. Will have to be moving soon. . . .

The farm on which DeLoach had been living since 1925 sold again, and this time he had to move. In January, 1937, he moved to the farm he bought from the Halsell Land Company in September, 1936. The farm he lost in January, 1936, had nothing to do with the move.

· Thurs 10. Sold 5 bales cotton to Jeff Rudman for 8½¢. . . . Finished cotton to day.

· Wed 23. . . . Mrs. Ruby called to see me about selling me the 12 × 28 house. I told her I would call on her in the morning and check it over.

· Thurs 24. I went up to see Mrs. Ruby about the house. I figured up all the lumber in it and at used lumber prices. (I told her I could not use it only at ½ used lumber prices.) I offered her $55.00 for it. She accepted. I payed her $30.00 on the bill. We left for Ralls at 10 A.M. . . . We arrived Ralls at 4 P.M. . . . We had a swell Christmas tree. All the kids were happy. All went to bed about (well) from 12 to 2.

· Fri 25. We were all up by 8:30 A.M. Had breakfast. Then the girls started in to fix the big feed. Mr. & Mrs. Coward and Grandma Coward came about 10 A.M. Some 25 were there for dinner. Jimmie had never had the responsibility of fixing such a big dinner. When one puts the feed bag on so many one has to do something, however she handled the affair fine. Sleeping all of us was no child's play, either. Raining now, 9:30 P.M. We did not have any trouble coming home.

· SAT 26.   I was up town early. Saw Henry Lee at bank about getting the money to pay Halsell Land Co. $250.00, balance on down payment. He told me to draw on bank. I went on over to Amherst. Gave check, got note. Sold two mules for $135.00. . . .

· MON 28.   Bill & I went up to the Ruby place. Lifted up the house. It is ready to load on the wagons.

· TUES 29.   They had a sad time in Sudan this early A.M. A fire broke out in the movie house. Destroyed the show, a drug store, and several other businesses. Last, but not least, Mrs. Clifton lost her life in the fire. She & her husband owned the show. I borrowed one wagon off Lloyd Olton, also one from Curt Pierce. Two boys of the light people loaded the house and moved it to new building site. I had Lloyd Olton's tractor to pull it. . . .

1·9·3·7

DeLoach was tired. He was tired of nature's indifference, tired of government programs, and tired of walking behind a mule.

J·A·N·U·A·R·Y

· FRI 29. Arlois [*Jimmie's husband*] & Jim and Bill left early. Bill is out on his own. Hated to see him go away, but I could not help him go to school and he wanted to try the job Arlois spoke about, so all he can do is to try it out. Hope he pulls the grade. Bill is a kid that wants to do something on his own and I will not be any stumbling block in his way. He told me to hire someone in his place to work the feed. All I told him when he left was to "shoot square" and he knows what I meant. If he shoots square and straight with all people he comes in contact with he will be O.K. I hated for him to go away and no money in hand, but I could not help it at this time.

Bill's leaving marked the second of DeLoach's three sons to leave the farm in search of a livelihood. See diary entry for October 29, 1927. According to demographic studies, 70 percent of the youth living on farms in 1940 were in town by 1950. Prior to 1937 the state's rural population did not decline as rapidly as it did nationally, but during the 1940s the rate of change was greater. In contrast to the movement of the 1920s, these people moved to cities within the state's boundaries, because the industrial economy was expanding rapidly enough to easily absorb rural youth being displaced by machinery (See Skra-banek, *Characteristics and Changes in the Texas Farm Population*; R. L. Skrabanek and Gladys K. Bowles, *Migration of the Texas Farm Population*).

M·A·R·C·H

· WED 3. . . . We sure do get lonesome. No one here but Sallie & I. Just like we started out, but not the kick we had when we started out. Now that is just too bad.

M·A·Y

· TUES 25. Some time last night a flood fell. I found this morning that my contoured rows broke and flooded my Sudan pasture and some of my cotton. The water would have not broke over if the place west of me had been contoured. My contoured rows could not take care of the water off the other place and my place too. I dug up some Johnson grass spots on bank of borrow pit this A.M.

On the South Plains the worst drought years were 1934–37. In Lamb County the drought broke with 5.07 inches of rain in May; the yearly total was 23.72. (Hurt, *The Dust Bowl*, pp. 87–101; *Climatological Data, 1937*, p. 100). Contour-ing is curving furrows to fit the lay of the land instead of making straight fur-rows up and down slopes in the field. Terraces and contoured rows held most of the rain on the land where it fell, resulting in more evenly distributed crop stands and better yields because of the additional moisture stored in the soil. Runoff water from land plowed in straight rows also caused erosion problems on adjoining farms, making it important for all of the farmers in a district to practice conservation measures. A borrow pit is an area from which soil is bor-rowed to build up another area. Soil was borrowed from the ditch to build the road higher so that rainwater would run off into the ditch and make the road passable.

J·U·L·Y

· THURS 1. I harrowed all day. Boy! was it hot? Some say 108° in shade, but we did not have to stay in the shade. Was awful hot walking be-hind a drag harrow. I could not ride it. The ground was too soft and

Contour plowing helped save what rain might fall and slowed erosion in flat, dry land.

besides old Jack could not do his part if I rode. Am awful tired. . . .

· THURS 22. . . . Had some hell about money. Never crosses one's mind to try to save a dollar, but after they are all gone then the itemizing is in order. Wants to know what was done with it.

· FRI 23. I hoed all day. Not with much heart. I can't do anything with any heart with such surroundings. I even can't write any more. My nerves are all shot just to be the paying teller and nothing more is bad. Not an affectionate gesture since I went to Washington, D.C. in April, 1936. . . .

In April, 1936, DeLoach, his two sons, and son-in-law spent a month traveling to Washington, D.C. seeking a patent for his collapsible chicken coop. After nearly a decade of financial difficulties caused by a depression and drought, it would be understandable for Sallie to be skeptical of an invention that was having problems "getting off the ground."

A·U·G·U·S·T

SUN 29. We all made ready and went down to the Friendship Church. The Christian people put on the feed bag and the dinner was fine and the day same like old times. We used to gather and spread dinner. All had a big time, but this is the first time that the people have gotten together at a function of that kind since July 15, 1933. . . .

S·E·P·T·E·M·B·E·R

· MON 13. . . . The price of cotton is going so low one does not have much heart to gather it. However, one must go forward and not look back. . . .

The rains returned and West Texas farmers rejoiced that the drought was broken, but their trouble was not over. The Soil Conservation Act, as administered in 1937, did not adequately control production, and acreage increased across the Cotton Belt. Not surprisingly, the price immediately fell when estimates of a bumper crop, over 18 million bales, were released by the government in August. By harvesttime cotton was down to eight cents a pound, considerably below the market of fourteen cents during the summer. Farmers were apathetic to production controls, due to their independent nature and the return of better prices. Failure to demand a cotton program from Congress subjected them to the same old downward spiral that had proved so ruinous in the past. The Editor of the October, 1937, *Progressive Farmer*, asked, "Will we ever learn?"

O·C·T·O·B·E·R

· SAT 30. . . . I had returns on the bale of cotton I put in the Government loan, $40.08, cost $1.00 for the grading and making out papers. . . . all went to town tonight. Sallie and Dot went to the Harley Sadler show. I did not care to go. . . .

During the previous spring cotton sold for nearly $70 a bale, compared to the $40.08 DeLoach got for this bale (See *Semi-Weekly Farm News*, Apr. 30, 1937, p. 6). Sallie and Dot went to see "Rose of the Rio Grande," a comedy drama in three acts. During the twenties and thirties Harley Sadler and his tent show "trouped" across Texas, providing clean and wholesome entertainment. Tent shows represented a brief but important phase of the American theater that brought entertainment and culture to more people than any other aspect of the industry (See Clifford Ashby and Suzanne DePauw May, *Trouping through Texas: Harley Sadler and His Tent Show*, pp. 1–4, 63–84; *Lamb County Leader*, Oct. 21, 1937, p. 6).

N·O·V·E·M·B·E·R

· Mon 1. . . . The argument came up again about the freeze that came in 1925. Some said the 9th, some said the 19th. I said it was on the 27th of Oct, 1925, an account of which will be found on that date in Ledger #4.

· Tues 30. . . . Tim King and Bruce Price came out at near night and told me I had been elected on the cotton committee. Well, I am just like I used to be about it. If I can do the man that has been penalized [*some good*] I am ready to go. If I can't I will get out. Tim King is chairman of the com. I am vice-chairman. Cold all day.

The "penalized man" DeLoach referred to was the farmer who voluntarily balanced his cropping plans by reducing his cotton acreage before 1933, then discovered that cotton allotments under the Agricultural Adjustment Act were based on a farm's production history during the years of diversification (1928–32). Most West Texas farmers felt their practice of diversification worked against them under the current method of allotting cotton acres. To prevent this inequity, they advocated a plan that would permit farmers to raise cotton on a specified percentage of their acres under cultivation.

D·E·C·E·M·B·E·R

· Fri 3. Before I was out of bed Tim King called for me to go to Amherst. The local cotton committee met with the county com. Mr. King was elected on county com. and I became chairman of local com. . . . We met at Amherst at 9 A.M. Finished by noon. I cut feed this P.M.

· Sun 19. . . . Bud said he had closed the deal for the Henry place at $38.00 per acre.

Farmers who purchased land prior to the 1950s saw their investment appreciate when land values rose during the 1970s. By the early 1980s, the land that cost Bud $38 per acre was selling for as much as $1,000 per acre (See *Lubbock Avalanche-Journal*, Feb. 6, 1982, sec. C, p. 7).

1·9·3·8

By 1938 the effects of low prices and a severe drought were showing on even the strongest West Texas farmers, especially those of DeLoach's generation. Thinking back, they realized that the past two decades should have been the most productive years of their life. Looking ahead, they saw changes in farming that were frightening. Family farms were being replaced by cotton empires. Mechanization, permitting one man to work more land than ever before in history, brought four thousand more Texas farmers to the ranks of those farming over five hundred acres. The family farmer's way of life was disappearing.

J·A·N·U·A·R·Y

·Tues 11. . . . I pulled 231# bolls to day. I am sure tired out tonight. Sallie plays and we sing some. That cheers us up so much. I come in tired and she plays the piano. . . .

F·E·B·R·U·A·R·Y

·Mon 28. . . . A poor fellow (an old man) came here today, about 11 A.M. Said he wanted something to eat. Sallie told him to wait and she would have dinner ready by 12 noon. So he sat down out in the yard and she fixed him some dinner. He sure did enjoy the feed. He said anything to eat was lots to him. Poor old fellow. What has he in view? Old, wore out and no place he can call home. Nothing to eat, only what he begs. That is awful. Those white locks looked so pitiful. I just can't turn a hungry person away, especially an old fellow that is down and out, now 10:30 P.M.

M·A·R·C·H

· Tues 1. . . . Went down town and on over to Amherst with Bruce Price. We did not learn much. The main speaker did not know much more about the new Government farm bill than the county committeemen or the local committeemen. However, we need all the dope any one can put out. The main issue he stresed was the voting on the quota issue March 12th. No one knows just how to vote on that subject, because no one at this time knows what he is voting for. Hope they will clear this up soon. Came back home. . . .

The 1938–39 Agricultural Adjustment Act was an attempt to combine the best features of earlier programs into one program that would be within the powers of Congress, as determined by the Supreme Court. Marketing control was substituted for production control since Congress had the power to regulate interstate and foreign commerce. The soil conservation and allotment features of the 1936 act were retained, including provisions for increasing the size of payments for small farming operations and limiting payments to ten thousand dollars.

Surpluses were to be controlled through parity payments, marketing quotas (subject to approval by two-thirds of the voting producers), and nonrecourse loans that enabled growers to hold crops off the market if prices were too low. The loan rate (between 52 and 75 percent of parity) could be reduced to discourage continued high production. The loan rate was set each year by using a specified formula that would maintain an "ever-normal granary" to provide reserve stocks for emergencies. The act also had provisions for reducing accumulated surpluses through the distribution of surplus farm commodities to the needy and the establishment of a school lunch program, low-cost milk program, and a food stamp plan.

The 1938 act became the basis for future agricultural programs. A point of similarity, however, in all of the government programs of the 1930s was their inability to truly control production. Acreage control was offset by better seed and fertilizers that sharply increased yield per acre (See USDA, *Agricultural Adjustment, 1938–39*, pp. 50–53; Tweeten, *Foundations of Farm Policy*, pp. 304–305; Benedict, *Farm Policies*, pp. 375–80).

Mon, Feb. 28... a poor fellow (an old man) came here today, about 11 A.M. Said he wanted something to eat... he sat down out in the yard and Sallie fixed some dinner. He sure did enjoy the feed.

· Sᴀᴛ 12.   I went down to Sudan. Opened polls at Co-op gin for the referendum vote on the quota plan. . . . We closed polls at 7 ᴘ.ᴍ. 233 yes
votes and 28 no votes were cast. . . .

All producers (tenants as well as owners) were allowed to vote. Over 88 percent of the Texas farmers who voted were in favor of marketing quotas. Penalty for marketing in excess of quotas was $.02 per pound, and reports indicate
penalties totaling $780,000 were collected (See USDA, *Agricultural Adjustment,
1938–39*, pp. 50–53; USDA, *Agricultural Adjustment, 1937–38*, pp. 108–11).

· Sᴀᴛ 19.   Did not plow. Sallie was all broke down. She has spells and
seems she can't control herself. I am in such a state of mind I do not
know what do do. We have had so much trouble the last years. . . . I
have something coming on my left ear. I think sometime it is a cancer.
That and all the other trouble sure makes it hard to carry on. . . .

Like the wind-eroded land they were working, Plains farmers were wounded
and hurting. West Texas farm women defined their worth in terms of being good
homemakers. The depression began to undermine their self-confidence when
scarcity of money delayed purchases or amusements. Frustration turned to de-
spair during the drought as day after day dust sifted in, finally staining everything it settled on and doubling their workload. They suffered great stress and
emotional discomfort; however, they managed to carry on even after conditions
became demoralizing (See Ruby Winona Adams, "Social Behavior in a Drought
Stricken Texas Panhandle Community," [Master's thesis, University of Texas,
1939]).

M·ᴀ·ʏ

· Tʜᴜʀꜱ 19.   I went down town to settle up with the bank. I made a new
note $203.00+. If that was all I owed it would not be so much, but I
owe other people and a land note of $226.80. In all it seems I am in
bad debt, but all I can do is try to get out. . . .

J·ᴜ·ɴ·ᴇ

· Tʜᴜʀꜱ 16.   . . . I went down town and insured my cotton. 21 A. at $10.00
per A. That will be a protection if hailed out and won't be so much if
not. . . . Cost me a note of $27.45. . . .

J·U·L·Y

· Mon 18. . . . I gave the *Sudan News* some dope out of my diary account
in the years of 1925, 1926 and 1927.

· Sat 23. . . . We went by Joel Wesson's place and voted. I voted for
O'Daniel for governor. I do not know that he is the man to put in,
but it will be a change. . . .

Breaking all records as a vote-getter, W. Lee "Pappy" O'Daniel dominated Texas
politics from 1938 to 1946. A shrewd flour salesman who quickly recognized the
potential of radio advertising, O'Daniel sold politics like flour. His noontime
radio program, featuring the Light Crust Doughboys, introduced him to thousands of rural Texans, who still comprised 60 percent of the state's population
in 1938. When prosperity returned and disillusionment with the New Deal
began to surface, Texans returned to voting for colorful personalities instead
of issues. O'Daniel entertained his audience while deriding professional politicians, who thought he was a joke until the votes were counted (See Seth Shepard McKay, *W. Lee O'Daniel and Texas Politics, 1938–1942*, pp. 9–44, 576–618;
McKay and Faulk, *Texas after Spindletop*, pp. 152–81).

· Sat 30. . . . Mr. Milam and his daughter-in-law called by. She wanted to
buy our place. I told her what I would have to have per A.—$50.00
with crop. Was so sudden I did not have time to think it over. . . .

Even though a drought hampered farming in West Texas during the 1930s,
Lamb County's average lint yield history was among the highest in the state,
making government payments quite hefty for some farmers. Landlords quickly
realized the advantage of taking land back from tenants or buying more. Farming a third more land brought their cotton acreage back to what it was before
the days of government control. They needed no more labor than formerly
used—less if they owned tractors—and the price-supported cotton greatly increased their income. DeLoach would have been a prime target because he
farmed only 68 acres and still used mules. Many farmers in his situation were
either selling out or renting their land to mechanized operators, who were using
improved seed and fertilizer to increase production per acre.

A·U·G·U·S·T

· Fri 12. . . . About 3 P.M. Mrs. Milam called and said she would take the
place at $50.00 per acre. She is to pay 1938 taxes and land payment. I

am to pay 1937 taxes. I am to give her possession not later than Sept. 10, 1938. I sure do hate to sell out, but we have had so much trouble here for the last two years that I think a change will do both of us good.

· SAT 13. I am lost not to work a little each day, but I guess I am sold out. I saw Judge Dunham and he told me the Milams were in to see him. They wanted him to examine my abstract, which he would do Monday P.M.

· FRI 19. We did not go any place today. . . . The people have not showed up that wanted to buy me out. I guess they have backed out. Well, I do not care. It is not pleasant when one sells one's home. . . .

S·E·P·T·E·M·B·E·R

· WED 28. . . . I helped Bud cut feed. He promoted me. Let me drive the tractor. First time I ever run a tractor. . . . I did not feel like cutting heads today. In fact, I am down and out. Have not energy to do any thing. No pride for nothing we raise.

· FRI 30. . . . new boy at Bud's house. Robert Edwin, they named him. We all went down to see him. That makes 3 grandsons & 2 granddaughters.

N·O·V·E·M·B·E·R

· TUES 8. We made ready in forenoon to go to Amherst. I as a local committeeman was called to meet with all, both county and local committmen of Lamb County. The meeting was all bunk. Too many long drawn out statements of two big shots. I don't think the big boys talks accomplished much. . . .

· FRI 11. . . . 20 years ago I planted wheat. The big guns at Ft. Sill, Okla began to shoot [*announcing armistice for World War I*] and I did not know what it was all about. . . .

D·E·C·E·M·B·E·R

· SAT 10. I went down town early to open polls for election at City Hall. 211 votes cast, 145 yes, 66 nos. 4 votes over the 2/3 majority. . . .

The vote was for cotton quotas in 1938–39. The large opposition indicates disillusionment with the New Deal programs.

1·9·3·9

Hard times were back. Growing surpluses, rising expenses, and increased use of synthetic fibers were hurting cotton producers. The conflict in Europe only made the picture darker. In the early stages of war the price of exported products, such as cotton and wheat, is usually hurt by blockades. It looked like the depression had returned.

J·A·N·U·A·R·Y

· THURS 19. . . . We are reading the book, *Gone with the Wind*. It is no wonder the people of Georgia had it in for Sherman and the Yankees. I have heard my mother tell about how Sherman's men put every thing they could not carry away in ashes. This book tells it in a way that would make any one mad that lived there.

According to DeLoach, his parents were Georgia plantation owners who lost everything in the Civil War. Perhaps he also reacted strongly because, after the 1930s, the title had an added meaning for him.

M·A·R·C·H

· WED 22. . . . I went down town to shop around for a used tractor. Too high. I guess I will not get a tractor. . . .

·Thurs 30.   . . . went down to Bud's for his tractor. I pulled it behind my
car. . . . Bud came up and we started plowing. I could not make a very
pretty row when I started out, but am doing some better now. . . .

Dorothy's marriage didn't last, and in April she returned home with her
child. At first, DeLoach was uneasy about the arrangement, but the baby
quickly won his heart. "The baby girl is a black haired baby. She is a pretty little thing." Almeda Faye took to her grandpa just as fast.

A·p·r·i·l

·Thurs 6.   . . . I sent money order to Washington, D. C. ($5.00) to the Patent
Attorneys Chartered Institute of American Inventors. I want to see
what they can do about my invention. . . .

Sallie had always been proud of her chickens and the money earned from
eggs. Now with Dorothy at home to help, she had an idea for earning extra
money that would be needed if the dire forecasts were true for cotton prices.

M·a·y

·Mon 8.   Sallie & I went to Sudan. While there Sallie went to bank.
Made dope for money to buy 500 baby R. I. [*Rhode Island Red*] chickens
and to feed them till 8 wks old. . . .

An important part of the balanced agriculture advocated by farm leaders,
poultry ranked fourth in agricultural income in Texas, generating approximately
$45 million a year during the late thirties. Requiring only a small investment,
flocks began producing income in eight or nine months. The Rhode Island Reds
that Sallie raised were popular egg-layers, averaging two hundred eggs per year.
These heavier chickens were also preferred because the cockerels made good
fryers. Even though the poultry industry in Texas was a small flock industry with
each farm carrying approximately forty-five hens, by 1940 thirty-six million eggs
and three thousand pounds of dressed poultry were shipped annually out of
Lubbock, which was a regional marketing center for the South Plains (See
A. H. Demke, "Count in the Hen," *West Texas Today* 21, no. 7 [Sept., 1940],
p. 8; H. S. Hilburn, "Cow, Sow, and Hen," *West Texas Today* 22, no. 11 [Jan.,
1942], p. 6; Frank E. Mitchell, "The Things You Want to Know about Baby
Chicks," *Progressive Farmer* 54, no. 2 [Feb., 1939], p. 56).

· Mon 15. I put the brooder stove up this forenoon. Sallie and I went to
Muleshoe for the baby chicks this P.M. 500 is too many little chicks for
my brooder house, but we can scatter them out in 2 weeks. They cost
$40.00; 4 feeders 35¢ each, $1.40; 200# chick starter $5.70; 1 bottle dope
for water faucets, 40¢. . . .

· Tues 16. We worked with the chickens in forenoon. Took Sallie down
town. She had a date with bank. Made her note for $72.50. . . .

· Fri 26. . . . Have planted all my cotton seed. Think maybe I will finish
planting with Paymaster seed.

In 1929 Anderson, Clayton and Company started breeding a strain of cotton that could be profitably produced during the Llano Estacado's short growing season. Paymaster cotton was the result. Developed from an early-maturing
Guatemalan cotton called Kekchi, Paymaster had large bolls that matured early;
a 15/16-inch staple from dry land; and a 40 percent lint turnout. Selection and
improvement continued until a stormproof variety, known as Paymaster "54,"
was developed in 1945 (Dr. Richard Sheets, cotton research manager, Paymaster Research Farm, interview with Janet Neugebauer, Aiken, Tex., Mar. 21, 1988).

J·U·N·E

After a visit on Sunday, June 11, Jimmie took her mother back to Ralls to
help with the birth of her second child.

· Tues 13. Had card from Sallie stating Jimmie's baby was born Monday,
6 A.M., 12th. Well that is the first time I ever saw a woman go 90 miles
for the midwife and take her home and then deliver the baby. A boy
[*Stanley Arlois*]. Hope they get along O.K.

· Sat 17. . . . I had to get some more chicken feed, so I bought laying
mash. Now won't it be just too bad if those little pullets start laying.
Well, it is cheaper than growing mash and I can't see why it will not do
the job. . . .

J·U·L·Y

· Sun 2. . . . He [*Arlois*], Jim, Bill and his girl and little ones came about
10 A.M. Bud and his folks did not come till about 11 A.M. Robert E. fell
out of his hi chair and mashed his nose and then all the babys sun

191

burned out in the park [*Mackenzie Park in Lubbock*]. Was hot, but we had lots of shade. Ida Rene brought the fried chicken, Jim the ice tea, Sallie the cake. Bill's girl brought his pillow for him. All seemed to have a good time. . . . I went to an old Sacred Harp singing up in District Court Room at Lubbock. Sure did have some fine singing. Those old people sure do enjoy themselves.

Sacred Harp Singing Conventions were held in a courthouse during the summer. The courtroom held the large group and the high ceilings kept the room cool.

A·U·G·U·S·T

· TUES 1. . . . Had to go to town this afternoon for feed and something to eat. Seems like it takes more for us to live on than it did back when all the kids were at home. Hit the bank up for $20.00. Bought gro. $5.20 feed bill last month $2.30, Gas bill last mo. 75¢. . . .

· SAT 19. . . . We all went to town this P.M. Have no money to buy anything. Would like to buy some peaches to can, but have to buy chicken feed and gas and pay insurance. Seems that I can never get a $ in my pocket that I can keep till I get another one to add to it.

· TUES 22. . . . Had to shut the old sow up so the chickens could not get to her. She ate several before I did. The chickens have an awful appetitie. They eat two big arm loads of heads [*grain sorghum*] each day.

· WED 23. The check up boys came out to measure the cotton I had to plow up to be in compliance. They found I had plowed up 2 A. and I was over planted 1 9/10 A. They told me about Clint Dawson killing himself at the grain elevator. Shot himself with a shot gun. We went to Sudan to wash this P.M. Heard some more about Dawson, but all hear say. No one knows just what he did that for. . . .

· SAT 26. Hoed and plowed in forenoon. Went to Sudan in P.M. Heard another fellow passed out the shot gun route early this A.M. 3 days, about to the hour two went that way. A Mr. Smithers, the latest suicide in town. It must be catching. One shot in head, other near head.

S·E·P·T·E·M·B·E·R

· WED 20. . . . I have nothing to say about the European war. Only that I hope the U.S. keeps out of it. . . .

DeLoach's comment reflected the feeling of most Americans; however, a situation was developing from which there could be no escape either through isolation or neutrality.

· Mon 25. . . . Sallie drove the car some this P.M. Think she needed attention when she quit.
· Fri 29. . . . We went back to the cooking school [*DeLoach took Sallie and Dot*]. A Mrs. Franks is the head cook and teacher. Boy! but she slings a wicked cabbage. One gets hungry, but alas! she does not serve. . . .

O·C·T·O·B·E·R

· Sat 7. . . . We caught up 30 young chickens. We took them to Sudan this P.M. Sold for 30¢ each. Sallie paid $12.90 on her bank note, $20.70 paid up to date. . . .

Diary entries do not give the total amount Sallie earned from the chickens she raised. Some were sold as fryers, the rest kept as hens. However, when the chickens began to produce a profit, DeLoach referred to them as "our chickens."

· Fri 13. . . . I sold Jeff Rudman 3 bales cotton 8.16¢ per lb., $125.36. Payed $80.00 on bank note, bal. $93+. . . .

N·O·V·E·M·B·E·R

· Thurs 23. . . . The mail man did not come. The Post Office Department observes this Thursday, Nov 23 as Thanksgiving Day. Mr. Rosevelt's New Deal on the days.

Twenty-six states, including Texas, celebrated Thanksgiving the last Thursday in November despite President Roosevelt's decree moving it to the fourth Thursday. Governor O'Daniel left the choice to Texans individually, and tradition won out in most cases. Roosevelt's scheme to add six additional days to the Christmas shopping season was labeled "Franksgiving" by West Texans. Regardless of local sentiment, however, the closing of government offices and schools on the fourth Thursday provided a clear indication of which day would ultimately become the national holiday, and in 1941 Congress adopted a joint resolution setting Thanksgiving on the fourth Thursday in November (See *Lubbock Avalanche-Journal*, Nov. 23, 1939, p. 1, Nov. 26, 1939, p. 5, and Nov. 30, 1939, p. 1; *Dallas Morning News*, Nov. 23, 1939, sec. 2, p. 2 and Nov. 30, 1939, sec. 2, p. 4).

D·E·C·E·M·B·E·R

· SAT 16. . . . We all went to Sudan this P.M. Nothing new. The same old faces and about the same talk. Hard times and the war is all people know. . . .

· MON 18. . . . I had supper and went into town. I opened the meeting of electing new Community Com. Men only. 17 voters came to meeting. I was put on as Chairman of the Local Committee. . . .

· SAT 30. . . . I took the butter to town, 4 lbs, 30¢ per [*pound*]. I did not stop long in town. I just can't hardly go to Sudan any more. The people are so different now. A new bunch and all the old timers have nearly all left, died or moved away. . . .

1·9·4·0

Lamb County farms continued to grow in size and decrease in number. Larger farms meant more money from additional cotton acres, and larger incomes allowed those who expanded to buy still more land. This was hard on small farmers, most of whom were not mechanized and found it difficult to work additional land with teams. Lacking the necessary collateral to borrow money for machinery, their best option was intensive use of their small acreage through chickens, cows, and hogs.

J·A·N·U·A·R·Y

· Sun 14. Thirty seven years ago today Sallie and I were married near Duke, Okla. We have had our five (5) children, (3) boys and (2) two girls to marry. The boy baby, Billy, was married last night at 9 p.m. at Lubbock, Texas to Miss Noma Jean Seeds of Ralls, Texas. They came up to day arriving about 11 a.m. They will make it O.K. I know they will. . . .

· Wed 17. We cut up the meat and packed it away. Cut up the lard and rendered it out by noon. . . . Sallie made soap. . . .

Packing cured meat in cottonseed oil prevented its becoming rancid, even during warm weather. The oil didn't add a flavor of its own, but only preserved the flavor of the meat, which was then stored in a cool, dry place, preferably a well-ventilated cellar (See *Semi-Weekly Farm News*, June 14, 1940, p. 3). Rural families were encouraged to use fats left over at slaughtering time for homemade soap, thereby reducing the drain on the national supply of fats and oils that would otherwise go into commercially produced soap. Sallie made her soap outdoors in a cast iron wash pot, using cow chips because they made a very hot fire (See *Lubbock Avalanche-Journal*, Dec. 24, 1941, p. 13; Jimmie DeLoach Moorhead, interview with Janet Neugebauer, Lubbock, Tex., Oct. 23, 1987).

> · FRI 19. . . . I threw a mad fit when the cows would not come up. I had to quit my work and go for them. I rode the black mare and run the cows all the way home. Bess did not give any milk tonight. Well if a fellow would just stop and think "what good does it do?" one would not get mad that way, only to hate it and be sorry that one did it. I am going to try and not pull a fool stunt like that any more. . . .

Milk is made and stored in the udder in little cavities or compartments called alveoli. If a cow is startled just before or during milking, the milk won't come down. It does not drain out of these cavities by gravity, but remains there until squeezed out (See W. C. Lassetter, "How to Make Livestock Pay," *Progressive Farmer* 58, no. 1 [Jan., 1943], p. 24).

> · SAT 20. . . . We went down town this P.M. I sold my Government loan (1938) cotton to Henry Lee. Eight bales $1.50 per bale. . . .

Cotton prices rose to $.10 a pound, and DeLoach withdrew cotton he put in the government loan in 1938 when the price dropped to nearly $.05. In order to secure possession of the warehouse receipts, he had to pay face value of the note plus interest and storage charges. After the charges were paid DeLoach netted $1.50 per bale on the eight bales he put in the loan in 1938. His 15/16-inch (staple length) cotton qualified for the top market price (See *Lamb County Leader*, Jan. 25, 1940, p. 9).

M·A·R·C·H

> · THURS 7. . . . A very pleasant day. Sallie fixed her hot bed. The hens layed 73 eggs today.

Hotbeds, usually three feet by six feet and covered with a glass window, were used to start early vegetable plants. A five-inch layer of soil could be heated to eighty-five degrees when placed on a bed of fresh horse manure (See L. A. Niven, "Next Month's Gardening," *Progressive Farmer* 54, no. 12 [Dec., 1939], p. 43).

DeLoach built a new outdoor toilet before the workload increased at planting time, and the whole family was on hand to supervise!

· WED 13.   . . . I worked on the toilet and did not get it finished. Sallie
    came out in the afternoon and said for me to make the counter 20
    inches high, 20 inches deep. Well, I did and it looks like a shelf in a dry
    goods store. Little ones will have to carry a stool to get up on the
    blame thing when they want to make a deposit. But that is the way she
    wanted it and she and Dot are the ones to please. . . .
· THURS 14.   I finished the toilet and what a job. Sallie asked me what I
    made the commode so large for. I told her if that fat lady ever called
    on her I wanted to have accommodations for her. And boy! Am I fixed
    for her. . . .
· MON 25.   . . . Bud came by at noon. He had a wind charger. . . .

The earliest electricity available to Lamb County farmers came from windchargers on the windmill. Six or twelve volts of electricity, generated by the
turning of the two-propeller mill, was stored in a battery. Because it was relatively inexpensive, most families used a standard car battery which could store
about a ten-hour supply of power. This was usually adequate to supply one or
two bulbs, which was a lot of light in those times. Lack of wind sometimes interrupted the flow of electricity; nevertheless, it was quite an improvement over
kerosene lamps (Scott, *A History of Lamb County*, p. 49).

A·P·R·I·L

· SAT 6.   . . . We all went up town this P.M. Sold 17 doz eggs at store, $2.04,
    12¢ per doz. Sold 175 eggs, $1.75 to be set in a hatchery. Set one hen
    17 eggs, besides what we ate. $3.79 worth sold, cream $1.04, $4.82 for
    income. Thanks.
· TUES 9.   . . . I sure wish I had a tractor. I think would put new life in me.
    To think about going away over to that land I have rented [*30 acres*]
    and put it up with these 3 horses. I could put it up in 1½ days with
    tractor and with team will take me a whole week, but I have not the
    tractor and don't see how I can get one.

This entry reflects the bind in which small farmers were caught. Cotton reductions had reached a point where there was little profit in their farming operation because of their small output and high production expense. Continued
reduction of their money crop was making many of them insolvent. Attempts

to increase their acreage, and their cotton allotment, were difficult because they lacked the machinery necessary to handle additional acres, and without increased acreage they could not secure credit to purchase tractors. See diary entry for December 5, 1940. Work sheets from the county agent's office indicated the average size of a Lamb County farm was 166 acres.

> · WED 10. . . . Did think I would plant some cane today, but I put in most of afternoon reading W. Lee O'Daniel's *News*. Boy he hits those old capital rats [*politicians holding state offices*] a hard blow. . . .

W. Lee O'Daniel borrowed a leaf from Jim Ferguson's notebook when he started a weekly political newspaper to convince voters of his honesty and economy of government. It was published in Fort Worth. Subscription rates were twenty-five cents for four months or one dollar per year (See *The W. Lee O'Daniel News* [Fort Worth, Tex.], Apr. 8, 1940, pp. 1, 8; *Semi-Weekly Farm News* [Dallas, Tex.], Mar. 29, 1940, p. 5; McKay, *W. Lee O'Daniel and Texas Politics, 1938–1942*, pp. 268–81).

> · SAT 20. . . . We went to town early. I had to be in the co-op Gin office by 2 P.M. I took 40 applications for the mattresses. I know some of them will be turned down, but the applicants signed the blank. I know that some did not answer the questions truthfully, however that is their funeral. Some that I know should have applied that did not. Mr. Barley came over early and brought all the application blanks. I put the returns in the Post Office about 6:30 P.M. We had a very nice day.

Under the supervision of County Home Demonstration Agents, rural families whose gross income was $400 or less, with 50 percent coming from the farm, were provided materials and instructions for making mattresses. An eligible family of three persons received two mattresses and an eligible family of five persons received three. The program was in effect during 1940 and 1941. Every family receiving mattresses was also entitled to receive materials for the same number of cotton comforters that were also made in community centers. Materials were furnished by the Surplus Marketing Administration and over 550 Lamb County families took advantage of the program. Families that were later declared ineligible were required to pay $6.55 for the mattress and $1.35 for the comforter or return them if unused. In addition to aiding low-income families, the program was intended to use surplus cotton owned by the government. The program operated in conjunction with the stamps, issued to low-income families, that could be redeemed for retail merchandise made of cotton (See *Lamb County Leader*, May 23, 1940, p. 1, Jan. 16, 1941, p. 2, Mar. 6, 1941, p. 3,

Mar. 13, 1941, p. 9; *Semi-Weekly Farm News*, Jan. 2, 1940, p. 4 and Feb. 13, 1940, p. 4).

· SAT 27. . . . I sent my 1940 gin tickets to County Agent's office, Amherst, for a check up on my last year's production. Also sent back the description of my patent or invention, Fig #1, which is in the hands of the American Patent Corporation, Washington, D.C.

Marketing quotas were in effect in 1939, and DeLoach had to verify that the bales of cotton he sold were within the quota allotted to him.

· MON 29. . . . The census taker came.

M·A·Y

· WED 1. . . . I went on to Amherst to a meeting of all local and county committeemen. We were in session from 1 P.M. to near 6 P.M. Its a bad looking deal for the cotton planter. The lint poundage will be cut again and the local committeemen will stand in the mouth of the gun, but we can pass the buck to the County committee.

Since the introduction of cotton acreage controls, Texas, Oklahoma, and Arkansas had assumed 88 percent of the nation's total acreage reduction, even though they produced only 33 percent of the total crop. Texas had assumed 54 percent of the reduction, from nineteen million acres to nine million acres. Southeastern congressmen argued that the expansion of cotton into Texas and the Southwest was largely responsible for the overproduction, hence this area should suffer the greater burden of acreage reduction. Southwestern cotton spokesmen, rejecting this argument, believed reduction had simply followed the path of least political resistance because the older cotton-growing area had four times as many senators and twice as many representatives as the Southwest (See *Semi-Weekly Farm News*, Jan. 30, 1940, p. 1, Feb. 2, 1940, p. 4, and Mar. 12, 1940, p. 2).

· SAT 11. . . . Has been a warm day. Cotton ought to sprout quick since the weather is favorable.

DeLoach was planting cotton seed that had not been delinted, and it would normally have sprouted in five or six days if the temperature of the soil surrounding the seed was at least seventy-five degrees (Dr. James Supak, agronomist, Agricultural Extension Service, interview with Janet Neugebauer, Lubbock, Tex., Apr. 4, 1988).

· Sat 25. . . . I did intend to insure my cotton, but decided I would not. I may get hailed out. They scheme to beat one some way or other, and from the looks of the war, cotton will be a dead weight this fall if things don't change. If the Allies are whipped people will be thinking in terms of defence instead of cotton and if something radical does not happen over there the Germans will finish plowing and planting in 30 days.

DeLoach is remembering how the cotton market collapsed in the early days of World War I. See entries during August, 1914.

· Wed 29. . . . I went to town this P.M. to see about some one to plant that land near town for me. A fellow with a John Deere tractor said he would plant it for 40¢ per A. if he could run in 3 gear and 45¢ if second gear was used. . . . The war of Europe is looking bad. Hitler is going to lick the world if he is not stopped and it looks like France and England can't stop him.

The situation in Europe looked serious for the Allies. France had already fallen to the Nazis, and Germany's army was advancing toward the English Channel. Fearing an invasion, England implemented emergency measures; President Roosevelt emphasized the urgency of national preparedness.

J·U·N·E

· Thurs 6. . . . The same old saw. Money matters. I can't make the grade. Will have to rob a bank I guess. Plowed feed this P.M.
· Wed 12. . . . The big war is getting to be bad. I can't help but think the Allies will win out for might is not right. The two big war dogs, Hitler & "Muso," they think they will take the Allies and make them like it.
· Wed 19. No Negroes worked today. I plowed for a while this forenoon. . . .

On June 19, 1865, Maj. Gen. Gordon Granger landed at Galveston and read the Emancipation Proclamation. Since that date blacks have observed June 19 (Juneteenth) with dances, parades, and speeches extolling the importance of freedom for all people. At first these celebrations were held far away from the eyes of curious whites; however, by the mid-1980s Juneteenth had become a public celebration, a day for honoring black heroes in addition to the usual festivities (See Alwyn Barr, *Black Texans: A History of Negroes in Texas, 1528–1971*, pp.

65, 106; Alwyn Barr and Robert A. Calvert, eds., *Black Leaders: Texans for Their Times*, pp. 70–71; Gerry Burton, "Unveiling of Bronze Sculpture to Depict Black History," *Lubbock Avalanche-Journal*, June 19, 1986, p. 12).

· THURS 27. . . . The Dalby truckers delivered the ice box from Lubbock. $1.11 was the charge. . . .

Wartime blockades and increased use of the barter system in Europe closed foreign markets for American agricultural products. Growing surpluses and weakening prices dramatically emphasized the importance of finding new domestic uses. The National Cotton Council waged a war of its own with a "fighting fund" campaign to raise one million dollars for research into new uses for cotton. Farmers were asked to contribute five cents per bale to help the council reach its goal of raising the domestic consumption to ten million bales annually.

J·u·l·y

· SUN 28. . . . I went down to Sudan for election returns. With what dope the press had O'Daniels is "it" with out a run off. About 54% of what votes has been tabulated. Well, I am truly glad. I do not think he is too hot for the Governor, but the way these hi birds in politics have slung mud, I am glad he beat the whole field. 6 or 7 I think was in the race.

A·u·g·u·s·t

· SAT 3. I put up my water m. stand in forenoon. I put a bunch of melons in it. Sallie sold $4.40. I had to go to town. The water melon thieves raided my patch again, but did not do as much damage as they did last Monday night. . . .
· WED 7. Was in the "dumps" when I got up. I felt so bad having to put up with some body coming in my water melon patch and cut and slash my melons. I set up till midnight, but they came in after I came in. . . . The stand did not make but $4.05. . . .

DeLoach operated two watermelon stands from his farm which was located on a highway. In 1940 he made $236.04 from the melons, averaging 40 cents per hundred pounds.

S·E·P·T·E·M·B·E·R

· WED 4. . . . The gas man put in the meter and Dot cooked dinner on the
gas stove. Sure does the job.

· SUN 29. . . . Dot had to stay all P.M. [*in the watermelon stand*]. She sold
2 for 25¢, total for the day $1.40. I do not believe women are good
watermelon sellers. . . .

N·O·V·E·M·B·E·R

· TUES 5. Election day. Roosevelt, Dem., Wilkie, Rep. I do believe that this
will be a close race between these two men. I did not go and vote. I
could not vote for a Republican and I would not vote for F.D.R. . . .

Many Texas farmers were frustrated with the Democratic ticket because they
thought the state's cotton acreage had been unfairly cut. This produced a large
number of "Willkie Democrats," but European war clouds gave FDR a nearly
700,000–vote lead over the inexperienced Republican Wendell Willkie (See Mc-
Kay, *Texas Politics, 1906–1944*, pp. 397–431).

· WED 6. . . . Roosevelt was elected by a land slide. . . .

· MON 18. . . . Bud and folks were here. He was driving a new V-8 car. Not
new, but new to them. . . .

· SUN 24. Every thing covered in ice and sleet. It rained and sleeted all
night. The highway trees are breaking down, so much ice on them. Boy
the gas is the tops. I do not have to go out for kindling or coal, nor oil.
I do not know just what the next bill will be. I may wish I had the coal
stove and oil stove back.

D·E·C·E·M·B·E·R

· THURS 5. . . . We decided we would go to Littlefield. I wanted to see a Mr.
Kerr about his loan plan. Kerr told me that my reg application would
not go through on account of I did not operate enough acres. . . . More
hell at home because I went to Littlefield. If I had any other business
other than meal ticket I could not attend to it. Nuff said.

1·9·4·1

During World War II food became a weapon of war—as vital as planes, guns, or munitions. When the dairy and hog centers of northwestern Europe were captured by the Axis powers, it was clear that without constant shipments of food England would be forced to surrender Europe to Nazi control. It was no longer wise to restrict American agricultural production; it needed to be increased, and fast. Guaranteed prices encouraged farmers to increase production by more than one-third; however, they negotiated a better deal than during World War I. They demanded the continuation of price supports for two years after peace was signed, to avoid a post-war depression.

Private supplies in regular commerical channels could not supply the enormous amounts needed to sustain the Allied efforts, but the "ever-normal granary" held enough food and fiber crops to meet the demand while farmers geared up for maximum production. This ready supply strengthened the confidence and morale of the Allies and Americans.

J·A·N·U·A·R·Y

· THURS 2. . . . Has been cold all day. . . . I sure had a pleasant surprise today when I received my statement from the gas co. I thought the bill would be at least $5.00, but it was only $3.05, less 15¢ interest on my $10.00 meter deposit. The bill is $2.90. I think that is cheap enough the way the weather has been the last month. That is a lot cheaper than oil and coal.

· SUN 12. We went down to spend the day with Mr. & Mrs. Crain [*parents of Ida Rene, Bud's wife*] at Friendship. Sure did enjoy the good dinner Mrs. Crain served us and we all enjoyed being in their home for the visit. Like old times when we used to go and stay all day with people in the Friendship Community. . . .

· MON 20. . . . President Roosevelt did something today no other president ever did. Taken office oath for President the third time or for the third term. Well, I guess that is O.K.

F·E·B·R·U·A·R·Y

· FRI 21. . . . Had letter from H. G. wanting us to get him a birth certificate. I do not know just how to go about getting it. They did not make certificates when he was born.

M·A·R·C·H

· SUN 9. . . . I bought 30 little Chinese elms at 3¢ each. . . .

Chinese elms were widely used for windbreaks or shelterbelts in Texas and Oklahoma. DeLoach did not plant the traditional shelterbelt consisting of rows of trees of varying heights, but he did plant trees around his house and barn to reduce the wind velocity. Windbreaks reduced home heating costs, in addition to protecting gardens and other tender vegetation. Nurseries, established as part of Roosevelt's Shelterbelt Program, sold seedlings raised for about one-fifth of the price charged by commercial nurseries. A windbreak thirty-five feet high could reduce a thirty-mile-per-hour wind by 50–60 percent, at ground level, for a distance of two hundred feet (See Wilmon H. Droze, *Trees, Prairies, and People: A History of Tree Planting in the Plains States*, pp. 136–37, 142–63).

A·P·R·I·L

· TUES 15. . . . The R.E.A. [*Rural Electrification Administration*] people unloaded the electric poles here this A.M. Bud & I went to Muleshoe to see about wiring my house. I also made application for $40.00 R.E.A. fund for wiring purposes. Will see about it later. . . .

· SAT 19. Boy things were sure covered in sand when we got up. . . . We went to town this P.M. Eggs down [to] 17¢ doz, cream 30¢ lb. 17 doz, $2.89, cream $2.10. . . .

· THURS 24.   I rigged up the trailer, loaded Bess Cow. Took her to Mule-shoe. She weighed 945#, sold for $5.70 per hundred, $53.87, $1.10 yard fees & Com. $52.77 my check. . . .

· WED 30.   I shelled out some peanuts for seed. Almeda [*Dorothy's daughter*] helped me. She wants to help me do every thing I do. . . .

M·A·Y

· THURS 8.   . . . Went to town to get Mother something for Mother's day. A dress, handkerchief.

· WED 14.   . . . The quilting ladies gathered in afternoon and did quilt and talk. 8 or 9 came. . . .

· TUES 20.   I brought out the 200 pullets, 211 in all. Paid $34.60 for them. . . . We bought 25 two wk old cockrels 7¢ each.

The Department of Agriculture decided to increase the number of laying hens by 10 percent during 1941 to meet the lend-lease requirements for eggs in dried, frozen, and shell form. Early in the year price supports of twenty-two cents a dozen for eggs (Chicago basis) were announced. From April to August 4.5 million cases of eggs were purchased by the government, boosting the price 50 percent over the same period for the previous year. By the end of 1941, the poultry industry was closer to defense requirements than most other branches of agriculture (See USDA, *Report of the Secretary of Agriculture, 1941*, pp. 112–14).

· SUN 25.   We were not hurt till last night. A hard rain fell that ruined the planted crops and washed out places in my field. . . . The Rudd lake is over the highway. Highway truck is pulling the traffic across. We all went to Sudan this P.M.

More than eleven inches of rain fell in May, 1941, and total precipitation for the year was almost twenty-six inches above normal. Even though it caused problems at the time, the deep-level moisture provided the basis for good crops for the next two years. For once the elements and the market showered their blessings at the same time. During the war agricultural prices were at an all-time high.

· THURS 29.   . . . Think I will look around and trade for a tractor. It would not eat only when it is at work, but these blooming horses just eat all the time.

Wed 30... I shelled out some peanuts for seed. Almeda helped me. She wants to help me do every thing I do....

· Fʀɪ 30.   I made up my mind that I would get me a tractor. I traded the
four (4) head of stock in on a $450.00 Farmall F-12. "I call it the Master
12." They allowed me $150.00 for stock, tools, & harness. The first time
I have been out of stock since December, 1912. . . .

Most implement dealers engaged the services of a mule trader, on a regular
basis, to sell the mules and animal-drawn equipment that was taken in as down
payments on tractors. There was a ready market for the mules of the Plains in
the Old Cotton Belt where mechanization had not yet developed, and many
implement dealers sold their tractors at cost, making their profit on the mules
(See Gordon, "The History and Development of Irrigated Cotton," pp. 171–73).

J·u·n·e

· Fʀɪ 13.   . . . My back hurts me. Think it is the shake up of the tractor.
· Sᴀᴛ 28.   . . . I gave Sallie her first lesson in tractor driving. She just
knocked down one corner post. We went to town this ᴘ.ᴍ. . . .

J·u·ʟ·ʏ

· Sᴀᴛ 19.   Mr. Milam came by early and wanted to know if I wanted him to
bring my tractor home. I need to be plowing, but none of the cotton I
am hoeing that I could help with the plow. I told him to have it here
by Monday morning. I do not know, but I don't think there is many
fellows that would loan a neighbor his tractor and outfit. I think he
would help me any way he could. . . .
· Sᴜɴ 20.   We went to Sudan to church. The people seem to just wonder
"what are you doing here." The modern set up I guess. Have nothing to
say or hardly speak to one another. Bud & folks came out for a pop call.
· Wᴇᴅ 30.   Mrs. Travis came out to hoe. She and the boy. . . . I told her I
would give her $2.00 per day and boy $1.00, or 20 cents per hr for her
and 10¢ per hr for boy. They put in about 8 hours today. . . . Mrs. Travis
killed a rattlesnake. She stepped on it. A wonder it did not bite her.

A·u·ɢ·u·s·ᴛ

· Sᴀᴛ 9.   I did plow 40 rows of cotton. That was done so quickly I like to
have forgotten about it. . . .

Fri: 30... I made up my mind that I would get me a tractor. I traded the four (4) head of stock in on a $450.00 Farmall F-12.... They allowed me $150.00 for stock, tools and harness. The first time I have been out of stock since December, 1912.

·Wed 13.   . . . I strained my grape mash and put it in a keg. I have a 10 gal.
   keg full. I used 20# sugar. . . . The wine is working off nicely. . . .

O·c·t·o·b·e·R

·Thurs 30.   The rain started falling after we had gone to bed last night
   and rained near all night and rained at different times till noon. Then
   snow started falling and is still snowing now, 9 P.M. The first snow that
   I have any record of coming in October. . . .

N·o·v·e·m·b·e·R

·Fri 21.   . . . paid my first tractor note of $51.68. Went up to school house
   and signed up on the farm defence plan.

Farmers signing the Food-for-Freedom pledge indicated the amount and kind
of production to be expected of them in the following year. This practice continued throughout the war and kept Washington officials informed about the
intentions of farmers. When necessary levels were not projected in crucial crops,
price incentives were implemented to stimulate production.

·Wed 26.   We finished the bale by noon. I took bale to Gates Gin, 1890#
   gin wt, 1764# field wt, bale wt 555#, 780# seed, sold at 43.90 per ton,
   $5.67, ginning $2.00, wrapping $7.67, rebate check $7.54. . . .

Cottonseed, which sold for twenty dollars per ton in 1940, was bringing close
to fifty dollars per ton in 1941. Defense spending greatly increased consumer
income, allowing consumers to use fats and oils in greater volume than ever
before. As a result the price of cottonseed oil rose 115 percent from 1940 to 1941,
causing a corresponding rise in the price farmers received for cottonseed (See
Lamb County Leader, Oct. 23, 1941, p. 2).

·Sat 29.   The weather is just as trickey as a domino player. Has been
   cloudy and mistey near all day. . . .

D·e·c·e·m·b·e·R

·Fri 5.   . . . The bookkeeper told me Gates had sold my bale of cotton. I
   saw Gates in Sudan. He told me he sold it for $14.75 or $15.00 per
   hundred lbs. . . .

· Sun 7. . . . During the funeral (Lynn Catt's) Owen Templeton had his pick up radio on and got the news of the Pearl Harbor—Japanese blow up.

· Mon 8. . . . The U.S.A. declared war on Japan at 3:10 p.m. C.S.T. Roosevelt signed the declaration of war at the executive mansion. Miss Rankins, Rep. of Montana, cast the only negative vote in both houses. . . .

Jeanette Rankin, Democratic congresswoman from Montana, was also among the few who voted against the 1917 declaration of war against Germany.

· Tues 9. . . . The war news is real bad. Japan is still trying to slip up on U.S. again. I think all Japs that is not proven good ought to be rounded up and cut their heads off. . . .

This is written by the same man who thought the 1936 execution of Hauptmann, for kidnapping and murdering the Lindbergh baby, was legalized murder. The entry illustrates the emotional response to fear, especially fear of the invasion of one's homeland. Newspapers of the time contained articles about gas masks for people living in coastal areas and finding protection from air raids. This was useful information because invasion of the U.S. seemed possible after Pearl Harbor; however, it also intensified feelings of fear. Fear was then used effectively to mobilize and unify the general population for a united front in the war.

· Wed 10. . . . Since 8 a.m. 8 or 9 long army trains have passed loaded with men and equipment, trucks & trailers. The war hum is in the air and people are real mad about the double crossing that Japan gave United States. Dirty.

· Thurs 11. . . . The troop trains came by to day, 5 or 6. . . .

· Tues 16. . . . They have out quite a few hundred pounds on the 6th bale. I believe now I will get 7 bales. . . .

· Sat 20. We were off to Clovis early. Sold cream for 33¢ per lb. Eggs were down to 25¢ cash or 27¢ trade. I bought two qts of whiskey. One for a Mr. Stapleton of Sudan and one for my self. $2.25 per qt. We bought some grocieries at the Safeway chain store. Mr. Milam came by and I gave him a drink. He gave us some more of the frozen venison.

· Sat 27. They had the wiring ready for the meter by noon. We went up to Muleshoe and bought a few extra appliances. Brought out the meter. The tempo[rary] inspector passed on the job, with a few minor adjustments, which we had to go to town to get. The $2.50 inspection fee and other extras has run the bill up to $22.80 [$17.25 for materials]. Mr. Perry turned the juice on and we have nice bright lights now. Bill and wife have gone down to Bud's. Arlois and Jim plan to go home tomorrow. In all we have had a very nice Christmas. Bud came up for a while Christmas Day. Cold all day. My pen went out. Will have to send it to the Shaffer Co. for adjustment.

The Rural Electrification Administration, established in 1935 to bring electricity to rural areas, was placed under the direction of the Secretary of Agriculture in 1939. It was only a lending agency. Cooperatives were formed to borrow funds, construct, and operate rural electric systems. In addition to raising the standard of living for farm people, electricity also played a major role in improving rural community life. Churches, schools, and community centers could be used after dark. Lights and controlled heat also enabled rural schools to equal urban schools in student benefits. DeLoach received electricity from the Bailey County Electric Cooperative, which was organized in 1938 (See Robert T. Beall, "Rural Electrification," in *Farmers in a Changing World: Yearbook of Agriculture, 1940*, pp. 790–809; Bailey County Electric Cooperative Association, Records, Reference File, SWC).

· SUN 28. . . . We went to town for some dope for the hens. Have lost two. The produce man said they had the chicken pox. Well the lights and gas heater sure makes a snug room. They come pretty high, but maybe we can meet the bills.

1·9·4·2

Agricultural prices reached a record high, and American farmers pulled out all the stops, even tailoring their output to suit the need. They shifted rapidly from the usual exports of cotton and wheat to meat, eggs, dairy products, and oil crops. Yet demand outstripped supply, and civilian restrictions were necessary to ensure adequate food for military requirements and lend-lease purchases. Americans were frustrated by rationing, especially when they had more money to spend on food and consumer items than at any previous time in their lives.

J·A·N·U·A·R·Y

· THURS 8.   . . . I went to town for a while. I will have to quit going to town if I have no business. Can't get any more new tires now. Will have to have my old ones recapped. All rubber is going to Government war equipment, I guess. That is what it says. . . .

One of the effects of war in the Pacific was the loss of Philippine rubber imports, causing tire rationing. Lamb County received thirty-eight car and seventy-five truck tires in January. Farmers were eligible to apply for truck tires and tubes to carry farm products to market (*Lamb County Leader*, Jan. 8, 1942, p. 11 and Jan. 29, 1942, p. 5).

· WED 21.   . . . We went to wash this forenoon. While at the wash house, Mr. & Mrs. Litton (They operate the Helpy-Selfy wash house) gave me

213

a big ledger for my diary. It is so much larger than my other ledgers that I will have to fix a place to keep it. However, it will be some time before I will need it as I will use this book till it is finished. . . .

· SAT 24.   One year ago today I smoked my last cigarette. I did not know when I said I would smoke no more that I would do it, but I have not used tobacco in any way since. . . .

· WED 28.   . . . Almeda stays out in the wind and sun with me all the time. She rides the tractor and says she is my tractor driver. She sure does eat when she comes to the table at night and she is ready to go to bed when she finishes her supper.

· FRI 30.   A northwest wind started blowing early. Some sand changed ownership. I rigged up the trailer and took the hog to Sudan. Sold him for $11.40. No, that was tops. My hog was too heavy for a top hog. 11.15¢ per lb. is what I got. 265 pounds, $29.54 [*top weight was 200–40 pounds*]. I put my tax money (state & county) in bank, $90.22. I paid $14.85 school tax. Not too cold tonight.

F·E·B·R·U·A·R·Y

· SUN 1.   Another birthday, 62 years young. Well, I can't kid anyone, only my self. I am not the young buck I was 28 or 20 years ago, but I can still carry on as usual. . . .

· THURS 5.   . . . I read in *Star-Telegram* of a woman in or near Charlotte, N.C. (Mint Hill, N.C., Mrs. L. B. Hough) who has kept a diary for 31 years. I will have kept this diary 28 years the 28th of March, 1942. I would like to talk to her and see her books. . . .

· SUN 8.   I worked on my tractor for a while this forenoon. I think I have it now where it will plow like I want it to. I took a bath and cleaned up P.M. We stayed home all day. Save rubber and gas. Help defense. The hens helped out today to the tune of 80 eggs. Maybe so we will be getting 100 eggs per day soon.

Texas egg producers were asked to produce at least fifteen hundred more train carloads of eggs in 1942 than they did in 1941. Eggs were purchased by the government, broken, and put through a fast drying process, and shipped to Britain under the lend-lease program. Lamb County farmers did their part, selling over eight hundred cases in two days to only one of several Littlefield produce companies (*Lamb County Leader*, Jan. 29, 1942, p. 10 and Feb. 5, 1942, p. 12).

· Fri 20. . . . The gas man did get here today. 55 gal. @ 9¢ per gal. 4¢ per gal. rebate for tractors.

Gas tax, used mainly to maintain Texas highways, was rebated to farmers because tractors were not driven on the highways. The average farmer received from fifty to seventy dollars annually in rebates (See "Down at Austin," *Progressive Farmer* 58, no. 3 [Mar., 1943], p. 9).

· Sat 21. . . . We all went to town this late P.M. Sold 56½ doz eggs. Only collected for 53½ doz. The grocery man counted us out of 3 doz. 25¢ trade, 24¢ cash, cream $1.75 . . . the egg controversy [*being cheated*] coming up sure does upset me.

M·A·R·C·H

· Tues 10. . . . Bill made his Tuesday call. He did not seem so down in the dumps about the war. No use for one to be bothered about it.
· Fri 13. I helped Sallie and Dot cull the hens [*culls were used as fryers, or for stewing*] and cut off one wing. That is the wing feathers, to keep them from flying over the garden fence. . . .
· Mon 16. . . . Went to town near night to pay Sallie's, Dot's, and Almeda's insurance. I left the money, $1.00, at Jackie Wilkinson's barber shop. I also told McCoy I left it. . . .
· Mon 23. . . . I went over to the A.A.A. office at Amherst. I wanted to see about the peanut planting. I signed up to plant 5 R[*ows*].

Peanuts were considered an important war crop, and Texas farmers were asked to plant a million acres to supply badly needed oil. More than half the world's supply of fats and oils was in Japanese hands, causing a critical shortage for the Allies during World War II.

A·P·R·I·L

· Sun 12. . . . I had a fight with one of my cows early this A.M. The cow won out in round 1. She mashed my left hand against a cross beam. Boy did it hurt.
· Fri 17. We fixed up some new nests in the laying house, but I think the hens will not use the new nests. They do not like a nest that is swinging.

· SAT 18. I think I will move all those new nests out and put the old ones back in laying house. We only gathered 65 eggs today. They break and eat the eggs. I caught three hens eating eggs. Only sold 56 doz. . . . I bought another 100# sack of the concentrate $4.10.

M · A · Y

· TUES 12. I planted watermelons this forenoon. I guess about four (4) A. Little over half of them are Black Diamond melons, bal. Tender Sweets. . . .

Black Diamond watermelons are large red-meated melons and Tender Sweets have yellow meat. Both varieties are popular in Texas.

· WED 13. I started in to plant cotton. I planted about 8 or 10 A. Mr. Wittman brought the gilt over. Boy, I could take 3 $1.00 bills and wrap her up. I can grow out if hogs stay up [*DeLoach paid $30 for the very young gilt*].

Farmers were asked to plant full cotton allotments. The percentage of acres planted in cotton in Texas had declined to 82 percent of the allotment in 1941. Low cotton prices, in comparison with other agricultural commodities, and scarcity of laborers at harvesttime accounted for the reduction (See *Lamb County Leader*, Mar. 26, 1942, p. 8).

· WED 27. . . . I paid Ball in A.A.A. Office $1.20 for shelling my 200# of spanish peanuts. They (AAA) Office are sending to Portales, N.M. Friday. . . .

Peanuts sold for fifty-five to ninety dollars per ton, depending on the grade. In 1942, Lamb County farmers grossed approximately $150,000 for peanuts, more than any previous time in history (*Lamb County Leader*, Dec. 3, 1942, p. 1).

J · U · N · E

· THURS 18. . . . I stopped in Sudan. I wanted to see about the sugar deal. I bought my 4 pounds. No. 4 stamp was used. . . .

Sugar was the first food to be rationed during World War II. All sugar sales in the United States were suspended at midnight April 27, 1942, for approximately one week, then rationing began. Initially each person was allowed half a pound per week, but when allotments were increased in varying amounts, for canning, the program became so flexible that it was difficult to administer (See Office of Price Administration, *Sugar Rationing Regulations*, Rationing Order no. 3; *Lamb County Leader*, July 16, 1942, p. 5).

J·U·L·Y

· FRI 3. . . . The Chick Overton cow bloated up. I went to see if Pope knew just what to do. He said tie a stick in her mouth. I also went to see Mr. Milam, but he was gone from home. I tied a stick in her mouth, let it stay 30 or 40 minutes. She was OK. . . .

· TUES 28. . . . Had first mess of roasting ears. They sure were good and sweet. Will have plenty of them in a few days. I am real tired.

A·U·G·U·S·T

· SAT 15. . . . We were eating dinner just before starting to town. Some one drove up and it [*was*] Harold, Dellie and Wayne. They did not let any one know they were coming. . . .

· WED 19. Harold & Dellie came up and said they had bought the place south of Bud's place. He also said that if the trade went through he had rented it to Bud. . . .

During the war years, when wages were unusually high and consumer items were restricted, Harold put his money in land. Bud was close enough to farm it, and the high price of agricultural commodities helped make land payments.

S·E·P·T·E·M·B·E·R

· THURS 17. . . . The F.S.A. supervisor Phil Howard with offices at Little- field called this P.M. I made application for $310.00 to build a chicken house and put in a water system. Wind mill, tank and pipe to put water in house, in hog lot, and out to chicken yard.

The Farm Security Administration, F.S.A., was established under the Bank- head-Jones Farm Tenant Act of 1937. Its emphasis shifted to the Food-for- Freedom drive by making food production, rather than the rehabilitation of low income families, a top priority. Loans, limited to $500, could be used to purchase supplies and equipment or make necessary repairs. The money was lent to small farmers to help them increase their production of meat, milk, eggs, fruits, and vegetables. Increasing these commodities had a dual benefit. The standard of living improved for the farmer's family, and a substantial amount that was produced was available for sale. The Department of Agriculture relied heavily on small farmers for help in reaching established goals for food and fiber. Large farms, because of labor and equipment shortages, actually produced less in 1942 than in 1941. In contrast, small farmers usually had adequate labor within the family, but were short of capital to invest in the means of production. During the first six months of 1942, $78,332 were loaned to Lamb County farmers, bringing to 196 the total number of farmers in the county served by this agency.

The regional director for the Farm Security Administration reported record-breaking collections from Texas borrowers, most of whom were considered poor credit risks by other lending agencies. DeLoach made the final payment on his loan in 1948 (See USDA, *Report of the Secretary of Agriculture, 1942*, pp. 206–209; *Lamb County Leader*, Jan. 25, 1940, p. 6, Apr. 24, 1941, p. 1, Apr. 16, 1942, p. 5; *Semi-Weekly Farm News*, Apr. 5, 1940, p. 1).

- SUN 20. . . . Bud & Ida came up for a pop call.
- MON 28. I felt so bad that we decided I would go to Hospital at Amherst. The Co-op. We did and we also took membership. Cost $50.00 for the four of us. I paid $10.00 on the $50.00 and paid $6.00 dues till the first of December. Then the dues will be $25.00 per year. Well the Doc gave me a bunch of medicine. I went my first time to a hospital.

Texas' first cooperative hospital was built in Amherst, Texas, and by 1943 membership had grown to a thousand families. The co-op received no government grants or loans; each family paid a $50.00 lifetime membership in addition to annual fees, to cover the cost of the building and equipment. Twenty-eight rooms accommodated fifty to sixty patients at a time. Two doctors and ten nurses, hired on a salary basis, staffed the hospital. Patients paid $2.50 per day for a semi-private room and $3.00 for a private one. A major operation, such as an appendectomy, cost about $20.00, maternity cases were $10.00; a minor operation, such as a tonsillectomy, was $10.00. Lower costs encouraged people to seek preventative medical care, rather than waiting until serious problems developed. The cooperative movement was widely accepted in Lamb County, where 80 percent of the population was rural. By 1943 there were eleven cooperative gins, a consumer cooperative, a rural electric cooperative, three co-op frozen food lockers, and a certified seed grower's cooperative (See C. E. Bowles,

"Lamb County Pioneers in Health Co-op," *Progressive Farmer* 58, no. 7 [July, 1943], p. 9).

· Tues 29.   . . . I did go to town for a little while. I had to take the peas to the elevator. Sold 339# at $3.10 per hundred. . . .

DeLoach planted black-eyed peas to add nitrogen to his soil.

The biggest cotton crop in Lamb County history was ripening in the fields. Ideal growing conditions and good subsoil moisture, following a wet year in 1941, allowed cotton plants to produce a deep root system that could easily sustain them between rains. Throughout the summer, blooms appeared as if by magic, and in the fall, heavy, loaded stalks bent nearly to the ground. High prices rounded out a picture of prosperity. The fly in the ointment, however, was a shortage of labor for harvesting since military duty and defense industries drained laborers out of rural areas.

O·c·t·o·b·e·r

· Wed 7.   . . . Bud came up going to Littlefield to see about getting some tires so I went with him. We got the certificate, however Bud said he would go back to Littlefield tonight to see if he could get 3 tires.

Local rationing boards were given final jurisdiction for issuing certificates to eligible persons (such as farmers) for purchasing tires.

· Fri 9.   . . . We killed 11 chickens, dressed them, and I took them to Locker box. Payed $3.00 for 3 months rent on the frozen food locker box. Don't think we will put any more chickens in box. The cartons are too bulky.
· Mon 26.   I took a hog to the frozen food locker. They will kill it tomorrow. . . . Bill and Noma Jean came in just now. Bill has quit his job and volunteered for the Army. He will be stationed at the Lubbock Air Base. I think that was the thing for him to do. He knows now just what he is going to do. He will go to Ft. Sill, Okla. for the inoculating. Will be the 3 days. He will be two that has been dressed up for the U.S. Army of ours, H. G. and Bill. An account of Harold's induction is found in Book #2 of my diary. 1920 (spring).
· Fri 30.   . . . Sallie & I pulled cotton all p.m. I pulled 231 lbs, she pulled 131 lbs. My hands are tired tonight.

N·O·V·E·M·B·E·R

· THURS 19.   . . . We (Sallie) went to town. Sallie to wash, I to do the gas
rationing act. I could not do any thing since I did not have my
glasses. . . .

Gas rationing went into effect November 22, with a basic ration of slightly
under four gallons per week. Automobile owners registered at filling stations
and were required to certify that they owned no more than five tires (See *Lamb
County Leader*, Oct. 22, 1942, p. 1).

· TUES 24.   We pulled cotton all day, or near all day. We finished the thick
cotton on the west side. Near 1100# on the 3rd bale off that 3 or 3¼ A.
Made good cotton.

· WED 25.   I went to town to see if I could get someone to help me pull the
balance of my cotton. Also to see if I could get a combine to cut some
feed. I am afraid a high wind will put it on the ground. I could not find
any help for either job. . . .

Labor shortages during World War II forced many Lamb County schools to
close for most of November, allowing students to help harvest the bumper crop.
Students did not complain, as earnings ranged from fifteen to twenty dollars
per week. However, cancellation of the Thanksgiving and Christmas holidays,
to make up the lost time, was disappointing (See *County Wide News*, Nov. 5,
1942, p. 8).

· MON 30.   I was up early. Met Overton in Sudan and we started to Littlefield. We stopped at Amherst to get sacks for our peanut crop. I purchased 25 at 20¢ each. . . . I think I bought just half enough. We went
on to Littlefield. Signed up for the extra gas and tractor gas. I had letter from Farm Security Administration stating my loan application had
been approved. That means a trip to Olton. I went over to Richard
Overton's for a team. I cut some maize. . . .

The AAA office in Amherst, Texas, was the agent for the Southwestern Peanut Growers Association in handling peanuts produced in Lamb County. A
government-licensed grader was on hand to grade the peanuts. Producers were
issued a marketing card labeled "oil peanuts," because marketing quotas were
in effect for peanuts.

Tues 24... We pulled cotton all day, or near all day.
We finished the thick cotton on the west side. Near
1100# on the 3rd bale off that 3 or 3½ A.
Made good cotton.

D·e·c·e·m·b·e·r

· Mon 7. One year since "Pearl Harbor." Lots of changes since then. . . .
   Bill came up tonight. He had a 7 day leave. He will have to return to
   his base tomorrow.
· Sat 12. I had to go to town for some meat. Took the cream to town. 50
   test, $0.50 per lb, $10.00. . . .
· Thurs 17. We were off to Littlefield early. I got the loan money from U.S.
   Improvement Loan, $290.00. . . .

DeLoach applied for a $310 loan. Apparently interest and processing charges
accounted for the difference. The manager of the Lamb County FSA office reported that borrowers in the county increased their production of a number
of foods. This increase provided needed supplies of meat, lard, and eggs for the
Food-for-Freedom campaign, a basic part of national defense. In addition, these
people learned the value of keeping better records of their farm and home operations (See *Lamb County Leader*, Jan. 22, 1942, p. 10).

· Mon 21. . . . Milam & I went to Littlefield this P.M. I had to go by Amherst for my peanut marketing card. We will load the Milam truck with
   my peanuts. Will take them to Olton tomorrow if nothing happens. I
   think they will be dryed out.
· Thurs 31. I went over and helped Milam unload the feed. We came
   home and loaded up the peanuts. Corey Ruby helped us. We were in
   Olton by 1:30 P.M. Had lunch and tested and graded the nuts. They
   graded $80.00 per ton. Oil 50 ct., gas $4.25, eats $1.25, sacks $14.40,
   threshing $22.28, seed $10.00. These items are to be charged against the
   $199.40 I received for peanuts. . . .

1·9·4·3

Food, food, and more food. The needs of the Allies and consumers seemed inexhaustible, but American farmers were equal to the demands. Even though they were using old equipment, inexperienced "hands," and hauling their crops to market on worn out tires, they met their quotas.

J·a·n·u·a·r·y

· WED 13.   I was off to Littlefield early. I did not have to have the tires inspected the second time. Cisco made out my papers for one new tire and one recapped tire. The new tire will cost me $11+. The recapped tire $6.00. I came back by Sudan. I payed Higginbotham & Bartlett for the Red wood overhead tank $60.00, drawn on the "Special fund." The first check on that Government money [*Farm Security Administration loan*].

· THURS 14.   . . . I went to Sudan for the Negroes. Brought out 5. One pulled 180 lbs and quit to catch a bus to Clovis, N.M. I paid him his $1.82 and $4.10 that one of the other Negroes owed him. When I took them back to Sudan tonight another one had to have his money. So I paid him $3.00. Boy these negroes can wart one. I do not know how to handle the black boys. . .

A shortage of workers was one of the farmer's greatest problems in World War II. Farm leaders warned Congress that two hundred thousand more work-

223

ers were needed in 1943 than were available in 1942 if established goals were to be reached. Black pastors used the pulpit to encourage blacks to work in the harvest by reminding them that if white Americans lost the war so would black Americans (See Eugene Butler, "What's New in Agriculture?" *Progressive Farmer* 58, no. 2 [Feb., 1943], p. 4; "Negroes and the Harvest," *Progressive Farmer* 58, no. 11, [Nov., 1943], p. 9).

F·E·B·R·U·A·R·Y

· Mon 1. Well another birthday, 63 years. Yes, sometimes I feel my age. Like today. We ground feed quite a lot. I feel tired and my eyes hurt me. . . .

Older farmers worked at a grueling pace during 1942 and 1943. Many who were ready to reduce their workload could not do so because younger men were in military service (See "Labor and Other 1944 Farm Needs," *Progressive Farmer* 58, no. 11 [Nov., 1943], p. 5).

· Tues 16. We loaded up the calf and we went to the farm sale at Mr. Dunagan's, near Circleback. I bought a cow and calf. Red 4 yr old cow, with white face heifer calf at side, $127.00. I sold my bull calf for $43.00, com. on my side $2.15, left a bal. of 40.85. . . . That was the highest sale I ever attended.

Dairy products brought 21 percent more income in 1942 than they had in 1941. This was largely due to substantial governmental purchases to meet military and lend-lease requirements. The price of breeding stock also rose (See USDA, *Report of the Secretary of Agriculture, 1943*, pp. 148–51).

· Wed 17. We decided to kill and dress the roosters. Killed 11. Cooked them and will make hot tamales and chili. . . .

M·A·R·C·H

· Wed 10. Mr. Bowers came over. Said he would take his tractor to work for me, but we had to go to town to sign up for the work sheet for 1943. . . . Bill came up from Lubbock Air Base. He has a 3 day furlough. Bud, Ida and Robert called for a while. Mr. & Mrs. Robert Overton, Mrs. Archie and two little ones called for a late bed time call.

We sure do appreciate their calls. We played Monoploy till 1:30 A.M. this morning. We sure did not sleep much.

The Farm Plan Work Sheet "mobilized" farmers for war. With the help of county committeemen, farmers participating in the Agricultural Adjustment Administration commodity adjustment program were required to list the 1942 acres of each crop and the number of livestock; their 1943 crop and livestock goals; and what was needed in the way of shelter, fencing, machinery, fertilizer, credit, labor, and housing in order to reach these 1943 goals. Secretary of Agriculture Wickard used this information to persuade the president that as a "war industry," agriculture must have adequate supplies and supports if food production was to reach the desired level. In response, American farmers again broke all production records, marking 1943 as a year of phenomenal livestock production (See Butler, "What's New in Agriculture?" *Progressive Farmer* 58, no. 2, [Feb., 1943], p. 4; USDA, *Report of the Secretary of Agriculture, 1943*, p. 12).

· WED 24. ... Had a card from Sallie stating the birth of a girl named Glenda Lee Coward. Born 2:30 A.M. Monday 22. All doing OK. Sallie said she would be home soon.

A·P·R·I·L

· FRI 2.   I went over to Milam's to help him shear his goats. Boy that is one job. I never sheared a sheep or goat. We sheared 8 and I was willing to call it a day. . . .
· TUES 6.   I worked near all day on the clothes closets. Put up two [*indicating farmers' increased affluence during World War II*]. I did not hang the doors. . . .
· MON 12.   ... I took out 50% insurance on my cotton. Government cotton insurance. Made my farm acreage allotment. . . .

The Federal Crop Insurance Corporation, established under the Agricultural Adjustment Act of 1938, insured only wheat farmers until 1942. When wartime demands emphasized the importance of all food and fiber crops, cotton producers were also allowed to insure their crops against natural disasters. Coverage was for 50–75 percent of the average yield. Generally, farmers insured their crops only when risks were exceptionally high, and losses soon exceeded premiums. Congress withdrew funding in 1944, but re-instated it, with modifications, in 1945. Crop insurance was another source of credit for replanting expenses after drought, hail, or insect damage. The contract also became collateral for loans to meet current farming expenses. County committees wrote the policies, measured the acreage, adjusted losses, and settled the claims. This was a practical arrangement because committee members understood local practices and conditions (See USDA, *Report of the Secretary of Agriculture, 1943*, pp. 231–35; Benedict, *Farm Policies*, pp. 381–84).

· Fri 23.   I worked all day on the hen house. . . . I will have a better hen house than I thought I would when I started in to remodel the old one. The way it stands now is 30 ft long, 12 ft wide, 7 ft high, front, 5 ft back. . . .

· Sat 24.   . . . Sallie sold 27 dozen eggs. Dot 6½ dozen, total $10.38 at 31¢ per doz. . . .

Increased consumer demand, made possible by high wages in defense industries, played a key role in the high prices farmers received for their commodities. In 1943 egg consumption was 345 eggs per person, compared with 320 eggs in 1942; chicken consumption rose to 28 pounds per person from 22 pounds during 1942 (See D. F. King, "Around My Chicken Yard," *Progressive Farmer* 58, no. 12 [Dec., 1943], p. 43).

· Mon 26.   . . . loaded 4 head of my hogs. 3 of the black ones and one of the black and white spotted gilts. . . . The 4 head brought $109.35. I bought two U.S. War Savings Bonds of the $25.00 denomination. Made to me and Sallie. . . .

Lamb County was charged with raising $428,000 during the month of April, 1943. This was the Second War Loan drive. Residents were encouraged to consume less of everything and devote at least 10 percent of their income to the purchase of war bonds. Farmers were asked to invest a certain sum for crops and animals they were raising. They were also encouraged to buy War Bonds as a hedge against the deflation that would likely follow the war. Equipment, being worked to the last nut, bolt, and bearing, could then be replaced without undue hardship (See *Lamb County Leader*, Apr. 8, 1943, p. 1; "The Farmer's Share in the War Bond Drive," *Progressive Farmer* 58, no. 10 [Oct., 1943], p. 9).

M · A · Y

· Thurs 6.   . . . "The March of Time" is on now.

"The March of Time" was seen monthly by moviegoers from 1935 to 1951. The newsreel that showed Americans the world and themselves used insightful narrative to bring the events of the day into focus (See Raymond Fielding, *The March of Time, 1935–1951*, pp. 3–26).

· MON 10.   We had a fine rain some time in the night. I went to town for some hen roost lumber and to pay my gas bill (natural). But I for got to pay it and had to make another trip this P.M. $2.15. I had them to put my name on the list that they check on. It is lots of trouble and no trouble to them to write a check for the amount on the 10th of each month. . . .

J·U·N·E

· SUN 13.   I was up early. Went over to Milan's to Dr. Harmon's cow. She had some screwworms. Back home. We got ready and started for Friendship. The Church of Christ had a real nice program and preaching and dinner spread. Seemed like old times when we first built the Friendship Union Church. Lots of big feeds we would have then. That was back in 1928 to 1934. . . .

According to the Department of Agriculture, screwworm infestations in Texas and Oklahoma had reached serious proportions by 1944. Livestock had to be examined regularly for wounds and treated immediately with Smear 62 (See *Progressive Farmer* 59, no. 9 [Sept., 1944], p. 57).

· WED 16.   I plowed in afternoon. I helped Dot hoe in the peanuts in A.M. Just work all the time. Seems I can never catch up. Sallie drove the car from the field to the house. Watch her strut.

J·U·L·Y

· SAT 24.   . . . The thunder and lightening sounds like it might come a big rain. Well it has started falling. We had to move the bed back in the house. It is raining hard now, 10:15 P.M. This one will make the feed and the other crops too, I think.

Beds were moved into the yard for sleeping during summer nights. Nights are cool in an arid region, and the constant breezes of the Plains made sleeping outdoors quite pleasant. Houses that heated up during the day were slow to cool.

A·U·G·U·S·T

DeLoach visited his brother, Ed, in Del Rio, Texas, and helped with the sheep roundup on the ranch. He and Ed also went across the border to shop in Villa Acuna, Mexico.

> · THURS 12. . . . We decided we would go over across the Rio Grande River for a visit. We were over there 2 or 3 hrs. Bought two pairs of lady's hose $2.00 each. They are the nylon, $6.00 to $8.00 in U.S., when one can find them. Also 2 qt of All American whiskey $2.00 per qt. Ed one and me one. That too is $8.00 or $10.00 in U.S.

It was almost impossible to buy nylon hose during World War II. When word got around that a shipment had arrived long lines formed at stores, and scuffles were not uncommon as women pushed and shoved each other to get their hands on this scarce item. Prior to World War II, silk stockings were used by 90 percent of American women, but after the Pearl Harbor attack far eastern imports ceased, and cotton stockings, the alternative, were never popular.

> · FRI 20. . . . Picked up some canned goods the women put up at the U.S. cannery. Sallie & I went to Sudan. On way back home I blew out my recapped tire. I am now on the rim. I can't get a truck to move my melons. They will all be ready to go in a few days.

In 1943, the cannery that was located in Littlefield, Texas, was one of the busiest places in Lamb County as farm families and townspeople processed the vegetables grown in their Victory gardens. Fifteen percent of the finished product went to the cannery, while the remaining 85 percent belonged to the producer if labor was furnished by the producer. If labor was furnished by the cannery, workers and producers divided the 85 percent equally. Anyone willing to help could come to the cannery and work for a percentage of the vegetables canned. Workers, producers, and the cannery each furnished their respective percentage of the containers. Food processed in this manner supplied many Lamb County families and at the same time allowed food processed in commercial channels to be used in the war effort (See *Lamb County Leader*, July 25, 1940, p. 1 and *County Wide News*, Aug. 6, 1942, p. 10).

· SAT 21.   I went over and told Milam my trouble about the tires. He had
the one we got over at Burn's, so now I have two of his tires on my
car. . . .

S·E·P·T·E·M·B·E·R

· FRI 17.   . . . Bud came up and we started for Littlefield early. I received
two certificates for tires. One #1, one #3. I found #1 in Littlefield,
$13.01, one inner-liner $4.95. . . .

O·C·T·O·B·E·R

· FRI 8.   . . . I went to Littlefield to see about my tube certificate and to see
about the canning sugar. We got 70 pounds of sugar [*to can fruit*]. . . .
WED 20.   . . . I wanted to go to Littlefield so Milam went with me. I could
not get my certificate for a third line tire changed. I will have to get a
"C" gas card to get a 1st line tire. . . .

The basic ration was the "A" book that contained 48 coupons. Drivers who
could prove to their local rationing board that they needed additional occupa-
tional mileage, in excess of the basic 470 miles, were issued "C" ration books.
Farmers received extra coupons in order to haul their crops to market (See Office of Price Administration, *Gasoline Rationing Instructions, July 1942*, pp. 8–9).

· MON 25.   I went up town early to see Jess Salter [*chairman of the local ration board*] about my "C" card (gas). He took my application and will
recommend a "C" card for me when the ration board meets soon at
Littlefield.

N·O·V·E·M·B·E·R

· MON 1.   . . . I went to town to see if I could either get some cotton pullers
or sell the cotton in the field. I could find neither. The Andrews came
over and pulled cotton today. . . .

The drain of young men for active duty during World War II created a shortage of agricultural labor. There were about 200,000 fewer Texas farm workers
in 1943 than in 1939. The fullest use of all available people supplied less than
half the workers needed on the South Plains (See Motheral, Metzler, and Du-

coff, *Cotton and Manpower,* p. 11; C. Hohn, "Texas Farm Labor," *Progressive Farmer* 59, no. 3 [Mar., 1944], p. 5).

· WED 10. I went to town for a while this early A.M. I did think I would get a sled (cotton puller) and pull the balance of my cotton, but the pullers came in at noon. . . .

As long as farmers could secure laborers at harvesttime, interest in mechanical harvesters was generally lacking. During the labor-scarce war years, however, combines and homemade mechanical cotton harvesters grew in popularity. Cotton seed was selling for $60.00 per ton, and it cost $21.90 to gin and wrap two bales.

· FRI 12. I took Sallie to town early to get her hair fixed. I also got my suit. We came home, made ready and went to Littlefield. We had some pictures made of ourselves, $6.75.
· SUN 14. . . . We went to see Attaway the tire man. I bought a new 600 × 16 synthetic rubber tire, $18.17. But I now have 3 tires that are all you might say are new. I took Milligan's tire home tonight. . . .
· SAT 20. . . . I paid Andrews for his cotton pulling. He claimed I owed him $34.41. I could do nothing only pay him. Those last 3 bales cost me about $75.00 to get it pulled. . . .

In 1944, the estimated cost of machine-stripping cotton was six dollars per bale, saving approximately $18 per bale over hand harvesting. A two-row, tractor-mounted stripper, costing approximately nine hundred dollars, would pay for itself with the first fifty bales of cotton. A small farmer, such as DeLoach, who produced less than ten bales per year would have had a difficult time paying for this equipment unless he did custom work for other farmers (See Eugene Butler, "Mechanical Cotton Harvesting," *Progressive Farmer* 59, no. 10 [Oct., 1944], pp. 14, 29; Eugene Butler, "Mechanical Harvesting Costs," *Progressive Farmer* 59, no. 11 [Nov., 1944], p. 22).

· SUN 21. Today is Bill's birthday. We did not get the photos in time to send them so he could have them on his birthday. However, he will have them and the box of goodies in a few days. . . .
· WED 24. I was up by 6 A.M. I went to town, hired Pat (Oh hell, I can't think of his name.) We loaded up and took off. I sold the peanuts at Amherst, 5888 lbs. at 7½ per pound, check $441.60. . . . I paid him $7.50 for hauling. The peanuts graded #1, test 76%. . . . [*DeLoach produced 83 sacks of peanuts.*]

1943

D·E·C·E·M·B·E·R

· Mon 6. . . . The three bales brought $239.44. I still have 3 more out and one in the field. . . .
· Wed 8. . . . I went by Gabel's gin for a warehouse receipt, but they had sent it in to town. Loan middling 13/16 staple, 15.19¢ per lb. $65.77. . . .
· Fri 10. . . . I went to town this late P.M. to send a war bond to Bill and Noma Jean. . . . Bill is now stationed Altus, Okla.
· Wed 15. . . . I paid my installment on the U.S. Farm Security Loan $68.00 (Sixty-eight dollars) + interest, total $70.31.
· Sat 18. . . . Harold & Dellie sent me a new ledger, however I will not need it for some time as I am only about ½ through this one.
· Mon 27. The cold snap hit here some time last night. The whole face of the earth was covered with snow and ice and the cold wind sure was blowing. . . .

1·9·4·4

High commodity prices and good production records helped mask the cost of wartime prosperity. Increased taxation and rationing irritated the farmers' independent spirit, but in time they realized that everything had a price.

J·A·N·U·A·R·Y

· MON 3.   . . . I called at bank to see what my balance was, $313.02. So I decided I would go to Amherst and take up two of my land notes, which I did. Note #7, $181.54, principle and interest, note #8 $117.88, total for the two notes, $299.42. . . .

During 1943–44 the Federal Land Bank of Houston recorded the largest payoff in its twenty-six year history. Across the nation, farm mortgage debt declined, which was a reversal of the trend during World War I. For the first time in over two decades, farmers had discretionary income, and with consumer items in limited supply they began doubling up on land payments (See Sterling C. Evans, "The Land Boom Is Here," *Progressive Farmer* 59, no. 5 [May, 1944], p. 50).

· TUES 4.   I took the Bess cow, the Overton calf, and the red heifer I got from the Dunagan sale last Feb. to the Fisher sale. I only got $80.35 for the 3 head. This time last year they would have sold for $150, but that is the way things go. . . .

· FRI 7.   . . . The radio said two or three times today that this is the worst blizzard in 43 years or since 1898 (Feb), but the cold Friday and Saturday in February, 1899 was the correct time, but this was not a comparison to that blizzard. I was working out of Midland, Texas at that time as a cow hand and lots of cattle froze to death and lots of them lived, but their feet were frozen off. That also happened in Jan, 1918. Lots of cattle froze. All in the Southwest. . . .

· Fri 14.   . . . I was asked if I would take $75.00 per A. for my little place. I need to do something else for I have lost all interest in the farm and besides we ought to be near some town where Dot could be at work. She will have to be by herself some time and she had better begin to make her own way.

Even though land prices increased 15 percent during 1943–44, land was still a good investment considering the value of farm commodities. Farmers were urged, however, to remember the drop in agricultural prices after World War I and exercise caution about overextending themselves. Unlike the non-farm buyers, who were responsible for 36 percent of all land purchases, farmers had to depend on the earning capacity of the land to meet operating expenses and liquidate indebtedness (Evans, "The Land Boom Is Here," *Progressive Farmer* 59, no. 5 [May, 1944], p. 50).

· Wed 19.   . . . I went over to Mr. Buckner's south place for his sled bolling machine. Think maybe I can pull the balance of my cotton tomorrow. . . .
· Fri 21.   I finished the cotton pulling. I think maybe I have as much as 2000 lbs. . . .

F·E·B·R·U·A·R·Y

· Tues 8.   We had to be out at the base [*Altus, Oklahoma*] by 9 A.M. . . . The Graduating Class had 234 fine young men. A fine looking body of young men. Bill had to stay at the base for assignment, but they will assign him when he returns on the 17th. We had dinner at the Rainbow. We, Sallie & I decided to stay over till tomorrow.
· Sat 12.   . . . Bill & Noma Jean came in about 6:30 P.M. . . . They will be with us till the 16th inst. Bill has just dressed in his flying toggs. Boy! all that make up is a load, but they do not have to walk with it. Bill gave me a pr. of shoes. They are good ones. Thanks.
· Mon 21.   I went up town early to get Bud to come out and help me load my hogs. I have seen the day I could load them alone. He and Robert

came out. We loaded 4. They weighed 530 lbs at 8¢ Check $42.40. . . .

· FRI 25. I did not plow much today. Was too cold. Well, I just did not want to plow.

M·A·R·C·H

· MON 6. I went down town early to sign up my work sheet for my farm. . . .

In 1944 the AAA was under attack for insisting that farmers sign up for the Triple A program or risk losing their gas rations and draft deferments. Work sheets were used by Selective Service boards in allotting deferments and by ration boards in making gasoline allowances. Because of the charges, the House Agriculture Appropriation Bill was amended. The amendment denied salary payments to any person demanding that a farmer join the Triple A "as a condition of draft deferment, or for the granting of a priority certificate for any rationed article or commodity" (See Eugene Butler, "What's New in Agriculture?" *Progressive Farmer* 59, no. 5 [May, 1944], p. 6).

· FRI 24. . . . I popped off and sold my red cow and her baby calf. I said I would take $100.00 for them. A cow buyer came out and looked at her and came back and gave me a check for the $100.00 for her and calf. I did not want to milk her and I decided I would sell her. Cold.

A·P·R·I·L

· WED 5. I worked till noon then I had to go for some more dope, some of the tile and underground pipe, total $21.55. This bath will cost aplenty before I get finished, but we will have it to enjoy.

· THURS 20. . . . About 6 P.M. I declared the bath duly opened and qualified to take care of all parties of this family. . . .

M·A·Y

· FRI 5. . . . Went out to Tim King's for 100 lbs of Martin maize seed, $2.82. . . .

In 1943 W. P. Martin was recognized as *Progressive Farmer*'s "Man of the Year" for his development of Martin's Combine milo maize. During the late 1930s

May to August, 1944... Planted quite a bunch of Martin Maize.

Martin began planting Wheatland maize because its straight neck made it adaptable to combine harvesting. Wheatland's one big drawback, however, was its vulnerability to Pythium root rot. In 1936 Martin found one green plant in a field that was withered and blasted by the disease, and from this one head he developed a supply of seed that was resistant to root rot. By 1943 he was selling over two million pounds of Martin's Combine maize seed, which produced uniform plants, three to four feet high, that could be machine harvested at the rate of twelve to fifteen acres a day. This was a big improvement over the old, labor-intensive method of row binding and threshing. Many South Plains farmers found grain sorghums, which often returned thirty to forty dollars an acre, more profitable than cotton that required scarce, high-priced hand labor. This timely development helped assure a plentiful supply of grain sorghums that were widely used to feed the cattle, hogs, and poultry that were so vital to the Allies during World War II (See "Men of the Year in Texas Agriculture," *Progressive Farmer* 59, no. 1 [Jan., 1944], p. 10; Eugene Butler, "How Farmers Are Meeting Wartime Problems," *Progressive Farmer* 58, no. 2 [Feb., 1943], p. 11).

· Sᴀᴛ 6. I got started about 9:30 ᴀ.ᴍ. to planting Martin maize. I planted quite a bunch of it, maybe 10 acres. . . .

DeLoach, Sallie, Dot, Almeda, and Bud and family drove to Big Spring, Texas, where Bill was stationed after graduation. It was their last visit with him before he was shipped to West Palm Beach, Florida, and then overseas.

J·ᴜ·ɴ·ᴇ

· Tᴜᴇs 6. . . . I was out cutting weeds when Sallie called me and said, "The invasion is on." Well, I listened to that for a while. . . . The second invasion of Hitler's Europe. . . .

DeLoach is referring to the invasion of Normandy. Under General Eisenhower's command American and British troops invaded northern France, ultimately routing Hitler's army and leading to German defeat.

· Fʀɪ 30. Nothing to do. Yes, I have plenty to do, but am getting too lazy to do it. . . . I went down town for a while this ᴘ.ᴍ.

J·ᴜ·ʟ·ʏ

· Fʀɪ 21. . . . We had two letters from Bill today. He stated that he had his first mail on the 10th of July since he left Big Spring, Texas. One letter from us and one from his wife, Noma Jean, at Belin N.M. He is still some where in India. Stated it is awful hot and rains quite a lot. [*Bill was a transport pilot in the China-Burma-India Theater.*]

A·ᴜ·ɢ·ᴜ·s·ᴛ

· Wᴇᴅ 9. . . . I went to town this ᴘ.ᴍ. No business, just to shoot the bull with the fellows.

· Tᴜᴇs 22. We received the long looked for letter from Bill. He wrote it the 7th of Aug. All seemed to be OK with him. . . .

· Wᴇᴅ 23. The awful blow hit us about 6 ᴘ.ᴍ. A Mr. Lowrey drove up and said he wanted to speak to me. I went out to his car. He said he had a death message from Washington, D.C. Well, I knew what it was. I had to be a little diplomatic about it, for I knew how Sallie and Dot would take it. I waited to get some neighbor women in before I told them that

Bill had been killed. I got in the car with Mr. Lowrey and went for the two Overton women and Mrs. Pope. Well, when we drove up and Mrs. Pope and Mrs. Overton got out of the car Sallie knew something had happened to Bill. Robert Overton went down to tell Bud. They came right up. Cody Overton took me to town to send wire to Noma Jean (Bill's wife). I also wired Mother at Sweetwater, Mr. C. C. Newton, Sallie's Dad, of Olustee, Okla. T. L. DeLoach of Houston, H. G. De-Loach & wife of Los Angeles. But before I did this wiring I received the telegram in person. It stated that Bill was Missing in Action. Well, that was a great relief. We hope he bailed out safely. The house is full of our loving and kind friends. I feel better about it and I know the balance do too. I called Jimmie and Arlois at Ralls. They said they would be up sometime tonight.

In December, 1941, the Japanese overran Burma, closing the Burma Road that linked China with the Bay of Bengal and supplies from the outside world. The Allies were faced with finding a new route into China. Plans called for a military road to be constructed from Assam (India) to Myitkyina in northern Burma, under the command of Gen. Joseph W. Stilwell. Myitkyina was crucial because after its capture airfields were constructed allowing the air ferry into China to follow a route that avoided the Hump and had fighter protection throughout. The campaign began in January, 1944, but Myitkyina was not captured until August 3. Bill was stationed at Moran, Assam. His ill-fated flight was one of the first missions of the air ferry along the new route into China (See Raymond Callahan, *Burma, 1942–1945*, p. 47; Frank Dorn, *Walkout: With Stilwell in Burma*, pp. 244–48). According to Army Bulletin #29, issued from Moran, Assam (India), a C-47, #767, from the 12th Combat Cargo Squadron, took off from Moran at 0630 hours Indian Standard Time on August 9, 1944, for Myitkyina, Burma. The last radio contact was at 0730 IST, when #767 was "on course." Six people were believed on board, four crewmen and two men on pass. The copilot was 2d Lt. Billy Roland DeLoach. No further report was heard from this aircraft (Army Bulletin #29, issued Aug. 17, 1944, at Moran, typescript in possession of editor).

· THURS 24.   I went to town to see if any more news had arrived. None. . . . All we can do now is wait for the best or the worst. . . .
· FRI 25.   . . . We decided we would go to Belin, N.M. and see how Bill's wife is, so we got started about 4 P.M. Arlois, Sallie and I. We arrived in Belin about mid-night. They were all O.K. In her condition she could not afford to take the news of Bill's Missing in Action too hard, how-

Wed., 23... The awful blow hit us
about 6 P.M. A Mr. Lowrey drove up
and said he wanted to speak to
me. I went out to his car.
He said he had a death message
from Washington, D.C.

ever she is holding up OK. [*Noma Jean was pregnant and was staying with her parents, who were living in Belen, New Mexico.*]

· THURS 31. Had several letters from different ones. All sympathy expressions which we sure appreciate.

S·E·P·T·E·M·B·E·R

· MON 4. . . . I received a letter from the Honorable George Mahon, M.C., Washington, D.C. offering his assistance and co-operation any way in behalf of Bill, asking us to write him if we need him. "Thanks.". . .

· SUN 17. I felt bad this early morning. I looked at Bill's pictures. Three of them of different poses, and it is an awful thought what has become of him? All we can do is to hope and pray that he is on his way back. . . .

· WED 20. [*Harold, Dellie, and Wayne came in from California.*]

· MON 25. . . . Melon money in bank and on hand $523.50. [*DeLoach made approximately $634.00 from watermelons in 1944.*]

· FRI 29. . . . We still look for a letter or telegram from some one about our Billy. He has been missing near two months. . . .

O·C·T·O·B·E·R

· MON 2. . . . Had letter from War Department stating Bill's ship went down in northeastern Burma. Quote "They used parachutes." They did not say who or how many used them. Well, we know one thing now. He did not crash, or hit a high peak. There still is a hope that he will show up later. . . . Bud sold Harold's place to Claude Benham, $52.50 per A. He made a nice little profit $14.00 per acre. . . .

· MON 16. I took Harold to town to go to Lubbock with Bud. I did not intend to go, but they both had so much business to attend to, that I thought that I had better go and see about getting the car doors my self. . . . When I got back home an iceberg had floated over the whole house. It is hell when a man of my age can't go any where with out asking the whole female outfit. . . .

N·O·V·E·M·B·E·R

· WED 1. Overton came over and cut quite a bunch of grain (Red top Martin maize). I put up about 7½ or 8 tons. The balance will be put on the ground. I think it will make about 1600 or 1800 lbs per A. Well, that is not too bad. . . .

Lamb County farmers planted over half of the total cultivated acres in grain sorghums in 1943 (See "South Plains Travelogue," *Progressive Farmer* 58, no. 10 [Oct., 1943], p. 16).

· Tues 7. We made ready early. Went by town, on out to the Henry voting box. I voted the Dem. straight through. I did not make up my mind until I went to vote. I could not vote the Jimbo way [*Republican*], hence the Jack Ass route [*Democrat*]. I have not forgotten how we had to do when Hoover was the Big Boy, 1930, 1931, 1932. We went on to Little-field to talk with the Red Cross executives. The lady said she could not find out a thing if Billy was a Jap prisoner, for the Japs would not tell a thing, for they have no Red Cross set up.
· Tues 21. 27 years ago today Billy Roland DeLoach was borned at Olustee, Okla. We lived near Crosbyton, Tex. then. . . .
· Sat 25. We had announcement card from Noma Jean stating the birth of a son. He arrived 11:42 P.M. November 21st, 1944. That date is Billy's birthday, 11-21-1917. She and Bill agreed on a name. If a boy name Billy Roland DeLoach. If a girl Susie Ellen. . . . Has been cold and windy all day. . . .

D·E·C·E·M·B·E·R

· Tues 14. I was off to Littlefield early. I went by Amherst to turn in my seed sample to the AAA people of my loan feed which I have in my granary. . . .

There was a bumper crop of grain sorghum in the South Plains in the fall of 1944, when the thirty-six Panhandle-Plains counties produced over 65 percent of the two-hundred-million-bushel total for Texas. Shortages of labor, combines, and railroad cars slowed the movement of this huge crop to market, which was also sluggish because buyers believed that holding off would force the price down. Farmers who had government-approved buildings stored their grain, hoping to receive the ceiling price set by the Office of Price Administration—$2.08 per 100 pounds at the farm (See "An Avalanche of Grain Sorghums," *Progressive Farmer* 59, no. 10 [Oct., 1944], p. 52).

Will, Sallie, Dot, and Almeda went to Olustee, Oklahoma, for Christmas.

· THURS 28.   We were up early to start home, but when I looked out everything was covered with snow. We did not know just what to do. Darla came over to Mr. Newton's and said she had just talked to Jimmie at Ralls. Jim told her that Noma Jean, Bill's wife, would stay over another day for us to come on if we wanted to see the baby (Bill's baby) and of course we wanted to see him. So we made ready and started for Ralls at 11 A.M. We arrived Ralls at 3:30 P.M. Well, we knew that something was wrong as soon as we went in Jimmie's home. They had the dreaded telegram from the War Department stating that Bill was killed in action on the day he was reported missing, 9th August. The telegram came here to me the day we left Ralls, Dec. 22. Bud received it for me. He gave it to Arlois & Jimmie when they came up to get the pony at my place on Saturday, 23. They did not know just what to do, so they did not send it to Olustee, Okla. Well, we have had hopes he would show up alive and well, but that wire blasted our hopes. Noma Jean and her baby came over to Arlois' home. We had a good look at the baby boy. He is named for our Billy. . . .

Army Bulletin #36 issued on October 27, 1944, at Moran confirmed the crash. The Air Jungle Rescue Unit located the wreckage of aircraft #767, which was completely burned except the middle of the fuselage and the tail. The numbers on the tail were easily discernable. Six men were aboard at the time of the crash and all were declared dead. During World War II, 581 men and women from Lamb County, Texas served in the armed forces. Sixty-two people lost their lives (See *Service Book, Lamb County, Texas: Second World War, 1941–1945*; Army Bulletin #36, issued Oct. 31, 1944, at Moran, typescript in possession of editor).

· FRI 29.   We started for home. Jimmie and children came home with us. It was awful to come in this house and have those pictures of Bill smiling at us, but after all there is nothing we can do about it, only wait for the War Department report which we were looking for. Mr. & Mrs. Seeds and daughter brought Noma Jean and Baby Billy by and stayed over night. The live at Belen, New Mexico.
· SUN 31.   . . . Cody Overton and Betty Huff came out from church and stayed all afternoon. They are good neighbors.

1·9·4·5

The shock of Bill's death left DeLoach despondent. He rented the farm to a neighbor, Cody Overton, a younger man with good equipment who wanted more land to work. Other farmers his age were also quitting. Perhaps they remembered how prices fell after World War I and decided to quit while they were ahead. Maybe they knew their way of farming was over, or they were just tired of the endless round of chores. The high salaries in defense jobs were tempting, but they soon learned that working for the public is different.

J·A·N·U·A·R·Y

· FRI 5.   The awful sting of Bill's death in that slaughtering war is not so great as it was. Time heals all trouble, but it is awful to think about. . . .

· WED 10.   We stayed close at home in forenoon. The Major Smith from the Lubbock Air Base did not arrive till near 12 noon. He told us lots of things to do and lots of things not to do. Among others he said for us to be careful what we signed and not send money to some one that would write "That he had some thing to tell that Bill said if they had the money to come to see us." As a whole he was a very! very! nice fellow. He said he would go to see Noma Jean. . . .

When a member of the Army dies on active duty or after retirement, the Department of the Army appoints a Survivor Assistance Officer to provide assistance to the next of kin of the deceased. Assistance might consist of coordination with transportation facilities to have the body delivered to the funeral home specified by the family; payment of fees for portions of the service; submission of forms needed to enable survivors to receive benefits from the Veterans' Administration; or appropriate cautions to people who are receiving a relatively large amount of life insurance without a strategy for prioritizing their purchases. If people misrepresent themselves to bereaved families, the Survivor Assistance Officer will act in the families' best interests by letting them know of any such misrepresentations, as the officer did who visited the DeLoach family (Maj. Daniel M. Ostendorph, U.S. Army, assistant professor of military science, Texas Tech University, interview with Janet Neugebauer, Lubbock, Tex., Feb. 10, 1988).

· THURS 25.   . . . I had to have the carburator worked on $5.50 worth. It won't be long now no matter where I am I can get a job done for nothing. I have had it worked on at Post City, Lubbock, Littlefield and Sudan. They all said, "If it does not work bring it back. I will fix it some more. No cost to you." The trouble is I am never in the same town when it fails.

· SAT 27.   . . . We had letter from Noma Jean. She had a letter from a 1st Lt. based in India. He said Bill and the 5 boys with him were killed. The Lt. letter stated the plane was blown off course and crashed into the side of a mountain and all six men were killed. I do not believe it. I still believe Billy will come back to us. He also said that the bodies were given a military funeral. That is hard to write when I can look up and see three of Bill's pictures just in front of me and to think I never will see him again and what was he killed for? For a bunch of money grubbing skunks. I am loyal to the U.S. flag, the constitution of the U.S., but the bunch of legalized hi-jackers and grafters in Washington, I am not loyal to them, for I think just as much of a Jap as I do a Chinaman and think they would double cross us just as quick.

The Air Jungle Rescue Unit sent volunteers from the 90th Fighter Squadron to the scene of the crash. Lt. Roger McDonnell, a pilot and ordained minister, was in charge. He kept a diary of his trip through the jungle, and in 1987 his widow sent a typescript of the diary of Jimmie DeLoach Moorhead. Natives were taken along as guides, interpreters, and bearers. The group had to cut their way through the dense jungle vegetation, kill a huge bull elephant that attacked them, allow their bearers time off to smoke opium, and finally bury the remains of the men on C-47 #767. Three of them, including Lt. Billy De-Loach, were killed instantly. One tried to bail out, but didn't make it out of the plane; one lived for some time in the back of the plane, as his body was less decomposed than the others; and one left the scene of the wreck, nothing more being known of his whereabouts. A lean-to had been built about a quarter of a mile from the wreckage, and a trail had been cut away from the crash about three months before the group arrived. Because the lean-to was not made of bamboo but was made of trees that were hacked by an inexperienced cutter, Lieutenant McDonnell believed an American had built it. The group could not follow the trail because it was overgrown with vines and bamboo. The entire trip took twenty-five days (A typescript of the account is in possession of the editor).

F·E·B·R·U·A·R·Y

· Sat 10. . . . I made Cody Overton two propositions on renting my place. First, No. 1, that I would rent for $500.00 cash, or I would rent for the most of the land to be put in cotton, say 50 A. and balance in water-melons. . . . I also told him he could have ½ of the fruit and me the other ½, that is if the freeze did not kill it. . . .

· Tues 13. . . . Three men came soon after I arrived home wanting to buy my tractor. Well, I priced it at $550.00. They took me up. I have no tractor now. . . .

M·A·R·C·H

· Tues 6. . . . Had telegram from Harold telling me to come on to Los Angeles. Had job for me at $14.96 per day. That sounds big. I do not know just what to do. . . .

DeLoach went to California alone, on the train, and found work in a ship-yard at San Pedro.

· Tues 20. . . . I am really tired. That work is a little heavy for me, but the $1.57 per hr. is good pay. . . .

· Sat 24. An other full day and time and ½ for Saturday work, which is $2.45 pr hr. We will work tomorrow. That will be double time, or $3.15 per hr, or $25.20 per 8 hr day.

· Mon 26. I decided that I would check out and not work any more, so I went up to Van Nuys to see George Witt and sister Fannie. . . . Harold brought my check in. . . . check was for $87.00 after all Gov. deductions, which [were] about $20.00. In all I am not dissatisfied with the pay.

According to Jimmie DeLoach Moorhead, her father was dissatisfied with the integrity of his co-workers. They rowed a small boat up under a pier and hid out most of one day to avoid working. He quit, just as he had in 1924 when he discovered his boss was dishonest. After a brief visit with family he returned to Sudan.

A·p·r·i·l

· Tues 3. . . . I guess I will not go to Odessa [*an oilfield supply center*] to work. I do not want to go alone and I can't get a house and I won't leave Sallie here alone. I guess we will just stay at home.

Sallie was not in favor of leaving her farm home. She felt that Will had always been too anxious to move on.

· Thurs 12. . . . I heard just before I left town that Pres. Roosevelt died in Warm Springs, Ga. Quite a shock to the nation and the people in general, however the Great must die too. . . .

In the third month of his fourth term, President Franklin D. Roosevelt died of a cerebral hemorrhage in Warm Springs, Georgia. As long as he lived, DeLoach blamed Roosevelt for World War II and Bill's death. In this entry it sounds like he might have received some consolation from Roosevelt's death.

J·u·n·e

· Tues 5. Just eat breakfast, milk cows, then read and sleep, then eat dinner. Set around a while then go to town. I went to town to get a hair cut. Hot, dry. High wind.
· Sat 16. . . . I was offered $2.00 per hundred lbs for my grain in Muleshoe and Sudan, but I think I will just pay the loan off and keep it for a while. Maybe I can get a little above the hauling. . . .
· Tues 19. I was down town for a while in A.M. I paid my grain Government loan off. It was $878.40. I can sell or I can hold my grain now as I want to. . . .
· Fri 22. . . . I made arrangements to go to work on a Government job. That is adjusting this cotton that is Gov. insured, $6.50 per day, 8 hrs, 4½¢ per mile for the car. I am to start work tomorrow.

Community committees were charged with handling the Federal Crop Insurance at the local level. See diary entries for April, 1943. DeLoach would have had no trouble getting a job because he served on the Community and County Agricultural Committee many years during the 1930s.

- Fri 29. ... I received from the War Department a little diary of Lt. Billy R. DeLoach. He kept it from the time he left Florida (I think about the 16 of May, 1944) until July 24, 1944, and he was killed on August 9, 1944. Boy it was sad to read it.

J·U·L·Y

- Fri 13. Today is Sallie's birthday. She thinks that the 13th is ill luck enough, but when it falls on Friday that is just too bad. However, I think there is nothing to her fear of the date. I told Hazel (Forman) Catts [*owner of the local dress shop*] to pick her a nice birthday present. She did in a dress with all the trimmings. ...
- Mon 16. He [*Cody Overton*] planted all the land on my place that he had in cotton.
- Tues 17. ... We looked around at the resident lots in Muleshoe. Maybe we will buy one.
- Thurs 31. I had backed out of the house deal. I don't think I want to put my self in debt for $2,000.00. Not at this time. I do not know just how to do nor just what to do. But I feel that a change of some kind will have to be made.

A·U·G·U·S·T

- Thurs 9. ... I am thinking about selling my grain. It could go down. The market could break in two.
- Fri 10. I was up town all day. I took Shaver up on his offer of my grain, $2.10 per hundred. ...
- Tues 14. The Japs said that the fight was off, but one can't believe them. I think they are just stalling for time to do something dirty. They can do it. That is the dirty stuff. ...

After suffering the devastation of atomic bombs on Hiroshima and Nagasaki, the Japanese government announced its surrender. World War II ended

with the United States in an unprecedented position of power and influence, but the cost in human suffering had been staggering. DeLoach must have been thinking that if this had happened a year earlier his son's life might have been spared.

· Fri 17. We moved all the grain, 51,190 lbs, $1039.15 after the hauling
    taken off. $35.83 for the haul, $1074.98. I made some money by holding
    the grain. . . .

The price DeLoach received when he put the grain in the loan was $1.71 per hundred pounds. He sold it for $2.10 per hundred and earned an additional $196.58, or 22 percent profit.

S·E·P·T·E·M·B·E·R

· Sat 1. . . . I have just been listening to the signing of the surrendering
    documents of Japan. They took place aboard the battle wagon Mis-
    souri. . . .

Japanese officials signed the articles of surrender aboard the American battleship *Missouri*, anchored in Tokyo Bay. General Douglas MacArthur received the formal surrender on behalf of the United States.

· Sun 2. We all went to church. As we came out of town I bought our first
    watermelon. It was a very good one. This is the first year since 1937
    that we have not had plenty of melons and plenty to sell, but we have
    none this time. . . .
· Tues 18. . . . I was down town this P.M. I saw H. G. & Bud in town. They
    had been to look at a place near Littlefield. We went to see a fellow at
    Muleshoe, about a deal. He has a very good equipment for farming, 4
    cows, 15 hogs, 200 chickens and other things. A feed crop, some Sudan
    grass. I think H. G. will buy it.

For the first time in two decades, agricultural prices were high enough to make farming attractive. Harold moved to California in the late 1920s because he couldn't make a decent living on the farm. Now the situation was right to return and sink his roots into the soil again. His return was timely because DeLoach was getting into the winter of his years, and having his sons nearby to help with the heavy work was comforting, especially during his grief over Bill's death.

O·c·t·o·b·e·r

· THURS 4. He [*Harold*] saw McCabe. They had a final settlement. . . . The people (McCabe) left just as soon as they could settle up. Harold moved in.

· TUES 23. . . . The grain on my place is good. That is for this year. Dry and late planting.

· SAT 27. . . . We all went to Littlefield in afternoon. Sallie sold 6 doz eggs for 50¢ per doz. Boy that is high eggs. They are not worth it.

N·o·v·e·m·b·e·r

· FRI 9. . . . Harold got in a hurry and would not stop the motor on the baler while he made a belt adjustment, so he got his middle finger caught in the pulley and cut the end off. The Dr. had to take the finger off at the first joint. He said he did not know when the Dr. cut it off. So we will not bale any more of the Sudan hay.

· MON 12. I had a call to come to the 3 A office. . . . I forgot about Armistice Day. All were closed. . . . I heard that George Witt, my oldest brother-in-law died in Van Noyes, Calif, the 8th of Nov.

This is the brother-in-law DeLoach rented a farm from when he moved to the Texas Plains in 1913 (See entries for March–November, 1914).

· SAT 17. . . . We made ready to go to Lubbock to Little Billy Roland's [*Bill's son*] birthday dinner. Sallie & I bought him a Victory Bond, $18.75.

D·e·c·e·m·b·e·r

· TUES 18. . . . I heard today that I had been put back on the Local Committee of the A.A.A. The election was held on 8th of December. I had forgotten about it.

· SUN 23. We all went to church, or the folks did. On down to Bud's for dinner. Ida gave a good dinner and boy was it a good one. Guess we will have a feed Christmas day. I think all the kids will be here. All but one. He will never come.

1·9·4·6

Grain sorghum production rose until over half of the nation's total came from Texas in 1946. According to the *Texas Almanac 1947–1948* (pp. 204–205), Lamb County led the state in production and yield per acre. Two developments played a key role in the rapid development of this industry. After farmers mechanized, feed that was formerly used for draft animals went onto the market; and the introduction of dwarf, straight-necked varieties, which could be harvested with combines, made it possible to increase acreage over the days of hand harvesting. Approximately 60 percent of the crop was sold on the grain market, and the remainder was marketed through livestock or as seed. South Plains farmers were fortunate to have a crop they could easily shift to when cotton fell on hard times. In 1941, cotton and grain sorghum acreages were about equal on the Llano Estacado, but by 1945 sorghum was planted on nearly three million acres, and cotton acreage was reduced to approximately four hundred thousand. The trend reversed as cotton prices rose after World War II.

J·A·N·U·A·R·Y

· Fri 11.   I went down town early. Mr. Al Mitchum wanted me to take him to Littlefield to see the old age welfare worker or agent or what ever his status is or name. Any way, I do not want any of it. Even if I could get it, it would have to be a have to case. One to qualify has to be a pauper or tell a doz. lies, and has to keep telling lies the balance of his life, so I will try to make out with out it. . . .

251

· SAT 19.   . . . I heard while in Muleshoe that Mr. P. E. Bosen, the Dad of
Sudan, passed away yesterday at 1 P.M. He was a good friend to the
needy man, if the needy man "toted" fair. He founded the First National Bank of Sudan, Tex back in the late 'teens' or early twenties. I
never asked this bank for a loan that I did not get. Pete Bosen just paid
up yesterday.

F·E·B·R·U·A·R·Y

· FRI 1.   Another birthday for me, 66. Mother passed away today at 10:30
A.M. Quite a concidence, 11 years today Dad died. Both died on my
birthday and the day of the week each died Friday. Dad was buried on
Sunday the 3rd and Mother was buried on the 3rd of Feb. The funeral
of each was preached in the Baptist Church of Ira at 2 P.M. on Sunday.
(I am writing this on Sunday night, the 3rd).
· THURS 21.   I fixed a flat and went to town, on down to see the tractor
that Erwin Badgett has for sale. I decided if I had to pay $850.00 for a
used Ford tractor as old as his I just would not do it. I will get me a
new one if I can find it. Slagle Tractor (International people) is trying to
find me one. . . .
· THURS 28.   . . . Mr. Hendricks came over. He wanted to rent my place, but
I can't rent out. I have too much expense and responsibility to not
make a crop myself.

M·A·R·C·H

· MON 4.   . . . Cody Overton came out just at night to tell me about a new
Ford tractor at Littlefield that I could get, so I have just made up my
mind that I will take the tractor. . . .
· TUES 5.   . . . I went to Sudan and met the man that had the tractor. I
made a deal with him. We went to Littlefield. They had the tractor
ready. I drove it home. . . . I am well pleased with it, cost $1297.70.
· SAT 9.   I went to Muleshoe. Had my tax report made out, $2.50. I came
back and Sallie & I went to Mr. Henry's to vote on the court house
removal. . . .

After three elections and fifteen years of trying, Littlefield finally won the
county seat, and the records were moved there in 1946. Olton, designated the

county seat in 1908, was located in wheat country. Littlefield, to the south, was located amidst smaller cotton farms, and the area had two-thirds of the county population by 1930.

M·A·Y

· FRI 31. . . . The rain seems like won't come. We are in for another dry year like last year.

J·U·N·E

· SAT 15.   I was down town early. The election of the S. C. [*Soil Conserva-tion*] set up. We opened at 8 A.M., closed at 7 P.M. 40 votes cast, 20 for and 20 against.

In 1937, the Texas Legislature began authorizing the establishment of con-servation districts to improve productivity of the land through such measures as erosion control and water conservation. The Soil Conservation Service fur-nished technical advice, but responsibility for conservation rested with local farmers and ranchers, as it still does. In 1946, 71 percent of the farmers voting were in favor of establishing a conservation district in Lamb County; how-ever, only 186 people voted throughout the county. Apathy appeared to be the problem—one of the voting boxes did not even open because everyone forgot about the election. DeLoach also reported a small turnout (See Bennett, *Our American Land*, pp. 8–9; *County Wide News*, June 20, 1946, p. 1; *Lamb County Leader*, June 20, 1946, p. 1).

· FRI 21. . . . This adjusting is a pain and headache.
· SAT 22.   I got ready early and got started late. I had a caller to see if I could let him start planting with out an inspection. I did because I could write up the contract later and they all want to get started planting this late crop of feed. Not too much moisture any way. Also another fellow called wanting to be "set free." They want their cake and eat it too. . . .

DeLoach was adjusting claims for farmers whose crops were insured by the Federal Crop Insurance Corporation. Lack of moisture prevented an acceptable stand of cotton before the cutoff date of June 15. Cotton seed that sprouted from a rain after that date would not have time to mature before frost. Farmers were therefore anxious to have their claims adjusted so they could plant grain sorghum, which would mature during the remaining frost-free days.

· SUN 23. Well, the long looked for rain came today. Maybe 3 inches.
Water every where. . . .

J·U·L·Y

· FRI 5. I took Sallie to see a Mr. Mulloy at Littlefield. A lady, Mrs. Quinn
of Sudan, told her that she could get the same pension money she
(Mrs Quinn) is getting, so she went with us. They made contract with
Mulloys. He told her all she would have to do would be for us to get
our wedding certificate, also Bill's birth certificate and ours too. They
will have to make up one for us, I guess, for I don't think any records
were kept of births when we were born. However, we will try. We might
as well have it as other parents that lost a boy. For what? Nothing,
only to make it better for the grafter and war minded. If I had my way
I would kill all who wants war.

The National Service life insurance policy, issued by the Veterans' Administration Insurance Center, provided compensation to both a widow and parents,
if the parents could prove they were dependent on the serviceman.

A·U·G·U·S·T

· SAT 31. . . . We all went to the blow out in Sudan. We had to stay tonight till it was over. I parked next to the roped off vicinity of the Indian stomp platform and I could not get my car out. However, we enjoyed the Indian stomp dancer and the old fiddlers contest. We were
home by 11 P.M.

Each fall, a two-day festival in Sudan opened with the burning in effigy of
"Old Man Gloom." After this, gaiety reigned over the crowd that gathered to
enjoy parades, Indian dancers, an old fiddlers' contest, and horse shows. The
Boy Scouts displayed their skills, and politicians were on hand to sandwich a
few words in between the other events (See *Lamb County Leader*, Sept. 5, 1946,
p. 9).

S·E·P·T·E·M·B·E·R

· THURS 5. . . . Dot picked 496 lbs of peas today.

According to the previous day's entry, Dot picked black-eyed peas for a neighbor and was paid a penny a pound. Texas ranked third among the seventeen states producing black-eyed peas in 1945, and by 1947 this was considered a cash crop on the South Plains, often generating as much as a hundred dollars per acre. Buyers liked the quality of West Texas black-eyed peas, because the fuller pods yielded more cans of peas per ton. An additional benefit was the nitrogen this plant added to the soil (See *Texas Almanac and State Industrial Guide, 1947–1948*, p. 209; *Southwestern Crop and Stock* 1, no. 3 [Mar., 1947], p. 34).

· Mon 16. . . . The fat insurance agent was here to collect. Sallie paid him up to Nov, I think it was. I am really tired looking at that bird. The check was made for $6.00.

· Sat 21. . . . Received salary check from Crop Insurance Corporation for $50.86. . . .

O·c·t·o·b·e·r

· Thurs 10. . . . Only 5 more days till the condemned Germans will be hung by the neck until they are dead, dead, dead. I guess they think of the thousands of men, women, and little children that they caused to be murdered.

DeLoach is referring to the execution of Nazi leaders, at Nuremberg, Germany, in expiation of war crimes. The executions were the first ever ordered by an international tribunal and established the history-making precedent of individual accountability for waging warfare. DeLoach was bitter toward the political and military leaders of World War II because his youngest son was a casualty of the conflict. The length and details of the news article about the death of these eleven war criminals indicate the execution was something of a catharsis for many Americans who suffered losses from the war (See *Dallas Morning News*, Oct. 16, 1946, p. 1).

· Wed 16. Well the murders of Germany were hung by the neck till they were dead, dead. All, but one, Herman Georing. He beat them "to the draw." He killed himself by the poison route. That was what [*showed*] him up to be a dirty cur and a coward. He could kill little children and women, but he could not stand up and take it. . . .

· Thurs 24. . . . I was on the look out for some land, but I did not find any [*with a new tractor, DeLoach could handle more land, and the additional income would make it easier to pay for his equipment*]. . . .

N·O·V·E·M·B·E·R

·Tues 5. . . . They came for the hog. She weighed 310 lbs at 24 ct., $74.40.
That is a lot of money for 1 hog. My cost for pig $6.00.

Under the stimulus of wartime demands, the hog industry in Texas expanded
until the state ranked ninth in the nation in the number of swine on farms. By
January, 1946, the total was 1,857,000. The old adage that when cotton declines,
hogs prosper proved true during World War II. Hog prices rose, and most farmers increased their acreage planted in feed grains that were marketed through
hogs. In contrast to hog-producing states in the Corn Belt, thousands of Texas
farms produced a few hogs, but few farms produced a large number (See *Texas
Almanac and State Industrial Guide, 1947–1948*, p. 232; Kincannon and McNeely,
An Economic Appraisal, pp. 3, 41–49).

·Sat 9. . . . We all went to Sudan this P.M. I got my Insurance (cotton)
check. $1012.23. I paid $171.24 premium. A total of $1185.47, less the
$171.24. . . . 3090 lbs at 38.30 cts. per lb.

The Federal Crop Insurance Corporation had a net loss of $50 million in the
six years that all-risk insurance was offered. Officials considered the feasibility
of covering "out-of-pocket" cost to farmers for planting crops, and in 1946 this
was tried on an experimental basis in several wheat counties. Apparently De-
Loach collected for cotton lost due to drought. Rain came about June 20, which
is too late for cotton. The price he received, $.383 per pound, had not been
equaled since 1919, shortages kept prices high throughout the season. DeLoach
had insured his crop in previous years, but this is the first record of receiving
payment for loss (See commentary on entry of April 12, 1943; *Country Gentleman* 116, no. 9 [Sept., 1946], p. 12).

·Fri 15. . . . We had a "very good" sand storm today. I had to go to Littlefield for the wind mill part. . . . I put the mill to pumping. I had a little
scare. The wind broke a cord I had the mill tied off with. I went up on
top of tower and tried to cut the mill off by hand. The tower began to
shimmey about. I could not let go of the fan. I did not know what to
do. I caught the little brake lever and finely stopped the wheel. I did
not get scared till it was all tied off. Mills are dangerous in high winds. I
will have to quit climbing up on them in high winds.

·Thurs 28. I worked here on my granary till near 1:00 P.M. I shaved, ate a
bite and took off for Littlefield to see my first foot ball game, Sudan-
Littlefield. Well, I am bound to admit that it is real exciting. Littlefield

Fri 15... had a little scare. The wind broke a cord I had the mill tied off with. I tried to cut the mill off by hand. The tower began to shimmey about.

beat them (Sudan) 35 to 14, but they hurt 4 of the Sudan team. That is they had to retire. The gate showed some 5,000 fans saw the game. Some came over the fence.

D·e·c·e·m·b·e·r

· Mon 2. Ray Overton started early to combining. Cody Overton combine came in just at noon. They both cut and threshed quite a lot. They can get me finished by tomorrow, Wed p.m. I believe I will make 60,000 lbs. . . . I had letter from the Veterans Administration Branch Office, #10, Dallas, Texas. $45.00 allowed from 1-14-46 to 8-31-46. $54.00 allowed from 9-1-46.

· Tues 10. . . . I put the insurance money in bank 50-50 with Sallie $251.25 each.

· Tues 17. . . . Had to go to town for Almeda. She went to the Brownie [*a junior division of Girl Scouts of America*] meeting at Mrs. Ned Warren's home after school. They have quite a bunch of little girls. She reported a good time.

· Mon 30. . . . I paid my land interest at Halsell Land Co Office, $35.36. They had me charged with $40.36. I figured it out and found I only owed $35.36. . . . Well, I saved $5.00 by doing a little figuring my self.

1·9·4·7

Agricultural prices reached a peak just after peace was declared, as they had after World War I. Increased national consumption after the end of rationing, as well as government shipments to the war-torn countries of Europe, kept the market strong. The ongoing labor shortage forced more farmers to use mechanical harvesters, and high commodity prices brought commercially manufactured cotton strippers within the range of most producers. Increased production of consumer items and an adequate income also allowed farmers to update the family car and take long-delayed vacations.

J·A·N·U·A·R·Y

· WED 1. . . . The first monthly pension check came to day $54.00, 50–50 each ($27.00 each).

· SAT 4. I had a reading of zero inside of my garage. . . . About 1 P.M. my main water line froze up. I had to get water out of over head tank. . . .

· SUN 5. [*DeLoach thawed the water in the pipe.*] . . . I do not see how we did without a piped in water supply.

· THURS 30. All is quiet along the "Sand Front." All except the house wives. Boy, are they on the prod. Cleaning out sand is the order of the day. All reports this one (yesterday) was equal to any we have any record of. . . .

Thurs. Jan. 30 — all is quiet along the "Sand Front." All except the housewives. Boy, are they on the prod. Cleaning out sand is the order of the day!

1947

F·E·B·R·U·A·R·Y

· Thurs 20. . . . Down town for a while this P.M. Shaver Elevator offered
me $43.00 per ton for my grain, but I think it will go higher, as wheat,
corn, and hogs are higher. Hogs I think are the highest in the history
of the live stock exhanges, $27.50 per hundred lb live wt.

Relaxed wartime restrictions and continuing high wages caused unusually
large consumer demands for meat. The small pig crop in 1946 was not sufficient
to meet this demand, and hog prices reached an all-time high in 1947 (See
Southwestern Crop and Stock 1, no. 3 [Mar., 1947], p. 7).

· Mon 24. . . . I bought two [*pigs*] at $12.50 each. . . . All feed and wheat
took a high jump. Also cotton was up $3.00 per bale. I will hold my
feed I guess till the price breaks $2.15 or $2.20 now. If it gets to $2.25 at
home I may sell. I would like to get $2.50.
· Fri 28. Well I had to borrow $50 or sell my grain. In as much as grain is
on the up grade I decided to borrow the $50.00. . . .

M·A·R·C·H

· Thurs 13. I went to Sudan and sold my grain $2.60 per hundred. . . .
Moved in 3 loads, 46570#, $2.60 per hundred, $1212.50, hauling 7¢ per
hundred, $32.72 less=$1182.72.
· Mon 17. Cloudy and looks like rain, now 9:20 A.M. I just shot a pole cat
and I think since I came in house that I got a little too close to him.
· Fri 28. This is the diary's birthday. The 28th of March, 1914 I started
writing my diary, 33 years ago. Jimmie was 3 months old. Billy's birth
record is the only one of the 3 boys & 3 girls in the family that I have
a record of birth. . . .
· Mon 31. Bud came up 7:30 A.M. We arrived Amarillo about 11:30. We
looked at a few cars before we ate dinner. We decided on a 1941 Chev.
We tried it out and made a deal with Conley Motor Co., Amarillo,
Tex. We traded. His prices were $1205.00, the little '37 Sport pick up
$287.50 and my check for $912.50. We arrived home about 5:30 P.M. All
are well pleased so far with the new car. That is it is new to us. . . .

This entry, when compared to those of March 21 and March 30, 1918, clearly
illustrates the problem farmers face with rising non-farm expenses, known as
the cost-price squeeze. In 1918 DeLoach paid $500.00 for a new Ford, and cot-

ton was selling for $.30 per pound. In 1947 cotton was again selling for $.30 a pound, but the six-year-old car he bought cost $1205.00. Furthermore, in 1918 DeLoach farmed with mules that required only homegrown feed, but, by 1947 he was farming with a tractor that cost $1297.00 and used gasoline. As the profit margin shrank, farmers had to increase yields and acreage to make money. Small farmers had difficulty generating enough profit for a decent living.

A·P·R·I·L

· Tues 1.   I worked on my garage. I had to extend the length. I made it 24″ longer. . . .

J·U·N·E

· Tues 3.   I had to go to town, but I had forgotten about Jeff Davis' birthday. The bank did not open.

Jefferson Davis was president of the Confederate States of America, and for many years his birthday was recognized as a holiday in those states that once belonged to the Confederacy.

J·U·L·Y

· Fri 11.   . . . we went to Littlefield. . . . We bought some eats. Last, but not least a 100 lb sack of sugar. The first one I have bought in several years. The sugar, $9.33.
· Tues 29.   . . . I am off my feed. No milk. Bess cow is supposed to freshen 8th of August. Will I be glad!

A·U·G·U·S·T

· Fri 8.   We began to make preparations to get off early for the Carlsbad Caverns. . . .

Carlsbad Caverns, a national park twenty-eight miles southwest of the city of Carlsbad, New Mexico, is a popular tourist attraction. Originally discovered in 1901, it was not very well known until President Coolidge proclaimed it a national monument in 1923. The Big Room, the largest of several underground chambers, is 750 feet below ground. It is large enough to hold fourteen football fields and tall enough to hold a twenty-two-story building. The Caverns is open daily for tours, which are three miles long and take nearly four hours to complete, including a rest stop in the underground dining room (See Jim White, "Carlsbad Cavern, Scenic Wonder of the World," *The Historical Encyclopedia of New Mexico* I, pp. 54–55).

· Sat 9. . . . Well, it is an underground trip that one will never forget. . . . Ate in the lunch room 750 ft underground.

S·e·p·t·e·m·b·e·r

· Mon 1. . . . Ed and I went to Clovis N.M. to a ropeing contest. Boy was it good! Eleven contestants roped in the contest for the jack pot of $115.00. . . .

Much of the land around Clovis, New Mexico, is ranch land, and contests involving the skills of that industry are a popular pastime. The roping contest DeLoach and his brother attended was part of the Labor Day Rodeo.

· Sun 21. . . . I think I will cut some more of my feed tomorrow. The price has gone down now. I might be able to get $3.00 per cwt. Was up to $3.30.
· Mon 29. . . . We finished cutting the grain. Shaver paid $3.00 per hundred to day, total yield 4000 – $1006.92.

O·c·t·o·b·e·r

· Sat 4. . . . I paid Bud $100.00 for feed combining.
· Thurs 9. No hands to pull cotton. I was down town, but found no one that I could hire. They do not want to work.
· Sat 11. I went down town early. Back home. Ate lunch. Then we all went to Sudan. Maybe so I will get a pulling machine to pull my cotton.
· Thurs 14. The cotton pulling man came about 10 a.m. We pulled cotton balance of day. Could not do a real good job. . . .

The lack of small mechanical harvesters for family farms and the lower grade of stripper-harvested cotton retarded full mechanization of the harvest. Also, branches that clogged the machine left a mess of scattered lint everywhere. Some farmers, such as DeLoach, did not believe that the lint wasted in stripper harvesting cost less than paying hands to gather every single boll. Despite these factors, the five thousand cotton strippers used on the Texas High Plains and in Oklahoma indicated a transition to mechanized harvesting. Savings in man-hours and expense encouraged the trend. A two-row, tractor-mounted stripper could harvest nearly a bale per hour, while the average person needed approximately seven days to gather a bale; stripper harvesting cost twenty-five dollars per bale less than hand snapping. A completely mechanized harvest did not exist, however, until after 1951 (See Motheral, Metzler, and Ducoff, *Cotton and Manpower*, pp. 17–20; Ernest Stewart, "How Far Mechanized Cotton Farming?" *Progressive Farmer* 63, no. 10 [Oct., 1948], p. 82).

· THURS 16. . . . They finished the cotton about 2 P.M. I now have it in the pile or dump rows. I think I will have 8 bales. . . .

N·O·V·E·M·B·E·R

The large amount of machine-harvested cotton crowded the gins in the fall of 1947, and farmers had to stack their cotton on the ground or in stalls at the gin. When cotton is harvested with a stripper, the entire stem is stripped clean. The stem generally contains green bolls that cause problems if stacked in piles that prohibit air circulation.

· MON 3. I went down to gin to see about my sled or puller cotton. It really is getting hot. . . .
· FRI 7. I loaded up a load of the pulled cotton and took it to co-op gin. They could not gin it, so I left it. They said it would be ginned off about 10:00 P.M. tonight.
· SAT 8. I was up early. Went down to gin to get my trailer. Boy was I knocked down when the office man told me I only had a bale wt of 385 lbs, 510 # seed. The gross wt was 1770 lbs. . . .

It is difficult to separate lint from burrs when cotton is damp or contains green bolls. Consequently, a lot of lint is burned in the burr-pit instead of going into the bale.

· MON 24. . . . Bud & Ida and Wanda & Buster came by to night. They had a new "48" Ford. Sure is a nice job. Cold tonight.

D·E·C·E·M·B·E·R

· MON 22. . . . I went by for a settlement with the "Farm Security U.S. people." [*Farm Security Association*] I payed off my $300.00 loan. I only owe $82.00 now. My payment today was $172.00. . . .

· WED 24. I was down town in the forenoon. I had to mail some more Christmas cards. . . .

· THURS 25. . . . We had a good old fashion dinner here at home. Back bones cooked to a turn. Beats any body's turkey for good eating.

· FRI 26. Well another Xmas day has come and gone. Soon we will start on another New Year and that also will pass away fast. . . .

1·9·4·8

Moisture was inadequate, but continuing high prices made up for the short-fall in yield.

J·A·N·U·A·R·Y

· WED 14.   Today 45 years since, on the same day of the week, Sallie & I were married. That seems a long time, but it is not. We have always gotten along O.K. She does not look now as she did then. I have a picture of her before me, is the reason I know. Picture made Sept, 1901, Mangum, Okla.

F·E·B·R·U·A·R·Y

· FRI 6.   This is the first green ink I have used in several years, 22 or 23 years, I think. . . .
· WED 18.   . . . A high of 80° today. . . .

M·A·R·C·H

· TUES 9.   . . . Boy the cold wave has moved in, now 10 P.M., 10° above.
· THURS 11.   . . . The Co-op gin manager gave me a check of $368.95 for my last cotton. The 8 bales brought $804.90 [*cotton grown in 1947*].

1948

Dot and Almeda were living in Littlefield, and Sallie spent a week in Oklahoma nursing an older sister who was bedridden with pneumonia.

· FRI 12. . . . I bought Bosco two cans of dog food. He ate one can this afternoon. He seemed to like it. Well, it looks good enough for man to eat. If Sallie does not hurry back I may take the other can my self. The reason I had to get dog food was Bosco did not like my cooking.

A·P·R·I·L

· WED 21. San Jacinto day. No other state enjoys this holiday. . . .

The battle of San Jacinto, on April 21, 1836, was the concluding battle of the Texas Revolution. It lasted only eighteen minutes; however, when measured by its results, San Jacinto was one of the most decisive battles in history. Texas' freedom from Mexico led to annexation and the Mexican War, from which the United States acquired almost one-third of its present area. Ultimately nearly a million square miles of territory changed sovereignty (See Webb and Carroll, eds., *The Handbook of Texas* 2, p. 554).

J·U·N·E

· FRI 4. . . . We all went up to Frank's and Curtie's. [*Curtie's husband, Hardy Witt, died, and she married Frank Wagnon.*] The oil lease "hound" was there talking to Frank. They made the deal. Five and ½ dollars per A. $1760. That was on 320 A. Well that was just like finding that much money. . . .

A "lease hound," officially known as a landman, is hired by an oil company to lease land suspected of containing pockets of oil below the surface. Surface rights are retained by the owner, who generally continues to use the land in the same manner. If oil is found, the property owner receives a portion — during the 1940s this was commonly one-eighth — and the oil company keeps the rest. Expenses for production and sale of the oil are assumed by the company.

A·U·G·U·S·T

· FRI 13. . . . I heard a hail storm hit in or near Bud's crop. We are sure dry.
· SUN 15. . . . Crops as a whole are in bad shape. Only the irrigated ones look good.

Lamb County recorded only ten inches of rain in 1948, less than half the normal amount (See *Climatological Data, 1948*, p. 372).

S·E·P·T·E·M·B·E·R

· SAT 25.   I do not want to pull it [*cotton*] with the cotton puller if I can help it.

DeLoach's experience with machine-harvested cotton in 1947 had not been good (See entries for October and November, 1947).

· MON 27.   . . . No cotton pickers and don't look like I will get any till all the other boys finish.

Because hands were paid by the pound, farmers with small acreages or light yields had difficulty finding and keeping laborers at harvest time.

· TUES 28.   . . . I can't find any one to pull my cotton. I will build me a cotton picker's house.

Dissatisfaction with housing was really not as important as it had been during the 1920s and 1930s. Migratory crews often established headquarters on a farm having adequate housing facilities and worked both there and on other farms in the neighborhood. DeLoach's problem was his small cotton acreage (See Motheral, Metzler, and Ducoff, *Cotton and Manpower*, pp. 32–36).

O·C·T·O·B·E·R

· MON 4.   . . . Went for Mr. Newton in Altus, Okla.
· FRI 29.   The Negroes finished their part of the cotton by 1 P.M. I had 5 big bales off of the 20 A. block. The whites will finish tomorrow if nothing happens. I may get 9 bales in all. I payed off the Negroes $205.90. That is over for this year.

It was costing DeLoach approximately forty dollars per bale to have his cotton harvested by hand.

N·O·V·E·M·B·E·R

· TUES 2.   We all went by the voting box at Mr. Jess Henry's Sallie & I voted. . . . I had to help hold the election in the afternoon, now 10 P.M. I think the whole thing will go Democratic.

The 1948 voter turnout was the largest for a general election in the history of Lamb County, where Truman received an eight-to-one majority over Dewey. Texans voted Democrat all the way, giving Truman the state's twenty-three electoral votes and sending Lyndon Johnson to the U.S. Senate.

· Mon 8. . . . I sold my 8 bales of cotton to Curtis Robbins, 27.21¢ per lb., $133.48 [*per bale*]. I did not want to put it in the loan.

In late November DeLoach and his sons went deer hunting on brother Ed's ranch near Del Rio, Texas, where they killed five white-tailed deer. This game animal thrives so well that overpopulation often causes problems, thus a kill of nearly 40,000 was encouraged in 1948. Deer hunting, a popular sport in Texas, provides meat that is generally used in sausage or in chili.

November... deer hunting on
brother Ed's place down by Del
Rio... got 5 deer.

1·9·4·9

High prices and adequate moisture meant a record-breaking year for farmers on the South Plains. Adequate moisture in West Texas, however, meant severe weather—ice storms, tornadoes, and hailstorms; but by fall, the warm dry weather was ideal for harvesting bumper crops.

J·A·N·U·A·R·Y

· WED 26. . . . Snow & sleet falling now, 11:50 P.M. Quite a lot of thunder & lightening now. Like an April shower cloud.

Old-timers in West Texas believed thunder during a snowstorm was a sign of prosperity for the coming year. Quite possibly the belief stemmed from the fact that adequate winter moisture was a key factor in producing a good yield. Many people, however, attributed this concept to Indian lore.

A·P·R·I·L

· SUN 10. Cold this early A.M., well all day. We went to church. I did something this Sunday I have not done in a long time. I took the sacrament [*communion*] at church. I think it is my duty to do that.

Bill's remains arrived home for a final burial. The fading of the family's hopes over the previous five years did not lessen the sting they felt now that they faced the certainty of his death. The last doubt was erased, and they had to perform the task they all dreaded.

- · SAT 16.   We were up and ready to go to Littlefield. We were down there by 10:00 A.M. The train was 2 hrs late in arriving in Lubbock, so the funeral coach was 2 hr late in reaching Littlefield. At last it arrived. Another sad hr. . . .
- · SUN 17.   [*Easter Sunday*] The good people of the Sudan vicinity brought in the good food for the noon lunch. We had lunch and all went to the funeral home and soon we were on the way to the church (Baptist) in Sudan. Everything went off all O.K. On out to the cemetery. The Legion boys took charge and put on their part after the church services. . . .

M·A·Y

- · SAT 7.   . . . I went to Hartman's Funeral Home and paid my bill, $45.00.
- · TUES 17.   . . . I am going to dig me a storm cellar. Too many cyclones passing through the country.
- · FRI 20.   I planted cotton till noon. I used all the D. P. L. cotton I had. . . .

DeLoach planted Delta Pine and Land cotton, which was rated by the Lubbock Experiment Station as having the highest average yield of the dryland varieties tested from 1947 to 1950. The average yield was 320 pounds of lint per acre; eighty bolls were required to produce a pound; lint turnout was 41 percent; and staple length was one inch (See D. T. Killough, E. F. McFarland, T. R. Richmond, and F. C. Elliott, *Performance of Cotton Varieties in Texas, 1948–1950*, pp. 10–12).

J·U·N·E

- · THURS 9.   Well, the rain, wind and hail came up about 9:00 P.M. last night so this early A.M. I went out for a look. I have nothing left. My crop was washed out, covered up and ruined. Well, it hit me below the belt, but I have looked for it for some time. Things were too good to be true. . . . No damage S.W. and south of Sudan. My melon patch was like a flower bed. Nothing now.

J·U·L·Y

· Mon 11. . . . I had to make another trip in P.M. with the 2 hogs. They
weighed total 349# at 20.5¢ per lb., check $71.55. I now want 2 more
pigs. I kept those two 4 months 10 days. First cost $25.00, feed $10.00=
$35.00. A profit $36.55. Good interest on $25.00 investment.

O·C·T·O·B·E·R

· Thurs 6.   The operation [*gallbladder*] so far was a success. Sallie was O.K.
up to this late P.M. . . . . Jim stayed with her tonight.
· Wed 19.   I was up early. Over to the hospital by 10 A.M. like the nurse
told me, but Sallie was ready and had been for some time. Waiting for
me. We made ready after I saw the Business Manager and settled up
the bill, which was $136.10. We arrived home about noon. Sallie had to
lay down. She is weak.
· Fri 21.   Worked in house, cleaning. I thought I had things clean, but
Sallie has snooped around and found some dirt behind the door. Then
she had me on the beam balance of day. . . . Sallie is doing O.K.

N·O·V·E·M·B·E·R

· Mon 7.   A little cool today. Nothing doing today. I do not want any cotton hands now. Will pull the cotton with a puller. . . .
· Tues 8.   . . . We went on to town, on down to Friendship store. I wanted
to see Eloy Templeton, but he was down in the Bull Lake country. I
saw his wife at Friendship store. I told her what to tell Eloy. I want him
to pull my cotton. He has one of the new John Deere pullers. Cold
tonight.

Eloy Templeton did custom harvesting for other farmers in the Sudan area.
This made it profitable to own expensive equipment when the small acreage he
farmed did not justify the expense.

· Wed 9.   I went down to see the man with the cotton puller. He said he
was booked up where he can't say when he would. . . .

In 1949, a seventy-county area in West Texas produced over three million bales
of cotton, the largest crop in the history of the region. To get the cotton out of
the fields as quickly as possible, more mechanical harvesters were used than ever

before, and men doing custom machine harvesting were booked up far in advance (See *West Texas Today* 30, no. 11 [Jan., 1950], p. 7).

·Thurs 10.   Rex Bowers came down to see me about pulling my cotton with the puller he used 2 years ago. He said if he could get to it Monday he would bring the outfit down Sun. Hope he can come. My threshed grain is on the ground and can't get a truck to move it to elevator, and the cotton needs to be gathered.

·Fri 11.   . . . I visited the cotton field and the wind has filled the cotton full of feed leaves. I will now try to get some one to hand pull it. Can't pull it with any kind of a cotton pulling machine. Has rained some tonight.

·Sat 12.   . . . The Mexicans got moved in. . . .

·Thurs 17.   I was in Sudan early. Got the report on the 2nd bale of cotton ginned. It lost 163 pounds. I could not stand that, so I came home and fired the whole lot of them. They said they would not take gin weights, so I paid them up and told them to move. I do not know yet what the third bale will do. Any way, I took 230 pounds to gin and put on the bale. Will see what that does. . . .

·Sat 19.   I guess our Vice-president is not dead this morning. He is an old man to take on a young widow of 35 years. They were married yesterday 11 A.M.

Alben William Barkley, vice president of the United States, married Mrs. Carleton S. Hadley. Both had been widowed. Based on the attention given to the couple, news reporters appeared to be as interested as DeLoach in the fact that Barkley was 71 and Hadley was 38 (See *New York Times*, Nov. 19, 1949, pp. 1, 3).

·Fri 25.   Dennis came over with cotton stripper. We tried it out. I did not like it. So I will get some hands and hand pull it. . . .

·Mon 28.   The Negro men were out pulling a little after day light and they pulled till sunset. They pulled 1161 lbs. . . .

·Tues 29.   . . . I picked up two bales of cotton tickets and compress certificates. One was a low grade, worth 16.94 cts in the loan. I sold it for a 17.94 cts per lb. I put the other one in the loan (U. S. cotton loan) at 23.90 cts per lb. . . .

Sat. 16... the funeral coach was 2 hr. late in reaching Littlefield. At last it arrived. Another sad hr....

· Fri 2.   We moved all the grain that I have to sell, 61,670# at Muleshoe, 15,440# at Sudan. I made 82 or 83,000 in all [*DeLoach grossed $1999.40 on the grain*]. Maybe more. A little cold tonight.

· Sun 4.   . . . We went to church. After church we went down to Littlefield to see how Dot & Almeda were getting along. We all went to the cafe for lunch. That restaurant food—I can't hardly eat it. 85¢ per plate for a spoon of English peas, a spoon of canned corn, a helping of mashed potatoes and two little finger tips [*of*] veal. Coffee free? For desert 3 little slices of peaches and 1 cake about the size of an old silver dollar. I would rather of had a hot dog and coffee. . . .

· Thurs 8.   . . . The boys finished the cotton pulling about 2:30 P.M. I went to town, took two bales of cotton. I have one more to go to gin. That will be the 9th bale [*DeLoach averaged slightly over one-half bale per acre*]. . . .

· Wed 21.   . . . I bought a waffle iron (electric). A real nice Christmas present. . . .

1·9·5·0

By 1950 more Texans lived in towns than on farms. The general pattern of movement was not to large cities but to towns within the counties where these people formerly farmed. Older farmers welcomed the trend because they could move to town without being completely separated from the land that was part of their identity.

J·A·N·U·A·R·Y

· Tues 17. . . . Was in town this afternoon. Heard Bud bought him another place of 113 A. . . at $70.00 per A. It ought to be good land. I sure would like to see a good rain. . . .

By 1947 farm land on the High Plains was among the highest real estate in the state (See "Texas Land Prices Start to Level Off," *Southwestern Crop and Stock* 3, no. 11 [Nov., 1949], p. 27).

· Thurs 19. . . . I went down to Sudan this P.M. Just to go was all. Well, I did get a hair cut and a bawling out when I got home. Well, I guess that is O.K. . . .

· Sun 22. We all (Sallie & I) went to church. Mr. N. [*Newton*] would not go. Bud, Ida, Wanda, Robert and his little boy friend, son of Mr & Mrs. Gil Belmont came home with us for lunch, but wanted to take us to see the place he bought a few days since. We drove around up in that part of the high plains. He bought land off of the old Syndicate land. The old XIT outfit. The Capitol Land Co.

In 1885 the XIT Ranch was established by the Capitol Syndicate, a Chicago corporation, in exchange for building the state capitol at Austin. The land, which covered all or part of ten Texas counties, was ranched until the early 1900s when farmers began settling West Texas. Bud did not buy land from the Capitol Syndicate but bought land that had at one time been part of the XIT Ranch.

· Mon 23.   . . . I renewed my driving license, 75¢. . . .

F·E·B·R·U·A·R·Y

· Sat 4.   . . . I payed the two last notes on the little home, No. 14, No. 15. The amount of the check $237.16, notes, interest. The little home is mine, or ours, as it should be. I owe nothing on it, or any thing else that I know of. . . .

M·A·R·C·H

· Thurs 2.   Another state holiday. This one the banks close up Independence Day for Texas. We all had our checks, but could not cash them. . . .

On March 2, 1836, delegates to the Convention of 1836 assembled at Washington-on-the-Brazos, a short distance from the present city of Navasota, and adopted a Declaration of Independence. The Republic of Texas was created by this document and lasted ten years; it was then annexed to the United States (See Webb and Carroll, eds., *Handbook of Texas* 1, pp. 479–80).

· Tues 14.   . . . Well, I smoked two ready rolls yesterday. Over 9 years that I did not smoke. I think I will get some tobacco and make my own. I never did like ready made cigarettes. . . .
· Sat 18.   I finished a part of the land that blew so bad, but by noon I could not tell where I had chiseled. Boy, it was really covering things up. . . . We went to town in afternoon. We stayed in the car most of the time while in town. We voted in the bond election. Yes, against it. A school bond of $125,000. . . .

During the drought-ridden 1950s farmers took every measure to avoid the wind erosion problems that plagued them in the 1930s. They discovered that one of their best weapons was the chisel plow. It had large sweeps attached to a tool bar that turned the soil to a depth of ten inches, throwing up clods that held the land against the wind (See Arlee Gowen, "There Goes That Farm Again," *Southwestern Crop and Stock* 3, no. 1 [Jan., 1949], pp. 10–11). The bond issue carried by a majority of four to one. DeLoach voted against it because the tax rate on his farm would be raised from $1.30 to $1.50 per hundred dollars valuation. The new rate was not unusually high; it was the same level as the surrounding school districts (See *Lamb County Leader*, Mar. 21, 1950, p. 7).

A·p·r·i·l

· Fri 7.   A pleasant surprise when I went to the mail box. A few days ago I requested K.G.N.C., Amarillo, to broadcast a request for an old 1890s Texas History. "Uncle Jack" did. So this mail brought one in. It came from the Hon. Donald Ziegler an Atty of Tulia, Texas. The history is the same as I studied back in the middle '90s. I lost the one I used, but all the things of those battles fought in those early days brought back memories to me when I read this history. Any Texas boy will, as a man, get a thrill when reading of the valiant fighting of those men, especially of the Alamo, "The Seige of the Alamo." Did nothing today, only read.

KGNC is a radio station popular with farmers because it is heavily oriented toward agricultural news. When compared to DeLoach's comments about World War II on January 27, 1945, this entry suggests that one's feelings about "history" and personal experience are often inconsistent.

· Mon 10.   . . . Bud came up to help me put up Bill's grave marker that Army Aviation furnished, but I looked at it after we had the hole dug for the base and I decided I would not use it. It looked too cheap and phoney. Bill deserves a better monument than that. If that is all he could [get], having lost his life, I will not have it.

· Thurs 20.   . . . We stayed close to the radio. We wanted to hear the evidence of the star witness of the McCarthy, Latimore Senate investigation. . . .

Soviet military power, loss of the monopoly of atomic power, the Korean War, and horror stories about spies sent a wave of fear through the American people in the decade following World War II. Reacting very much as people did during the Red Scare of the twenties, many Americans supported Senator Joseph McCarthy's sensational rampage to find people who could be accused of being communists and causing the turmoil that is typical of the adjustment period following a worldwide conflict. Professor Owen Latimore of Johns Hopkins University was a victim of McCarthy's investigative hearings.

· TUES 25.   We were off for Lubbock by 8:30 A.M. . . . We went to all the monument shops in town. We made a trade with the South Plains Monument people. We picked out a stone at $340.00. They are to put it up and also place the Gov. stone that is for Bill's grave. All at the above price to be put up inside of 2 weeks. . . .

M·A·Y

· THURS 4.   The wind and sand started about 10 A.M. By 4 P.M. we thought it was at its high, but by 7 P.M. the sand was so thick that visibility was 100 yds or less. The worst sand storm we have had since Thanksgiving 1926. It is banked up some places 2 ft high. We need a rain to stop the wind and sand blowing. I stayed home all day. In fact a man is just foolish to get out on the high way.
· FRI 5.   We cleaned sand out of house by 11 A.M. It sure did blow in around doors and windows. . . .
· TUES 16.   I went to get mail at 11:15 A.M. I was bouyed up when I got letter from Ed. It had a check in it for $300.00. That is for the oil lease on the Scurry Co. land we own there. Ed leased it according to his letter, for $150.00 per acre. $50.00 cash, $100.00 payable in oil. . . .

This land, near Ira, Texas, belonged to DeLoach's parents while they were living. Scurry County, Texas, located in the northeast corner of the Permian Basin, is a prehistoric sea that contains some of the richest oil deposits in the world. Discovery of the Canyon Reef Field in 1948 touched off a boom. Leases ran as high as two thousand dollars per acre in good territory, and people who had been battling debts all of their lives soon wiped the slate clean (See Hooper Shelton, comp., *From Buffalo to Oil: History of Scurry County, Texas*, pp. 261–66).

· THURS 18.   I did some work around house. . . . I ought to be planting. But no moisture to do anything in the field. . . .

J·U·N·E

· FRI 16.   At home all forenoon. I went down town about 2 P.M. Jackie Williamson and Clay Polk came out to house as I went into town. They brought out a telegram from Houston stating the death of Bro. Tom of Houston. He passed on at 8:30 A.M. today. The funeral will be held at or on the afternoon of Tuesday, June 20th. I went up to Muleshoe to see if Sister Curtie could go. We made arrangements to take the afternoon train out of Sudan on Sunday 18th. Will stop overnight at Bro. Bowden's in Snyder. Only 6 of the 9 of us left now. Two of the girls and 1 of the 5 boys have passed away. The telegram did not say what was the cause of his passing. Heart trouble I am afraid.

J·U·L·Y

· SAT 1.   Too late! Too late! for a cotton crop and if we could get a feed crop planted now everything would have to favor it for it to make a grain crop. . . .

· MON 3.   . . . It is a little more favorable tonight for a rain, but don't know. We have been fooled before.

· TUES 4.   Well, we thought when we got up that we had had another ¼" of rain, but before night we decided as much as 1" fell. I heard early that all the Friendship vicinity had a flood, so Sallie & I pulled out for Bud's, Ida. Sure enough they had a wash out. I told Bud he could come up with his 4 row John Deere and plant my place in a day's time. We did not intend to plant till tomorrow. That would let the moisture go down, but he started about 5 P.M. I started little Robert to cutting stalks ahead of him. They worked till about 7:00 P.M. Robert stayed here tonight. He sure is thrilled to drive the Ford tractor and cut stalks [*he was also pleased with the $4.75 his grandfather paid him for the work*].

Officially, Lamb County recorded 18.59 inches of moisture in 1950. Nearly half of the total, 8.44 inches, fell in July. The hard, washing rains destroyed crops that were in the path of the runoff water, and all of this happened when it was much too late to plant cotton and risky even for grain sorghums (See *Climatological Data, 1950*, p. 397). Stalks from the previous year's crop were left standing to reduce wind erosion. A stalk cutter broke them into small pieces, adding humus to the soil before a new crop was planted.

· SAT 22.   . . . Has rained several of those "widely scattered showers" that the weather man speaks of. . . .

A·U·G·U·S·T

· Tues 22. Sallie and I went to Littlefield. Closed the trade for the Sudan
    house. Paid off. I had put in a Federal Home Loan for $2500.00, paid
    cash of 1750.00.
· Wed 23. The first month's rent coming to me was due today. . . . Mr.
    Wolf payed the $50.00 house rent. The rent is payable in advance.

S·E·P·T·E·M·B·E·R

· Fri 29. . . . The oil man came out to see me again. We made a trade,
    $5.00 per A. $1.00 rental per year. check was $316.90. I credited Sallie's
    account at Bank with one half, $158.45.

DeLoach leased his land to an oil company. Leases were for a specified number of years and dollars per acre, which was paid when the lease was signed. One
dollar per acre rental money was due each succeeding year until the lease ended.

O·C·T·O·B·E·R

· Wed 4. . . . I listened to the ball game. The National League, New York
    Yanks, Phil vs Yanks game 2 to 1. . . .
· Thurs 19. I fixed the rats. I put the tractor up against the grain bin,
    stopped all holes around the bins, put a pipe on the exhaust of tractor,
    put it under bins and started the motor and I think it killed all the
    rats. . . .

N·O·V·E·M·B·E·R

· Fri 3. Well, what we have been looking for and hating to see came in
    last night. A freeze. The temperature was down to 29° at 6:30 A.M.
    [average date for first freeze is November 10]. . . .
· Tues 14. . . . H. G. & Dellie came by for a pop call. He is helping Bud
    cut his feed. I am going to try and get a combine in mine tomorrow.
    A few hard winds will put it down.
· Sun 19. Well, the sand storm struck here about 4:00 A.M., but did not
    get real bad until around 10:00 A.M. and by noon all the feed was

blown down. A total loss if combine men can't find some kind of attachment to pick it up off the ground. That is real disappointing. All the good feed on the ground and I sure did need it. I do not know just what I can do about it. Nothing.

The freeze dried the moisture out of the feed stalk, making it quite brittle and subject to being knocked over by a strong wind.

D·E·C·E·M·B·E·R

· Sat 16. . . . I will put a hot wire around the stalk field when I get the heads cut out. Mr. Hilton wanted to rent my place and buy my tractor. I told him I would take $850.00 for tractor and equipment. He said he would see me soon.

DeLoach salvaged some of the maize heads that were knocked to the ground in the windstorm of November 19 by letting his cow eat them.

1·9·5·1

The highest prices in history for crops—and the highest expenses for raising them—were predicted for 1951. The reduced margin of profit meant that it was wise for small farmers to rent their land to larger operators who could spread the cost of production over many acres.

J·A·N·U·A·R·Y

· Fri 19.   Another set around and do nothing [*day*], but there are lots of such day's ahead since I have rented out. The ear marks of an other dry year are in the making. . . .

Total rainfall for 1951 was only 2.35 inches below average, but weather reports indicate the area in which DeLoach lived received less than 2 inches of moisture from October, 1950, through April, 1951. Winter moisture is vital for raising bountiful crops in West Texas (See *Climatological Data, 1950*, p. 397; *Climatological Data, 1951*, p. 379).

F·E·B·R·U·A·R·Y

· Sat 10.   Mr. Hilton came over and started plowing. We decided to put the rows on the same contour as highway. By doing that the short rows are cut to a minimum. [*Short rows were bothersome for tractor work, because of the constant turning.*]

M·A·R·C·H

· THURS 15. . . . Sallie went for the eggs. The Pet cow made a pass at her.
I decided Pet needed attention, so I went over to Harry Williams'. He
came for the cow. We put her in with [a] muly gentleman cow, so now
maybe she won't be attacking women.

A·P·R·I·L

· FRI 13. . . . I called to see how Percy Mercer was getting along. He seemed
to be some better. He said I could plant 5 acres of water melons on his
land if I wanted to, and we would split the money 50–50. That would
give me a job.

· WED 25. . . . The sewing club met here this P.M.

· FRI 27. . . . I was in Sudan for a while this P.M. Had to report. If one of
the old coons are missing they think he is sick, hence the reporting.

M·A·Y

· TUES 1. A hard sand storm blew all day. Lots of land changed hand. No
deeds issued. The wind does not require a deed.

· TUES 22. . . . I made a run to town for some chicken feed. . . . This buying feed sure gets old. A man that don't put up feed should not keep
any thing that eats.

J·U·N·E

· TUES 5. . . . near night a heavy bad cloud started making up in N.W.,
about 4:00 P.M. and by 6:00 P.M. it hit here and I mean it hit. The worst
hail storm I ever saw. In my 52 years on the plains I never saw such a
hail storm. It beat the limbs off the trees. . . . Two cars of people ran in
here for shelter. The hail was so bad they could not get out. . . .

Dry spells characteristically break with violent weather in a semi-arid climate.
This one broke on the night of June 5 when a supercharged thunderstorm raged
across the South Plains, dumping flood-like rains and walnut size hailstones.
Over three hundred thousand acres of young cotton were damaged in Lamb
County.

· FRI 22. . . . I sent by Bud for some radiator fluid. He reported he had a
    good well. They finished it out this P.M. . . .

Rising farm prices during the 1940s and the development of powerful pumps
led to an increased interest in irrigation to offset the erratic rainfall of the Plains.
Wide variations in production and farm incomes, caused by undependable rainfall, became a critical problem as production costs increased. The thick, underlying layer of water sands, known as the Ogallala Aquifer, brings water close
enough to the surface to be economical for irrigation on the Llano Estacado.
By 1951, 180,000 acres in Lamb County were irrigated with seventeen hundred
wells (See C. A. Bonnen, W. C. McArthur, A. C. Magee, and W. F. Hughes,
Use of Irrigation Water on the High Plains, pp. 1–43; and TAES, *Irrigation Survey
of the High Plains of Texas,* cited in Gordon, "The History and Development of
Irrigated Cotton," p. 359).

J·U·L·Y

· WED 4. . . . Hilton ran the sand fighter over my place. The sand would
    have damaged the cotton if it had not been done. He is very consider-
    ate of my place.

A sandfighter is a piece of equipment that has spiked teeth welded onto a
long tool bar. As it is dragged across the land it breaks the crust after a rain and
reduces the possibility of blowing sand which would kill tender, young cotton
plants in a few minutes.

· FRI 13. Sallie's birthday. She is 67 years old today. I am 4 yrs, 5 mo., 12
    days older than she. We hoed in the corn patch while it was cool. . . .
· FRI 20. I was ready to hoe cotton here on my place for Mr. Hilton. I put
    in 7 hrs. . . . It was awful hot, but just about as cool out in the field as
    in the house [*Hilton paid DeLoach seventy-five cents per hour*]. . . .
· SAT 21. . . . About 11:00 A.M. Harold, Dellie and Wayne, their youngest
    son just back from the war front Korea, came in. We all were glad to see
    Wayne back and looking so well. . . .

A·U·G·U·S·T

· MON 13. . . . the 15th that is Dad Newton's birthday. . . . The old fellow
    will be 96 yrs old. Sallie's dad.

N·O·V·E·M·B·E·R

·THURS 8. . . . I met Melba Bozeman in bank and talked with her about
the liability insurance. She told me it would cost me $25.00 per year to
carry $15,000 on my car. . . .

This is the premium for liability insurance (See diary entry for December 31,
1951).

·FRI 16. . . . Sallie & I went to Sudan in P.M. We had to get some milk.
Boy that is a pain in the flank. Buying milk is something I have not
done in 38 years, only just a few days at a time when I turned cows dry.

·FRI 30. . . . We came by Mrs. Wilmon's for some butter. "Cow butter."
This "oleo" stuff, can't hardly look at it. . . .

D·E·C·E·M·B·E·R

·SUN 2. . . . Mr. Hilton finished the cotton harvest yesterday. He will make
18 bales +. That is of 500 lb bales. That gives me 4½ bales to my part.

DeLoach received $790.87 rent from the cotton produced on his farm. This
was slightly more than the gross income ($787.00) from his entire cotton crop
a decade earlier. High market prices favored the land owner, who did not have
to bear the correspondingly high expense of production.

·THURS 6. Mr. Hilton sold 8 bales of cotton off my place. 195 (1/3 of 859
lbs at 35.15¢ per lb).

·THURS 20. . . . I stamped and posted a bunch of Christmas cards. . . .

·SAT 22. . . . I have been watching the Pet cow all afternoon. She dropped
her calf about 7:00 P.M. A big roan she calf. . . .

·MON 31. The last day of 1951. I went to town early. Made application for
the law insurance on my car, the liability insurance. . . .

Texas' Safety Responsibility Law, which went into effect January 1, 1952, required any owner whose vehicle was involved in an accident causing property
damage of a hundred dollars or more, or injury or death to a person, to produce fifteen thousand dollars in cash or securities. Insurance, while not man-
datory, was a method of providing the necessary coverage. Premiums, set by the
state, were twenty-five dollars for Lamb County residents, and failure to meet
the financial obligations meant suspension of the operator's license and regis-
tration plates (See Lubbock Avalanche-Journal, Dec. 31, 1951, p. 1).

1·9·5·2

High commodity prices and another drought confirmed DeLoach's decision to retire, but not working on a regular basis required some adjustments. His feeling that the time clock was running out was noticeable—he wrote in November, "I wanted a new car. If ever we aimed to have a new car, now was the time to get it. We can enjoy it while we are not too old to drive it."

F·E·B·R·U·A·R·Y

· Sun 17.   . . . We have been here looking at the same scenery all day. The same old thing. Enough to put any one in a nut house. Bud & Ida came up for a pop call late.

M·A·R·C·H

· Wed 5.   A boy born to Jim & Arlois [*Bill*].
· Wed 26.   . . . We got the joint Will that atty. Dunham drew up for us.

M·A·Y

· Thurs 22.   . . . Sallie & I went to Sudan this P.M. I needed a hair cut. The first one I have had in barber shop since they went up to $1.00 per head. . . .

289

J·U·N·E

· Sat 14. I was down town for a while this A.M. Just to visit with the boys. Well, all of my old friends are boys to me. All of us were in town this P.M. All people talk about is dry weather and it is getting real serious. Lots of people have not planted a seed of any thing and it is going to be too late for a feed crop soon. It is too late for cotton now, unless every thing suits it. It is real unsatisfactory, but nothing can be done about it. . . .

J·U·L·Y

· Fri 11. . . . Eisenhower was nominated GOP tail twister today on the first ballot. I think I will vote for him. Any thing to stop that boy slaughter pen in Korea.

This entry reflects the frustration felt throughout the nation over the stalemate in Korea. DeLoach is also remembering the pain of losing his own son in World War II. Eisenhower, a military hero and president of Columbia University, won the hearts of the American people when he promised, if elected, to go to Korea to work out a solution (Herbert S. Parmet, *Eisenhower and the American Crusades*, pp. 102–44).

· Thurs 24. We (or I) did nothing much this day, only listen to the Demo. Convention and I did not know any more when I turned off at 9:10 P.M. than when I tuned in at 1:35 P.M. . . .

· Fri 25. . . . The convention started at about 12 noon and I stayed with it till 9:10 P.M. The steam roller came down the line in the 3rd ballot. And no candidate had a ghost of a show, only Stephenson of Ill., so I went to bed after I saw that Russell, of Ga., was out.

In 1952 the Democratic party staked its hopes on the intelligence and sophistication of Adlai E. Stevenson, governor of Illinois. His major obstacle was Eisenhower's popularity. The Texas delegation to the Democratic national convention favored Senator Richard Russell of Georgia for president, hence DeLoach's interest in this contender. Leaders of the party in Texas refused to support Stevenson partly because he had Truman's endorsement. Truman lost favor in Texas when he refused to acknowledge the state's claim to the tidelands, an oil-rich ten-mile strip extending out from the coast. Eisenhower's support of the state's claim, and his birth in Texas, cemented the opposition (See McKay and Faulk, *Texas after Spindletop*, pp. 216–18).

A·u·g·u·s·t

· Tues 19.   . . . I went up to Muleshoe to have my car inspected. The new
   law is to have the inspection done by Sept. 6, 1952. I think it is an un-
   just law, but it is a law and no use to defy it. There is nothing to do to
   my car. It passed all the tests. Cost me $1.00 for the windshield sticker
   tag. Was a hot day.

· Tues 26.   We went down to Littlefield. . . . I wanted to talk with the Federal Loan people, a Mr. Stowe. I am thinking about an irrigating well.
   A well means the difference between a crop and no crop.

· Wed 27.   . . . We drove over and took a look at their [*Harold and Dellie's*]
   irrigated cotton. Boy it is fine. All watered cotton is good. . . .

S·e·p·t·e·m·b·e·r

· Wed 3.   . . . Bud & I went up to see Harold's cotton on Bud's place. It is
   throwing off some squares. But I do not think watering it at this time
   would do it any good. . . .

"Squares" are buds made of three triangular leaves. They enclose and protect the flower before it opens, which happens about twenty-one days after
squares appear. The first flowers open low on the plant; the next ones are higher
and farther out on the branches. On first opening, flowers are a creamy-white
or yellow. At the close of the first day they are pink, and by the second day they
are red. On the third day they fall off and the bolls begin to grow. The average
time between bloom and open boll ranges from 46 to 65 days, depending on
the variety of cotton and weather conditions. When cotton plants are under
stress, they throw off their fruit (squares, flowers, or bolls) in an attempt to sustain the life of the plant. Harold's cotton plants could have been shedding because of deficient moisture or because the plant already had all of the fruit it
could carry. Shedding is common near the end of the season (See Harry Bates
Brown, *Cotton*, 1938 edition, pp. 91–95, 123–26).

O·c·t·o·b·e·r

· Sat 11.   We, Sallie, Dot, and Almeda, went to Littlefield. I drove by the
   voting box at the F. O. Masten headquarters to vote on the $6000.00
   court house and jail bond. Sallie & I were the first votes cast. We voted
   against the issue, but I guess it will carry. We were in Littlefield till

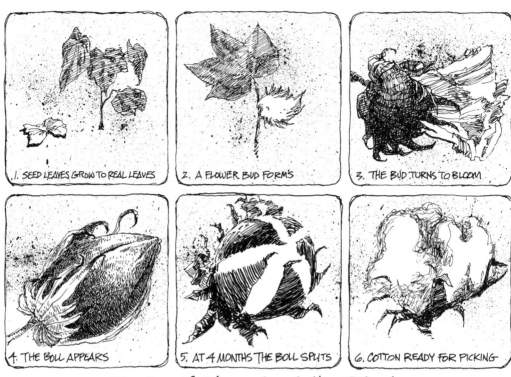

1. SEED LEAVES GROW TO REAL LEAVES
2. A FLOWER BUD FORMS
3. THE BUD TURNS TO BLOOM
4. THE BOLL APPEARS
5. AT 4 MONTHS THE BOLL SPLITS
6. COTTON READY FOR PICKING

The Growth Stages of a Cotton Plant

about 4:00 P.M. The town is full of Mexicans. They are here to pull cotton. The cotton harvest will be in full swing in a few days.

In 1952, 51 percent of the cotton crop was still handpulled the first time over to receive better prices in an early market. Then, approximately ten days after a heavy frost, stalks were stripped by machine (See William G. Adkins and William H. Metzler, *Tenure and Mechanization of the Cotton Harvest, Texas High Plains*, pp. 3–11).

· WED 29. . . . Mr. Newton passed away about 10:00 P.M. The old fellow did not suffer any. He just passed away so easily.

· THURS 30. . . . We picked out the casket, a steel one. Had an old suit that Mr. Newton requested to be buried in, (He never wore it but a few times), cleaned and pressed. It is a nice suit. The casket and all the undertaking services, $724.00. Sallie bought a blanket of flowers, $25.00, total, $749.00. Mr. Newton had saved up $475.00 that we applied on the account. Balance for us to pay, $249.00. The good people had brought in a great deal of food when we came in. Harold & Bud were quite a lot of help today. The funeral services will be held at 2:30, Friday, Oct. 31, 1952.

N·O·V·E·M·B·E·R

· Mon 3. . . . I was down town this P.M. I voted a straight Ike ticket. I do not know who Sallie voted for. . . . We got all the elections up to the time Stevenson conceeded Ike was the winner, hence a Republican President for the next 4 years.

Eisenhower won 442 electoral votes to Stevenson's 89; however, this landslide was not reflected in congressional elections. Obviously, Eisenhower was more popular than the party as a whole. Texas voters turned out in record numbers and "Eisenhower Democrats" carried the state by a sizeable margin, but in Lamb County he averaged only nine votes per box over Stevenson. Apparently many farmers still remembered the New Deal benefits during their plight in the 1930s (See Parmet, *Eisenhower and the American Crusades*, pp. 145–49; McKay and Faulk, *Texas after Spindletop*, p. 220; *Lamb County Leader*, Nov. 6, 1952, p. 1).

· Wed 5. I went down town with Ed [*a brother*]. . . . I wanted to put a thank you notice in the paper. . . .

1·9·5·3

DeLoach leased his farm for cash, instead of renting for a share of the crops, and beat the odds imposed by a full-blown drought. He sold the house in Littlefield. Dot and Almeda moved back to the farm to help prepare for the family's move to Sudan. With the worries of farming behind him, DeLoach's attention focused on family activities and current events.

J·A·N·U·A·R·Y

· Mon 19. ... Sallie & I went up to Muleshoe to attend the Electric Co-op meeting. They gave away several nice electrical appliances. One a T.V. set, but we did not draw a lucky no. ...

M·A·R·C·H

· Wed 4. ... The wolf killer and all out bad man Joe Stalin of Russia is reported in bad shape. I don't suppose he would be missed if he dies. ...

· Thurs 5. ... Sallie has been sick all day. We heard just now that the "Uncle Joe Stalin" died at 1:00 P.M. our time. Well, my bladder is too full for my eyes to shed any tears for him. ...

· Thurs 19. ... I subscribed for *Crop & Stock*, a magazine that is published in Lubbock. It treats on the early days of Crosby and Lubbock Counties. Things that I knew of back in the late 90's.

DeLoach is referring to a series of articles by his friend, Nellie Witt Spikes, that appeared monthly. Mrs. Spikes also wrote one of the first histories of Crosby County (See footnotes for 1914–17). *Southwestern Crop and Stock*, published in Lubbock from the late 1940s through the 1960s, provided the latest information about ranching and agriculture in the Southwest.

A·P·R·I·L

· TUES 28. The wind came out of the west early and by noon visibility was at times almost 0. . . . The wind got up so high that school kids could hardly walk down the streets.

M·A·Y

· FRI 1. . . . We called on the Roy Whit's for 1 hr of wrestling. They have a "T.V." set. We really did enjoy it.
· MON 11. . . . Radio report, a tornado struck San Angelo about 2:00 P.M. Then about 5:30 or 6:00 P.M. an other report (radio) that about 4:00 P.M. another tornado struck near Waco. That town was hit in the business center. The death toll is unknown at this time. Only 3 deaths have been reported in the San Angelo storm as of this time, 10:15 P.M. . . .

The Waco tornado broke all records as the single most disastrous weather occurrence in the history of Texas. Deaths totaled 114, and 597 people were injured. In addition, property damage exceeded $41 million. At San Angelo 11 people were killed and 159 injured; property damage amounted to more than $3 million. The intensity of these storms helps explain Sallie's lifelong fear of tornadoes (See *Texas Almanac and State Industrial Guide, 1954–1955*, pp. 146–48).

J·U·N·E

· SAT 13. I took Almeda down to the Valda Clark drug store. She works there on Saturdays and afternoon on Sundays.
· SAT 20. . . . we went to the open air show [*drive-in movie*] at Muleshoe, a very good show. The picture, the greatest "Show on Earth," Ringling Bro. Barnham, Bailey. A lot of improvement from the first show Barnham & Bailey show for me in 1894.

J·U·L·Y

· Mon 6. . . . We took Almeda over to the Hospital for a tooth extraction. Cost $3.00. The first tooth I ever had pulled cost Dad 25¢ in Greenville in 1888. I never will forget it. Of course, they did not have the equipment then they have now. The dentist just sat me down and pulled it. Now they have to make an exray picture and deaden the gum, but I guess it is O.K.

· Wed 8. . . . We bought 200 lbs of onions out north of Muleshoe. They sold for 50¢ per hundred. That is cheaper than one can raise them. . . .

· Wed 15. . . . Then we all went to a field where they had dug the potatoes. They gave one all the spuds one could pick up behind the digging machines. We picked up possibly 400 lbs. They lost lots, but it did not pay them to hire them picked up, hence the gift.

With the development of irrigation, vegetable crops increased in West Texas. Produce distributors from the Rio Grande Valley and California furnished seed, fertilizer, and equipment. They paid farmers ten dollars per acre at planting time plus another ten dollars per acre at harvesttime. The company harvested, processed, and marketed the crop. Vegetables grown on the Plains were being sold when older vegetable-producing areas were idle. Because only vegetables of uniform size and quality were selected for market, the culls were given away or left in the field to rot. This is another illustration of the changes taking place in farming. The small margin of profit per unit encouraged the integration of several phases of production to guarantee a dependable flow to year-round urban markets. This is in sharp contrast to the days of general farming, when vegetables of varying quality were enjoyed on a seasonal basis (See *Southwestern Crop and Stock* 2, no. 7 [July, 1948], p. 14).

A·U·G·U·S·T

· Fri 7. We went up to Harold's, Dellie's. . . . He told me that his hoeing bill was $1041.00. That is quite a hoe bill. . . .

S·E·P·T·E·M·B·E·R

· Mon 14. . . . We are spending our first night in Sudan. I think it will be O.K.

People 65 years of age and older who migrated from Texas farms had a tendency to move to small towns near their farms. In contrast, young people moved to the larger cities or urban areas (See Skrabanek, *Characteristics and Changes in the Texas Farm Population*, p. 14).

· Tues 15.   We have been on the go all day. I went out to the place (Our old home on the farm will be known here after as "The Farm"). . . .

· Sat 19.   We made ready and left for Littlefield about 11:00 A.M. Sallie did her grocery shopping and we started back home. We were down in Sudan for a while this P.M. We went over to the Pete Mercer's home for the T.V. program. We wanted to see Bud's and Ida's picture and the irrigated cotton on his place up in Parmer County, but they could not tune in on Amarillo. . . .

The dependability that irrigation gave to farming was welcomed and lauded across West Texas. After farmers suffered through the Dust Bowl days, good crops made the news during the drought-ridden 1950s.

In October Will & Sallie went to San Antonio, Texas, to attend a Baptist convention. They also did some sight-seeing. After retiring they had time and enough money from the rent to do a little traveling.

N·O·V·E·M·B·E·R

· Tues 24.   . . . Got the groceries and the green S&H Stamps at the Piggly Wiggly store. . . .

S&H Green Stamps, received for the purchase of groceries, could be redeemed for household items, recreational gear, or articles of clothing. Many grocery stores offered double stamps during the week, usually on Tuesday, and this practice changed the usual shopping day from Saturday to a weekday.

1·9·5·4

Even though he had formally retired, DeLoach reduced his work load gradually, avoiding the loss of self-esteem that often accompanies abrupt, forced retirement. Substituting leisure for work is often not satisfying in a society that values work. Retired farmers had their rented-out land to oversee and were welcomed as extra hands during peak rush times.

M·A·R·C·H

· Thurs 25. I made up my mind to have my place deep broke. . . .

After tractors replaced mules, soil compaction became a problem. To combat this, a one-way plow was used to break the land to a depth of ten to twelve inches. Deep breaking also reduced soil erosion from high winds during the drought-ridden 1950s.

A·P·R·I·L

· Sat 3. . . . Everything in the food line is going up all the time. I never buy the grocieries. Sallie has done that for so long. I gave her the right to check on me since I have had money in the bank, some 10 or twelve years ago. She generally has money in her own name for the household expences.

· Mon 5. . . . I stopped at the A.A.A. office at Amherst to see about my application for the deep breaking money of $150.00 [*government payment for conservation measure*]. They told me the county committee would have a meeting Tuesday, 6th at 2:00 P.M. and for me to be there. . . . $2.50 per A., $150.00 payment [*total cost to deep break 60 acres was $450; renter paid $300*].

· Mon 12. . . . I had a check from the sale of the old home in Scurry Co. Each part $444.44. . . .

In the settlement of the DeLoach estate, the farm near Ira was sold.

O·c·t·o·b·e·r

· Thurs 21. Sallie & I went out to Ray Overton's and pulled some cotton. I pulled 166 lbs, she 125, but I don't think we will pull any more. I will have to be tailed up in the morning. Too much for us.

· Mon 25. . . . Have quit smoking today. . . .

N·o·v·e·m·b·e·r

· Mon 22. . . . I worked in the trailer keeping the cotton pushed back [*DeLoach was helping a former neighbor*]. . . .

D·e·c·e·m·b·e·r

· Thurs 9. . . . I signed up for a permit to put down a well. An irrigation well. . . .

· Tues 21. . . . Joel Dillon told me that he had a buyer for our little farm. He asked me what I would take for it. I told him $250.00 for A. he asked me if I would take $200.00. I told him no.

Mon 22... I worked in
the trailer keeping the
cotton pushed back...

1·9·5·5

By the 1950s, capital had replaced labor as the primary input in farming. The days were gone when a man and his family formed a partnership if he wanted to farm. Now a farmer had to join hands with a bank or some other lending institution.

J·A·N·U·A·R·Y

· THURS 6.   . . . I sent check for renewal of *Star-Telegram*, $13.95 today [*he paid $3.25 per year for his first subscription in 1914*].

· MON 10.   . . . went to Littlefield this P.M. I wanted to get my well permit. It was properly signed up. I put up a check for $10.00. This check will be refunded. The permit is good for 120 days. I did not see the Loan man. Too many in his lobby waiting to see him and one has to take his turn. . . .

· THURS 13.   . . . I went up to Muleshoe in afternoon to see Elmer Crosby, the Trading Post Manager. I wanted to list my farm with him to sell. We have decided to sell out the farm while the land prices are good, but I could not see him. He was out of town and his office was closed. . . .

Land values reflect farm income more than any other economic activity; rising land values in the southwestern states reflected the strength of commercial agriculture in that area. Prices began climbing in 1946 when farmers started spending money they had accumulated due to record-breaking prices during

World War II. In Texas the value of land generally doubled from 1941–45; the growth of irrigation and commercial farming caused values on the Llano Estacado to double again from 1946–54. Although land prices reached record highs, this was not a speculative activity similar to that of the 1920s. Farmers remained the primary buyers, and the widely held goal of ownership of farmland by those who till it was probably closer to realization than at any time since Texas was settled. However, the increase in land values significantly raised the capital requirements for farming and restricted the number of young operators who could enter agriculture. Most of the land was purchased to enlarge operating farm units, which continued the trend toward fewer but larger farms (See John H. Southern, *Farm Land Market Situation in the Southwestern States, 1946–1954,* pp. 3–12).

·Tues 25. . . . An Amherst driller looked me up and gave me an estimate on a well. $3210.00 for a 225 ft well. A turn key job. . . .

·Wed 26. . . . We came back to Littlefield and talked with the Federal Land Bank people. They could not finance the well as I did not have enough acres. So that is it, I can't get a well.

·Thurs 27. Here all day. Down & in the dumps. I just can't get the needed money to put down a well. . . .

F·e·b·r·u·a·r·y

·Mon 14. . . . Almeda is gone every night to basket ball games or some school program. . . .

M·a·y

·Thurs 19. . . . Bud & Ida and Buster were here today. They went to Littlefield with us to buy a T.V. set. We, or Sallie, bought a Zenith, 17 inch, $221.30. It has been going since 6:00 P.M., now 9:35 P.M. Bud bought a new Ford.

O·c·t·o·b·e·r

·Mon 24. . . . Killing frost.

·Tues 25. We made a drive out to farm this P.M. The cotton leaves are all killed and the cotton is sure opening fast. Mr. Overton thinks he will have 8 hand pullers in the field by tomorrow. I hope he does. The cotton is in a fine state to pull now with all this sunshine and S.W. wind.

· WED 26.   . . . Sallie & I drove down to the city park to see the "Cousin Jody" and his troupe, a part of the "Grand Old Opera" of Nashville, Tenn. The whole show was good for sore eyes. Quite a comedy. . . .

N·O·V·E·M·B·E·R

· TUES 22.   . . . We have had a hard west sand storm all day. They had a bad fire in the compress cotton yard. They estimate 1000 bales of cotton burned. I do not know just what the loss will be. The fire department could do nothing with the fire only keep it from spreading. The high wind from the west pushed the fire through the entire width of the cotton yard. Some 22,000 bales of cotton on the yard. Ray Overton had cotton returns on the cotton raised on my place. My rent on the 12 bales was $461.80 [*twelve bales were produced on DeLoach's farm*]. Rebates on seed to be settled yet.

D·E·C·E·M·B·E·R

· FRI 30.   . . . I bought some reading glasses.

Wednesday, October 26 — Sallie and I drove down to the city park to see the "Cousin Jody" and his troupe, a part of the "Grand Old Opera"....was good for sore eyes. Quite a comedy....

1·9·5·6

Winter snow renewed everyone's hope for relief from the droughty conditions of the previous six years, but hot, dry winds in the spring blew the hope away, along with the rain clouds. By planting time, only those farmers with irrigation were able to get a crop started. Even though enough irrigation wells were pumping in Lamb County to keep county production records high, dryland farmers were suffering.

F·E·B·R·U·A·R·Y

· Sat 4. I think snow fell all night. Some 10″ to 12″ in on the level. Drifts look like from 2′ to 3′. . . . This is the worst snow storm I have seen in the last 50 years on the plains. The 1906 blizzard is thought to [be] worse. I do not think so.

M·A·R·C·H

· Tues 13. Sallie & I went for the mail and stayed in town for the John Deere free feed. They put it on every year. They also had a moving picture show. . . .
· Tues 20. . . . Almeda's birthday. She is 17 years old. I can't hardly believe it. She has been with us all of her life. She and her mother were to themselves for 2 years, but they were close enough that we could see about her from as much as once a week.

Plains Farmer

A·P·R·I·L

· Mon 9. . . . Out of tobacco, 3 smokes. No smoking. I quit only today. One after each meal.

· Fri 13. In house most of the day. I had a new book to read. "The History of Parker County." I get quite a kick out of reading it as I knew and know lots of the subjects that is recorded in it.

M·A·Y

· Tues 8. . . . A cloud came up in S.E., but we did not get any rain from it. Every irrigated farmer is planting cotton, but near all of the dry land men don't have enough moisture to plant. This has been the same set up since 1949. That is the last year that we had any early rainfall. Six dry years in a row.

· Thurs 10. The day started out pretty, but by noon a "cat" of a sand storm moved in. . . .

· Thurs 17. . . . I worked most of the day in the garden. Just to have something to do. I love to have something to do. I like to see things growing. . . .

J·U·N·E

· Sun 10. The folks all went to church. I do not go any more for I can't hear the preacher. I do not like to ask any one to repeat and I do not like to say huh. . . .

J·U·L·Y

· Tues 31. . . . we had a nice "cotton shower". . . .

S·E·P·T·E·M·B·E·R

· Sat 1. I went down to Community House to vote on the water bond. I voted against it. I have not heard how it went at this time, now 9:00 P.M. . . .

Lamb County voters were deciding whether or not to create a water control district. The intention was simply to retain Lamb County water in Lamb County. Bailey County, an adjoining county, did not have a control district, and nearby Lubbock officials bought water rights from individuals to supply growing municipal needs. As the number of irrigation wells increased, people were becoming aware of the importance of monitoring the use and distribution of underground water, but, as the election illustrates, not everyone understood this immediately (See *Lamb County Leader*, Aug. 30, 1956, p. 1).

· Sun 2. I heard early that bond issue lost out. That is remarkable. All the other bond issues carried by a large vote. . . .

· Mon 3. . . . The crop on my place is in bad shape as well all other dry land crops. Too dry.

· Wed 26. . . . I went down to elevator to see if Overton brought the grain in last night. He did. 3450 lbs at $1.75 per hundred. Check—$59.50. Not much for a feed crop, but nothing I can do about it. It just burnt up. No water.

O·C·T·O·B·E·R

· Mon 22. . . . I went out and pulled cotton . . . 153 lbs. I am a little tired tonight.

Even though DeLoach was exhausted, he could not stay away from the farm during planting and harvesting. The cycles of the crops had become an important part of his life.

N·O·V·E·M·B·E·R

· Mon 19. I sold my 7 bales of cotton this A.M. 3575 lbs at 26.48 cts for lb. $956.66 less charges, $11.50, draft $935.16. . . . Paid Bud $30.00 cash for pulling cotton. 2 B/C [*bales of cotton*] at .75 cts per 100 lbs or for 4000 lbs. I put one bale in Gov. loan, $119.01. It may make some money or it may not. . . .

· Fri 30. . . . I paid Ray Overton for pulling six bales total at 75¢ per 100 lbs $78.30.

Despite a bad year because of deficient moisture, DeLoach settled his debts and wrote in December, "All taxes paid for 1956." Taxes amounted to $119.82 for his farm and house in Sudan.

1·9·5·7

J·A·N·U·A·R·Y

· Fri 11. . . . I went to see the Federal Land Bank Sec, a Mr. McKelly. I can get the loan now to put down a irrigating well. I also called the Adams Pump Co. people and had them figure on the equipment, drilling, caseing, pump, and in all a turn key job. . . .

· Sun 13. We were up early. Had breakfast and I went up to Muleshoe for Curtie. The girls did not come, but Bess, Bowden's (our brother's) wife and Lowell Martin and Sue his wife were there. So Curtie said she would come with them after lunch. I came on home. Others began to come in. Sallie's nephew, Cecil Drake and wife, came in about 11:00 A.M. They live in Houston, Tex. In the afternoon they began to come in and callers were so thick we could not keep up with them. There were some 150 registered. It was the most enjoyable time of our 54 years of marriage for us. And the gifts were just wonderful. All of our children and grandchildren that live in Texas were here. Also one great-great-grandson. . . . In all it was a very happy get together. With all the old neighbors & friends it sure was a fine gathering.

· Mon 21. . . . I went out to farm. The soil conservation man was there, a Mr. Kiser. To look the place over and the best place for the well location. However, there is so much red tape to it I am about ready to back out of it. I am too old to try to compete with the young fellows that is at the head of these loan agencies and Government set up's.

· Fri 25. . . . I let the contract to Adams Pump & Supply Co. for a turn key job, $2,745.50. I am getting the money from the Littlefield National Loan Association. . . .

F·E·B·R·U·A·R·Y

· Thurs 12. . . . I went to Littlefield in afternoon to see Mrs. Kirby. She is making out Social Security papers. 1956 is the first year I have my credit. Can't use 1955 crop year at all, so I will have to use 1957 in order to qualify for the Social Security. I went to the Water District meeting at the high school auditorium.

In 1950 the Social Security Act was extended to cover people engaged in agriculture. Initially only hired hands were included, but passage of the 1956 Amendment to the Act covered farm landlords who substantially assisted in the production of crops or livestock on land farmed by renters if they had a net profit of four hundred dollars or more in 1956. This revision covered virtually all self-employed persons except medical doctors (See R. L. Skrabanek, Loyd B. Keel, and Louis J. Ducoff, *Texas Farmers and Old Age and Survivors Insurance*, pp. 3–12).

M·A·R·C·H

· Tues 12. These ball point pens are all out of ink. A hand full of them. No ink in any of them. . . .
· Thurs 14. . . . I have felt bad today. At times I can hardly breathe [*DeLoach had emphysema*].
· Thurs 28. . . . Ray Overton & I had an understanding about our respective interest in the partnership of the 1957 crop on my place. My part will be 1/3 of all crops raised on my place. Overton 2/3.

Rent was typically one fourth of the cotton crop and one third of the grain crop, but it was common practice to raise the cotton rent for irrigated land. Studies indicate irrigation increased cotton yields by more than 60 percent during years of deficient rainfall (See E. L. Thaxton, Jr., and N. P. Swanson, *Guides in Cotton Irrigation on the High Plains*, p. 5).

A·P·R·I·L

· Tues 30.   . . . Mr. McCord, the man that sold me the Layne pump from Littlefield rendered his bill. The amount for the job, $590.35, less $68.00. . . .

M·A·Y

· Sat 18.   . . . Ray Overton drove to tell us about the tragic death of friend Sam Stacy. He was killed about 2:00 P.M. He fell off his tractor and was caught under a 15 foot disc one way. It almost severed his body. Sand storm.

S·E·P·T·E·M·B·E·R

· Wed 4.   . . . The poison spray plane [*for leaf worms in the cotton*] got to us about 2:30 P.M. He had us sprayed by 4:00 P.M. The charge on my place was $1.85 per acre, area total of $48.10. I gave Ray Overton a check for 1/3 of $48.10. $16.00, my part.

· Sat 21.   . . . "The farm" will be listed in this Diary as "Ex home" regardless as to how it is used. . . .

· Tues 24.   . . . Ray Overton came in and paid me the rent on the feed or gave me the deposit slip, which was $233.05. Total weight was 48,280 pounds.

O·C·T·O·B·E·R

· Thurs 24.   . . . They got the peas at Bud's (a son) place. "Soil Bank."

The Soil Bank, established by the Agricultural Act of 1956, resembled the programs of the 1930s by taking farmland out of production to reduce surpluses. There were two parts to the program. A short-range part (Acreage Reserve) paid farmers for participating on a year-by-year basis, and a long-range part (Conservation Reserve) had farmers entering into contracts for up to ten years. In some areas business communities were disrupted when a large number of farmers put their entire farm in the Conservation Reserve. In 1956, Lamb County farmers put over four thousand acres in the Soil Bank and received approxi-

mately twelve dollars per acre of rent annually (See Baker, Rasmussen, Wiser, and Porter, *Century of Service*, p. 386; *County Wide News*, Oct. 28, 1956, p. 8).

D·E·C·E·M·B·E·R

· MON 16. . . . Ray & Susan [*Overton*] were here before noon. He had finished the cotton pulling. A total of 22 bales. That is under a bale per acre. . . .

1·9·5·8

The average per-acre value of U.S. farmland increased 337 percent from 1940 to 1964, and 1958 was one of the peak years in rising values (Tweeten, *Foundations of Farm Policy*, pp. 254–57). This appreciated value provided older farmers with money for retirement, capital improvements, or more land. More importantly, it barred many from entering farming, an occupation that was rapidly becoming over-stocked with operators.

F·e·b·r·u·a·r·y

· Mon 24.   . . . We worked in the garden cleaning, digging, and planting. We are tired tonight. We can't take it as of old, but such a pretty day. We just could not stay in doors. We had to get out and dig in the dirt.

J·u·n·e

· Thurs 12.   I went down to Post Office for my mail. I had letter and check under separate cover. Check $855.00, which was a surprise and a pleasant one, too. . . . Social Security Check.
· Sat 14.   . . . We went to Muleshoe this P.M. I bought the $110.00 air conditioner and Harold & Walter brought it out and put it up. It sure does the job, keeping the house cool. I had to buy 50 ft. of 5/8″ hose. Some of my old hose is wore out.

The air conditioner DeLoach bought was an evaporative cooler, which was installed in a window. Hot, dry, outside air was drawn through wet excelsior, or other water-absorptive material, and blown into the house as cool, moist air. A window on the opposite side of the house was opened to create a draft. As a pump circulated water to keep the excelsior pads wet, five to ten gallons of water per hour were used to cool an average-sized house (See USDA, *Yearbook of Agriculture, 1965*, pp. 56–60).

· Mon 23. . . . I put some papers in my safety box at bank.

A·U·G·U·S·T

· Fri 15.   This has been one hot day. . . . The paper said something about 102 at Childress and 105 Wichita Falls, Lubbock high maximum 98, minimum 68. . . . We did not get out much. In house most of the day with the "wind box" [*air conditioner*] turned on at high speed. . . .

S·E·P·T·E·M·B·E·R

· Sat 6.   . . . Just heard that gulf storm "Ella" was moving further into central and West Texas. Hope Ella, the latest storm from the Gulf does not storm too much out here.

Hurricanes that come into the Texas Gulf Coast often cause heavy rains in West Texas.

· Sat 13.   . . . We were off for Muleshoe in afternoon. I saw Harold after a while. He had bought 8 shotes out at the auction sale ring. . . . They were Red Durocks and a good color of Red. He has 50 or 60 head now of different sizes & ages. They are doing fine on the school lunch room garbage. He has a contract with Muleshoe School Board to move all the school garbage & slop.

O·C·T·O·B·E·R

· Mon 13. . . . I made ready and went to the funeral of another of the old friends, Chester Whitman. He was the village blacksmith of Sudan since 1927. . . .

· THURS 16.   . . . I think I will go up to Muleshoe tomorrow to look at an
   80 A farm for sale at $300.00 per A. I think I will go see about it.
   I have the money to make a $10,000 payment, and borrow $14,000.

The money DeLoach had in savings did not all come from his farm. His
brother, Ed, who ranched near Del Rio, willed part of his estate to his remaining brothers and sisters. DeLoach's first thought was to invest this money in
farmland.

· WED 22.   When Daniel McClary came by before breakfast and told me
   that Mr. Shot would trade on his terms. The least was $22,000 down
   and he would carry the balance of $2,000. That means for me to put
   up $12,000 and get a $10,000 Federal Farm Loan for the $10,000. . . . I
   still think it is a good buy.

N·O·V·E·M·B·E·R

· THURS 13.   Mrs. Chas. Swift, one of the Lamb County United Way Fund
   solicitors, called to see us. A check for $10.00 paid. . . .
· MON 17.   Mr & Mrs. D. A. Shot came up and we finished the sale of the
   80 acres of Bailey County land. I payed him the $22,000.00 in cash.
   Made him (Shot) note for $2,000.00 payable in 5 years at $400.00 per
   year at 5%. The land is now my own. We ate dinner at Harold's &
   Dellie's. Now 7:00 P.M. . . . I rented place to Harold, 3rd, 4th rent.

D·E·C·E·M·B·E·R

· TUES 9.   I went to see one Colin Terry, Chairman of the County Com-
   mittee. I wanted to move my cotton acreage off of my place here west of
   Sudan, to the place I bought N.W. of Muleshoe. He said the Lamb Co.
   Committee would release me if Bailey Co. would accept me. . . .
· SAT 20.   Red Wooten came over and wanted to see if I would sell my
   home place out west of Sudan. . . .
· TUES 23.   We, Sallie & I met over at Atty. E. J. Dunham, also Mr. Red
   Wooten and fixed up all the papers for the sale of our farm 5 miles
   N.W. of Sudan. We sold out to Wooten for $19,000.00. $5,510 is 29%
   down and balance of 12 notes of principal sum of $1124.17 each. All of
   even date. Said notes to provide 5% interest, payable annually. . . .

DeLoach paid $35 per acre for this farm in September of 1936. The sale price, of slightly over $279 per acre, vividly illustrates the large capital gain farmers realized from land that was continuously rising in value. DeLoach always believed he could improve his lot in life through the ownership of land, and this transaction must surely have confirmed his belief.

· WED 24.   I paid my first installment of $63.50 interest on the Bailey County loan, also $45.00 to Bobby for legal services.

1·9·5·9

As farmers became producers instead of husbandmen, their nonfarm purchases steadily increased. By 1959 they were spending, as a group, over forty billion dollars annually for goods and services. This was three times as much as two decades before. Even though only 12 percent of the population lived on farms, agriculture was the nation's largest industry. Forty percent of the total labor force was either serving agriculture or processing and distributing agricultural commodities, according to the USDA's *Report of the Secretary of Agriculture, 1959.*

F·E·B·R·U·A·R·Y

· Mon 9.   The day came in nice and quiet, but by 9:00 A.M. the wind came out of the southwest at from as high as 80 m.p.h. I don't think we had any higher than 40 to 50 m.p.h. here, but the different reports were that 40 to 80 in districts further to the northeast. Anyway it was real bad. Visibility from 0 to ¼ miles. We had more sand in the house than any time in the last 2 or 3 years. Good bye to this Ledger, No. 10, as I will start on No. 11. No. 11 will be a 360 page book of my diary. . . .

· Sat 28.   . . . I would love to see a good rain, but we have none to speak of the first two months of this year, 1959. About .03 and that is not enough to count. However, Harold is watering every day on my place north west of Muleshoe. That is one thing I have on that place, abun-

317

dance of water. The first watering on the place I bought northwest of Muleshoe.

M·A·R·C·H

· Thurs 19. . . . From now on when I mention going to the farm that will mean the farm I bought northwest of Muleshoe. . . .

· Sun 22. . . . Bud & Ida came in for a chat. They asked me to go to the fund raising meeting they had called to get the necessary money ready to start on the new Baptist Church. I think there was about $14,000.00 pledged. I gave my check for $400.00. That is what I felt like I could give because we need the church to be rebuilt [*the old church had burned*].

A·P·R·I·L

· Wed 22. We worked today in the garden. We are just planting every-thing that grows in a garden and we have said that we would not plant any thing much that calls for work and water, because this watering a garden runs into $. But we get a lot of pleasure out of seeing things grow.

· Fri 24. . . . I ran into Walter McMahan and went out to his place for some eggs. He and Peggy gave me, I guess, 5 or 6 doz. eggs. I did not count them. They can't sell their eggs since they are not caged eggs, so they give them away. . . .

After the mid-1950s, egg production in Texas changed from small barnyard flocks to large-scale commercial production, where flocks ranged from fifteen hundred layers upward. Generally, the chickens were housed in individual cages containing mechanical feeders and waterers. Eggs were gathered three or four times daily, cleaned, graded, and packed in cartons for retail outlets. By 1957 approximately half a million caged eggs were produced weekly by Lamb County farmers for urban markets, where buyers paid as much as a twelve-cent premium per dozen over ungraded yard eggs (See A. C. Magee, B. H. Stone, and B. C. Wormeli, *Planning for Profitable Egg Production*, pp. 3–16).

· Mon 27. The day came in fine. No sign of a windy, but soon one could see signs that all old timers know when a sand storm is in the making and by noon it was really bad. . . .

M·A·Y

· TUES 5. . . . I bought Sallie a watch and a diamond ring for Mother's
Day. . . .

J·U·N·E

· TUES 2. We had .4″ of rain at near mid-night. I was up watching clouds.
I had T.V. on to hear any weather reports, but none came over the
air. . . .
· THURS 18. At home all day. Only to Post Office and maybe so 2 hours at
the "clipping club," which is operated by one Jack Cushing and helper
Tom Maxfield. A good place to "shoot the bull," and catch the gossip.

The local barbershop, or "clipping club," was a favorite place for men to gather
and catch up on all the town gossip.

J·U·L·Y

· WED 1. I went to Muleshoe school tax office for interview with the
Equalization Board, but all I could hear was we can't make any adjustment or change in the valuation. So I could get no help from the
Equalization Board. Quite a lot of difference from last year's school tax
of $61.00 and for this year, which will be near $169.00. Legalized high
jacking system. But why belly-ache? The big boys say you will have to
pay or else. . . .
· SAT 11. . . . Bud cut our grass. He has a gas pull mower. Sure does a good
& quick job.
· MON 13. . . . I was down to the "gabbers hold out." A very learned
bunch of old coons, but we have quite a time when all are there.

A·U·G·U·S·T

· WED 5. [DeLoach had some carpentry work done on his house.] . . . They
made very good progress today. The head carpenter brought another
helper, Joe Reed a $2.00 an hr. man. They have to have the "coffee
break" that is ¼ hr. at least. At $6.25 an hour ¼ or 15 minutes is $1.26,
two times a day is $2.50 for them to drink coffee, but that is the custom.

Thursday, June 18 ... 2 hours at the
"clipping club," ... a good place to "shoot the bull" and
catch the gossip.

Monday, July 13... I was down to the "gabbers hold out."
A very learned bunch of old coons.

· Tues 25.   . . . Sallie & I went to the Lamb County Pioneers [*Reunion*]. Who came to [*Sudan*] 1925 or before. We moved to Sudan, Lamb Co. in 1925, March 15th. I came out in Nov. 1924. . . .

S·E·P·T·E·M·B·E·R

· Tues 1.   . . . I had my August water report and it was the largest water bill I have had since I lived in Sudan, $9.00. So I will have to quit so much garden watering. . . .
· Sun 6.   . . . We all went to the First National Bank of Sudan. They had their general opening since the repair job. Boy, the general arrangements of the bank is something the town should be proud of. The water melon feast was sure nice. The melons were cut in City Park, by the Bank. 500 melons came from my farm. . . .
· Mon 7.   . . . This is another Labor Day. The first time I remember a Labor Day was in September, 1903, first Monday. The day the miners (coal) was organized into the "United Mine Workers of America," and the big coal miner strike followed. I was not a miner at that time, but all miners came out on strike and my job was terminated. So I had a young wife about 5 months pregnant and no job, but we made it, but not too good. It was not long till I had another job. That was 56 years today. The Texas & Pacific Coal Co. Mines were shut down. The Co. would not recognize the Miners Union, but did in about 6 weeks.
· Tues 8.   . . . I made my daily trip to the farm.
· Fri 25.   . . . Harold & Dellie also came down. He gave me another check for $81.37, watermelons. That makes my amount of the crop of melons $846.86 up to this date. . .

O·C·T·O·B·E·R

· Mon 12.   Have been at home most of the day. . . . This sure is tiring. Just to have nothing to do that one wants to do.
· Tues 20.   . . . Edgar Chaney and a Mr. Samson of the Lubbock Christian College called on us. We had decided about two weeks ago to buy some bonds that are being issued to complete campus projects. They pay 6% interest, while we are only getting 3% in our savings account at the first National Bank of Sudan. We will let the college sell us from $2,000.00 to $4,000.00 worth of the above named bonds. . . .

· SAT 31.   . . . Back home. Had supper, then the Halloween kids began to rap on the door, and we were tied up watching the Perry Mason program. The kids seemed to have a very high heel time. Sallie did not [*get*] enough apples to go around, but plenty.

N·O·V·E·M·B·E·R

· SUN 1.   . . . We went to church for morning services. I went into the church on a statement. I joined the Baptist Church in August, 1895 in Parker County at Post Oak Point. The Rev. Chasteen of Earthland baptized me, along with 8 or 9 others. . . . That has been 64 years this last August. The Post Oak Church was discontinued some 40 years ago. I don't know just how many of that number are living.

· SAT 7.   . . . Mrs. Salter brought me a book that is being put out by the Texas Technological College of Lubbock, which has a mention of 5 times of my Diary, which I have given to the Texas Museum Association when I am through with it. Thanks for the book. [*The diary was actually given to the Southwest Collection rather than the Museum.*]

· TUES 10.   He [*carpet man*] came about I'll say 9:30 A.M. He had the carpet layed by 12:00 noon. He ate dinner with us. He looked surprised when I told him to get ready for dinner. Anyway he acted like people were not supposed to ask them to eat. Anyway he enjoyed the feed. . . .

· WED 18.   . . . I talked with Harold about renting him the farm for cash rent. . . .

· MON 23.   . . . I want to put out a lot of peaches, plums, apricots, and grapes. For I want that place to be a fine looking farm home. We, Sallie and I, may never live there, but I want it to be a credit to my estate. To our estate.

· SUN 29.   . . . I do not get much out of my visits with boys and their wives for they talk to one another, as I can't hear such low talk. I hope and pray that they will never lose their sense of hearing. I feel like "a motherless calf at a round up."

D·E·C·E·M·B·E·R

· MON 7.   Well the long looked for stucco man came in early A.M. before we ate breakfast and ready to do the finishing job on the stuccoing of our home. . . .

· THURS 17.   The day came in with clearing skies, but the sun was "mil-
dewed." Has been cloudy and misty to rain and snow for the last week,
but the moisture that has been put in the ground is worth lots to
farmers. . . .

· FRI 18.   . . . Red Wooten paid his No. 1 note off to day, $1792.51, on place
we sold him 12–23–58.

· SUN 20.   . . . Lubbock is metropolis for size.

By 1960 Lubbock boasted a population of 128,691; it had been 1,938 in 1910
(See *Texas Almanac and State Industrial Guide, 1914*, p. 307; *Texas Almanac and
State Industrial Guide, 1961–1962*, p. 609).

· SUN 27.   I did not feel very good, but we went to church. I to the first services held in the new church. It sure is a nice building. The interior
looks so good and nice. All the seats & furniture & choir set up is
nice. We have had a sand storm blowing since about 9:00 A.M., but I
have not heard Sallie say one word about the sand getting in the
house. The stucco job and the sealing of the windows really got the job
done. . . .

· THURS 31.   . . . So much for the year 1959. I got to checking back on my
age and it has been 70 years in the last October or November when my
father moved to Parker County. And believe me that was in real "West
Texas." Then he moved to Scurry Co. in 1906 and that was a real frontier county at that time. He took up land 14 miles southwest of Snyder,
a small inland town of possibly 500 people. I came through the town of
Snyder in June 1899 on a freight wagon going to Crosby Co. Old
Emma was the county seat at that time with a frame court house, 2
ranch stores. Witt and Spikes ran one, Ed Covington, the other. Dr.
Carter, the only Dr. east of Lubbock as far as Dickins City.

1·9·6·0

"Such is life. We have to take it," wrote DeLoach after an October hailstorm severely damaged the cotton in Lamb County. That entry described his general outlook as the aging process ran its course.

J·A·N·U·A·R·Y

· Fri 1.   The day came in clear, but real cold. If the year 1960 is as good to the South Plains people as 1959 was, no one will have any gripe to make unless it is some of the Roosevelt, Truman "die hards." I think it got Truman's goat when he selfinvested his self to make the one half circle around the world with the present administration, but Ike did not recognize his wishes. . . .

· Wed 6.   We all stayed in bed till near 7:30 a.m. Was reported 8° below zero. . . .

· Thurs 21.   . . . Telephone man installed my phone today. The No. 3062.

· Mon 25.   . . . I decided last night I would not keep the hearing aid. I would never be satisfied with the aid for two reasons. First, I could never get my self used to that grinding noise and last, but not least, I do not feel like being highjacked, $295.00 for such a price is robbery and I shall take the "aid" back to them. . . .

F·e·b·r·u·a·r·y

· Mon 1.   Well, I am an old man from the standpoint of years. 80 years 'young'. I do not feel like some men of that age and look younger. I don't know how they feel, but I can't realize the fact that I am 80 years old. . . . Harold and Dellie gave me a watch chain. Just what I needed, as I was using a shoe string.

M·a·r·c·h

· Sat 26.   . . . I had a kind of embarassing episode in Littlefield. I went to coffee shop. Drank my coffee and started back to my car. I thought I was getting in my car. The woman under the wheel was dressed like Sallie's dress and another woman on front seat, that I took for a car visitor, so I piled in back seat. The lady in front left side said, "Well, where to now," I had not yet noticed them and I said, "I parked right here." About that time I noticed her and boy did I feel hacked. Two strange women, but we made comedy out of the situation. All had a big laugh. They told me not to think anything about it. They were very nice and congenial about it, so I excused myself and beat it.
· Thurs 31.   The last day of March, 1960 came in "like a lamb, but believe [me] it went out like two lions fighting." The wind all forenoon would blow hard for a few minutes, but about 12 or 1:00 P.M. it started to blow hard and kept it up till sunset and into the night. It was hard on me to get my breath. The dust, my bronchial trouble.

M·a·y

· Fri 13.   This is a black cat day. According to the old southern darkies, one can have any kind of bad luck. . . .
· Sat 28.   At home till after the ball game, which ended about 3:00 P.M. We then took off for Muleshoe. We were not long in M'shoe. We had to be back home by 6:30 for the Perry Mason, T.V. program. . . .
· Mon 30.   Memorial Day. . . . We put wreaths on Bill's grave. Also Mr. Newton's. . . .

The custom of placing flowers on the graves of the war dead began in 1866 in New York. After World War I it was extended to include paying homage to deceased friends and relatives, both military and civilian.

1960

The summer consisted of attending old friends' funerals, celebrating Sallie's 76th birthday, tending the vegetable garden, and watching baseball games and the political conventions on TV. In September DeLoach had hemorrhoid surgery and afterwards wrote "the nurses and some others called for me on a lay down contraption and took me to the operating room." There were no entries during his week's stay in the hospital. In November he voted for Nixon and Lodge, the Republican candidates, as did many other Texans. Kennedy and Johnson won the election, but they carried Texas by only a small margin. The large Republican vote signaled the beginning of two-party politics in the state.

D·E·C·E·M·B·E·R

· Sat 24. . . . Sallie is busy getting her Christmas dinner ready. She has the turkey in the electric cooker now. It will be done by 8:00 p.m. That is a lot faster than the old time coal, wood or "cow chip" stoves we used to have to use here on the Western Plains, but all were happy when the Christmas day dinner was served whether a crowd or just the family.
· Mon 26. . . . I cut out of *Avalanche-Journal* (Lubbock) a write up of a Mrs. Edith Hoover, 3919 59th St., Lubbock, has a diary that she has kept for the last 27 years. Since 1933. My first issue of my diary March 28, 1914. Soon 47 years.
· Sat 31. . . . Word came of the passing of Pruitt DeLoach [*a brother*]. Grandfield, Okla.

1·9·6·1

DeLoach was forever on time, behind time, or ahead of time. He spent time, wasted time, and killed time, but he never seemed to have enough time until he was too old to use it.

M·A·R·C·H

· FRI 24. . . . I wanted a book that Ida told me about in the Lamb County Library. "Good-bye to a River" [*included in A. C. Greene's list of the fifty best books about Texas*]. So Sallie & I pulled out and went to the Library for the book. I have read 4 chapters of it and like it as I have some things in common with the book's history of the Brazos River in Palo Pinto, Young, and Parker Counties. As I lived near this river in my youth.

A·P·R·I·L

· TUES 4. This day is the election day for the senate race. I went down early, but did not vote till about 10:00 A.M. I voted for the lone Republican John Tower. Jim Wright's talk last night seems like he wanted to promise just too much, hence my vote for Tower. . . .

· WED 12. We worked quite a lot. Just to be doing something. I planted

some radishes, and watered the berry patches. . . . does not take long
to do what ever we have to do. If I have something to do, I am better
satisfied, but no use in thinking about being dissatisfied for we have a
long road of do nothing to travel if we live and both of us are in very
good health. . . .

· MON 17.   I did some piddling work around the house. Now the definition
for piddling is some little job like repairing a screen door or cutting
weeds out of the black berry patch, or any little job.

M·A·Y

· THURS 18.   . . . We have one of the prettiest back yards we have ever had
at this time of year.
· WED 24.   . . . Sister Curtie Wagnon passed away at or near 9:30 P.M.
· THURS 25.   . . . Brothers & sisters of this date: Will G. DeLoach of Sudan,
Texas, Brother, Bowden M. DeLoach of Snyder, Texas, one sister, Mrs.
Octave DeLoach Martin of Sweetwater, Texas. In order of their passing:
sister, Eunice DeLoach Orr passed away November, 1918, Fannie De-
Loach Witt, April, 1949, Thomas L. DeLoach, died 4-16-1950, Edward S.
DeLoach, died Oct. 28, 1957, John P. DeLoach, died Dec. 31, 1960.
Mrs. Curtie Witt Wagnon, died May 24, 1961.

J·U·L·Y

· SAT 15.   . . . I tuned in on the baseball game of the week. New York
Yankees–Chicago White Sox. The game went to the 10th inning. The
Yanks won 9 to 8. It was a good ball game, although my team lost. I
really enjoyed it. I am for the Chicago W. Sox.

A·U·G·U·S·T

· THURS 31.   At home all day. We did a little grass cutting and watering.
This lawn grass is a Job, with a capital J. We do not have anything to
do only just eat, sleep, go to Post Office, get the mail, if any, back
home, start all over again. This is the last of August of 1961.

S·E·P·T·E·M·B·E·R

· Fri 1.   The day came in sunshiney & clear. Also the day came in with a 2% sales tax. That is headache for some, and is about the only way to get the State out of the 'Red' as I see it. Any way one needs a pocket full of penneys if one buys a lot of different items. . . .

· Mon 25.   . . . But we (Bowden & I) got to looking through an old De-Loach Bible. . . . This Bible was handed down from son to son, but my dad, E. P. DeLoach, did not want it because some one that had access to it cut the family records out of it before it was sent to Dad from Chippley, Georgia. About the year 1925. So he kept it with out any interest until 1930, I think. When he told quote "This Bible is yours when I am through with it. Now I am through with it because the main thing is the records of the DeLoach family from the Revolution was in it. But my whole interest is not. I have no further use for it. You take it now.". . .

O·C·T·O·B·E·R

· Mon 23.   . . . Sallie & Dellie went over to Mr. Gosden's to see the new baby of Robert (Buster) DeLoach and Patty Ruth Gosden DeLoach. They reported a fine looking young son of the couple. He is the 12th Great-great-grandchild of ours. . . .

· Thurs 26.   . . . A lot of people are getting scared on account of this Russians Big shots they are talking about. I think there will be several fall out poison shelters built soon, but I can't see where that would do any good. "If the air and all food is contaminated, the shelters would have to have fresh air to live in them." And where would that come from? So I guess it is the way of the Lord to destroy the world. I am not scared enough to start building a shelter yet. I may try it, but not as of now.

N·O·V·E·M·B·E·R

· Sun 5.   . . . I took Sallie to church, but I did not go to church. I began to feel bad when I got ready, so I decided I would not go. Bud and Ida came by and wanted us to come on down for the Sunday dinner. We told them we would come, but we decided I was not in shape to go, so Sallie called Bud and told him I was sick and we would not come down. And I went to bed. Soon they came up. Bud called Harold and had him to make reservations at Green Hospital & Clinic at Muleshoe and they picked me up in the P.M. and took me to the hospital. I have written this entry on Tuesday Morning, November 14, 1961, as the time is a blank to me between the 5th and the 13th. I am about exhausted now.

· THURS 16. . . . The Speaker of the House of Representatives in Washington, Sam Rayburn, died at 6:00 A.M. today. He was a great Democrat. Over 17 years as Speaker.

When Speaker of the House Sam Rayburn died of cancer in 1961, Texas lost a strong voice in Washington. During the twentieth century, Texans played a leading role in national politics, but their power began to wane in 1960. Party rivalry, scandals in high places, and the president's assassination in Texas threatened the influence of Lone Star statesmen at the national level (See McKay and Faulk, *Texas after Spindletop,* pp. 225–226).

· SUN 19. . . . The pastor of Baptist Church, Rev. Allen called this P.M. A very pleasant caller. He had prayer before he left. Thanks so much for the kind words of his prayer. The cloudy cold weather all day.

· TUES 21. . . . Harold & Dellie came down for the day. They arrived just before noon. In the afternoon Jim Burnside came over. Then the big domino game was on. A 3 handed game. Jim B., Harold, & I. We played for about two hours. I won 2 games, Harold 1, Jim 1. We had a very pleasant afternoon. Harold & Dellie stayed till about 9:30 P.M. We enjoy their visits so much. . . .

Because of the high proportion of elderly people in most rural communities, social opportunities with others of their age were numerous. These activities made the aging process easier to accept and boosted the morale of older people. Moreover, DeLoach's adult children, who lived close enough to visit often, were a source of companionship and help.

· TUES 28. I heard at noon that Tim Kirby passed away about 10:00 A.M. today. He also had a heart attack. Another old timer gone. . . .

D·E·C·E·M·B·E·R

· SAT 9. I am not feeling too friskey. I mean Friskey with a capital "F." . . .

· SUN 24. We spent Christmas Eve at Bud's and Ida's. They had a big

Christmas gift opening. . . . All had a big fine time. The Christmas Eve dinner was a perfect set up in every way. . . .

· MON 25.   Another day of get-to-gethers with our sons & daughters, Robert DeLoach & Dorothy and Jimmie. Mrs. Dorothy Blackman and Jimmie Coward. Robert DeLoach and wife, Ida, Walter McMahan and wife, Peggy, and Lamona. Me and Sallie DeLoach, parents of the two boys & two daughters all met in the home of our oldest son Harold DeLoach & wife, Dellie, northwest of Muleshoe, Texas. This was the Christmas day get-to-gether and dinner. I was a little groggy after the all day set up, but we all enjoyed it. Thanks to both for the event.

· SUN 31.   The last day of the year. Nothing happened any more than any other day.

1·9·6·2

· THURS 1. Since the 5th of November 5, 1961 I have not kept a daily account of my events. I have been in and out of the hospitals at Muleshoe & Amherst and lost all of my desire to keep up my daily writings
which I started in March 28, 1914. But I [am] going to try and pick up
my interest in my daily writing of events of each day. . . .

· MON 5. . . . Sometimes I just wonder if I did really have a heart attack at
first on November 5, 1961? However, there was something wrong with
me at that time and I am still bothered with something. Short breath. . . .

· FRI 9. . . . Mr and Mrs. R. W. Pettey come over one day and we play
dominoes and have a good time and enjoy it. Then Sallie & I go over
to their house and play dominoes. That way we pass away lots of
lonely hours.

· SUN 11. . . . I have not attended church since my first heart attack the
fifth of November, I am getting so shakey I can't hardly write.

On Friday evening, March 16, the DeLoach clan gathered at Will's house for
a fish fry. Everyone had a good time and stayed until midnight playing dominoes and visiting. While recording the day's events in his diary, Will added his
recipe for catfish bait.

· Mix thoroughly 1 lb. of old, soft limburger cheese and 1 lb. of canned wall
paper cleaner (the doughy putty-like kind) Add 20 drops of anise oil.

335

Keep in a tight can or jar. The cleaning agent in the wall paper cleaner keeps bait soft. It stays on hooks and really takes the cat fish.

· SUN 25.   Just as we finished breakfast Ida called and announced that her father, Mr. Arthur Crain, had passed away at about 6 A.M. He died in his sleep. He has had a rough time for several years. . . .

A · P · R · I · L

· THURS 26.   [*sic*] Afternoon I decided I would go to [*the*] farm. . . . When I got up to farm Dellie was just fixing to go to Clovis, N.M. so I needed some whiskey, and I went with her to get it. I do not know but I think that is about as good medicine for this heart & broncial trouble as one can take. Just so long as one does not abuse it.

M · A · Y

· MON 7.   . . . In the P.M. Sallie & I went over to Amherst Hospital for a check up. The Dr. sure did check me up.

Lung X Ray	$10.00
Three different kinds medicine	12.75
Dr. Fee	3.00
	$25.75

I can't keep that kind of expense up long.

· FRI 25.   I was down in town before noon also in the afternoon, but all one can hear is Billie Sol Estes mess that is going the rounds for local, county, State and National scandal talk. Some of the big boys are beginning to look around for a tall building to jump off the window or from the top. And it is just started. Some local men are losing their grain elevators, farms, money and reputations. They asked for it. The prime idea is "Get something for nothing." Just where it will stop no one knows. . . .

Billie Sol Estes, the King of Texas Wheeler-Dealers, was indicted on charges that he made false statements to the Commodity Credit Corporation in order to secure contracts to store government grain and that he sent fraudulent mortgages for fertilizer tanks through the U.S. mail. There were also allegations that Estes was involved in the murder of a U.S. Department of Agriculture official and that some of the money made from his illegal business dealings went into a slush fund for government officials, including President Johnson. The Pecos, Texas, resident brought many people into his money-making schemes, and as the "house of dominoes" began to fall fear spread through West Texas. (See Pam Estes, *Billie Sol: King of Texas Wheeler-Dealers*, pp. 58–97; *Houston Post*, June 6, 1964, sec. 3, p. 19; *San Angelo Standard-Times*, Mar. 25, 1984, p. 8).

J·u·n·e

· Sun 17.   This darn pen is going hay wire. Too many ball points on the give away list. We went to church for the morning services. The second time I have been to church since I had my first heart flare-up. . . .

Will and Sallie went to Sweetwater to join his sister, Octave Martin, in the celebration of Octave's 50th Wedding anniversary. Will's brother, Bowden, and his wife, Bess, joined the group. Will, Bowden, and Octave were the only surviving children of Emmanuel and Elizabeth DeLoach.

· Fri 29.   . . . Our grandson, Robert, Bud and Ida's boy. He came in from Korea yesterday. He was here at mid-day dinner time. I don't think he looks as well as he did when he went away. He has lost some weight. We enjoyed his visit. Pattie did not come with him. He reported that she and baby were fine.

J·u·l·y

· Sun 8.   . . . Just as we finished eating supper Dellie called. Sallie took the message. . . . Dellie's son, Walter McMahan was killed. . . . His plane dived and killed he and his student pilot. . . . We called Bud & Ida. They came up and drove us all up to Harold's. . . .

Services were held in the Methodist Church at Muleshoe before Walter's body was taken to McKinney, Texas, for burial. Will and Sallie did not go to McKinney; the death was very painful for Will, and the trip was more than he could stand. Walter had been in the family since he was a small child (see May 24, 1924). Memories of their son Billy, who was also killed in a plane crash, made this death especially difficult. As DeLoach tried to record the names of family members who attended services in Muleshoe, he wrote, "Oh! I am so upset I can't write. I get names & events all mixed up." His grief was seen in his unsteady handwriting.

A·u·g·u·s·t

· Fri 3.   I am getting to the place where I make errors. I shake when I am writing. I can't help it. . . .

S·e·p·t·e·m·b·e·r

· Sat 15.   . . . The revival meeting closed tonight. I did not get to go any. My heart is still acting up. My Dr. warned me to keep out of crowds and not go to funerals.

· Sun 16.   We all went up to school building to take the first of 3 polio treatments. [*They were taking oral polio vaccine.*] I think everybody in this school district came out for the treatment, that was state-wide.

O·c·t·o·b·e·r

· Sun 21.   I had quite a heart flutter this early A.M. I liked to have not got my clothes on after my bath. . . . I feel fine after I take the tablets for such attacks. . . .

N·o·v·e·m·b·e·r

· Tues 13.   I am not writing for a while. I do not feel like it, so I will discontinue writing till some future date.

[*DeLoach made no further entries until January, 1963.*]

1·9·6·3

· Tues 1. This is Tuesday, January 2, 1963. I had Sallie call brother
   Bowden and Bess, his wife. She got them on the phone at once. I told
   he & Bess to come up and visit a few days. They came on.
· Wed 2. We had a long visit before we went to bed. . . .
· Fri 4. The folks left, real early, for home. They live in Snyder, Texas. We
   just sat around and did nothing.

M·A·R·C·H

· Fri 8. . . . Just at near night my only sister and husband, Mr. and Mrs.
   Tom Martin, of Sweetwater, came in for an over night visit. So nice to
   have them call. We did not go to bed till mid-night. [*When DeLoach's
   sister and brother-in-law started home, he and Sallie followed them part of
   the way.*]
· Sat 9. After we ate breakfast we decided we would go on as far as the
   Old Emma cemetery South of Ralls, Texas, 5 miles, where some of our
   kinfolks and any number of old settlers and friends of ours are buried
   there. The first person that was buried there to start the graveyard was
   a son of a widow James that had 5 or 6 boys. This son pulled a shot
   gun the wrong way and it went off and killed the young man, hence

339

the starting of the old cemetery. That was in year of 1892. Some of my people moved there in 1891, some in 1895 and some in 1898. I, W. G. DeLoach, moved to the little town of Emma in June, 1899. I was 19 years old. We looked everything over. Everything is changed so. Very few people live in the country now. All the fine grazing land now is in farms, the greatest cotton farms of the U.S. I saw no one that I knew. . . . And in the years from 1899 to 1917 I knew all the old timers. . . .

A·P·R·I·L

· THURS 11.   Down in town till noon. Finch Fike came by. He was going to Muleshoe to see about a pressure pump. He wanted me to go with him. . . . When I got home more sad news. Sallie had a call from Bro. Bowden's youngest daughter, of Odessa, stating Bowden, my only brother, had passed away this early A.M. I can't hardly write. Know nothing as to what caused his death.

· MON 15.   . . . We all went to the funeral home to take a last notice of deceased as they did not open the casket at the church. The burial was at the Ira Cemetery, southwest of Snyder, where the DeLoach family bought a home in the year of 1906. And both Dad and Mother died there and were buried in the Ira Cemetery. . . .

· MON 29.   Just as of all other days. Oh, I have forgotten just what happened.

A·U·G·U·S·T

Diary entries stopped until August.

· SAT 31.   After so long a time I will take up where I left off . . . no excuse. Just did not feel like writing.

O·C·T·O·B·E·R

· SAT 26.   As of today, [from] August 31, 1963 to this date Saturday, October 26, has been blank. I took Sallie to hospital at Amherst on October 5th. She was in surgery for gall bladder trouble, but she seemed to come out of it fine. Since the operation I have not kept up with any of the events of the current days, so I will just start over as of this date which is October 26, 1963. . . .

Sallie had her gallbladder removed in 1949, but she needed surgery to correct some complications caused by the first operation.

· SUN 27.   At home all day. Harold, Dellie, Dot were down for the afternoon. Also Bud & Ida. . . .

· THURS 31.   The last of October, 1963. We were at home. Nothing to do. Bud came up and stayed part of the afternoon. Sallie is doing fine. She is eating normally and sleeps good. I think she will be OK. Now a little soreness in side yet.

N·O·V·E·M·B·E·R

· FRI 22.   . . . I lay down for my afternoon nap, but I did not go to sleep at once. Sallie was called to the telephone. It was Mrs. Mirror calling to tell us of the shooting of President Kennedy. He was shot at 12:31 P.M. in Dallas, Texas. At this time the killer has not been caught. The time is now 10:20 P.M. It was one of the most cowardly murders of all times. According to T.V. reports the world is in deep mourning and all shocked.

Kennedy was in Texas to patch the differences between two warring factions of the Democratic party. Lyndon Johnson and John Connally were on the conservative side, while Sen. Ralph Yarborough and Rep. Henry Gonzalez were among the liberals (See Michael L. Kurtz, *Crime of the Century*, pp. v, 3–23).

D·E·C·E·M·B·E·R

· WED 18.   Early A.M. we decided to go to Littlefield. I went out about 8:00 A.M. to start the car and warm it up. I looked up and there stood Robert Jr., Bud's son. He took over. Got the heater regulated and we found left back tire flat. Robert changed tires and took the take off tire down for repair. He said he would drive us to Littlefield as he was afraid for us to get out on the slick road. . . . I payed my state & county tax on home here in Sudan, $12.63. I also payed the city tax & school tax. I think I am about all payed up here and at Muleshoe, too. We really enjoy "Buster." He is so pleasant and congenial, and helpful. . . .

1·9·6·4

The following thoughts were written on the same kind of tablet paper that was used for the entries during the summer of 1915. The two small pages, inserted in the front of the earliest ledger, he labeled Forward.

Years are the milestones that tell us the distance we have traveled and while each passing year robs us of something, we can always recapture it in memory. Strange to say, even the things that are hard to bear are pleasant to remember.

Through the medium of our written chronicles we can turn back the pages of time and review the events of yesteryears as they apply to our own lives. A lasting record of our activities, our experiences and our view points; a living memoir of things attempted and things done; a vivid story that is ever new and ever refreshing to us in hours of recollection.

This diary is designed for just such a purpose. This diary is dedicated to Sallie, my wife, as a living rememberance [sic] of her.

Will G. DeLoach

J·A·N·U·A·R·Y

· TUES 14.   Another wedding day. On this date Sallie Edna Newton and
W. G. DeLoach were married near Duke, Oklahoma, Tuesday, Jan. 14th,
1903. Now 61 years ago. All the years have been very pleasant and
congenial. Oh yes, a few quarrels & spats. Nothing that amounted to
anything.

1964

F·E·B·R·U·A·R·Y

· WED 26.   I have been on the lift all day. I have caught the nose dripping,
    whatever it is called, and I am now bothered with my old trouble.
    After all neither one of us is able to help the other up if we fell down.

M·A·R·C·H

· TUES 10.   Another day of do nothing. Too cold early to be out much any-
    way. The time when I will have completed my goal of 50 years of con-
    tinuous daily writing, which will be fully carried out on 28th of March,
    1964.
· SAT 28.   This is March 28, 1964. My first entry was made on March 28,
    1914, but I am getting so infirm in more ways than one. I have decided
    not to make any more entries. This is the 50 years that out side of a
    few days at different times I have kept a daily account of my where-
    abouts and work that I was doing. So good-bye, Diary. You have been
    lots of help in lots of ways.

Epilogue

William DeLoach died from emphysema on April 1, 1967. He was eighty-seven years old. During his last weeks in the hospital he told his daughter, Jimmie, he wished he had continued writing in his diary, but even a small task like that was too exhausting.

Funeral services were held in the First Baptist Church at Sudan, with burial in the Sudan Cemetery. Grandsons were pallbearers. DeLoach had ten grand-children and eighteen great-grandchildren when he died.

Sallie continued to live in Sudan. Life without Will was very different, but adapting had always been one of her strong points. She stayed busy with her housework, church activities, and her garden. She also traveled with Jimmie and Dorothy before Dorothy's death in 1968.

In 1975 Sallie laid her life with Will to rest peacefully when she returned his ledgers to the Southwest Collection. For sixty-four years he had been her hus-band, her workmate, and her best friend, but now he belonged to history.

Sallie died on April 18, 1980. She was ninety-five. Harold had already retired from farming, and shortly after his mother's death he returned to California to be near his children. Jimmie and Bud were the only two of Will and Sallie's children left on the Llano Estacado. Jimmie lived in Lubbock and Bud contin-ued to farm near Sudan.

During the 1940s and 1950s Bud put his trust in better equipment, irriga-tion wells, and increased acreage. He believed these would improve his lot in life just as his father had thought owning a farm would make life more secure. Initially, science and technology appeared to be blessings. Farmers learned how to farm more acres and produce more per acre until small family farms became big farms. Agriculture became dependent on expensive nonfarm inputs instead of the cheap family labor of times past, and when increased production created price-reducing surpluses, farmers felt one of the negative results of increased technology. Rising costs of production and low commodity prices brought even the most efficient farmers very close to the break-even point in their operation; others were driven out of business. In the 1980s, farmers across the nation were going broke and leaving the land to earn a living just as they had during the agricultural depression of the 1920s. For most, the break with their heritage was a wrenching one that followed years of struggle, frayed nerves, and even broken marriages or nervous breakdowns.

Bud invested in land early on, when the price was low enough that a farmer could pay for a place. Debt-free land and good management skills made it possible to earn a decent living, but he was the last of the family to farm. The next generation of DeLoach men broke a family tradition of growing cotton that was over two hundred years old. Deciding to avoid the huge capital investment required of beginning farmers, they entered the nonfarm economy. However, Bud's son, Bob (Buster in the diary), still lives on a farm that is worked by another farmer. He is following a pattern that has emerged across rural America, and like others who have made a similar choice, he believes he has the best of both worlds. He is close to the land that is an important part of his heritage, but he enjoys the security of a paycheck that is free from the fickle temperament of the weather and the market. The rental income from the land is ample to provide "extras" for his family.

Bud DeLoach died December 29, 1987. He was buried in Sudan. As I made my way to the gravesite after the services, I glanced at the names on the tombstones—names I recognized from Will DeLoach's diary—and knew that an era had ended. It was an emotional time for me, but as I drove home across the plains I realized that even in the midst of transitions as swift as those taking place in agriculture today, some things remain the same. I glanced down a row of dried cotton stalks and saw the wind making the sand "walk about" and "strut its stuff." I understood that the Llano Estacado had just been a stage on which so many pioneer farmers played their part until the land reclaimed its own. Then I thought of the diary, DeLoach's remarkably long record, and knew their story would live on.

Bibliography

U·N·P·U·B·L·I·S·H·E·D

Adams, Ruby Winona. "Social Behavior in a Drought Stricken Texas Panhandle Community," Master's thesis, University of Texas, 1932.

Anderson, Clayton, and Co., Promotional material. Reference File, Southwest Collection, Texas Tech University, Lubbock, Texas.

Army Bulletin #29 issued August 17, 1944, at Moran (India). Typed copy in possession of editor.

Arnold, Richard Wilson. "The History of Adaptation of Cotton to the High Plains of Texas, 1890–1947," Master's thesis, Texas Tech University, 1975.

Bailey County Electric Co-operative Association. Records, 1939. Southwest Collection, Texas Tech University, Lubbock, Texas.

Barr, Chester Alwyn. "Texas Politics, 1876–1906," Ph.D. diss., University of Texas, 1966.

DeLoach, Robert E., and Jimmie DeLoach Moorhead. Interview with Janet Neugebauer. Sudan, Texas, July 1, 1987.

DeLoach, Robert Edwin. Interview with Janet Neugebauer. Sudan, Texas, March 16, 1988.

DeLoach, W. G. family. Interviews with David Murrah. February 21, 1975, and March 18, 1975. Oral History Files, Southwest Collection, Texas Tech University, Lubbock, Texas.

Evans, Samuel Lee. "Texas Agriculture, 1880–1930," Ph.D. diss., University of Texas, 1960.

Garrison, Homer. Interview with Janet Neugebauer and Richard Mason. July 18, 1987. Oral History Files, Southwest Collection, Texas Tech University, Lubbock, Texas.

Gordon, Joseph F. "The History and Development of Irrigated Cotton on the High Plains of Texas," Ph.D. diss., Texas Tech University, 1961.

Hagens, Lloyd, vineyard master. Interview with Janet Neugebauer. Slaton, Texas, February 25, 1986.

Bibliography

Hayter, Delmar. "South Plains Agriculture: 1880–1950," Master's thesis, Texas Tech University, 1981.

Hewlett, Harry H. Interview with Richard Mason. March 31, 1982. Oral History Files, Southwest Collection, Texas Tech University, Lubbock, Texas.

Huddlestone, John David, "Good Roads for Texas: A History of the Texas Highway Department 1917–1947," Ph.D. diss., Texas A&M University, 1981.

Jones, D. L. "Cotton and the Texas High Plains." Reference File, Southwest Collection, Texas Tech University, Lubbock, Texas. Unpublished manuscript.

Kuhlers, Terry, cotton classer, U.S. Department of Agriculture. Interview with Janet Neugebauer. Lubbock, Texas, February 25, 1987.

Lowrance, Virniel Joseph, Jr. "Solmization: Historical Background and Contemporary Usage," Master's thesis, Texas Tech University, 1969.

McPherson C. M. Papers, 1962–1987. Southwest Collection, Texas Tech University, Lubbock, Texas.

Mahon, George. Papers, 1918–1981. Southwest Collection, Texas Tech University, Lubbock, Texas.

Maynard, Judson, professor of music, Texas Tech University. Interview with Janet Neugebauer. Lubbock, Texas, April 15, 1988.

Medlock, Claude W. Interview with Sylva Wesendonk. July 26, 1976. Oral History Files, Southwest Collection, Texas Tech University, Lubbock, Texas.

Moorhead, Jimmie DeLoach. Interview with Janet Neugebauer. Lubbock, Texas, October 23, 1987.

Ostendorph, Maj. Daniel M., U.S. Army, assistant professor of military science, Texas Tech University. Interview with Janet Neugebauer. Lubbock, Texas, February 10, 1988.

Sheets, Richard, manager, Paymaster Cotton Research Farm. Interview with Janet Neugebauer. Aiken, Texas, March 21, 1988.

Sherrod, Charles C. Interview with Jeff Townsend. April 11, 1974. Oral History Files, Southwest Collection, Texas Tech University, Lubbock, Texas.

Supak, James, agronomist, Agricultural Extension Service. Interview with Janet Neugebauer. Lubbock, Texas, April 4, 1988.

Teague, Fannie. Interview with David Murrah. July 1, 1975. Oral History Files, Southwest Collection, Texas Tech University, Lubbock, Texas.

Young, Stanley, county extension agent—agriculture, Lubbock County. Telephone interview with Janet Neugebauer. April 8, 1988.

P·U·B·L·I·S·H·E·D

Acheson, Sam. *Dallas Yesterday*. Edited by Lee Milazzo. Dallas: Southern Methodist University Press, 1977.

Adams, Arthur E. *Stalin and His Times*. New York: Holt, Rinehart, and Winston, 1972.

Adkins, William G., and William H. Metzler. *Tenure and Mechanization of the Cotton Harvest, Texas High Plains*. Texas Agricultural Experiment Station Bulletin no. 813. College Station: Texas A&M College, 1955.

Anglin, Bob. "Grain Sorghums: Facts You Want to Know." *Progressive Farmer* (Texas edition) 44, no. 3 (January, 1929).

Arneson, Edwin P. "The Early Art of Terrestial Measurement and Its Practice in Texas." In *One League to Each Wind*, edited by Sue Watkins. Austin: Texas Surveyors Association, [1964].

Ashby, Clifford, and Susanne De Pauw May. *Trouping through Texas: Harley Sadler and His Tent Show*. Bowling Green, Ohio: University Popular Press, 1982.

Atkins, J. L., Jr. "Hegari, an Adaptable Crop." *Progressive Farmer* (Texas edition) 44, no. 3 (January 19, 1929).

"An Avalanche of Grain Sorghums." *Progressive Farmer* (Texas edition) 59, no. 10 (October, 1944).

Bailey, Olga. *Mollie Bailey: The Circus Queen of the Southwest*. Edited by Bess Samuel Ayres. Dallas: Harben-Spotts Co., 1943.

Baker, Gladys L., Wayne D. Rasmussen, Vivian Wiser, and Jane M. Porter. *Century of Service: The First 100 Years of the United States Department of Agriculture*. Washington D.C.: U.S. Department of Agriculture, 1963.

Baker, T. Lindsay. *A Field Guide to American Windmills*. Norman: University of Oklahoma Press, 1985.

Ball, Carleton R. "The Grain Sorghums: Immigrant Crops That Have Made Good," U.S. Department of Agriculture, *Yearbook of Agriculture, 1913*. Washington, D.C.: Government Printing Office, 1914.

Barr, Alwyn. *Black Texans: A History of Negroes in Texas, 1528–1971*. Austin: Pemberton Press, 1973.

Barr, Alwyn, and Robert A. Calvert, eds. *Black Leaders: Texans for Their Times*. Austin: Texas State Historical Association, 1981.

Bates, Carlos G. *The Windbreak as a Farm Asset*, USDA Farmer's Bulletin no. 1405, 1924.

Beall, Robert I. "Rural Electrification," in U.S. Department of Agriculture, *Farmers in a Changing World: Yearbook of Agriculture, 1940*. Washington, D.C.: Government Printing Office, 1940.

Benedict, Murray R. *Can We Solve the Farm Problem?* New York: Twentieth Century Fund, 1955.

———. *Farm Policies of the United States, 1790–1950.* New York: Twentieth Century Fund, 1953.

Bennett, Hugh H. *Our American Land: The Story of Its Abuse and Its Conservation.* USDA Miscellaneous Publication no. 599, 1950.

Berry, W. J., "Primitive Baptists." *Encyclopedia of Southern Baptists* 2. Nashville: Broadman Press, 1958.

Blandford, Percy W. *Old Farm Tools and Machinery: An Illustrated History.* Fort Lauderdale, Florida: Gale Research Company, 1976.

Blum, Daniel. *A Pictorial History of the Silent Screen.* New York: G. P. Putnam's Sons, 1953.

———. *A New Pictorial History of the Talkies,* revised by John Kobal. New York: G. P. Putnam's Sons, 1968.

Bomar, George W. *Texas Weather.* Austin: University of Texas Press, 1983.

Bonnen, C. A., W. C. McArthur, A. C. Magee, and W. F. Hughes. *Use of Irrigation Water on the High Plains.* Texas Agricultural Experiment Station Bulletin no. 756. College Station: Texas A&M College, 1952.

Boone, Lalia Phipps. *The Petroleum Dictionary.* Norman: University of Oklahoma Press, 1952.

Bowles, C. E. "Lamb County Pioneers in Health Co-op." *Progressive Farmer* (Texas edition) 58, no. 7 (July, 1943).

Brinkley, Alan. *Voices of Protest: Huey Long, Father Coughlin, and the Great Depression.* New York: Alfred A. Knopf, 1982.

Brown, Harry Bates. *Cotton.* New York: McGraw-Hill Book Co., 1927; revised edition, 1938.

Brown, Norman D. *Hood, Bonnet, and Little Brown Jug: Texas Politics, 1921–1928.* College Station: Texas A&M University Press, 1984.

Bryan, Lilla Graham. *The Story of the Demonstration Work in Texas.* Texas Agricultural Extension Service Bulletin B-93 (revised). College Station: Agricultural and Mechanical College of Texas, and U.S. Department of Agriculture, 1938.

Bryant, Keith L., Jr. *History of the Atchison, Topeka, and Santa Fe Railway.* New York: Macmillan Co., 1974.

"Bull Circles." *The Cattleman* 16, no. 8 (January, 1930).

Butler, Eugene, "How Farmers Are Meeting Wartime Problems." *Progressive Farmer* (Texas edition) 58, no. 2 (February, 1943).

———. "Mechanical Cotton Harvesting." *Progressive Farmer* (Texas edition) 59, no. 10 (October, 1944).

————. "Mechanical Harvesting Costs." *Progressive Farmer* (Texas edition) 59, no. 11 (November, 1944).

————. "What's New in Agriculture?" *Progressive Farmer* (Texas edition) 54, no. 11 (November, 1939).

————. "What's New in Agriculture?" *Progressive Farmer* (Texas edition) 58, no. 2 (February, 1943).

————. "What's New in Agriculture?" *Progressive Farmer* (Texas edition) 59, nos. 5 and 11 (May and November, 1944).

Caffey, David L. *The Old Home Place: Farming on the West Texas Frontier.* Burnet, Texas: Eakin Press, 1981.

Callahan, Raymond. *Burma, 1942–1945.* Newark: University of Delaware Press, 1978.

"Carlsbad Cavern, Scenic Wonder of the World," *The Historical Encyclopedia of New Mexico* I. Albuquerque: New Mexico Historical Association, 1945.

Carter, James D. *Masonry in Texas: Background, History, and Influence to 1864.* Waco: Privately published, 1955.

Chafee, Zechariah, Jr. *Free Speech in the United States.* Cambridge: Harvard University Press, 1942.

Chapin, Robert N. *Arsenical Cattle Dips.* USDA Farmer's Bulletin no. 603, 1914.

Christidis, Basil G., and George J. Harrison. *Cotton Growing Problems.* New York: McGraw-Hill Book Co., 1955.

Christman, Henry M., *Kingfish to America: Share Our Wealth, Selected Senatorial Papers of Huey P. Long.* New York: Schocken Books, 1985.

Cobb, Buell E., Jr. *The Sacred Harp: A Tradition and Its Music.* Athens: University of Georgia Press, 1978.

Cobb, Cully A. "Cotton Plow-up a Signal Success." *Progressive Farmer* (Texas edition) 48, no. 8 (August, 1933).

Cochrane, Williard W. *The Development of American Agriculture.* Minneapolis: University of Minnesota Press, 1979.

Colton, C. E. "Baptist Missionary Association." *Encyclopedia of Southern Baptists* 1. Nashville: Broadman Press, 1958.

Country Gentleman 66, nos. 8 and 9 (August and September, 1946).

Craik, T. W., and R. J. Craik. *John Donne: Selected Poetry and Prose.* London: Methuen and Co., 1986.

Crosby County Pioneer Memorial Museum. *A History of Crosby County, 1876–1977.* Dallas: Taylor Publishing Co., 1978.

Current, Richard N., T. Harry Williams, Frank Freidel, and Alan Brinkley. *American History.* Vol. 2, 7th ed. New York: Alfred A. Knopf, 1987.

Dale, Edward Everett. *The Cross Timbers: Memories of a North Texas Boyhood.* Austin: University of Texas Press, 1966.

————. *Frontier Ways: Sketches of Life in the Old West.* Austin: University of Texas Press, 1959.

Darnell, A. L. *Ground versus Unground Grain for Lactating Dairy Cows.* Texas Agricultural Experiment Station Bulletin no. 530. College Station: Texas A&M College, 1936.

Dary, David. *Cowboy Culture: A Saga of Five Centuries.* New York: Alfred A. Knopf, 1981.

Davidson, Donald. "The Sacred Harp in the Land of Eden." In *Still Rebels, Still Yankees, and Other Essays.* Baton Rouge: Louisiana State University Press, 1957.

Demke, A. H. "Count in the Hen." *West Texas Today* 21, no. 7 (September, 1940).

Dorn, Frank. *Walkout: With Stilwell in Burma.* New York: Thomas Y. Crowell Co., 1971.

"Down at Austin." *Progressive Farmer* (Texas edition) 58, no. 3 (March, 1943).

Drache, Hiram M. *Plowshares to Printouts: Farm Management as Viewed through 75 Years of the Northwest Farm Managers Association.* Danville, Illinois: Interstate Printers and Publishers, 1985.

Droze, Wilmon H. *Trees, Prairies, and People: A History of Tree Planting in the Plains States.* Denton: Texas Woman's University, 1977.

Dulles, Foster Rhea. *The American Red Cross: A History.* New York: Harper and Brothers, 1950.

Dunn, Roy Sylvan. "Agriculture Builds a City," *A History of Lubbock,* edited by Lawrence L. Graves. Lubbock: West Texas Museum Association, 1962.

The Earth. Dallas, Tex. May, 1933–March, 1934.

Ebeling, Walter. *The Fruited Plain: The Story of American Agriculture.* Berkeley: University of California Press, 1979.

Editorial Opinion. *Progressive Farmer* (Texas edition) 44, no. 3 (January 19, 1929).

Editorial Viewpoint. *Progressive Farmer* (Texas edition) 58, no. 10 (October, 1943).

Eighmy, John Lee. *Churches in Cultural Captivity: A History of the Social Attitudes of Southern Baptists.* Knoxville: University of Tennessee Press, 1972.

Elliott, Fred C., Marvin Hoover, and Walter K. Porter Jr., eds. *Cotton Principles and Practices.* Ames: Iowa State University Press, 1968.

Estes, Pam. *Billie Sol: King of Texas Wheeler-Dealers.* Abilene, Texas: Noble Craft Books, 1983.

Evans, Sterling C. "The Land Boom Is Here." *Progressive Farmer* (Texas edition) 59, no. 5 (May, 1944).

Farrall, Arthur W., and Carl F. Albrecht. *Agricultural Engineering.* Danville, Ill.: Interstate Printers and Publishers, 1965.

Ferguson, Charles W. *Fifty Million Brothers: A Panorama of American Lodges and Clubs.* New York: Farrar and Rinehart, 1937.

Fielding, Raymond. *The March of Time, 1935–1951.* New York: Oxford University Press, 1978.

Fite, Gilbert C. *American Farmers: The New Minority.* Bloomington: Indiana University Press, 1981.

————. *Farm to Factories.* Columbia: University of Missouri Press, 1965.

Fletcher, Sydney E. *The Cowboy and His Horse.* New York: Grosset and Dunlap, 1951.

Garraty, John A. *The American Nation.* Vol. 2, 5th ed. New York: Harper and Row, 1983.

"Get Ready for Lubbock's Meat Show." *Progressive Farmer* (Texas edition) 47, no. 6 (March 15–31, 1932).

Gillmer, Thomas C., and H. Erich Nietsch. *Clouds, Weather, and Flight.* New York: D. Van Nostrand Co., 1944.

Gowen, Arlee. "There Goes That Farm Again." *Southwestern Crop and Stock* 3, no. 1 (January, 1949).

Gracy, David B., II. *Littlefield Lands: Colonization of the Texas Plains, 1912–1920.* Austin: University of Texas Press, 1968.

Graves, Lawrence L., ed. *A History of Lubbock.* Lubbock, Texas: West Texas Museum Association, 1962.

————, ed. *Lubbock From Town to City.* Lubbock, Texas: West Texas Museum Association, 1986.

Grebler, Leo, Joan W. Moore, and Ralph C. Guzman. *The Mexican-American People: The Nation's Second Largest Minority.* New York: Free Press, 1970.

Green, Donald E. *Fifty Years of Service to West Texas Agriculture: A History of Texas Tech University's College of Agricultural Sciences, 1925–1975.* Lubbock: Texas Tech Press, 1977.

————. *Land of the Underground Rain: Irrigation on the Texas High Plains, 1910–1970.* Austin: University of Texas Press, 1973.

Greene, A. C. *The 50 Best Books on Texas.* Dallas: Pressworks Publishing, 1982.

Hale, Joseph W. "Masonry in the Early Days of Texas." *Southwestern Historical Quarterly* 49, no. 3 (January, 1946).

Haley, J. Evetts. *The XIT Ranch of Texas and the Early Days of the Llano Estacado.* Norman: University of Oklahoma Press, 1953.

Hall, Tom G. "Government Controls: How to Understand the Experience of World War I." In *Farmers, Bureaucrats, and Middlemen: Historical Perspectives on American Agriculture*, edited by Trudy Huskamp Peterson. Washington, D.C.: Howard University Press, 1980.

Haragan, Donald R. *Blue Northers to Sea Breezes: Texas Weather and Climate*. Dallas: Hendrick-Long Publishing Co., 1983.

Harrington, H. D. *Edible Native Plants of the Rocky Mountains*. Albuquerque: University of New Mexico Press, 1967.

Heady, Earl O., Edwin O. Haroldsen, Leo V. Mayer, and Luther G. Tweeten. *Roots of the Farm Problem*. Ames: Iowa State University Press, 1965.

Herrmann, O. W., and Chastina Gardner, *Early Developments in Cooperative Cotton Marketing*. Farm Credit Administration Circular no. C-101. Washington, D.C.: Government Printing Office, 1936.

Hilburn, H. S. "Cow, Sow and Hen." *West Texas Today* 22, no. 11 (January, 1942).

Hill, I. W. "Boys and Girls Clubs Do Pioneer Work in Improving Farm Life," U.S. Department of Agriculture, *Yearbook of Agriculture, 1927*. Washington, D.C.: Government Printing Office, 1928.

Hofstadter, Richard, William Miller, and Daniel Aaron. *The United States: The History of a Republic*. 2d ed. Englewood Cliffs, N.J.: Prentice-Hall, 1967.

Holden, William Curry. *A Ranching Saga: The Lives of William Electious Halsell and Ewing Halsell*. San Antonio: Trinity University Press, 1976.

————. *The Spur Ranch*. Boston: Christopher Publishing House, 1934.

————. *Why Use Dobe?* Lubbock: Texas Technological College, Research Publication no. 10, 1948.

Hohn, C. "Texas Farm Labor." *Progressive Farmer* (Texas edition) 59, no. 3 (March, 1944).

The Hub (official publication of the Lubbock Chamber of Commerce and the Board of City Development). Vol. 1, no. 1–vol. 3, no. 12. November, 1927–July, 1942.

Huey, Paul. "Best Bulls Only." *Progressive Farmer* (Texas edition) 43, no. 22 (June 2, 1928).

Hughes, William F., and A. C. Magee. *Changes in Investment and Irrigation Water Costs, Texas High Plains, 1950–54*. Texas Agricultural Experiment Station Bulletin no. 828. College Station: Texas A&M College, 1956.

Hunter, W. D. *The Pink Bollworm with Special Reference to Steps Taken by the Department of Agriculture to Prevent Its Establishment in the United States*. USDA Technical Bulletin 723. Washington, D.C., 1918.

Hurt, R. Douglas. *The Dust Bowl: An Agriculture and Social History*. Chicago: Nelson-Hall, 1981.

Hutchinson, Paul D. *Grain Sorghum in the United States*. Lubbock: Texas Tech University, 1977.

Joel, Arthur H. *Soil Conservation Reconnaissance Survey of the Southern Great Plains Wind-Erosion Area.* USDA Technical Bulletin no. 556. Washington D.C.: U.S. Department of Agriculture, 1937.

Jones, D. L., W. M. Hurst, and D. Scoates. *Mechanical Harvesting of Cotton in Northwest Texas.* Texas Agricultural Experiment Station Circular no. 52. College Station: Agricultural and Mechanical College of Texas, 1928.

Jones, Jesse H., with Edward Angly. *Fifty Billion Dollars: My Thirteen Years with the RFC, 1932–1945.* New York: Macmillan Co., 1951.

Karper, R. E. "Grain Sorghums: Facts You Want to Know about Hegari." *Progressive Farmer* (Texas edition) 44, no. 3 (January 19, 1929).

Karper, R. E., and D. L. Jones. *Varieties of Cotton in Northwest Texas.* Texas Agricultural Experiment Station Bulletin no. 364. College Station: Agricultural and Mechanical College of Texas, 1927.

Key, V. O., Jr. *Southern Politics in State and Nation.* Knoxville: University of Tennessee Press, 1984.

Killough, D. T., E. F. McFarland, T. R. Richard, and F. C. Elliott. *Performance of Cotton Varieties in Texas, 1948–1950.* Texas Agricultural Experiment Station Bulletin no. 739. College Station: Texas A&M College, 1951.

Kincannon, John A., and John G. McNeely. *An Economic Appraisal of the Texas Hog Industry.* Texas Agricultural Experiment Station Bulletin no. 749. College Station: Texas A&M College, 1952.

King, D. F. "Around My Chicken Yard." *Progressive Farmer* (Texas edition) 58, no. 12 (December, 1943).

Kirkendall, Richard S. *Social Scientists and Farm Politics in the Age of Roosevelt.* Columbia: University of Missouri Press, 1966.

Kleemeir, Robert W. *Aging and Leisure.* New York: Oxford University Press, 1961.

Kurtz, Michael L. *Crime of the Century.* Knoxville: University of Tennessee Press, 1982.

"Labor and Other 1944 Farm Needs." *Progressive Farmer* (Texas edition) 58, no. 11 (November, 1943).

Lasseter, W. C. "How to Make Livestock Pay." *Progressive Farmer* (Texas edition) 58, no. 1 (January, 1943).

Leuchtenburg, William E. *The Perils of Prosperity, 1914–1932.* Chicago: University of Chicago Press, 1958.

———. *A Troubled Feast: American Society Since 1945.* Boston: Little, Brown, and Co., 1979.

Loehr, Rodney C. "Farmer's Diaries." *Agricultural History* 12, no. 4 (October, 1938).

Lubbock Chamber of Commerce, comp. *Texas Technological College Locating Brief,* 1923. Southwest Collection, Texas Tech University, Lubbock, Texas.

Lubbock Cotton Exchange, comp. *Charter, Rules and Bylaws of the Lubbock Cotton Exchange,* 1951.

Lubbock Sudan Grass Seed Association, *Sudan Grass.* Lubbock: Lubbock Sudan Grass Seed Association, 1915.

McKay, Seth Shepard. *Texas Politics, 1906–1944.* Lubbock: Texas Tech Press, 1952.

————. *W. Lee O'Daniel and Texas Politics, 1938–1942.* Lubbock: Texas Tech Press, 1944.

McKay, Seth Shepard, and Odie B. Faulk. *Texas After Spindletop.* Austin: Steck-Vaughn Co., 1965.

McLain, J. H. *Eradication of the Cattle Tick Necessary for Profitable Dairying.* USDA Farmer's Bulletin no. 639, 1914.

McReynolds, Edwin C. *Oklahoma: A History of the Sooner State.* Norman: University of Oklahoma Press, 1964.

Magee, A. C., B. H. Stone, and B. C. Wormeli. *Planning for Profitable Egg Production.* Texas Agricultural Experiment Station Bulletin no. B-1012. College Station: Texas A&M University, 1964.

Magee, A. C., C. A. Bonnen, W. C. McArthur, and W. F. Hughes. *Production Practices for Irrigated Crops on the High Plains.* Texas Agricultural Experiment Station Bulletin no. 763. College Station: Texas A&M College, 1953.

Mallory, Randy. "The Abiding Art of Sacred Harp." *Texas Highways* 34, no. 8 (August, 1987).

Marburger, Harold J. *Texas Elections, 1918–1954.* Austin: Texas State Library, 1956.

Marshall, James. *Santa Fe: The Railroad That Built an Empire.* New York: Random House, 1945.

Martin, John H. "Sorghum Improvement," U.S. Department of Agriculture, *Yearbook of Agriculture, 1936.* Washington, D.C.: Government Printing Office, 1936.

Mason, Richard. "The Cotton Kingdom and the City of Lubbock: South Plains Agriculture in the Postwar Era." In *Lubbock From Town to City,* edited by Lawrence L. Graves, Lubbock: West Texas Museum Association, 1986.

"Men of the Year in Agriculture." *Progressive Farmer* (Texas edition) 58, no. 1 (January, 1944).

Merk, Frederick. *History of the Westward Movement.* New York: Alfred A. Knopf, 1978.

Merrill, Gilbert R., Alfred R. Macormac, and Herbert R. Mauersberger. *American Cotton Handbook*, 2d rev. ed. New York: Textile Book Publishers, 1949.

Miller, William C., and Geoffrey P. West. *Encyclopedia of Animal Care*. Baltimore: Williams and Wilkins Co., 1967.

Mitchell, Frank E. "The Things You Want to Know about Baby Chicks." *Progressive Farmer* (Texas edition) 54, no. 2 (February, 1939).

Mock, James R., and Cedric Larson. *Words That Won the War*. Princeton: Princeton University Press, 1939.

Montgomery, Robert Hargrove. *The Cooperative Pattern in Cotton*. New York: MacMillan Co., 1929.

Morrison, Samuel Eliot, and Henry Steele Commager. *The Growth of the American Republic*. Vol. 2, 6th ed. New York: Oxford University Press, 1956.

Morton, W. J., Jr. *Snowstorms, Dust Storms, and Horses' Tails*. Dumas, Tex.: Privately published, 1966.

Motheral, Joe R., William H. Metzler, and Louis J. Ducoff. *Cotton and Manpower—Texas High Plains*. Texas Agricultural Experiment Station Bulletin no. 762. College Station: Texas A&M College, 1953.

Musselwhite, Lynn Ray, "Texas in the 1920's: A History of Social Change," Ph.D. diss., Texas Tech University, 1975.

Nall, Gary Lynn, "Agricultural History of the Texas Panhandle, 1880–1965," Ph.D. diss., University of Oklahoma, 1972.

"Negroes and the Harvest." *Progressive Farmer* (Texas edition) 58, no. 11 (November, 1943).

Niven, L. A. "Next Month's Gardening." *Progressive Farmer* (Texas edition) 54, no. 12 (December, 1939).

Nourse, Edwin G., Joseph S. Davis, and John D. Black. *Three Years of the Agricultural Adjustment Administration*. Washington, D.C.: Brookings Institution, 1937.

Office of Price Administration, *Gasoline Rationing Instructions, July 1942*. Washington, D.C.: Government Printing Office, 1942.

Office of Price Administration, *Sugar Rationing Regulations*. Rationing Order no. 3. Washington, D.C.: Government Printing Office, 1942.

Olien, Roger M. *From Token to Triumph: The Texas Republicans since 1920*. Dallas: Southern Methodist University Press, 1982.

Orr, Elsie. "Radio—the Farmer's Liberator." *Progressive Farmer* (Texas edition) 51, no. 2 (February, 1936).

Parmet, Herbert S. *Eisenhower and the American Crusades*. New York: Macmillan Co., 1972.

Poe, Clarence. "What's New in Agriculture?" *Progressive Farmer* (Texas edition) 48, no. 6 (June, 1933).

Quimby, J. Roy. "The Development of Grain Sorghums." *West Texas Historical Association Yearbook* 33 (October, 1957).

Rasmussen, Wayne D., ed. *Agriculture in the United States: A Documentary History*, Vols. 2 and 3. New York: Random House, 1975.

Richardson, Rupert Norval. *Texas: The Lone Star State*. New York: Prentice-Hall, 1943.

Richardson, Rupert N., Ernest Wallace, and Adrian N. Anderson. *Texas: The Lone Star State*. 3d ed. Englewood Cliffs, N.J.: Prentice-Hall, 1970.

Rister, Carl Coke. *Oil! Titan of the Southwest*. Norman: University of Oklahoma Press, 1949.

Rohrer, Wayne C., and Louis H. Douglas. *The Agrarian Transition in America*. New York: Bobbs-Merrill Co., 1969.

Rosenburg, Norman J. "Climate of the Great Plains Region of the United States." *Great Plains Quarterly* 7, no. 1 (Winter, 1987).

Schlebecker, John T. *Cattle Raising on the Plains, 1900–1961*. Lincoln: University of Nebraska Press, 1963.

Schlesinger, Arthur M., Jr. *A Thousand Days*. Boston: Houghton-Mifflin Co., 1965.

Scott, Evalyn Parrott. *A History of Lamb County*. Lamb County Historical Survey Committee, 1968.

Serratt, Joe. "My Home Town – Sudan." *West Texas Today* 16, no. 7 (September, 1935).

Service Book, Lamb County, Texas: Second World War, 1941–1945. Vernon, Texas: Greenbelt Publishing Service, n.d.

Sevareid, Eric, ed. *Candidates 1960*. New York: Basic Books, 1959.

Shelton, Hooper, comp. *From Buffalo to Oil: History of Scurry County, Texas*. Scurry County Historical Survey Committee, 1973.

Shideler, James H. "Flappers and Philosophers, and Farmers: Rural-Urban Tensions of the Twenties." *Agricultural History* 47, no. 4 (October, 1973).

Shinkle, R. D. "Tops for Texas – Lubbock Leads in Butter Manufacture, Egg Shipments." *West Texas Today* 21, no. 7 (September, 1940).

Skrabanek, R. L. *Characteristics and Changes in the Texas Farm Population*. Texas Agricultural Experiment Station Bulletin no. 825. College Station: Texas A&M College, 1955.

Skrabanek, R. L., and Gladys K. Bowles. *Migration of the Texas Farm Population*. Texas Agricultural Experiment Station Bulletin no. 847. College Station: Texas A&M College, 1957.

Skrabanek, R. L., Loyd B. Keel, and Louis J. Ducoff. *Texas Farmers and Old Age and Survivors Insurance.* Texas Agricultural Experiment Station Bulletin no. 886. College Station: Texas A&M College, 1958.

Slagel, A. B. "Cotton Growers Open Fight for Survival." *Southwestern Crop and Stock* 10, no. 2 (February, 1956).

Slocum, Rob R. *Standard Varieties of Chickens: The American Class.* USDA Farmer's Bulletin no. 806, 1917.

Smith, H. P., D. T. Killough, D. L. Jones, and M. H. Byrom. *Mechanical Harvesting of Cotton as Affected By Varietal Characteristics and Other Factors.* Texas Agricultural Experiment Station Bulletin no. 580. College Station: Agricultural & Mechanical College of Texas, 1939.

Smith, M. Lynwood. *Give the World a Smile: A Compilation of Songs by Frank Stamps with a Story of His Life by Mrs. Frank Stamps.* Wesson, Mississippi: M. Lynwood Smith Publications, 1969.

Southern, John H. *Farm Land Market Situation in the Southwestern States, 1946–1954.* Texas Agricultural Experiment Station Bulletin no. 797. College Station: Texas A&M College, 1955.

"South Plains Travelogue." *Progressive Farmer* (Texas edition) 58, no. 10 (October, 1943).

Spence, Mary Lee. "They Also Serve Who Wait." *Western Historical Quarterly* 14, no. 1 (January, 1983).

Spikes, Nellie Witt, and Temple Ann Ellis. *Through the Years: A History of Crosby County, Texas.* San Antonio: Naylor Company, 1952.

Stephens, A. Ray. *The Taft Ranch: A Texas Principality.* Austin: University of Texas Press, 1964.

Stevenson, Adlai E. *Major Campaign Speeches of Adlai E. Stevenson, 1952.* New York: Random House, 1953.

Stewart, Ernest. "How Far Mechanized Cotton Farming?" *Progressive Farmer* (Texas edition) 63, no. 10 (October, 1948).

Talbot, M. W. *Johnson Grass as a Weed.* USDA Farmer's Bulletin no. 1537, 1928.

Texas Agricultural Experiment Station. *Irrigation Survey of the High Plains of Texas.* Lubbock: TAES, 1951.

Texas Almanac and State Industrial Guide. Dallas: A. H. Belo Corporation, 1914–63.

Texas. *General Laws of the State of Texas.* Senate Bill no. 69, March 1, 1915.

———. *General Laws of the State of Texas.* 34th Leg., Reg. Sess., Jan. 12, 1915–Apr. 20, 1915. Austin: A. C. Baldwin and Sons.

Texas Jurisprudence: A Complete Statement of the Law and Practice of the State of

Texas. Vol. 39, *Statutes to Swindling and Cheating.* San Francisco: Bancroft-Whitney Company, 1936.

"Texas Land Prices Start to Level Off." *Southwestern Crop and Stock* 3, no. 11 (November, 1949).

Texas State Highway Department, comp. *A Guide to the South Plains of Texas.* N.p., 1935.

Tharp, Max M., and E. Lee Langsford. "Where Our Cotton Comes From," U.S. Department of Agriculture, *Yearbook of Agriculture, 1958.* Washington, D.C.: Government Printing Office, 1958.

Thaxton, E. L., Jr., and N. P. Swanson. *Guides in Cotton Irrigation on the High Plains.* Texas Agricultural Experiment Station Bulletin no. 838. College Station: Texas A&M College, 1956.

Thibodeaux, B. H., C. A. Bonnen, and A. C. Magee. *An Economic Study of Farm Organization and Operation in the High Plains Cotton Area of Texas.* Texas Agricultural Experiment Station Bulletin no. 568. College Station: Agricultural & Mechanical College of Texas, 1939.

Traweek, Eleanor Mitchell. *Of Such as These: A History of Motley County and Its Families.* Quanah: Nortex Offset Publications, 1973.

Truman, Margaret. *Harry S. Truman.* New York: William Morrow and Co., 1973.

Tune, Carlton Lee. "The Dust That Darkens the Sun." *Southwestern Crop and Stock* 1, no. 3 (March, 1947).

Tweeten, Luther. *Foundations of Farm Policy.* Lincoln: University of Nebraska Press, 1970.

U.S. Bureau of the Census. *Cotton Production in the United States, Crop of 1916.* Washington, D.C.: Government Printing Office, 1917.

————. *Cotton Production in the United States, Crop of 1920.* Washington, D.C.: Government Printing Office, 1921.

————. *Fifteenth Census of the United States, 1930.* Vol. 1, *Population.* Washington, D.C.: Government Printing Office, 1931.

U.S. Department of Agriculture. *Agricultural Adjustment* [1933–34]. Washington, D.C.: Government Printing Office, 1934.

————. *Agriculture Adjustment in 1934.* Washington, D.C.: Government Printing Office, 1935.

————. *Agriculture Adjustment* [1938–39]. Washington, D.C.: Government Printing Office, 1939.

————. *Agriculture Adjustment* [1937–38]. Washington, D.C.: Government Printing Office, 1939.

————. *Agricultural Adjustment* [1933–35]. Washington, D.C.: Government Printing Office, 1936.

————. *Climatological Data for the United States by Sections*. Vol. 1, Part 5: Annual Summary. Washington, D.C.: Weather Bureau, 1914–63. In 1940 the Weather Bureau was transferred from the Department of Agriculture to the Department of Commerce.

————. *Report of the Secretary of Agriculture*. Washington, D.C.: Government Printing Office, 1941–60. Reports were included in *Yearbook of Agriculture* until 1941.

"U.S. Soil Bank Moves into Operation." *Southwestern Crop and Stock* 10, no. 7 (July, 1956).

Vinall, H. N. *Johnson Grass: Its Production for Hay and Pasturage*. USDA Farmer's Bulletin no. 1476, 1926.

Vinson, James, ed. *Twentieth Century Western Writers*. Detroit: Gale Research Co., 1982.

Walton, W. R. *The True Army Worm and Its Control*, USDA Farmer's Bulletin no. 731, 1916.

Ware, J. D. "Plant Breeding and the Cotton Industry," U.S. Department of Agriculture, *Yearbook of Agriculture, 1936*. Washington, D.C.: Government Printing Office, 1936.

Warth, Robert D. *Joseph Stalin*. New York: Twayne Publishers, 1969.

Webb, Walter Prescott. *The Great Plains*. New York: Grosset and Dunlap, 1971.

Webb, Walter Prescott, and H. Bailey Carroll, eds. *The Handbook of Texas*. 2 Vols. Austin: Texas State Historical Association, 1952.

Welch, June Rayfield. *The Texas Courthouse Revisited*. Dallas: G.L.A. Press, 1984.

Welch, June Rayfield, and J. Larry Nance. *The Texas Courthouse*. Dallas: G.L.A. Press, 1971.

Widsoe, John. *Dry Farming*. New York: Macmillan Co., 1911.

Wilcox, Walter W. *The Farmer in the Second World War*. Ames: Iowa State College Press, 1947.

"Will We Ever Learn?" *Progressive Farmer* (Texas edition) 52, no. 10 (October, 1937).

Williams, T. Harry. *Huey Long*. New York: Alfred A. Knopf, 1970.

Willoughby, William Franklin. *Government Organization in War Time and After*. New York: D. Appleton and Co., 1919.

Worster, Donald. *Dust Bowl: The Southern Plains in the 1930s*. New York: Oxford University Press, 1979.

Wright, W. C. *Religious and Patriotic Ideals of the Ku Klux Klan*. Waco: Grove Publishing Co., 1926.

Youmans, E. Grant, ed. *Older Rural Americans: A Sociological Perspective*. Lexington: University of Kentucky Press, 1967.

Index

Index

United Way Fund, 315
U.S. Radio Farm School, 108

veterans, benefits for, 259
Veterans Administration, 254
veterinary medicine, 128

washday, 13, 213–14
washing machine, 159
water, costs of, 324
water control districts, 306–307
watering troughs, 110
water use, 25, 28
weather: effects of, 87, 137–38, 171, 283–84; expressions about, 306, 326; and folklore, 30, 35, 151, 272; and soil erosion, 142, 162; unseasonable, 266; West Texas, xxi, 28, 85, 272–73. *See also specific types of weather*
wells. *See* farming methods, irrigation

wheat, 21, 42, 55, 58, 104, 105–106
Wheatland maize, 234–36
Wilbarger County, Tex., 73
Wildey, Thomas, 30
Willkie, Wendell, 202
wind, 29, 61, 76, 82, 142–43, 317, 328
windbreaks, 204
windchargers, 197
windmills, 25, 28, 75, 76, 87, 256–57
wolves, 7–8
Woodmen of the World, 4
World War I, 8, 35, 38, 39, 42, 46, 47, 50, 188
World War II, 192–93, 200, 226, 245; domestic effects of, 201, 203, 205, 210, 213, 214, 216, 217–18, 219, 220, 225, 228, 229–30; military aspects of, 211, 236–37, 247, 249, 250, 255
Wright, Jim, 330

XIT Ranch, 76, 279

Plains Farmer was composed into type on a Compugraphic digital phototype-setter in eleven and one-half point Goudy Old Style with two and one-half points of spacing between the lines. Goudy Old Style was also selected for display. The book was designed by Jim Billingsley, typeset by Metricomp, Inc., printed offset and bound by John H. Dekker & Sons, Inc. The paper on which this book is printed carries acid-free characteristics for an effective life of at least three hundred years.

TEXAS A&M UNIVERSITY PRESS : COLLEGE STATION